]
Michael.

REGICIDE
Michael. Marley. Murder.

Analyzing the Assassinations of Two Kings

Wesley Muhammad, Ph.D.

A-Team Publishing
Chicago

reg·i·cide – *noun* 1. The purposeful act of killing a king.

This work is humbly dedicated to the Jackson Family and the Marley Family.

Table of Contents

Book I
Killing The King of Reggae

Book II
Killing The King of Pop

Book I

Killing The King of Reggae

Bob Marley, 36, king of reggae

By MICHAEL BROWNING
Herald Staff Writer

Jamaican reggae music king Bob Marley died Monday of cancer at Cedars of Lebanon Hospital in Miami. He was 36.

Hospital spokeswoman Karen Buchabaum gave no details concerning Marley's death, other than saying he was admitted to the hospital last Thursday and died at 11:45 a.m. Monday. She said his family was with him at the last.

Marley, a soft-spoken man who belonged to the Rastafarian cult, believed the Last Judgment was imminent and, until recently, had smoked about a pound of marijuana a week. He had been undergoing treatment for lung cancer since last fall and had spent time at the

mother was black. When Marley was nine, his family moved to the Kingston ghetto neighborhood, Trenchtown. This teeming slum was where he grew up.

He quit school at 16 to become an electrical welder. In 1963 he formed his singing group, Bob Marley and the Wailers. They released their first song, Judge Not, in 1963. It flopped. Marley received $50.

It was in the 1960s that reggae music evolved in Jamaica. It united the rock and roll rhythms of American black pop singers like Fats Domino and James Brown with the native Caribbean song patterns. Reggae was the musical idiom Marley made peculiarly his own.

Reggae is also bound up with the Rastafarian religion, a cult that

cialist candidate Michael Manley in 1972 when Manley was first elected prime minister, but later grew disaffected with him. When Marley asked Manley to make reggae the national music of Jamaica, the request was refused.

He was shot and wounded at his home on Dec. 3, 1976, just before a concert. Though his assailants were never caught, Marley made it clear he believed they were Manley supporters.

Abroad, Marley's fame grew gradually. His early, Burnin', Catch a Fire, and Natty Dread, sold slowly but steadily. His Rastaman Vibrations, released in 1976, was the first reggae album to reach the Top Ten of the American pop charts.

By then other American artists,

Bob Marley: Died at Miami

The Miami Herald May 12, 1981

On Saturday May 9, 1981, an ailing Bob Marley arrived in Miami, Florida after spending six months in Bavaria, Germany undergoing alternative cancer treatment. He was taken immediately to Cedars of Lebanon Hospital (now the University of Miami Hospital). Marley was diagnosed in 1977 with acral lentiginous melanoma, a rare form of skin cancer, after developing a wound in his right big toe. Marley's melanoma was unusually aggressive. By 1981 it had reportedly spread to his vital organs, including his liver, throughout both lungs, and his brain. A doctor at the world-famous Sloan-Kettering Cancer Center in Manhattan, where Bob Marley's brain tumor was discovered, told Bob that he had more cancer inside him that he has ever seen in a live human being. That's saying a lot. "He's a dead man walking," the doctor said. On Monday, May 11, 1981, the King of Reggae died of a metastatic brain tumor.

Bob Marley had already survived a previous, violent attempt on his life. On December 3, 1976, a hit squad stormed his home studio at 56 Hope Road in Kingston. His wife Rita Marley took a non-fatal bullet in her head. Band employee Louis Griffiths took two bullets in his stomach. Bob Marley took a bullet across the chest and in the arm, but his manager Don Taylor, who was in front of Marley, took five shots in his back and legs. Everyone survived the ambush, but Bob left Jamaica for London in a self-imposed exile.

Bob survived the ambush with heavy gun fire at Hope Road, just to have hope dashed months later by a cancer diagnosis. "Momma, the doctor say I have cancer in my leg and maybe they have to cut it off," he told his mother Cedella Marley Booker. "Why would Jah give me cancer? I never do anybody any wrong; I never do anything that is wrong. What is it? Why?" Having no answer to her son's lament, Mother Marley could only ensure him, "Who Jah loveth, He chastiseth..."[1]

---

1 *Bob Marley: Freedom Road* 2007, Directed by Sonia Anderson.

Did Jah give Bob Marley cancer? There are legitimate questions in Bob Marley's case. Why was his melanoma so unusually aggressive, defying the normal behavior of that cancer? How did he even get the disease? Melanomas are typically found in whites who are 65 years old and older. How did the young, healthy and melanated Bob Marley get the disease? We are told that a recurring toe injury is the source. But as forensic pathologist Dr. Michael Hunter admitted, melanomas don't act that way.[2] Melanoma does not arise from injuries or scar tissue.[3]

Or did an enemy give this "Che Guevara of popular culture" the disease that will ultimately take his life? Professor Fred Zindi of the University of Zimbabwe raises the possibility:

> To our mind, it is absolutely plausible and extremely likely that cancer can be artificially induced in a specific target...Certainly we must realize that the causes, the mechanism of how various pollutants cause cancer, has been studied and understood with some of the billions and billions of research monies devoted to cancer over the past hundred years...In fact, many believe that is exactly how Bob Marley died. Cancer was inflicted through his toe. The only thing you have to entertain is whether you think it is possible; whether the technological understanding exists; whether the malice exists to give someone cancer and whether you think it was possible to do those things in the 1970s.[4]

Cancer artificially induced in Bob Marley? How? By whom?

Professor Zindi's credible remarks were made in 2015. Two years later, the *in*credible (and *dis*credible) site *YourNewsWire*.com published an explosive article: "CIA Agent Confesses On Deathbed: 'I Killed Bob Marley'."[5] The author

---

[2] *Autopsy: The Last Hours of Bob Marley* (Reelz TV Series). Aired February 25, 2017.

[3] Dr. Lowell Taubman in Roger Steffens, *So Much Things To Say: The Oral History of Bob Marley* (New York: W.W. Norton & Company, 2017) 287.

[4] Fred Zindi, "How Did Bob Marley Die?" *The Herald* (Zimbabwe) October 4, 2015.

[5] Baxter Dmitry, "CIA Agent Confesses On Deathbed: 'I Killed Bob Marley'," *YourNewsWire*.com December 1, 2017.

claims that a retired 29-year operative of the CIA was admitted on November 27, 2017 to Mercy Hospital in Main and, on his deathbed, confessed to having committed seventeen political assassinations on behalf of the Agency, including that of Bob Marley. The CIA operative, named Bill Oxley and pictured in his hospital bed with a breathing tube in his nose, claimed that *he* injected Bob Marley with cancer.

YourNewsWire.com
News. Truth. Unfiltered.

HOME   NEWS ˅   HEALTH   SCI/ENVIRONMENT   TECHNOLOGY   ENTERTAINMENT   CONSPIRACIES   CONTACT US
CONTACT US   TERMS OF USE   PRIVACY   ADVERTISE
HEADLINES ›   [November 30, 2017] Emmanuel Macron: Gender-Based Insults Now Criminal Offence In France › NEWS

CIA Agent Confesses On Deathbed: 'I Killed Bob Marley'

A 79-year-old retired officer of the CIA, Bill Oxley, has made a series of stunning confessions since he was admitted to the Mercy Hospital in Maine on Monday and told he has weeks to live. He claims he committed 17 assassinations for the American government between 1974 and 1985, including the music icon Bob Marley.

The story spread like wildfire. In 2018 rappers T.I. and Busta Rhymes both shared the story on their social media platforms.[6] The rappers were roundly criticized for spreading an alleged "debunked" conspiracy theory to their millions of followers.[7] It is indeed the case that the *YourNewsWire* article is completely bogus

---

6 Nick Reilly, "T.I. and Busta Rhymes claim Bob Marley was assassinated by the CIA," *NME* September 5, 2018.
7 Aaron Homer, "The Bob Marley Conspiracy Theory That Would Prove He Was Murdered By The CIA," *Grunge* August 25, 2021.

and has been successfully debunked.[8] The author included extensive quotes from the alleged CIA operative dying in Main but the article did not provide a single source for the quotations or for the story. "The writer doesn't say where he's getting his information from. Was he at Bill Oxley's bedside himself? Or did he hear the story from someone else? If so, who? He doesn't say."[9] No evidence of a Bill Oxley with an association with the Agency could be found and Mercy Hospital had no record of such a patient. What's more, the image of the white-haired gentleman in a hospital bed that accompanies the unsourced article – supposedly a picture of the confessing Bill Oxley in Main – is actually an edited stock image taken in Poland.

This article was *too easily* debunked. Nevertheless, we can defend T.I. and Busta's support of the claim that Bob Marley was murdered by the CIA. The *story* in the article – the "conspiracy theory" put in the mouth of the dying (but fictitious) "Bill Oxley" – is a very *defensible* conspiracy "theory" with strong evidential support. In fact, I strongly suspect that the whole point of this bogus and easily debunked *article* of the confessing operative was to discredit the strongly supported *story* of the CIA's actual involvement in the demise of the much-loved Bob Marley. This compelling story is not dependent on "Bill Oxley."

Professor Zindi concluded above: "The only thing you have to entertain is whether you think it is possible; whether the technological understanding exists; whether the malice exists to give someone cancer and whether you think it was possible to do those things in the 1970s."[10]

The answers to these questions, as we will now show with overwhelming evidence, are: Yes; Yes; Yes, and Yes.

---

8 Dan MacGuill, "Did a CIA Agent Confess to Killing Bob Marley?" *Snopes* December 3, 2017; Martin Williams, "No, the CIA didn't kill Bob Marley," *Channel 4 News* December 5, 2017.
9 Williams, "No, the CIA didn't kill Bob Marley."
10 Fred Zindi, "How Did Bob Marley Die?" *The Herald* (Zimbabwe) October 4, 2015.

Part 1

Weaponizing Cancer

Chapter One

America's Murder, Inc.

I.   *The Assassination Bureau*

Since the close of World War II, the U.S. has had in place an assassination apparatus. William Blum has outlined this "decapitation squad" operated by the CIA, the purpose of which was (and is) "killing heads of state and others."[11] This "decapitation squad" was referred to by former President Lyndon Baines Johnson as "Murder Inc." and he implied it was involved in killing his predecessor President John F. Kennedy.[12] A declassified 1953 CIA file entitled "A Study of Assassination" is a 19-page training manual or "how-to" guidebook in the art of political killing. It outlines techniques to efficiently carry out such "decapitations,"[13] and offers detailed descriptions of the procedures, instruments, and implementation of assassination. "Killing a political leader whose burgeoning career is a clear and present danger to the cause of freedom may be held necessary...Persons who are morally squeamish should not attempt (p. 6]," the document admonishes. The targets of these "decapitation" operations are those persons who threaten the

---

11 Bill Blum, *Killing Hope: U.S. Military and CIA Interventions Since World War II* (Monroe, Main: Common Courage Press, 2004).
12 Leo Janos, "The Last Days of The President," *The Atlantic* July 1973. See also Max Holland, "The Assassination Tapes," *The Atlantic* June 2004.
13 https://ia800904.us.archive.org/30/items/CIAAStudyOfAssassination1953/CIA%20-%20A%20Study%20of%20Assassination%20%281953%29.pdf (= *Ron Collins, The Secret CIA Assassination Manual: A Study of Assassination* [Lulu.com, 2015])

U.S.'s freedom to pursue her capitalist and colonial ambitions in Third World nations. This manual was used during Operation PBSUCCESS, which involved the overthrow of the democratically elected Guatemalan government of President Jacobo Árbenz in 1954 and the installation of *the* military dictatorship *of* Carlos Castillo Armas. "A Study of Assassination" was distributed to CIA agents and operatives.

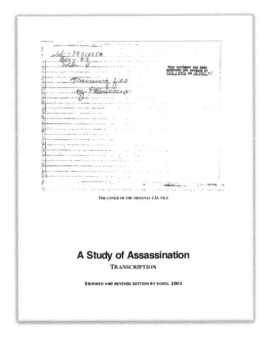

THE COVER OF THE ORIGINAL CIA FILE

A Study of Assassination
TRANSCRIPTION

EBOOKED AND REVISED EDITION BY SOKOL 2002

Retired Air Force Colonel Fletcher Prouty, who was chief of special operations for the Joint Chiefs of Staff during the Kennedy years and provided support for clandestine CIA operations from 1955 to 1964 (and who is also behind the character "Mr. X." in Oliver Stone's 1991 hit movie *JFK*[14]), tells us "uncounted times...enemies of the government had been killed by this 'Murder Inc.' quickly, cleanly and with precision...and without their apprehension and prosecution by anyone."[15] This government sponsored murder capability was a professional operation.

Teams of professional "hit men" are recruited, trained, equipped and provided with a complex of "real life" identities, by this government, in order that they may live this strange existence as normal individuals.

---

14 Mark Seal, "Can Hollywood Solve JFK's Murder?" *Texas Monthly* (December 1991): 128-133, 158-168.
15 L. Fletcher Prouty, "Lyndon B. Johnson, John F. Kennedy and the Great American Coup D'etat," @ http://www.prouty.org/johnson.html

They are always available for these special duties anywhere and against any target. They are skilled automatons who are set in motion by a code system that does not require the identities of those who have made the "Decision" ...These murder teams belong to an organization that is, in a special sense, timeless. Such murders are not arranged and carried out on an "ad hoc" basis. These teams are always ready.[16]

This murder capability of the United States was codified in 1960 as ZR/RIFLE, the code name for a documented systematic CIA assassination program.[17] ZR/RIFLE was a project to research and develop the means for overthrowing foreign political leaders, including a standing "capability to perform assassination" when required. This standing assassination capability, euphemized by the CIA as an "Executive Action,"[18] was requested by the White House.[19] The CIA has correctly been described as "the secret hand of the White House."[20] The project aimed at the "assassination of political leaders whose further existence impinged on U.S. interests."[21] Bill Harvey, known as the CIA's "Loaded Gun," ran ZR/RIFLE.[22]

---

16 Prouty, "Lyndon B. Johnson, John F. Kennedy and the Great American Coup D'etat."

17 Don Bohning, "Distorting History," *The Intelligencer: Journal of U.S. Intelligence Studies* 16:2 (Fall 2008): 67-76.

18 "The initial term of the CIA for assassination of foreign leaders was 'Executive Action'." Noel Twyman, *Bloody Treason: On Solving History's Greatest Murder Mystery: The Assassination of John F. Kennedy* (Rancho Santa Fe, CA: Laurel Publishing, 1997) 389.

19 *Alleged Assassination Plots Involving Foreign Leaders: an interim report of the Select Committee to Study Governmental Operations with Respect to Intelligence Activities, United States Senate: together with additional, supplemental, and separate views* (Washington: U.S. Government Printing Office, 1975) 182.

20 Daniele Ganser, *NATO's Secret Armies: Operation Gladio and Terrorism in Western Europe* (London: Frank Cass, 2005).

21 Stockton, *Flawed Patriot*, 370.

22 David C. Martin, "The CIA's 'Loaded Gun,'" *The Washington Post* October 10, 1976.

II.   *Israel: America's Assassination Ally*

The United States has taken the intelligence-gathering and assassination techniques developed in Israel as a model[23]

Prior to 1948 a Zionist underground ran surreptitious intelligence operations in the U.S. with a four-member commission that included two diplomats, a troubleshooter who traveled frequently to Palestine, and an American citizen.[24] This underground smuggled war materials to Palestine and passed classified information to Israel after the state was established.[25] Then a deal was struck in 1951 when Prime Minister David Ben-Gurion, father of the State of Israel, came to Washington and offered the CIA the services of Israeli intelligence. Reuven Shiloah, the founder of Israeli intelligence, came to D.C. with him. Shiloah met with his American counterpart, James Jesus Angleton, the CIA's counterintelligence chief, and the two of them worked out an arrangement of a CIA-Mossad collaboration. This agreement established "the foundation for the exchange of secret information between the two services and committed them to report to each other on subjects of mutual interest."[26] Thus began Operation Balsam, the intelligence sharing between the two countries on "subjects of mutual interest."

This official CIA-Mossad collaboration went well beyond simply sharing information. Andrew Cockburn and Leslie Cockburn, authors of *Dangerous Liaisons: The Inside Story of the U.S.-Israeli Covert Relationship* (2007), report,

---

23 Ronen Bergman, *Rise And Kill First: The Secret History of Israel's Targeted Assassinations* (Random House) xxiv.

24 David K. Shipler, "Close U.S.-Israel Relationship Makes Keeping Secrets Hard," *The New York Times* December 22, 1985.

25 Jeff McConnell, "Israeli Spies in the US," *MERIP Middle East Report* 138 (Jan-Feb 1986) 35-37, 45.

26 Ted Snider, "Israel-linked assassinations: How much is the US really involved?" *Responsible Statecraft* December 21, 2020.

there has been since almost the earliest days of the Israeli state and the earliest days of the CIA *a secret bond*, a secret link between them, basically by which the Israelis -- *the Israeli intelligence -- did jobs for the CIA and for the rest of American intelligence.* You can't understand what's been going on around the world with American covert operations and the Israeli covert operations until you understand that the two countries have this secret arrangement (emphasis added – WM).[27]

The link between and the linchpin of this collaboration was James Jesus Angleton. Beginning in 1951 Angleton managed the CIA's "Israeli desk" and he thus was the Agency's liaison with Israel's Mossad and Shin Bet (internal security) agencies. "The secret alliance between American and Israeli intelligence was born. On the American side, it was led by James Jesus Angleton, chief of the CIA's counterintelligence staff, a supporter of Israel...Through this channel, the CIA would obtain a great deal of Middle East intelligence, a practice that continues to this day."[28] For jobs which the CIA couldn't do or didn't want to be seen doing or *didn't want to do in this country*, things it was legally precluded from doing, Angleton would approach foreign intelligence allies, particularly Israel, to do them on the CIA's behalf, according to the Cockburns.[29]

Israel's intelligence services have built "the most robust streamlined assassination machine in history," according to *The Washington Post.*[30] Israel's "killing machine" "perfected the art of

27 Andrew Cockburn and Leslie Cockburn, *Dangerous Liaisons: The Inside Story of the U.S.-Israeli Covert Relationship* (New York: Harper Perennial 2007 [1991]); Andrew and Leslie Cockburn with Brian Lamb on *C-Span Booknotes* September 1, 1991 @ http://www.booknotes.org/FullPage.aspx?SID=20968-1
28 Bergman, *Rise And Kill First*, 57.
29 See also Jefferson Morley, "CIA and Mossad: Tradeoffs in the Formation of the US-Israel Strategic Relationship," *Washington Report On Middle East Affairs* (May 2018): 63-67; idem, *The Ghost: The Secret Life of CIA Spymaster James Jesus Angleton* New York, NY: St. Martin's Press, 2017)
30 Glenn Frankel, "How Israel's secret service built the most robust assassination machine in history," *The Washington Post* January 26, 2018.

assassination."[31] And Israel is a "targeted-killing junkie."[32] According to Ronen Bergman, who wrote the authoritative and exhaustive history of Israel's targeted killing operations, "the Jewish state and its pre-state paramilitary organizations have assassinated more people than any other country in the Western world."[33] Kidon (Hebrew: כידון, "bayonet" or "tip of the spear") is the Mossad department that handles assassinations. It is a "trigger-happy" agency.[34] Israel's robust assassination machine is guided by the Talmudic mandate (midrashic text Bamidar Rabbah): "If someone comes to kill you, *rise up and kill him first.*" Thus, as Bergman writes: "Summary executions of suspects *who posed no immediate threat, violations of the laws of Israel and the rules of war* – were not renegade acts by rogue operatives. *They were officially sanctioned extrajudicial killings.*"[35] Menachem Begin, Yitzak Shamir, Ariel Sharon, and Ehud Barak all rose to head of the Israeli government, and all committed extra-judicial, face-to-face murders, according to Bergman. And per the long-standing pact between the CIA and the Mossad, America and Israel often kill together, as they did in the hit on Iranian General Qassem Suleeimani in January 2020.[36]

31 Tom Leonard, "The killing machine," *Daily Mail* December 6, 2020.
32 Kenneth M. Pollack, "Learning From Israel's Political Assassination Program," *The New York Times* March 7, 2018.
33 Ronen Bergman, *Rise And Kill First.*
34 Tom Leonard, "The killing machine," *Daily Mail* December 6, 2020.
35 Charles Glass, "" 'Rise and Kill First' Explores The Corrupting Effects of Israel's Assassination Program," *The Intercept* March 11, 2018.
36 Ted Snider, "Israel-linked assassinations: How much is the US really involved?" *Responsible Statecraft* December 21, 2020.

Chapter Two

Death By Natural Causes

Israel's targeted killings are not usually simple assassinations. Israel likes theatrics. "Mossad operations are like Hollywood films."[37] Israel likes to send a message with these loud killings.

> Since World War II, Israel has assassinated more people than any other country in the Western world...The Mossad and Israel's other intelligence arms have done away with individuals who were identified as direct threats to national security and killing them has also sent a bigger message: If you are an enemy of Israel, we will find and kill you, wherever you are.[38]

All of Israel's targeted killings are not loud, however. Sometimes the Mossad opts for a quieter execution. For political reasons some targets cannot be seen to have been killed by Israel. Plausible deniability therefore requires a "Low-Signature" operation, an "execution without footprints."[39] This is why, as Tom Leonard reports, "Mossad likes to use poisons."[40]

YASSER ARAFAT

Wayne Smith, former head of the US interests' section in Havana, said concerning the CIA's decades-long obsession with

---

37 Tom Leonard, "The killing machine," *Daily Mail* December 6, 2020.
38 Bergman, *Rise And Kill First*, xxii, xxiii
39 Bergman, *Rise And Kill First*, 452.
40 Tom Leonard, "The killing machine," *Daily Mail* December 6, 2020.

assassinating Fidel Castro: "Cuba seems to have the same effect on *American* administrations that a full moon has on a *werewolf. We may not sprout* hair and howl, but *we* behave in the same way."[41]

What Castro was to America and the CIA, Palestinian Liberation Organization (PLO) leader Yasser Arafat was to Israel and the Mossad. "The hunt for the person who was codenamed The Head of the Fish, Yasser Arafat, was the most extensive and long term in the history of Israeli intelligence. It started back in 1964 and lasted for decades. Israel tried to kill him numerous times...defense minister of Israel, Ariel Sharon...was...obsessed to kill Arafat."[42] Much like Castro did to the CIA, "No target thwarted, vexed and bedeviled the Israeli assassination apparatus more than Yasir Arafat".[43] The U.S.'s attempts to kill Castro and Israel's attempts to kill Arafat are instructive; they throw light on the assassination of Bob Marley.

The Mossad's many attempts to kill Arafat fell to a taskforce codenamed Operation Salt-Fish. Defense Minister General Ariel Sharon directed the operation. Over the many years the operation included, for example, plans to plant a powerful explosive under the VIP seating area of a local stadium in Lebanon, the PLO headquarters, where the entire PLO leadership were expected to celebrate the new year and would therefore be wiped out. General Sharon approved the terrorist plan to blow up a stadium filled with innocents, but Prime Minister Menachem Begin was eventually impressed upon to cancel it because, "if it became known that we (Israel) were involved, the whole world would turn against us."[44]

---

41 Duncan Campbell, "Close but no cigar: how America failed to kill Fidel Castro," *The Guardian* November 26, 2016.

42 Ronen Bergman, "Journalist Details Israel's 'Secret History' of Targeted Assassinations," *NPR* January 31, 2018.

43 Ronen Bergman, "How Arafat Eluded Israel's Assassination Machine," *The New York Times Magazine* January 23, 2018.

44 Isaac Horoviz, "Killing Arafat//Author Ronen Bergman reveals the secret inside..." *Ami Magazine* January 31, 2018.

Instead, General Sharon launched an all-out war on Lebanon with the aim of wiping Arafat out "in his bunker." But the 1982 Siege of Beirut failed to kill the PLO leader, and with each failed attempt Arafat grew in political stature on the world stage. In 1974 he addressed the United Nations. This growing legitimization of the hated PLO leader put Israel in a quandary. Once Arafat became a man of international prominence and prestige, considered by much of the world as a statesman, "Gradually the awareness grew that Arafat was a political matter, and he must not be seen as a target for assassination," said brigadier general Amos Gilboa, head of AMAN's Research Division.[45] This means Arafat must not be seen as a target of *open* assassination.

> The problem with operation Salt Fish, for Sharon and for Israel, was that the entire world was watching. With each failed assassination attempt, Israel looked more and more like a military power overrunning a sovereign nation in a monomaniacal quest to kill a single man. Arafat, rather than being seen as a bloodthirsty terrorist, was now the hunted leader of a nation of refugees trampled by the Israeli war machine. Sharon had achieved precisely the opposite of what he wanted. Its main target now an object of global sympathy...Sharon realized that by this point, Arafat was such a popular figure that *an open assassination* would only make him a martyr to his cause. So, he instructed the intelligence organizations to intensify their surveillance of Arafat and to see if they could find *a more subtle way to dispose of him*. Operation Salt Fish morphed into Operation Goldfish."[46]

The aim of Operation Goldfish was still to kill Arafat, but not openly; kill him "without leaving an Israeli footprint."[47] This is what the Mossad calls a "low-signature" or a silent operation: "The killing could not cause a commotion, could not draw attention to the assassination, and, ideally, would make it look like [the target] had died of natural causes,"[48] as said by Israeli

---

45 Bergman, Rise And Kill First, 276.
46 Bergman, *Rise And Kill First*, 259, 267.
47 Bergman, "How Arafat Eluded Israel's Assassination Machine"; Bergman, *Rise And Kill First*, 452.
48 Bergman, *Rise And Kill First*, 454.

investigative journalist and author Ronen Bergman, who wrote the authoritative and exhaustive history of Israel's targeted killing operations.

Operation Goldfish seems to have had an evolving concept of a "low-signature" or silent operation to assassinate Arafat. For example, an early plan was to shoot down commercial flights that may be carrying Arafat, killing civilians along with the PLO chief.

> When the Mossad reported that Arafat was flying more commercial flights, with the PLO often buying up the entire first-class or business-class cabin for him and his aides, Sharon decided that one of those would make a legitimate target. He ordered [chief of staff of the Israeli Defense Forces Lt. General Rafael] Eitan, the air force, and the operations branch to come up with a plan to shoot down a civilian jetliner. Sharon sketched out the broad parameters. The flight would have to be shot down over the open sea, far from the coast, so that it would take investigators a long time to find the wreckage and establish whether it had been hit by a missile or had crashed due to engine failure. Deep water would be preferable, to make recovery even more difficult. Aviem Sella couldn't believe his ears. "It was a direct and clear order from him: Shoot the plane down," he said. "I had no problem with killing Arafat, who deserved to die, in my opinion. The problem was with shooting down a civilian airliner with innocent passengers aboard. That is a war crime."... The air force drew up a detailed plan to shoot down an airliner. Its representatives at the Goldfish forum explained that they had chosen a precise spot on the commercial air route across the Mediterranean, one where there was no continuous radar coverage by any nation and where the sea below was a daunting three miles deep. A salvage operation there would be extremely difficult, perhaps impossible, with the technology of the time. This complex plan set strict parameters for where the Israeli aircraft could shoot down Arafat's plane undetected, which meant there would be a fairly narrow window of opportunity for executing the attack.[49]

It may be hard to see how blowing up a commercial airliner classifies as a "silent" operation, but the elements that make this operation low-signature probably include:

---

49 Bergman, *Rise And Kill First*, 272.

- The Kill Zone would be a spot over the Mediterranean Sea where there is no radar coverage by any nation, so the scrambled Israeli F-15s could fire on the airliner undetected.
- The Kill Zone would be over an area of the sea three miles deep, making recovery of wreckage important for an investigation unlikely: "the plane would vanish forever."[50]

This operation was Low-Signature because the logistics made it unlikely to be traced back to Israel.

General Sharon scrambled such planes on five occasions, willing to down commercial flights carrying civilians in hopes of killing one man whom Jews saw as "Hitler Incarnate," Yasser Arafat. However, according to Bergman, each time the operation was sabotaged and finally abandoned because, if something went wrong, the mission "could ruin the state [of Israel] internationally if it were known that we downed a civilian airliner," as brigadier general Amos Gilboa warned the chief of staff of the Israeli Defense Forces, Lt Gen Rafael Eitan.[51]

Israeli intelligence moved on to an even more silent option: a poisoning that made Arafat's death look like he died of natural causes. Bergman sets the stage:

> In November 2002, in the wake of several horrific attacks against Israelis, Sharon gave an order to encircle the Mukataa, Arafat's headquarters, and to leave Arafat and some of his men besieged inside. His instructions were to make life miserable for "the dog from the Mukataa," as he called him—sometimes cutting off electricity, sometimes cutting off the water supply. Sharon then ordered a company of armored D9 bulldozers to demolish another wall of the compound every few days.
>
> Even still, there were disagreements about what, finally, should be done with Arafat. Some thought he should be made a target for liquidation and that Israel should strike against him. Some thought he should be hit covertly, without connecting the action to Israel. Others

50 Bergman, *Rise And Kill First*, 273.
51 Oliver Holmes, "Israel had plan to shoot down passenger plane to kill Arafat, book claims," *The Guardian* January 25, 2018.

were in favor of exiling him, while some said he should be left alone "to rot" in the Mukataa. After a grave attack in April 2002, Sharon and chief of staff Mofaz were overheard conducting a private conversation. They sat near microphones at a public event, unaware that a television crew was already connected to the microphones and was filming them from afar.

> MOFAZ: We've got to get rid of him.
> SHARON: What?
> MOFAZ: To get rid of him.
> SHARON: I know.
> MOFAZ: To take advantage of the opportunity now. There won't be another opportunity. I want to talk with you now.
> SHARON: When we act...I don't know what method you use for this (chuckles). But you put everyone to sleep...(becomes serious). We have to be careful!

It is unclear precisely which "act" Sharon was referring to here, but the IDF and the intelligence community did prepare contingency plans for each potential Arafat strategy. The commander of the air force, Dan Halutz, who was an enthusiastic proponent of exiling Arafat, picked out two small islands—one near the coast of Lebanon and the other near Sudan—as potential new homes for the president...

The deliberations surrounding Arafat eventually reached Washington. Bush administration officials feared that, just as Sharon had decided to liquidate Yassin, he would also order the assassination of Arafat. In a meeting at the White House on April 14, 2004, Bush demanded that Sharon promise not to harm Arafat. According to one of the participants in the meeting, Sharon told the president that he understood his request ("I see your point"). Bush saw that the prime minister was prevaricating, and he pressed on until Sharon explicitly promised not to kill Arafat.

Even before this promise, Sharon, in consultation with the heads of the IDF and the intelligence community, had reached the conclusion that *Israel must not be seen as being involved* in the death of Yasser Arafat in any way. This became even more important after he made the promise to President Bush.

AND THEN, SUDDENLY, THE man who had managed to elude death so many times succumbed to a mysterious intestinal disease and died.[52]

What made him die so suddenly?

---

52 Bergman, *Rise And Kill First*, 560-561.

While President Bush in April 2004 gave Prime Minister Begin a red light to Israel's plans to assassinate Arafat, reportedly *another* White House meeting occurred later, and the U.S. president finally relented to Begin's request. We learn of this second meeting form Uri Avnery, a former Israeli legislator and reporter. He reported in 2007.

> Just before he died last month, Uri Dan, Ariel Sharon's loyal mouthpiece for almost 50 years, published a book in France. It includes a report of a conversation Sharon told him about, with President Bush. Sharon asked for permission to kill Arafat and Bush gave it to him, **with the proviso that it must be done undetectably**. When Dan asked Sharon whether it had been carried out, Sharon answered: "It's better not to talk about that." Dan took this as confirmation.[53]

Uri Avnery, an Israeli journalist, and Yasir Arafat in Beirut in 1982. Anat Saragusti.

Kill him but kill him "undetectably." President Bush green lighted a "low-signature" assassination of Yasser Arafat.

On October 11, 2004, at approximately 11:30pm, two hours after he ate dinner, Arafat fell ill, vomiting. The next day his doctor diagnosed Arafat with viral gastroenteritis. On November 3

---

53 Uri Avnery, "If Arafat were still alive," *The Guardian* January 30, 2007.

he fell into a coma, dying eight days later at the Percy Hospital in Paris, France of internal bleeding in the brain. PLO chief Yasser Arafat died of natural causes, we are told.

In 2012 Arafat's widow Suha Arafat had his remains exhumed and an investigation initiated. Arafat's remains were sent to laboratories in Russia, France and Switzerland. Scientists from the Vaudois University Hospital Centre (CHUV) in Lausanne, Switzerland carried out a detailed examination of 38 items belonging to Arafat including his underwear and a toothbrush, Arafat's medical records, samples taken from his remains (blood, sweat and urine from Arafat's cloths) and items he had taken into the hospital in Paris where he died. The biological materials included pieces of Arafat's bones and soil samples from around his corpse. These were compared with a control group of 37 items of Arafat's that had been in storage for some time before his death. The toxicologists found higher than expected levels of a highly toxic radioactive material, polonium-210 - up to eighteen times higher - on Arafat's underwear, headwear, and toothbrush. Russian intelligence agent Alexander Litvinenko died of polonium-210 poisoning in November 2006. The Swiss scientists concluded regarding their investigation of Arafat's remains: "These findings support the possibility of Arafat's poisoning with polonium-210." They stressed that they had been unable to reach a more definitive conclusion because of the time that had lapsed since Arafat's death, the limited samples available and the confused "chain of custody" of some of the specimens.[54] The conclusions of the Swiss investigation were published in the *Lancet*, one of the world's premier medical journals, on October 12 under the title, "*Improving Forensic Investigation for Polonium Poisoning.*"[55] The Report Summary reads:

---

54 "Yasser Arafat 'may have been poisoned with polonium," *BBC* November 6, 2013.

55 Pascal Froidevaux, Sébastien Baechler, Claude J Bailat, Vincent Castella, Marc Augsburger, Katarzyna Michaud, Patrice Mangin, François O Bochud, "Improving forensic investigation for polonium poisoning," *Lancet* 382 October 12, 2013: 1308; Prof. Patrice Mangin et al., *Expert Forensics Report Concerning The Late President Yasser Arafat* November 5, 2013 @

On the evening of 12 October 2004, President Yasser Arafat developed acute gastrointestinal symptoms eventually resulting in death one month later. The numerous clinical investigations performed prior to his death did not yield a diagnosis.

The DNA analysis performed on the personal belongings and the body remains showed that they belonged to President Arafat. The toxicological examinations did not reveal the presence of poisonous substances. The radio-analytical evaluation established the presence of abnormally high quantities of polonium-210 that lead to the exhumation of the body in November 2012. Specimens of air, soil, shroud, residue of tissues and bones were collected.

More than nine months of measurements and analysis demonstrated the presence of abnormally high quantities of polonium-210 and lead-210 in various specimens collected in the tomb. Radon gas present in the tomb, tobacco smoking and body contamination with radium-226 did not explain the observations.

Taking into account all the observations – in particular the higher than expected activities of polonium-210 and lead-210 and the impurities present in a commercial source of polonium – and considering also the analytical limitations of the study – mostly time lapse since death and the nature and quality of the specimens – the results moderately support the proposition that the death was the consequence of poisoning with polonium-210.[56]

With the publication of the Swiss report a Palestinian committee was organized to investigate the death of Arafat headed by Fatah official Tawfik Tirawi, a retired general who served as chief of Palestinian General Intelligence in the West Bank and currently advised Palestinian Authority President Mahmoud Abbas. The committee released a seventy-page preliminary report. Tirawi summarizes the report's conclusions: "The crime has three

https://s3.documentcloud.org/documents/815515/expert-forensics-report-concerning-the-late.pdf
56 "Factsheet on forensics report concerning the late President Yasser Arafat," Press factsheet | Lausanne, November 10, 2013 @ https://www.curml.ch/sites/default/files/fichiers/documents/factsheet_arafat_2 01310081.pdf.

pillars: the first is the perpetrator, which is Israel. The second is the method, which is poisoning. The third pillar is the means of delivering the poison, which we will get to, God willing. Whether the tool was an Arab, a foreigner or a Palestinian makes no difference. When the investigation is completed, Israel will not be able to deny it."[57] Suha Arafat expressed the belief that somebody within her husband's own circle was involved. Mahmoud Habbash, Palestinian Authority Religious Endowments Minister declared in a broadcast on official Palestinian television that Arafat was martyred in the same way Prophet Muhammad was: by being poisoned by Jews. "Be satisfied, o mighty one, o Martyr Arafat, that you were killed the same way Allah's Messenger was killed," he reportedly said. [58]

Israel predictably denied the "preposterous" allegation that they poisoned Yasser Arafat.[59] Equally predictably, the French and the Russian investigations echoed Israel's denial, "finding" that Arafat died of "natural causes" rather than of poisoning. However, both of these investigations agree with the Swiss in finding higher than expected levels of radioactive polonium and radioactive lead.[60] The apparent contradiction between their first conclusion (Arafat died of natural causes and not polonium poisoning) and

57 Yifa Yaakov, "PA Minister: Jews poisoned Muhammad, Arafat," *Times of Israel* November 13, 2013.
58 Yaakov, "PA Minister: Jews poisoned Muhammad, Arafat."
59 "In Wake of Swiss Findings, Israel Vehemently Denies Poisoning Arafat," *Haaretz* November 7, 2013.
60 Kim Willsher and Harriet Sherwood, "Yasser Arafat died of natural causes, French investigators says," *The Guardian* December 3, 2013; Steve Gutterman, "Russia says Arafat died of natural causes," *Reuters* December 26, 2013.

their second conclusion (higher than expected levels of radioactive polonium and lead were found in Arafat's system) has not been resolved.

TWO MORE "NATURAL CAUSES" MURDERS

The State of Israel has mastered the silent operation or "death by natural causes" assassination. Two further cases are worth noting.

On March 29, 1978 Wadie Haddad, the Palestinian leader of the armed wing of the Popular Front for the Liberation of Palestine, died in an East Berlin hospital. *Time Magazine* Jerusalem correspondent Aaron Klein, in his 2005 book *Striking Back: the 1972 Munich Olympics Massacre and Israel's Deadly Response*, wrote of Haddad's "Slow, mysterious death" and noted that the 309-pound Palestinian leader was a food lover with a weakness for chocolate. Klein reveals that the Mossad worked with a close associate of Haddad to secretly give him his favorite Belgium chocolate laced with a poison.[61] Haddad was on Israel's "Hit List." Bergman likewise affirms that the Mossad was able to get very close to Haddad and contaminate another item of his with a poison that the Mossad called "the potion of gods."[62] Bergman's account is worth quoting at length.

FOR EIGHTEEN MONTHS AFTER the Entebbe raid, Wadie Haddad lived securely and very affluently in Baghdad and Beirut. The Mossad was apprehensive about using firearms in Arab capitals such as Baghdad, Damascus, and Beirut, however, because the risk of capture was simply too great. And so more silent methods of assassination were sought, ones that had a less visible signature and made the death appear natural or

---

61 The Associated Press, "Israeli assassination tool? Belgian chocolate," *NBC News* May 6, 2006; Aaron Klein, *Striking Back: the 1972 Munich Olympics Massacre and Israel's Deadly Response* (New York, NY: Random House, 2005).
62 Ronen Bergman, "Journalist Details Israel's 'Secret History' of Targeted Assassinations," *NPR* January 31, 2018.

accidental, the product of, say, a disease or a car crash. In such cases, even if there were to be a suspicion of foul play, by the time anything could be done, the killers would be long gone, whereas, in a hit using firearms, it is immediately clear that the killers are still in the vicinity.

The Mossad decided to exploit its deep intelligence penetration of Haddad's organization and to allocate the job of eliminating him to Junction. The assassination, using poison, was assigned to the agent Sadness, who had a high degree of access to his home and office.

On January 10, 1978, Sadness switched Haddad's toothpaste for an identical tube containing a lethal toxin, which had been developed after intense effort at the Israel Institute for Biological Research, in Ness Ziona, southeast of Tel Aviv, one of the most closely guarded locations in Israel. It was founded in 1952 and still serves as the facility where Israel develops its top-secret defensive and offensive biological warfare agents. Each time Haddad brushed his teeth, a minute quantity of the deadly toxin penetrated the mucous membranes in his mouth and entered his bloodstream. The gradual accretion in his body, when it reached a critical mass, would be fatal.

Haddad began feeling sick and was admitted to an Iraqi government hospital. He told the doctors there that in the middle of January he had begun suffering from severe abdominal spasms after a meal. His appetite faded, and he lost more than twenty-five pounds.

He was first diagnosed as suffering from hepatitis and, later, a very bad cold. Doctors treated him with aggressive antibiotics, but his condition didn't improve. His hair began to fall out and his fever spiked. The doctors in Baghdad were at a loss. They suspected that Haddad had been poisoned. Arafat instructed an aide to approach the Stasi, East Germany's secret service, to ask them for help. In the 1970s, the Stasi had provided Palestinian terror organizations with passports, intelligence, shelter, and weapons. The East German leader, Erich Honecker, and others in that country regarded Arafat as a true revolutionary, like Fidel Castro, and were ready to help him.

On March 19, 1978, Haddad was flown to the Regierungskrankenhaus, in East Berlin, a prestigious hospital that catered to members of the intelligence and security communities. His aides packed a bag for him with his toiletries, including a tube of the deadly toothpaste.

Intelligence material reaching the Mossad after he boarded the plane from Baghdad to Berlin gave cause for satisfaction. "Haddad was absolutely finished when he reached Germany," read a report at a Junction command meeting. "Biological Institute experts say he is a dead man walking."

He was admitted under the pseudonym Ahmed Doukli, forty-one years old, five feet six inches tall. He was indeed in bad condition:

28

hemorrhaging in many places, including subcutaneously, from the pericardium around his heart, at the root of his tongue, his tonsils, his pleural membranes, and inside his cranium, with large quantities of blood in his urine. Bone marrow functioning was suppressed, with a resulting drop in the red platelet count in his blood. Despite his being treated as a privileged patient, Haddad's condition continued to deteriorate. The military physicians, the best doctors in East Germany, put their patient through every conceivable test: blood, urine, bone marrow, X-rays. They believed he had been poisoned, either with rat poison or some heavy metal, perhaps thallium, but they could find no physical evidence. According to information reaching Israel from an agent in East Germany, Haddad's screams of pain reverberated throughout the hospital, and the doctors gave him increasing doses of tranquilizers and sedatives.

Wadie Haddad died in great agony in the East Berlin hospital on March 29, ten days after he had arrived. Shortly afterward, Stasi chief Erich Mielke received a full report, including results of an autopsy conducted by Professor Otto Prokop, of East Berlin's Humboldt University, one of the world's leading authorities on forensic medicine. He wrote that the immediate cause of death was "brain bleeding and pneumonia by panmyelopathy" and that, in view of the symptoms and the person under discussion, there was room for suspicion that someone had assassinated him. But in hairsplitting forensic medicalese, he was actually admitting that he had no idea what had killed Haddad.

At the time of his death, Haddad was effectively in command of an entirely separate organization from that led by George Habash. But Habash grieved his comrade's demise, and he had no doubt that Israel was behind it.

The Mossad and the leaders of the Israeli defense establishment were overjoyed at the operation's outcome. One of Israel's most potent and effective enemies had been neutralized. No less important, five years after the Lillehammer fiasco, the Mossad had returned to targeted killings, and had done so in an eminently sophisticated manner. This may have been the first time that the phrase "low-signature," to describe an assassination in which the death appears to be natural or by chance, entered the Mossad's vocabulary.

"I was very happy when I heard Haddad was dead," said Shimshon Yitzhaki. Because Israel never admitted that it had killed Haddad, he stressed, "Don't take my words as confirmation of involvement in the case," but he declared that "anyone who has Jewish blood on their hands is doomed to die. Without Haddad, incidentally, his organization couldn't exist. It was already functioning separately from

George Habash, and it split between Haddad's deputies and then kept on splitting until it melted away.[63]

Significant here is the fact that Haddad's condition showed symptoms of leukemia.[64] His autopsy described him as dying "from something that looks like a blood cancer"[65] and so the papers reported that Wadie Haddad "has died of cancer in a hospital in East Germany."[66] The fact that the Mossad possesses a chemical weapon which they call "the potion of the gods" which creates a condition in the target showing symptoms of leukemia, thus making it look like the target died of cancer, is of profound significance. Israel deployed this cancer-causing chemical weapon against Palestinian militant Wadie Hadad in 1978. The Mossad even has an instrument that uses ultrasound waves to inject this poison into a person without breaking the skin. The "potion of the gods" can thus be clandestinely delivered to a target during a routine non-invasive medical procedure, and he would be none the wiser, as the following case suggests.

Another Low Signature assassination was that of Mahmoud Al-Mabhouh, reputedly the chief of logistics and weapons procurement for Hamas's military wing, who was assassinated on January 19, 2010, in Dubai. The aim of the Israeli operation, called Plasma Screen, was "making sure it would appear that al-Mabhouh had died a natural death."[67] When al-Mabhouh returned to his hotel room at around ten o'clock on the evening on January 19, three members of the 27-member Mossad Kill Team were waiting there for him. The grabbed him in his room.

AL-MABHOUH TRIED TO ESCAPE back into the corridor. But two pairs of strong arms gripped him. A third man gagged him with one hand

---

63 Bergman, *Rise And Kill First*, 211-214.
64 The Associated Press, "Israeli assassination tool? Belgian chocolate," *NBC News* May 6, 2006.
65 Bergman, "Journalist Details Israel's 'Secret History' of Targeted Assassinations."
66 Raymond H. Anderson, "Wadi Haddad, Palestinian Hijacking Strategist, Dies," *The New York Times* April 2, 1978.
67 Bergman, *Rise And Kill First*, 613.

and, with the other, **pressed to al-Mabhouh's neck an instrument that uses ultrasound waves to inject medication without breaking the skin.** The instrument was loaded with suxamethonium chloride, an anesthetic known commercially as Scoline that is used in combination with other drugs in surgery. On its own, it induces paralysis and, because it causes the muscles used in breathing to stop working, asphyxiation. The men maintained their grip until al-Mabhouh stopped struggling. As the paralysis spread through his body, they laid him on the floor. Al-Mabhouh was wide awake, thinking clearly, seeing and hearing everything. He just couldn't move. Foam formed at the corners of his mouth. He gurgled. Three strangers stared at him dispassionately, still lightly holding his arms, just in case.

That was the last thing he saw.

The executioners checked his pulse in two places, as they had been instructed to do by a Mossad doctor, making sure that this time he was really dead. They removed his shoes, shirt, and trousers, placed them neatly in the closet, and put the body into the bed, under the covers. The entire episode took twenty minutes. Using a technique developed by the Mossad for such occasions, the team closed the door in such a way that it seemed to have been locked from the inside, with the chain slid into place. They hung a DO NOT DISTURB sign on the door handle, knocked twice on the door of 237 as a mission-accomplished signal, and then disappeared into the elevators. Folliard left one minute later, Daveron four minutes after that, then the surveillance team in the lobby. Within four hours, most of the team was out of Dubai, and none were left twenty-four hours later. In Tel Aviv, a mood of self-satisfaction reigned, an atmosphere that was later described as "the euphoria of a historic success." Everyone involved—Meir Dagan, Holiday, the hit team—believed another mission had been expertly accomplished. Dagan reported the kill to Netanyahu. "Al-Mabhouh," he said, "won't bother us anymore."[68]

---

68 Bergman, *Rise And Kill First*, 616-617.

II.   *The CIA's Low-Signature Operation*

Here in America, the CIA's Assassination Manual recommends "the contrived accident" as the best way to dispose of a target.[69] "For secret assassination, either simple or chase, the contrived accident is the most effective technique. When successfully executed, it causes little excitement and is only casually investigated," the manual says. The Agency also likes *medical assassinations*. On page 10 of the transcription of this document, we read: "In all types of assassinations except terroristic, drugs can be very effective. If the assassin is trained as a doctor or nurse and the subject is under medical care, this is an easy and rare method." The CIA's "Executive Action" program or "Assassination Bureau" operationalized this medical skullduggery: kill a target with a drug or poison clandestinely administered to him by a doctor or nurse under whose medical care the target happens to be.

The reported author of this 1953 CIA "Study of Assassination" was Sidney Gottlieb, known as the Agency's "black sorcerer" and "master of poisons."[70] Described as the CIA's very own "Poisoner In Chief" and "Dr. Death," Gottlieb was born in 1918 in New York to Jewish immigrants from Hungary and he was raised in an Orthodox Jewish home.[71] As a boy, he learned Hebrew and had a bar mitzvah, and in college he was described as "a very high type of Jewish boy."[72] Gottlieb's walk was affected by a defect with which he was born in which his foot was twisted out of shape. His CIA colleagues therefore called him the "clubfooted Jew."

---

69 David Wise, "The CIA – licensed to kill for decades," *Los Angeles Times* July 22, 2009.
70 Stephen Kinzer, *Poisoner in Chief: Sidney Gottlieb and the CIA Search for Mind Control* (New York: Henry Holt and Company, 2019) 252.
71 David B. Green, "This Day in Jewish History - 1999: CIA Dirty Trickster Dies," *Haaretz* May 7, 2014.
72 Kinzer, *Poisoner in Chief*, 5, 7.

Sidney Gottlieb. 'The first person ever to be drafted by the U.S. administration to find ways to control the human mind' Credit: AP

'America's Dr. Mengele': The Jewish Biochemist Backed by the CIA Who Experimented on Thousands

Sidney Gottlieb conducted tests on refugees and prisoners that were as brutal as those carried out by the Nazi doctor. 'He is undoubtedly the closest thing to Mengele in the history of the U.S.,' says author of his biography

Gottlieb was recruited to the CIA in 1951 for his expertise on poisons, "lured away [from the University of Maryland] to work at the CIA where he consulted on undetectable poisons useful in assassinations."[73] According to his lawyer Terry Lenzner: "Because of his expertise in poisons, Gottlieb told me that he was put in charge of assassination programs for the agency. He managed several attempts to assassinate foreign leaders..."[74] "As the CIA's sorcerer, Gottlieb had also attempted to raise assassination to an art form."[75] Ergo, the CIA "Assassination" training manual that he reportedly authored. He was "the CIA's master magician"[76] and served the CIA for 22 years "as the senior scientist presiding over some of the C.I.A.'s darkest secrets."[77]

On behalf of the CIA Gottlieb conducted or oversaw brutal and inhumane experiments on thousands of vulnerable citizens, causing writers to draw a comparison with the notorious Nazi doctor Josef Mengele, known as the "Angel of Death." "Gottlieb

---

73 Troy Lennon, "CIA's 'black sorcerer' scientist Sidney Gottlieb was a master of poisons and mind control," *The Daily Telegraph* (Sydney, Australia) August 3, 2018.
74 Kinzer, *Poisoner in Chief*, 224.
75 Ted Gup, "The Coldest," *The Washington Post* December 16, 2001.
76 Kinzer, *Poisoner in Chief*, 2.
77 Tim Weiner, "Sidney Gottlieb, 80, Dies; Took LSD to C.I.A.," *The New York Times* March 10, 1999.

is undoubtedly the closest thing to Mengele in the history of the United States."[78] His obituary in the *Times* of London read:

> When Churchill spoke of a world "made darker by the dark lights of perverted science," he was referring to the revolting experiments conducted on human beings by Nazi doctors in the concentration camps. But his remarks might with equal justice have been applied to the activities of the CIA's Sidney Gottlieb … Indeed, what Gottlieb and his CIA henchmen did was only in degree different from the activities which had sent a number of Nazi scientists to the gallows at Nuremberg in 1946…Drugs were not Gottlieb's only weapon against the CIA's enemies. He was also involved in assassination plots which at this distance read like something out of a Jacobean revenge play.[79]

BLUEBIRD

The CIA's Project BLUEBIRD, established in 1950, experimented with "Special Interrogation" techniques using drugs and chemicals on captured prisoners at overseas black sites such as Camp King, Fort Clayton, and Villa Schuster. Believing BLUEBIRD lacked a scientific grounding, CIA director Allen Dulles recruited Gottlieb to bring "an infusion of expertise and vision" to the project.[80] Gottlieb was named chief of the newly formed Chemical Division of the *Technical Services Staff* (TSS).

Camp King, the CIA's first secret prison that stood in Germany outside of Frankfurt, was run by Gottlieb. A few miles away was Villa Schuster, named after the Jewish family that built and owned it in 1906. In 1951 Villa Schuster became a black site for the CIA and the Army's Special Operations Division (SOD). It was the CIA's "torture house." "Expendables," i.e., persons whose disappearance the CIA believed would cause no inquiry, were sent to Villa Schuster from Camp King for special interrogation. In

---

78 Tzach Yoked, " 'America's Dr. Mengele': The Jewish Biochemist Backed by the CIA Who Experimented on Thousands," *Haaretz* December 12, 2019.
79 Quoted in Kinzer, *Poisoner in Chief*, 3.
80 Kinzer, *Poisoner in Chief*, 47.

1952 Dulles brought Gottlieb to Germany to oversee the interrogation of the "expendables" at the black site. The staff doctor at Camp King was General Walter Schreiber, the former surgeon general for the Nazi army. Later, these interrogations with "the use of drugs and chemicals" were CONDUCTED by Dr. Kurt Blome, the Nazi's director of research into biological warfare during World War II.

Nazi (Kurt Blome) and Jew (Sidney Gottlieb): Partners in Crime

MKULTRA

In 1953 the CIA initiated its infamous MKULTRA project and made Gottlieb its chief. What is MKULTRA? The CIA Inspector General's Report of July 26, 1963, says: "MK-ULTRA activity is concerned with the research and development of chemical, biological, and radiological materials capable of employment in clandestine operations to control human behavior."[81]   MKULTRA's aim was and is control of human behavior through scientifically sophisticated mind control techniques, particularly through the use of drugs. According to biographer Stephen Kinzer, MKULTRA was Gottlieb's brainchild. "He designed it, helped [Directorate for Plans Chief of Operations] Richard Helms draft the memo to Allen Dulles that brought it into being in 1953, conceived the 149 'subprojects' that pushed its mind control research into hitherto unimagined realms, and monitored the results of extreme experiments at detention centers on four continents."[82] According to journalist Tzach Yoked, "[MKULTRA] was inspired by the horrifying experiments conducted by the Nazis and by the Japanese military," and therefore Gottlieb "conducted tests on refugees and prisoners that were as brutal as those carried out by the Nazi doctor [Mengele]."[83] Besides CIA Director Dulles, Gottlieb's MKULTRA was known only to his boss Richard Helms, deputy director of plan Frank Wisner, and chief of counterintelligence James Jesus Angleton. This fact aided Israel in its assassination operations.

> The Israeli intelligence agency, Mossad, had an intimate connection to the CIA through James Jesus Angleton, the CIA officer who managed their relationship, and the two services often shared intelligence. As head of the CIA's counterintelligence staff, Angleton knew much about MK-ULTRA. Mossad was curious about one of the central MK-ULTRA goals: creating a programmed killer. Mossad officers thought this technique might help them assassinate the Palestinian leader Yasir Arafat.[84]

MKNAOMI

In 1943 the U.S. Army Chemical Corps Research and Development Command established the U.S. Army Biological Warfare Laboratories (USBWL) at Camp (later Fort)

---

81 J. S. Earman, CIA Inspector General's Report July 26, 1963.
82 Kinzer, *Poisoner in Chief*, 196.
83 Yoked, "'America's Dr. Mengele'."
84 Kinzer, *Poisoner in Chief*, 207.

Detrick, Maryland. The USBWL undertook the production and purification of biological agents for the U.S. offensive biowarfare program. In a secret October 1948 report on covert biowarfare the Pentagon's Committee on Biological Warfare noted that "Biological agents would appear to be well adapted to subversive use since very small amounts of such agents can be effective. A significant portion of the human population within selected target areas may be killed or incapacitated." The report listed potential delivery systems for these biological agents: "ventilating systems, subway systems, water supply systems...stamps, envelopes, money, biologicals and cosmetics...contamination of food and beverages."[85]

While military scientists at Detrick could design and concoct all manner of drug combinations, the military had no authority to use them in operations. On the other hand, the CIA "is an action agency."[86] Thus, the Army and the CIA reached an agreement in 1952 and "two of the most secret covert teams in Cold War America became partners."[87] In this joint project called MKNAOMI the Army Chemical Corps' Special Operations Division (SOD) of the Army Biological Laboratory at Fort Detrick partnered with the Technical Services Staff (TSS) of the CIA "in developing, testing, and maintaining biological agents and delivery systems." The Army would produce, and the CIA would operationalize these chemical and biological warfare (CBW) agents and delivery systems for purposes of incapacitation and elimination.[88] MKNAOMI was a secret $3 million project that (officially) lasted 18 years.[89] Twice a year, the SOD and TSS men

---

85 Scott Shane, "Buried Secrets of Biowarfare," *The Baltimore Sun* July 31, 2004.
86 Kinzer, *Poisoner In Chief*, 36.
87 Kinzer, *Poisoner In Chief*, 36.
88 *Project MKULTRA, The CIA's Program of Research in Behavioral Modification - Joint Hearing before the Select Committee on Intelligence and the Subcommittee on Health and Scientific Research Current Section: Appendix A: XVII. Testing and Use of Chemical and Biological Agents by the Intelligence Community,* 388-389
89 Nicholas M. Horrock, "Colby Describes C.I.A. Poison Work," *The New York Times* September 17, 1975.

who collaborated on MKNAOMI "held a planning session at a remote site where they could brainstorm without interruption."[90]

"Under MK-NAOMI," according to one investigator, "the SOD men developed a whole arsenal of toxic substances for CIA use. If Agency operators needed to kill someone in a few seconds with, say, a suicide pill, SOD provided super-deadly shellfish toxin."[91]

When CIA operators merely wanted to be rid of somebody temporarily, SOD stockpiled for them about a dozen diseases and toxins of varying strengths. At the relatively benign end of the SOD list stood Staph. enterotoxin, a mild form of food poisoning—mild compared to botulinum. This Staph. infection almost never killed and simply incapacitated its victim for 3 to 6 hours. Under the skilled guidance of Sid Gottlieb's wartime predecessor, Stanley Lovell, OSS had used this very substance to prevent Nazi official Hjalmar Schacht from attending an economic conference during the war. More virulent in the SOD arsenal was Venezuelan equine encephalomyelitis virus. It usually immobilized a person for 2 to 5 days and kept him in a weakened state for several more weeks. If the Agency wanted to incapacitate someone for a period of months, SOD had two different kinds of brucellosis.[92]

In August 1951 the inhabitants of the quiet village of Pont-Saint-Esprit in southern France suddenly fell ill, struck down with mass insanity and frightful hallucinations of terrifying beasts and fire. Five people died, dozens were interned in asylums, and hundreds were afflicted. For 50 years it was assumed that the outbreak was inadvertently caused by a local baker who unknowingly served the villagers bread contaminated with ergot, the hallucinogenic mould that infects rye grain. In fact, the local bread was deliberately contaminated with LSD by the CIA and the US Army as part of a human chemical warfare experiment.[93]

In 1955 and 1956 MKNAOMI targeted two black housing communities with offensive biological weapons. In Carter Village

---

90 John Marks, *The Search for the "Manchurian candidate": the CIA and Mind Control* (New York: Times Books, 1979) 79.

91 Kinzer, *Poisoner In Chief*, 37.

92 Marks, *The Search for the "Manchurian candidate,"* 81.

93 H.P. Albarelli Jr., *A Terrible Mistake: The Murder of Frank Olson and the CIA's Secret Cold War Experiments* (Walterville, OR: Trine Day LLC, 2009).

in Miami, Florida and in Carter Village in Chatham County, Georgia – both black housing complexes – swarms of *Aedes aegypti* mosquitos bred by the Army Chemical Corps at Fort Detrick laboratories and carrying both yellow fever and dengue fever were unleashed into the air on the Black residents.[94] The purpose of this experiment was to test the effectiveness of the mosquitos as disease vectors to be used as first-strike biological weapons against "the Soviets." 1,080 Miami residents alone came down with whooping cough, some died. This spike in local disease and death convinced the MKNAOMI operatives that the infected mosquitos indeed made effective bioweapons.

For sixteen years (1950-1966) U.S. Army scientists, as part of their germ warfare experiments, deliberately released the bacteria *Serratia marcescens* into the air of eight cities and military installations and then monitored the bacteria's spread. The bacterium was grown in Oakland, California at the U.S. Naval Biological Laboratory and tested in the Bay. In San Francisco, the Army scientists wanted to know if the Bay Area winds would carry the germs into the city. After the bacteria's release military personnel took air samples for testing. Within a week, San Francisco residents developed rare infections and at least one died. In another experiment conducted in the Bay code-named Operation Seaspray, the bacterium was put is a paste and then dropped into the water. The idea was to see if the breaking waves would toss the germs into the air where the winds would carry them into San Francisco or Oakland. The germs were carried into Berkeley and Oakland.[95]

---

94 Harriet A. Washington, *Medical Apartheid: the dark history of medical experimentation on Black Americans from colonial times to the present* (New York: Doubleday 2006)359-365.
95 "Army Tested Biological War in S.F." *Newsday* December 22, 1976.

III.   *Delivery Mechanisms*

According to John Marks, "To the CIA, perhaps the most important question was whether it could covertly deliver the germ to infect the right person. One branch of SOD specialized in building delivery systems".[96] Under the MKNAOMI agreement, "The CIA would ask the SOD to produce a delivery system and a compatible biological agent."[97] The "Agency had long been after SOD to develop a 'non-discernible microbioinoculator (micro + bio + inoculator)' which could give people deadly shots that...could not be 'easily detected upon a detailed autopsy.'"[98] SOD "came up with an array of James Bond weaponry that could use the shellfish toxin and other poisons as ammunition." [99] As dissemination devices the CIA considered cigarettes, chewing gum, cigarette lighters, wrist watches, fountain pens, and rings. "SOD also rigged up aerosol sprays that could be fired by remote control, including a fluorescent starter that was activated by turning on the light, a cigarette lighter that sprayed when lit, and an engine head bolt that shot off as the engine heated. 'If you're going to infect people, the most likely way is respiratory....Everybody breathes, but you might not get them to eat.'"[100] Charles Senseney, an engineer for the Defense Department, told the Church Committee in 1975 that he had devised dart launchers that were disguised as walking canes and umbrellas, as well as a device that fitted into a fluorescent bulb and spread a biological poison when the light was turned on.[101]

On September 16, 1975, the Senate Select Committee Hearing chaired by Idaho Senator Frank Church was scheduled to discuss with CIA Director William Colby the Agency's

96 Marks, *Search for the "Manchurian Candidate"*, 82-83.
97 *Church Committee: Book I - Foreign and Military Intelligence Current Section: F. Chemical and Biological Activities* 361
98 Marks, *Search for the "Manchurian Candidate"*, 82-83.
99 "Intelligence: Of Dart Guns and Poisons," *Time* September 29, 1975.
100 Marks, *Search for the "Manchurian Candidate"*, 82-83.
101 "Intelligence: Of Dart Guns and Poisons," *Time* September 29, 1975.

"Unauthorized Storage of Toxic Agents." At a certain moment during the Hearing Senator Church asked Director Colby if he had brought anything with him, at which point Colby's assistant produced a top-secret CIA weapon from out of a bag on the floor and handed it to Senator Church. It was a black pistol with a scope attached to the top. While it looked conventional enough, this weapon was actually an illustration of what Philip H. Melansen describes as the CIA's "state-of-the-art technology of murder."[102] This was the CIA's infamous "non-discernable microbioinoculator."

Frank Church, chairman of the Senate Committee on Intelligence and Senator John G. Tower of Texas

When the SOD was asked to design biological assassination delivery systems, Fort Detrick's engineers delivered five devices - including the non-discernable microbioinoculator - collectively known as the "Big Five." While detailed descriptions of the Big Five remain classified, documents show that they

102 Philip H. Melanson, "High Tech Mysterious Deaths," *Critique: A Journal of Conspiracies & Metaphysics* 4:3,4 (Fall/Winter '84/85): 209-220 (217).

included a biological dart-firing rifle that uses a pressurized air cartridge; a 7.62 mm rifle cartridge packed with anthrax or botulinum toxin that would disperse in the air on impact; a time-delay bomblet that would release a cloud of bacteria when a train or truck convoy passed; and a pressurized can that sprayed an aerosol of germs.[103]

The most infamous of this "Big Five" is certainly the non-discernable microbioinoculator displayed by Senator Church during the Hearing. Resembling a modified Colt .45 pistol equipped with a fat telescopic sight and an electrical firing mechanism, the gun was adapted to almost silently fire a special dart. The CIA developed a special type of poison that induces a heart attack and leaves no trace. This poison could be frozen into the shape of a dart and then fired at high speed from the modified pistol (the non-discernable microbioinoculator). The dart is tiny as to be almost indetectable — the width of a human hair and a quarter of an inch long.[104] The dart gun was capable of shooting the icy projectile with enough speed that it penetrated the target's clothing and left nothing but a tiny red dot on the skin. The target may feel as if bitten by a mosquito, or they may feel nothing at all. Once in the body the poisonous dart completely disintegrates. The lethal poison is then rapidly absorbed into the bloodstream causing a heart attack. The poison was developed to be undetectable by modern autopsy procedures. After the heart attack the poison denatures quickly and leaves no trace in a victim's body, so that an autopsy is very unlikely to detect that the heart attack resulted from anything other than natural causes.[105] The dart could be coated with a biological agent, such as a cancer-causing agent. This non-discernable micro+bio+inoculator is thus described as a "Heart Attack and Cancer Gun."[106] According to Mary Embree, the CIA agent who is most associated with the creation of this weapon, the

---

103 Scott Shane, "Buried Secrets of Biowarfare," *The Baltimore Sun* July 31, 2004.
104 "Intelligence: Of Dart Guns and Poisons," *Time* September 29, 1975.
105 "Intelligence: Of Dart Guns and Poisons," *Time* September 29, 1975.
106 Press Core, "Assassinations by induced heart attack and cancer," *Sign of The Times* December 16, 2010.

gun was successfully tested on both animals and human prisoners "to great effect."[107] Senator Church called the pistol "a murder instrument that's about as efficient as you can get."[108]

IV.   *Weaponizing Tuberculosis*

> The Central Intelligence Agency operated an 18-year, $3-million super-secret project to develop poisons, biochemical weapons, and such devices as dart guns to administer them, the agency's director testified today. William E. Colby, Director of Central Intelligence, told the Senate Select Committee on Intelligence that...in May 1952, the C.I.A. began a joint project with the special operations division of the Army Biological Laboratory at Fort Detrick, Md. During the course of this project, his testimony and documents disclosed, the C.I.A. stockpiled substances that would cause tuberculosis, anthrax, encephalitis (sleeping sickness), valley fever, salmonella food poisoning and smallpox.[109]

Attempts to weaponize tuberculosis began in earnest during the time of the Second World War and shortly before. Reputedly the world's first major biowarfare installation, Japan's "Unit 731" was established in 1932 as a small group of five scientists interested in biological weapons and was expanded around 1936 when General Shiro Ishii was given full command of the unit.[110] The lab was based at the Epidemic Prevention Research Laboratory in Japanese Army Military Medical School in Tokyo. Unit 731 consisted of eight subunits designed to focus on different topics of warfare. In the first subunit, which focused on biological weapons like bubonic plague, cholera, anthrax, typhoid, and

---

107 Morgan Dunn and Erik Hawkins, "The Disturbing Story Of The Heart Attack Gun Invented By The CIA During The Cold War," *All That's Interesting* January 31, 2022.
108 "Intelligence: Of Dart Guns and Poisons," *Time* September 29, 1975.
109 Nicholas M. Horrock, "Colby Describes C.I.A. Poison Work," *The New York Times* September 17 ,1975.
110 Robert Harris and Jeremy Paxman, *A Higher Form of Killing: The Secret Story of Chemical and Biological Warfare* (New York: The Noonday Press, 1982) 76.

tuberculosis, Dr. Hideo Futaki led the tuberculosis research squad. Bacteria was grown in vast numbers of aluminum tanks and prisoners were used as human guinea pigs and infected with tuberculosis.[111]

Similar research was being conducted in Nazi Germany. In 1944 at the Neuengamme concentration camp near Hamburg, Mycobacterium tuberculosis experiments were conducted on children sent there from Auschwitz. These Nazi experiments were overseen by Dr. Kurt Heissmeyer of the Hohenlychen Sanatorium, an SS hospital near Berlin. He applied doses from a TB bacteria culture to cuts in the children's skin. In another experiment, 25 men had a probe lowered into their healthy lung thorough the trachea and bronchia. The probe contained spittle contaminated with TB bacteria. "Heissmeyer introduced virulent TB bacteria into the healthy lung to obtain an infection induced artificially via the bronchia in favourable conditions for progressive infiltration."[112] Heissmeyer developed a technique "of intravenous injections of a suspension of live tubercle bacilli, which brought on acute military tuberculosis within a few weeks."[113] Jewish psychiatrist and key medical advisor during the *Nuremberg Trials* Leo Alexander gave a useful overview in 1949:

> In the course of ktenological research, methods of mass killing and mass sterilization were investigated and developed, as well as the methods for rapid and inconspicuous individual execution. A committee of physicians and medical experts, headed by Dr. Karl Brandt, developed various methods of extermination by gas. At first carbon monoxide was used; later cyanide gas ("Cyclon B"), and occasionally chemical warfare gases. Of methods for the inconspicuous execution of individuals the most widely used was the intravenous injection of phenol or gasoline. This, however, left a telltale odor with the corpse, which made it

---

111 John W. Powell, "Japan's germ warfare: The U.S. cover-up of a war crime," *Bulletin of Concerned Asian Scholars* 12 (1980): 2-17.
112 S. Kłodziński, "Criminal tuberculosis experiments conducted in Nazi German concentration camps during the Second World War," (trans. T. Bałuk-Ulewiczowa) *Medical Review – Auschwitz*. February 22, 2021.
113 Vadim J. Birstein, *Perversion of Knowledge: The True Story of Soviet Science* (Boulder, CO: Westview Press, 2001) 175.

undesirable in the case of prominent prisoners or high-ranking Nazis. The triumph along this line-a method that would produce autopsy findings indicative of death from natural causes-was the development of intravenous injections of a suspension of live tubercle bacilli, which brought on acute military tuberculosis within a few weeks. The method was worked out by Professor Heissmeyer, one of Gebhardt's associates at the SS hospital of Hohlenlychen. As a means of further camouflage, so that the SS at large would not suspect the purpose of these experiments, preliminary tests on the efficacy of this method were performed exclusively on children at the Neuengamme concentration camp. The 'cellulitis experiments" ... which were associated with intravenous injection of pus from the abscess produced, represent an earlier phase of the same research.

For use in "medical" executions of prisoners and of members of the SS and other branches of the German armed forces, the use of simple lethal injections, particularly phenol injections, remained the instrument of choice. Whatever methods he used, the physician gradually became the unofficial executioner, for the sake of convenience, informality, and relative secrecy. Even on German submarines it was the physician's duty to execute the trouble makers among the crew by lethal injections.[114]

Alexander makes a number of notable broader observations here. According to his account, the German military preference was to use the physician as the unofficial executioner of prisoners, trouble-makers from the ranks, and high-ranking Nazis. The standard method of these medical executions was via lethal intravenous injections of phenol or gasoline. But this left the corpse with a telltale odor. The Nazi's desired a more inconspicuous method of execution. The goal was to find a method that would produce autopsy findings indicative of death from natural causes. This goal was achieved through the development of intravenous injections of a suspension of live tubercle bacilli, which brought on acute tuberculosis within a few weeks.

---

114 Leo Alexander statement in Alexander Mitscherlich and Fred Mielke, *Doctors of Infamy: The Story of the Nazi Medical Crimes* (New York: Henry Schuman, 1949) xxxiii-xxxiv.

45

Thus, both Japan and Germany had succeeded in weaponizing TB during the war. Under the secret United States intelligence program called Operation Paperclip over 1,600 German scientists, engineers, and technicians – including many Nazi physicians - were secreted out of Germany to the U.S. for government employment after the end of WWII between 1945 and 1959.[115] Similarly, after the war Fort Detrick and Japan's Unit 731 scientists entered a "secret deal" in which the U.S. helped Japanese war criminals escape trial and punishment for war crimes in exchange for bioweapons research data allowing the U.S. to develop its own.[116]

> In a secret deal struck between September 1945 and November 1948, Fort Detrick of the U.S. Army spent 250,000 yen, about several thousand U.S. dollars at that time, obtaining data and medical papers on human experiments, bacterial tests, germ warfare, and toxic gas experiments conducted by Unit 731, according to Jin Chengmin, curator of the Museum of Evidence of War Crimes by the Japanese Army Unit 731. The United States subsequently used these data and medical papers to conduct research involving biological weapons...[117]

From 1945 to 1947, the U.S. dispatched four investigators from Fort Detrick to Japan to interrogate at least 25 members of Unit 731. "By offering them a chance to be exempted from trial, the US obtained data of human experiments, bacterial warfare and poison gas experiments...benefiting from the material from Unit 731, the US Army was able to accelerate its research and development of biological weapons at Fort Detrick."[118] From 1943 to 1969, Fort Detrick's research plan included Bacillus anthracis, Yersinia pestis, and Mycobacterium tuberculosis, the very disease

---

115 Annie Jacobsen, *Operation Paperclip: The Secret Intelligence Program to Bring Nazi Scientists to America* (New York: Little, Brown and Company, 2014).
116 "Secret deal between U.S. Fort Detrick, Japanese germ warfare unit revealed," *Xinhuanet* August 4, 2021.
117 Liu Caiyu, "Newly disclosed germ warfare archives reveal US helped Japanese war criminals escape trial in exchange for bio materials," *Global Times* August 16, 2021.
118 Caiyu, "Newly disclosed germ warfare archives."

weaponized by both Japan and Germany. The CIA maintained a supply of several weaponized toxins and bacterial and viral agents in ready-to-use form, include tuberculosis.[119] When President Nixon renounced U.S. production and use of bioweapons in November 1969, the CIA possessed stockpiles of Mycobacterium tuberculosis stored at Fort Detrick, as admitted by Director Colby in 1975. The TB was produced for covert offensive use. Appearing before the Select Committee to Study Governmental Operations with Respect to Intelligence Activities (The Church Committee) on Tuesday, September 16, 1975, and being questioned by Senator Walter Huddleston (D-KY) Colby said:

Senator HUDDLESTON: Now, most of the material there, the toxic material, was applied by some sort of injection. Consequently, you developed the dart guns and drill bits that you put in silver dollars and whatever. Was there also material there that would be administered in some other way?

Mr. COLBY: Oh, yes; there were various ways you could administer various of these materials, no question about it, both orally and under some kind of a guise and so forth.

Senator HUDDLESTON: And what devices were prepared for that kind of administration?

Mr. COLBY: It was really rather the development - to see what the effect of putting the particular material into another substance, what chemical reactions and stabilities were.

Senator HUDDLESTON: Now, the inventory for the first set of materials that were held at Fort Detrick included an agent that, I presume, was designed to induce tuberculosis. Is that correct?

Mr. COLBY: Yes. There is that capability.

Senator HUDDLEBTON: What application would be made of that particular agent?

Mr. COLBY: It is obviously to induce tuberculosis in a subject that you want to induce it in.

---

119 Powell, "Japan's germ warfare," 12.

Senator HUDDLESTON: For what purpose?

Mr. COLBY: We know of no application ever being done with it, but the idea of giving someone this particular disease is obviously the thought process behind this.[120]

The point of producing this stockpile of Mycobacterium tuberculosis is so the CIA could induce the disease in a targeted subject. Director Colby told Senator Huddleston that he knew of no application of this being done, but we know of at least two such applications.

In 1960 Sidney Gottlieb reportedly established within the CIA the ironically named "Health Alteration Committee," an internal committee of chemists who looked for unique and plausibly deniable methods of assassinating foreign leaders.[121] The CIA's Health Alteration Committee (HAC) interfaced with the Army's SOD scientists on many projects.[122] It passed on proposals involving the operational use of drugs, chemicals and biological agents. The HAC's "medicine chest at Fort Detrick contained ten biological agents that could cause diseases including smallpox, tuberculosis, equine encephalitis, and anthrax, as well as six organic toxins, among them snake venom and paralytic shellfish poison."[123]

In February 1960 the CIA's Near East Division targeted an Iraqi colonel (likely Colonel Fadhil Abbas Mahdawi) for "incapacitation." They turned to the Health Alteration Committee (HAC) for a recommendation of a technique "which, while not likely to result in total disablement, would be certain to prevent the target from pursuing his usual activities for a minimum of three

---

120 *Hearings Before the Select Committee to Study Governmental Operations with Respect to Intelligence Activities of the United States Senate Ninety-Fourth Congress. First Session.* Volume 1: *Unauthorized Storage of Toxic Agents September 16, 17, and 18, 1975* (Washington, D.C.: U.S. Government Printing Office, 1976) 27.
121 Kinzer, *Poisoner in Chief*, 204.
122 Albarelli Jr., *A Terrible Mistake*, 69.
123 Kinzer, *Poisoner in Chief*, 204.

months."[124] In April the HAC suggested to the CIA's Deputy Director of Plans that, for the planned "disabling operation," a gift monogrammed handkerchief be delivered to the Iraqi colonel. The gift handkerchief would contain an incapacitating agent capable of disabling the target. Gottlieb delivered the handkerchief poisoned with weaponized tuberculosis to the colonel. The operation worked, Gottlieb later admitted.[125]

The second case that we know of where the CIA planned to deploy its weaponized TB against a target was Fidel Castro (see below).

V.   *Indigenous Disease as Cover*

According to Marks, "If CIA officials wanted an assassination to look like a death from natural causes, they could choose from a long list of deadly diseases *that normally occurred in particular countries*."[126] Assassinating a target with an MKNAOMI-derived agent that mimics a disease indigenous to the target's locale ensures plausible deniability. SOD scientists prepared memoranda detailing what diseases were common in what areas of the world so that covert use by the CIA of biological weapons containing these diseases could easily go undetected.[127] An illustration of this "indigenous disease as cover" assassination technique is the U.S. plot in 1960 to kill the "Messiah of the Congo," Patrice Lumumba.

---

124 *Alleged Assassination Plots Involving Foreign Leaders. An Interim Report of the Select Committee to Study Governmental Operations with Respect to Intelligence Activities. United States Senate Together with Additional, Supplemental, and Separate Views. November 20, 1975* (Washington, D.C.: U.S. Government Printing Office, 1976) 181.
125 Kinzer, *Poisoner In Chief,* 226-227.
126 Marks, *Search for the "Manchurian Candidate",* 79-80.
127 *Church Committee: Book I - Foreign and Military Intelligence Current Section: F. Chemical and Biological Activities* 362.

An August 1960 cable from CIA Director Allen Dulles to CIA Station in Leopoldville, capital of the Republic of the Congo, stated: "We conclude that his removal must be an urgent and prime objective and that under existing conditions this should be a high priority of our covert action." The "he" here is the Congo's first democratically elected Prime Minister Patrice Lumumba. The West hated Lumumba's anti-colonialist posture which, with his noted "spellbinding" oratory, "magnetic public appeal" and the "ability to stir the masses of people to action," caused U.S. policymakers to view him with alarm.[128] White House officials characterized this as Lumumba's "messianic fervor."[129]

At a National Security Council meeting on August 18, 1960, U.S. President Dwight Eisenhower authorized CIA Director Allen Dulles to assassinate Prime Minister Patrice Lumumba.[130] Dulles allocated $100,000 for this Executive Action with the guiding principle: "[A]ny form of assassination would do, so long as it could not be traced back to the United States Government."[131] The CIA turned to its own "sorcerer" and "Master of Poisons," Sidney Gottlieb. For the "Lumumba Job," Gottlieb suggested that "biological agents were perfect for the task," the science historian Ed Regis wrote in his description of this plot. "They were invisible, untraceable and, if intelligently selected and delivered, not even liable to create a suspicion of foul play. The target would get sick

128 *Alleged Assassination Plots Involving Foreign Leaders: an interim report of the Select Committee to Study Governmental Operations with Respect to Intelligence Activities, United States Senate: together with additional, supplemental, and separate views* (Washington: U.S. Government Printing Office, 1975), 13, 18 n. 2; Madeleine G. Kalb, "The C.I.A. and Lumumba," *The New York Times* August 2, 1981.
129 *Alleged Assassination Plots Involving Foreign Leaders*, 53.
130 Office of the Historian, State Department, "Foreign Relations of the United States, 1964–1968, Volume XXIII, Congo, 1960–1968," @ https://history.state.gov/historicaldocuments/frus1964-68v23/d1; George Lardner, Jr. Did Ike Authorize a Murder?" *The Washington Post* August 8, 2000; Alex Duval Smith, "Eisenhower ordered Congo killing," *Independent* April 18, 2009; *Alleged Assassination Plots Involving Foreign Leaders*, 58; Kalb, "The C.I.A. and Lumumba."
131 Madeleine G. Kalb, "The C.I.A. and Lumumba," *The New York Times* August 2, 1981.

and die exactly as if he'd been attacked by a natural outbreak of an endemic disease. Plenty of lethal or incapacitating germs were out there and available..."[132]

Clandestine Services chief Richard Bissell asked Gottlieb to pick out an appropriate malady to kill the "Messiah of the Congo."[133] Bronson Tweedy, head of the African Division of the CIA Clandestine Services, told Gottlieb that this biological assault on the democratically elected leader of the Congo "had to be done *without attribution to the USA.*"[134] Gottlieb said "the CIA had access to lethal or potentially lethal biological materials that could be used" for the job. He then "reviewed a list of biological materials available at the army's Chemical Corps installation at Fort Detrick, Maryland, which would produce diseases that would 'either kill the individual or incapacitate him so severely that he would be out of action.'"[135] Gottlieb later told Senate investigators that he selected one from the list that "was supposed to produce a disease that was...indigenous to that area [of West Africa] and that could be fatal."[136]

> After receiving his assignment, Gottlieb began considering which "lethal or incapacitating germs" he would use. His first step was to determine which diseases most commonly caused unexpected death in the Congo... They turned out to be anthrax, smallpox, tuberculosis, and three animal-borne plagues. Gottlieb began looking for a match: Which poison would produce a death most like the one those diseases cause? He settled on botulinum, which is sometimes found in improperly canned food. It takes several hours to work but is so potent that a concentrated dose of just two one-billionths of a gram can kill. Working with partners at Fort Detrick, where he stored his toxins, Gottlieb began assembling his assassination kit. It contained a vial of liquid botulinum; a hypodermic syringe with an ultra-thin needle; a small jar of chlorine that could be mixed with the botulinum to render it ineffective in an emergency; and "accessory

132 Kinzer, *Poisoner in Chief*, 177.
133 Marks, *Search for the "Manchurian Candidate"*, 79-80.
134 *Alleged Assassination Plots Involving Foreign Leaders*, 24.
135 Kinzer, *Poisoner in Chief*, 226.
136 Marks, *Search for the "Manchurian Candidate"*, 79-80.

materials," including protective gloves and a face mask to be worn while conducting the operation.[137]

"Gottlieb concocted a blend of viruses to be injected into the toothpaste of Congo prime minister Patrice Lumumba"[138] In September 1960 Gottlieb flew into Leopoldville with a "first aid kit" in hand and met CIA Chief of Station in the Congo Lawrence Devlin at a safe house. Gottlieb told Devlin that the manner of Lumumba's assassination "had to be a way which could not be traced back either to an American or the United States government,"[139] and he reportedly said regarding the "kit": "With the stuff that's in there, no one will ever be able to know that Lumumba was assassinated."[140]

> Gottlieb coolly explained to Devlin what was in the poison kit and how to use it. One of Devlin's agents, he said, should use the hypodermic needle to inject botulinum into something Lumumba would ingest—as Gottlieb later put it, "anything he could get to his mouth, whether it was food or a toothbrush." Devlin later wrote that the kit also included a pre-poisoned tube of toothpaste. The toxins were designed to kill not immediately, but after a few hours. An autopsy, Gottlieb assured Devlin, would show "normal traces found in people who die of certain diseases.[141]

This operation required conscripting somebody within Lumumba's own circle that was close enough to him to place the special toothpaste in his bathroom. From brushing his teeth Lumumba would catch "a staggering polio" (the clinical pictures of botulism and polio are similar and can be confused[142]). Devlin

---

137 Kinzer, *Poisoner in Chief*, 177-178.
138 David B. Green, "This Day in Jewish History - 1999: CIA Dirty Trickster Dies," *Haaretz* May 7, 2014.
139 *Alleged Assassination Plots Involving Foreign Leaders*, 25
140 Kinzer, *Poisoner in Chief*, 178.
141 Kinzer, *Poisoner in Chief*, 178-179.
142 Larry M. Bush and Maria T. Vazquez-Pertejo, "Botulism," *Merck Manual* May 2021 @ https://www.merckmanuals.com/professional/infectious-diseases/anaerobic-bacteria/botulism; E. Vivian Lambert, "Botulism or Polio-encephalomyelitis?" *British Medical Journal* November 26, 1949, p. 1235.

found an agent who was thought to have such access to Lumumba and could, as he wrote in a cable to Washington, "act as inside man." The agent Devlin hired to slip Lumumba a tube of poisoned toothpaste, or to poison his food, proved unable to penetrate Lumumba's rings of security.[143] "Devlin...contacts his only agent within Lumumba's entourage. But the agent withdrew: he did not, he assured him, have access to the kitchens and private flats of an increasingly distrustful Lumumba."[144] Gottlieb left Africa on October 5, 1960, having failed the mission. Before doing so, however, Gottlieb dumped his exotic substance in the Congo River.[145] The "Messiah of the Congo" ended up being killed by firing squad.

VI.   *The Cancer Option*

H.P. Albarelli Jr. correctly notes: "The MKULTRA program also explored cancer and experimented with various techniques for 'inducing cancer.'"[146] "During the 1950's the CIA developed cancer-causing drugs for use in political assassinations—drugs that would produce what appeared to be 'natural' death," Philip H. Melansen documents as well.[147] The CIA was clearly investigating the weaponization of cancer as far back as the 1950s. This fact was confirmed by an important article in *San Francisco Chronicle* in 1979.

> At the height of the Cold War, the Central Intelligence Agency looked into ways to 'knock off key guys' through such 'natural causes' as cancer and heart attacks, it was disclosed yesterday. Heavily censored CIA

---

143 Kinzer, *Poisoner in Chief*, 178-179.
144 François Soudan, "DRC: How the CIA got Patrice Lumumba," *The Africa Report* January 13, 2021.
145 Kalb, "C.I.A. and Lumumba"; *Alleged Assassination Plots Involving Foreign Leaders*, 29.
146 Albarelli Jr., *A Terrible Mistake*, 292.
147 Philip H. Melanson, "High Tech Mysterious Deaths," *Critique: A Journal of Conspiracies & Metaphysics* 4:3,4 (Fall/Winter '84/85): 209-220 (217).

documents from a quarter-century ago show the agency even considered performing experiments on terminal cancer patients under the guise of "legitimate medical work."[148]

Death by 'Natural Causes'
10 San Francisco Chronicle ★ Mon., Apr. 2, 1979

CIA's Bizarre Ideas for Assassinations

Washington

At the height of the Cold War, the Central Intelligence Agency looked into ways to "knock off key guys" through such "natural causes" as cancer and heart attacks, it was disclosed yesterday.

Heavily censored CIA documents from a quarter-century ago show the agency even considered performing experiments on terminal cancer patients under the guise of "legitimate medical work."

The documents do not indicate, however, whether the talk about inducing cancer and heart attacks ever got past the memorandum stage.

The papers — released under Freedom of Information Act requests — were researched by Martin Lee of the Washington-based Assassination Information Bureau.

The CIA project apparently started with an undated, unsigned note indicating concern about the vulnerability of U.S. leaders to assassination by "natural causes."

The memo noted the "vulnerability of U.S. to unconventional attack" and referred to studies by the Office of Strategic Services, the World War II predecessor of the CIA.

"Knock off key people," the heavily censored document said. "How knock off key guys ... Natural Causes.

"Method produce cancer.

"Heart techniques ...

"Query — should facts on (blank) be dug up?

"Are they of interest to (blank). Probably yes.

"At any rate, we need know enough more about it to decide how much interest we have in it."

The next pertinent document was a Feb. 4, 1952, "draft" memorandum from "Chemical Branch, Research & Development."

The paper reported inspecting a lab for possible use in "medical research involving physiologically active chemical compounds."

"Human subjects would be available for work that could be carried out as legitimate medical research," it said. "Extensive animal facilities exist for other kinds of research."

The memo discussed the use of beryllium, a metallic element said to have "extreme toxicity" capable of inducing tumors.

"This is certainly the most toxic inorganic element and it produces a peculiar fibrotic tumor at the site of local application," the memo said.

It suggested "a study of the effect of inhaling small amounts of beryllium in the lungs, and other studies to evaluate the potentialities of beryllium as a covert weapon."

A document dated Aug. 4, 1954, showed the project was still receiving serious consideration at that time.

The unidentified writer provided a bibliography of such relevant works as "Chemical Induction of Cancer" and "Survey of Compounds Tested for Carcinogenic Properties."

"Methylcholanthrene is now recognized as probably the most potent known carcinogen (cancer-causing agent) in the production of tumors of various types," the memo said.

It suggested using "normal constituents of the human organism" to produce methylcholanthrene in the body "through a process of abnormal metabolism." A footnote gave the cost of the chemical as $4.40 a half gram, $8.25 a gram.

United Press

Copper Train Hit by Guerrillas

Salisbury

Black nationalist guerrillas derailed a train carrying Zambian copper through Rhodesia yesterday, injuring three crew members, a spokesman for military headquarters said.

The train was travelling on what has become Zambia's crucial supply line for badly-needed food and fertilizers and an important route for copper exports.

Reuters

One CIA document released under FOIA to the *Chronical* asks and answers: "How [to]knock off key guys" and gives the answer: "Natural Causes. Method produce cancer." A February 4, 1952, draft memorandum from the CIA's "Chemical Branch, Research & Development," reveals the Agency's interest in using "physiologically active chemical compounds," such as beryllium and methylcholanthrene to induce cancer. Beryllium is a metallic element said to have "extreme toxicity" capable of inducing tumors. "This (beryllium) is certainly the most toxic inorganic element, and it produces a peculiar fibrotic tumor at the site of local application," the draft memo said. The CIA conceived "a study of the effect of beryllium in the lungs, and other studies to evaluate the potentialities of beryllium as a covert weapon."

---

148 United Press, "Death by 'Natural Causes': CIA's Bizarre Ideas for Assassinations," *San Francisco Chronicle* April 2, 1979

An August 4, 1954, document noted as well that, "Methylcholanthrene is now recognized as probably the most potent known carcinogen in the production of tumors of various types," citing research works with titles such as "Chemical Induction of Cancer" and "Survey of Compounds Tested for Carcinogenic Properties." It says further: "If this hydrocarbon can be produced in the laboratory by chemical transformation of normal constituents of the human organism, it is possible that the substance may arise in the body through a process of abnormal metabolism – and initiate cancer." One SOD project was "developing 'the ability to induce cancer through covert means.'"[149] "Human subjects would be available for work that could be carried out as legitimate medical research," a CIA memo stated, indicating that this "cancer research" would be clandestinely carried out on unsuspecting patients in cooperating medical institutions.

Another important article, "Cancer Warfare" by Richard Hatch, was published in *Covert Action Information Bulletin* in 1992.[150] A particularly significant revelation from this article concerns the government and military studies on the *aerosolization of cancer*.

> The field of "aerobiology," or the transmission of disease organisms through the air, is essentially an outgrowth of [biological warfare] research. The military objective of exposing many people to a biological warfare agent and the ready susceptibility to infection by inhaling these agents make aerosol weapons the most practical form of transmission...The line between aerosol and biological warfare research was often fine. [151]

---

149 H.P. Albarelli Jr., *A Terrible Mistake: The Murder of Frank Olson and the CIA's Cold War Experiments* (Walterville, Oregon: Trine Day LLC, 2009) 68.
150 Richard Hatch, "Cancer Warfare," *Covert Action Information Bulletin* Number 39 (Winter 1991–92): 14ff.
151 Hatch, "Cancer Warfare," 16.

CancerWarfare

Richard Hatch

*Those who would
increase the potency of
biological weapons must
search for improved
methods of mass
production of organisms,
factors which will
enhance the virulence,
ways to prolong the
storage life of living
agents, ways to improve
aerosol stability, and
methods of producing
variant organisms by
recombination or by
other means.*

—Col. William D. Tigertt, former commander
of the Army's medical unit at Fort Detrick[1]

National Cancer Institute and the Fort Detrick Link

In 1969, President Richard Nixon ordered a halt to offensive biological warfare (BW) research and weapons stockpiling by the United States. The U.S. Army destroyed its toxins, viruses, and bacteria with heat and disinfectants by May 1972; the disposal of the scientific personnel was not so simple. Some of these biowarriors went to the CIA.[2] Others quickly found new support from the National Cancer Institute, particularly in its Virus Cancer Program (VCP).[3] The NCI funded and supervised some of the same scientists, universities, and contracting corporations—ostensibly for cancer research—which had conducted biological warfare research. Some of these medical research contracts ran simultaneously with the U.S. biological warfare program. When the military work ended, the civilian programs continued to expand on the same critical areas outlined by Colonel Tigertt.

The NCI's Viral Cancer Program—a highly politicized public relations effort—was launched in 1971 with great fanfare as part of Nixon's War on Cancer. The stated aim of the program was to organize experiments aimed at finding cancer-causing viruses.

Apparently this agenda was compatible with the incorporation into various units of the VCP of possibly dozens of

---

Richard Hatch is a research chemist with 12 years' industrial experience. He currently designs scientific instruments for use in biotechnology and related fields. Photo: Test chamber for secret chemical and biological aerosol spray weapons at Fort Detrick, Maryland. April 1967 (U.S. Army photo)
1. Charles Piller and Keith R. Yamamoto, *Gene Wars: Military Control Over the New Genetic Technologies* (New York: Beech Tree Books/Morrow and Co.), 1988, p. 50.
2. Louis Wolf, "This Side of Nuclear War," *CAIB,* (Summer 1982), p. 14.
3. The bureaucratic organization of NCI units changes. Some NCI con-

---

tracts began before the VCP actually started. For simplicity, these contracts are referred to as VCP contracts when they continue under the VCP effort.

Ohio State University is one of 80 U.S. institutions, including several universities,[152] that carried out projects for the

---

152 On the Military-Industrial-Academic Complex see Lisa Martino-Taylor, "The Military-Industrial-Academic Complex and a New Social Autism," *Journal of Political & Military Sociology* 36:1 (Summer 2008): 37-52 (39): "Universities involved in early gas and chemical weapons research included Catholic University, Johns Hopkins, Yale, Princeton, Ohio State, Wisconsin, Washington, Kansas, Michigan, Columbia University, Cornell, California, Rice Institute, Iowa State College, Bryn Mawr, Massachusetts Institute of Technology, Worcester Polytechnic, Vanderbilt, University of Wisconsin,

CIA's MKULTRA and MKNAOMI programs.[153] From 1955 to 1965, the Ohio State University College of Medicine conducted research for Fort Detrick into the aerosol transmission of biological warfare (BW) agents, including Tularemia ("rabbit fever") and Q fever. In some of these studies, prisoners from the Ohio State Penitentiary were used as guinea pigs. According to Hatch, between 1952 and 1969, the affiliated Ohio State University Research Foundation had eight contracts with the U.S. Army for BW research. Tularemia and Q fever were ultimately stockpiled by the U.S. Army. [154]

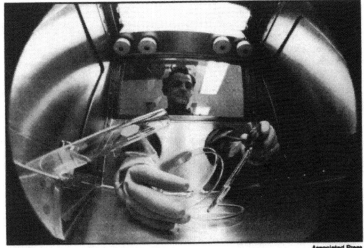

Biological warfare veteran Dr. Alfred Hellman at National Cancer Institute, 1970.

University of Illinois, and the University of Chicago (...). Harvard University began working on chemical gases in 1917; by 1918, 1,294 scientists nationwide were undertaking chemical research for the United States Army (...). The Chemical Warfare Service facility at Camp Detrick, Maryland had as its advisor Ezra Kraus, chairman of the botany department at the University of Chicago, where the chemical weapon Agent Orange was developed."
153 Peter E. Cole, "OSU prof linked to CIA work: Mind control pursued in '60s," *Arkon Beacon Journal* January 26, 1986; Jo Thomas, "Extent of University Work for C.I.A. Is Hard to Pin Down," *The New York Times* October 9, 1977.
154 Hatch, "Cancer Warfare," 16.

The National Cancer Institute (NCI) and the Office of Naval Research (ONR) collaborated in intensive studies of the aerosol transmission of cancer viruses. One such study involved sponsored experiments on "Aerosol Properties of Potentially Oncogenic Viruses"; another, titled FS-57 "Aerosol Properties of Oncogenic Viruses," was funded at over $100,000 a year.[155] Former U.S. Air Force virologist Dr. Alfred Hellman was the NCI project officer for much of this aerobiology research. He oversaw the 1971 $100,000 Naval Biosciences Laboratory (NBL) study on the "physical and biological characteristics of viral aerosols." Between 1965 and 1972 Dr. Hellman supervised an NCI contract for Ohio State University designed to study the aerosol transmission of cancer-causing viruses. The principal investigator for this work was Dr. Richard Griesemer, who eventually succeeded in giving tumors to mice and monkeys.[156]

In the mid-1950s and 1960s in St. Louis the U.S. Army conducted secret aerobiology weapons testing in impoverished Black neighborhoods. Using motorized blowers atop a low-income housing high-rise, at schools, and from the back of station wagons, the Army sent potentially dangerous chemical compounds – zinc cadmium sulfide - into the air in predominantly Black areas of St. Louis.[157] This was an "aerosol cloud study" and "Cadmium is a known carcinogen."[158] Residents of the targeted areas also remember the Army using planes to drop a powdery substance down on the landscape *and on the inhabitants*. Thousands of people were unwillingly exposed so that the Army could "test" the health effects of one of their potential chemical-biological warfare agents. Whole families came down with cancer after the

---

155 Hatch, "Cancer Warfare," 16.
156 Hatch, "Cancer Warfare," 16.
157 "Secret Cold War tests in St. Louis cause worry," *CBS News* October 3, 2012.
158 Lisa Martino-Taylor, "The Military-Industrial-Academic Complex and a New Social Autism," *Journal of Political & Military Sociology* 36:1 (Summer 2008): 37-52 (45).

experiment.[159] The Army used the claim of a "Russian-threat" as a smoke screen and lied even to local officials regarding the true nature of their activities in these segregated Black neighborhoods. The Army conducted the same aerosol cloud study with the carcinogen Cadmium in Minneapolis in 1953. One site that was targeted was a public elementary school.[160]

---

159 "Secret Cold War tests in St. Louis cause worry," *CBS News* October 3, 2012.
160 Reuters, "Minneapolis Called Toxic Test Site in '53," *The New York Times* June 11, 1994.

Part 2

Manufacturing Cancer

Chapter Three

"Under the Guise of Legitimate Medical Work"

A huge amount of weapons research was done for the Department of Defense (DOD) in the private sector, academia, hospitals and prison systems. Some biological weapons research has been done under the guise of disease, cancer, or pesticide research.[161]

In the course of the early animal cancer studies, methods of inducing tumors were developed so that their growth and interaction with the immune system could be routinely studied in the laboratory. In mice, tumors and leukemias were intentionally induced in various mouse strains through exposure to radiation or chemical agents. Cells from these induced tumors (or naturally occurring varieties) were typically filtered and grown in tissue cultures. These processed cells were then transplanted and grown in other mice. When cancer resulted from these transplanted cancer cells, cells from the new tumors would then be processed and cultured and the transplantation process would be repeated. (This process of refining and injecting cancer viruses was sometimes referred to as the "bio-assay" method of determining the cancer-causing potential of viruses)...As part of this research, scientists measured cancer susceptibility due to these viruses as a function of simultaneous exposure to immunosuppressive treatments such as radiation, chemicals, surgeries, and co-infection with other viral agents-including immunosuppressive viruses...Processes similar to those just described for inducing cancer in mice and cats were also applied in human cancer experiments... In experiments similar to those conducted in animals, researchers also studied the ability of these human cancer cell lines...to induce tumors in humans in combination with immunosuppressive treatments such as radiation and chemical treatments. For example, in some of these experiments human patients undergoing chemotherapy or radiation therapy were given cancer cell transplants...to see how the cancer cells grew as a function of immune system manipulation.

---

161 Lisa Martino-Taylor, "The Military-Industrial-Academic Complex and a New Social Autism," *Journal of Political & Military Sociology* 36:1 (Summer 2008): 37-52 (37-38).

In later cross-species human experiments, which were similar to those conducted in mice, researchers studied the cancer-causing potential of animal cancer viruses in human subjects...These studies also included determining how immunosuppressive treatments aided cancer growth due to animal cancer viruses...in addition to exploiting immune system damage from chemical and radiation treatments to enhance the growth of deliberately induced cancer in humans, researchers also used active immunosuppression caused by human immunosuppressive viruses in such studies...[162]

in one set of these cross-species cancer vaccine experiments, immunosuppressed rats *and humans* were given the same set of cancer-inducing virus injections so that the tumors that developed in each species could be systematically compared. In a similar set of immunosuppressive experiments, *tumors were deliberately induced in human subjects as a result of injections with monkey tumor and cancer viruses, so that researchers could compare the resultant human tumors with those that grew in the monkeys.*[163]

I.   *Cancer Injections I: Dr. Rhoads and the Puerto Rican Experiment*

In the early part of the twentieth century the International Health Division of The Rockefeller Institute for Medical

Investigations, as part of its Commission for the Study of Anemia in Puerto Rico, tested experimental treatments on the population under the pretense of a global fight against hookworm. Among the medical contingent that the Institute sent to San Juan was Dr. Cornelius Packard Rhoads. Arriving in Puerto Rico in 1931 with the carte blanche granted him by the Rockefeller Institute and working out of Presbyterian Hospital in San Juan,

162 Jerry Leonard, *How AIDS Was Invented* (Booklocker, 2001) 2-3.
163 Jerry Leonard, *AIDS: The Perfect Disease* (1st Books Library, 2002)

Rhoads "appeared to regard Puerto Rico as an island laboratory...a place to try out ideas while facing few consequences," according to Professor Daniel Immerwahr of Northwestern University.[164] Rhoads referred to his Puerto Rican patients as "experimental animals." Five months into his tenure at Presbyterian Hospital, Rhoads penned a letter to a Boston colleague, Fred Stewart,

Dear Ferdie:

The more I think about the Larry Smith appointment the more disgusted I get. Have you heard any reason advanced for it? It certainly is odd that a man out with the entire Boston group, fired by Wallach and as far as I know, absolutely devoid of any scientific reputation, should be given the place.

I can get a damn fine job here and am tempted to take it. It would be ideal except for the Porto Ricans—they are beyond doubt the dirtiest, laziest, most degenerate and thievish race of men ever inhabiting this sphere. It makes you sick to inhabit the same island with them. They are even lower than Italians. What the island needs is not public health work, but a tidal wave or something to totally exterminate the population. It might then be livable. I have done my best to further the process of extermination by killing off 8 and transplanting cancer into several more. The latter has not resulted in any fatalities so far. The matter of consideration for the patients' welfare plays no role here—in fact, all physicians take delight in the abuse and torture of the unfortunate subjects.

Do let me know if you hear any more news.

Sincerely, Dusty

"Dusty" here seems to be boasting of deliberately transplanting cancer to several Puerto Ricans under his medical care and killing eight of them. He composed the letter at the desk of hospital stenographer Betty Guillermety and then accidentally left it there. She found it after returning from lunch. The letter fell into the possession of lab technician Luis Baldoni, whom Rhoads tried to bribe with a "gift" to keep it under wraps before he

---

164 Daniel Immerwahr, *How To Hide An Empire: A History of the Greater United States* (New York: ThirFarrar, Straus and Giroux, 2019) 197.

(Rhoads) fled back to New York.[165] When Puerto Rican Nationalist Party leader Pedro Albizu Campos received the letter, he publicized it. He sent a copy to all of the newspapers, the League of Nations, the Vatican, and the American Civil Liberties Union. This prompted the colonial governor of Puerto Rico, James R. Beverley, to launch an investigation. Deeming the letter to be a "confession of murder," Governor Beverley took the matter seriously. Thirteen patients did die at Presbyterian Hospital during the time Rhoads was there. That investigation uncovered *another letter* which the governor viewed as "even worse than the first." However, "the [U.S.] government suppressed it, and it has never been found" – the second letter was destroyed.[166] Thus, the colonial investigation as well as an internal investigation by the Rockefeller Institute cleared Rhoads of any guilt. However, as Professor Immerwahr points out, "an investigation by a government that destroys incriminating evidence and doesn't even require the accused to participate can hardly be called fair or thorough."[167]

Rhoads' genocidal experiment envisioned a medical solution to the problem of the "degenerate Porto Rican": transplanting cancer. Rhoads' vision was actually consistent with "cancer science" at the time. As Susan E. Lederer points out in this context, "The idea that cancer could be transmitted through surgical means or via a microbe or virus surfaced repeatedly in the twentieth century in both expert and lay circles."[168] Therefore the

> effort to relegate the cancer transplantation [claim of Rhoads] to the
> world of fantasy was disingenuous. Not only had Rous established in

165 Immerwahr, *How To Hide An Empire*, 199; Susan E. Lederer, "'Porto Ricochet': Joking about Germs, Cancer, and Race Extermination in the 1930s," *American Literary History* 14 (2002): 720-746 (727).
166 Immerwahr, *How To Hide An Empire*, 200; Douglas Starr, "Revisiting a 1930s Scandal, AACR to Rename a Prize," *Science* 300 (April 25, 2003): 573-574.
167 Immerwahr, *How To Hide An Empire*, 201.
168 Susan E. Lederer, "'Porto Ricochet': Joking about Germs, Cancer, and Race Extermination in the 1930s," *American Literary History* 14 (2002): 720-746 (722).

1911 that chicken sarcoma could be transmissible by a viral agent, but the notion that cancer could be transmitted from one person to another was, in the words of the leading American oncologist James Ewing, "the oldest hypothesis of the origin of cancer". In his 1931 text on cancer, Ewing listed more than 100 microorganisms that researchers claimed to cause cancer after the organism was isolated, grown in a pure culture, and inoculated into a healthy subject. Moreover, Ewing described a series of experiments in which tumors were deliberately transplanted between "man and man," including the 1891 report by French physician A. V. Cornil on the successful effort by a male surgeon to transplant a fragment of spindle-cell sarcoma of the breast into his female patient's other breast (Lederer, Subjected to Science 10- 12). In an ironic twist to the cancer transplant story, Rhoads, after his return to the US, pursued the transmissibility of cancer as Ewing's successor as director of the leading cancer research facility, the New York Memorial-Sloan-Kettering Institute for Cancer Research.[169]

After ensuring Rhoads was cleared by any investigation in Puerto Rico, the Rockefeller Institute called on their public relations expert and spin-doctor, Ivy Lee, to establish media contacts and take control of the narrative in America. Rhoads was turned into a jocular hero rather than a genocidal maniac.[170] "Not only was he never tried, he wasn't even fired: he continued to work for the Rockefeller Institute."[171]

Lee's strategy seemed to work well for both Rhoads and the Rockefeller Institute. In December 1931 Rhoads resumed his duties at the institute;

---

169 Lederer, "'Porto Ricochet'," 729-730.
170 Lederer, "'Porto Ricochet'," 730. Ivy Lee was one of the founders of modern-day public relations spin-doctoring. By 1932 he had managed Rockefeller public relations for two decades, since the 1914 Ludlow Massacre when 24 men, women and children were killed during a labor riot at a Rockefeller-owned mine. In the Rhoads' case, Lee telephoned all of the newspapers and secured an agreement "not to publish anything on the subject without telephoning himself first." Lee had pre-publication access to the *Time* and *The New York Times* articles and he shaped the versions that were ultimately printed alleging that Rhoads' was simply "joking" in the letter. See Lederer, "'Porto Ricochet'," 730; "Medicine: Porto Richochet," *Time* February 15, 1932; "Dr. Rhoads Cleared of Porto Richo Plot," *The New York Times* February 15, 1932.
171 Immerwahr, *How To Hide An Empire*, 206.

in 1935 when several Boston institutions explored the prospect of bringing him to the city, Rockefeller Institute staff met repeatedly to discuss what incentives would be necessary to keep him in New York. Rhoads remained in New York, but not at the Rockefeller Institute. In 1939 he succeeded James Ewing as the director of the nation's preeminent cancer hospital, Memorial Hospital in New York City. [172]

In 1940 he was made director of Memorial Hospital in New York. In 1942 he was elected vice president of the New York Academy of Medicine. Then, with the United States at war, Rhoads was commissioned as a colonel in the army. The military was an interesting place for a man of his expertise. Ever since Fritz Haber released chlorine gas at Ypres in 1915, the threat of chemical warfare had hung in the air. Roosevelt pledged that the United States wouldn't be the first to use gas in the Second World War, but the military prepared for a chemical war nonetheless. That meant not only manufacturing poison gas but testing it, too. And the chief of the Chemical Warfare Service's medical division was Cornelius P. Rhoads.[173]

Rhoads continued to conduct secret race-based experiments with chemical warfare agents during World War II and Puerto Ricans seem to have been a choice guineapig.

Beyond the experimental use of Puerto Ricans in racial tests, the Chemical Warfare Service relied on them for field tests at its "jungle" testing site: San José Island off Panama, an entire island for testing chemical weapons. The Puerto Ricans weren't brought there because of their race per se. They were brought because they were easy to get. The Military Personnel Division refused to send enough men "from the Continental Limits" for the tests but was happy to send Puerto Ricans. One GI who participated in the tests on San José Island (and later developed stomach and throat cancer) observed that more than two-thirds of his fellow soldiers had Spanish surnames and couldn't understand the instructions in English.[174]

After the war Rhoads was awarded a Legion of Merit medal for "combating poison gas and other advances in chemical warfare." He will go on to establish in 1943 a Medical Division in

172 Lederer, "'Porto Ricochet'," 738.
173 Immerwahr, *How To Hide An Empire*, 206.
174 Immerwahr, *How To Hide An Empire*, 207.

the Chemical Warfare Service at Fort Detrick and Edgewood Arsenal in Maryland, and apparently also at Dugway Proving Ground in Utah and Camp Sibert in Alabama.[175] In 1944 the Chemical Warfare Service was charged with responsibility of biological warfare defense projects as well.

Despite (or because of) his exposed vision of and effort toward medical genocide in Puerto Rico, Rhoads became a highly celebrated American pathologist and oncologist.

Rhoads worked closely with industrial magnate Alfred P. Sloan and engineer Charles Kettering to create a new cancer research institute. The opening of the Sloan-Kettering Institute in 1948 prompted Time magazine to once again profile "Dusty" Rhoads. On 27 June 1949 he appeared on the cover of the magazine. Clad in a white coat, he stood with a glowing sword smashing into a ferocious crab (the comparison of cancer to crabs is as old as Hippocrates). Announcing the opening of the Sloan-Kettering Institute, Rhoads was no longer the rollicking young researcher but the zealous cancer warrior.[176]

175 Timothy Alexander Guzman, "Racism and 'Dreams of Extermination' in Puerto Rico: U.S. Biological Warfare and the Legacy of Dr. Cornelius Rhoads," *Global Research* March 28, 2020.
176 Lederer, "'Porto Ricochet'," 738.

II.   Cancer Injections II: Dr. Southam and the Negro Experiments

direct communication of cancer from one host to another has been documented, and transplanting cancer cells to another person in an effort to cause cancer is possible...[177]

For about a decade a team of cancer researchers led by Chester M. Southam of the Sloan-Kettering Institute for Cancer Research has been injecting human beings with live cancer cells in order to study human immunity to cancer.[178]

Cancer by the Needle

Healthy convicts in Ohio State Penitentiary are currently risking cancer by receiving direct needle injections of live cancer cells in their forearms. Through these tests, the first of their kind, cancer researchers at Ohio State University and the Sloan-Kettering Institute for Cancer Research hope to discover the secret of how healthy human bodies fight the invasion of malignant cells. Their findings may step up even more significant research in immunization against cancer by a person's own resistance to the disease (NEWSWEEK, July 25, 1955).

Dr. Rhoads' cancer-injection experimentation was continued and expanded by a mentee of his at Sloan-Kettering: Dr. Chester M. Southam. Southam began training at Memorial Hospital/Sloan-Kettering Cancer Hospital in 1948, where Cornelius Rhoads was director. Southam was soon appointed director of the hospital's Division of Virology/Immunology.

---

177 Leonard F. Vernon, "Tuskegee Syphilis Study not Americas only Medical Scandal: Chester M. Southam, MD, Henrietta Lacks, and the Sloan-Kettering Research Scandal," *Online Journal of Health Ethics* 16:2 (2020): 1-8 (1).
178 Elinor Langer, "Human Experimentation: Cancer Studies at Sloan-Kettering Stir Public Debate on Medical Ethics," *Science* 143 (February 7, 1964): 551-553.

Southam's research concentrated on two main questions: whether cancer could be transmitted from person to person and whether certain virus antibodies had anti-neoplastic properties. "To answer these questions," Leonard Vernon informs us, "[Southam] would utilize society's most vulnerable citizens, including patients already diagnosed with cancer and undergoing gynecological surgery at Memorial Sloan-Kettering Cancer Hospital, incarcerated inmates, and frail, chronically ill nursing home patients (22 elderly Black woman.)[179]

Southam's government-funded research investigated the role of the human immune system in cancer susceptibility, and it involved inducing cancer growth in humans by exploiting immunosuppression. He created model cancer infections in human subjects for the purpose of vaccine research. Southam discovered that while healthy subjects rejected tumor cell injections, immune-impaired subjects were able to sustain tumor growth from the cancer implants for a longer period of time. This suggested to him that a healthy immune system could ward off cancer in healthy subjects and that immunocompromised subjects are susceptible.

Southam's work started in Africa where he injected severely ill cancer patients with a combination of rare and common diseases, including mumps, dengue, Semliki Forest virus, and West Nile Virus.[180] Southam injected West Nile Virus into more than 100 people with advanced cancer to see if it can "be 'trained'

---

179 Vernon, "Tuskegee Syphilis Study not Americas only Medical Scandal," 4.
180 Michael Schymanski, "Case Study Number 3: Brooklyn Chronic Disease Hospital," *Health & Inequality Website Project Race And Health* July 4, 2015 @ https://raceandhealth.weebly.com/1963-jewish-chornic-disease-hospital-study

to eat cancerous tissue without harming normal tissues."[181] Southam continued his cancer research in the United States.[182]

> In 1953, Southam began what appear to have been his first human experiments to test his theory about virus antibodies with anti-neoplastic properties. To do this, he and various colleagues routinely inoculated cancer patients with dangerous viruses, including West Nile, Ilheus, and Bunyamwera viruses...Beginning in February 1954, Southam and his colleagues initiated their first human experiments in cancer immunology by injecting 14 previously diagnosed terminal cancer inpatients at the Memorial Hospital (which became Sloan-Kettering in 1948) with cancer cells.[183]

The teacher and the student, Cornelius Rhoads and Chester Southam, along with Alice Moore, partnered in studies that injected 600 sick and healthy subjects with cancer cells.[184] The test subjects' immune system was modulated during these experiments with the use of chemotherapy and radiation, allowing Southam et al. to measure the effects of cancer transplants as the subjects underwent various forms of immunosuppression.

---

181 "Deep Cancers Temporarily Shrunk By Rare Nerve Virus From Africa," *The New York Times* April 15, 1952; Kent Sepkowitz, "A Virus's Debut in a Doctor's Syringe," *The New York Times* August 24, 2009; Chester M. Southam and Alice E. Moore, "Clinical Studies of Viruses as Antineoplastic Agents, with Particular Reference to Egypt 101 Virus," *Cancer* 5 (September 1952): 1025-1034; idem, "Anti-Virus Antibody Studies Following Induced Infection of Man with West Nile, Ilhéus, and Other Viruses," *The Journal of Immunology* 72 (1954): 446-462.
182 Michael Schymanski, "Case Study Number 3: Brooklyn Chronic Disease Hospital," *Health & Inequality Website Project Race And Health* July 4, 2015 @ https://raceandhealth.weebly.com/1963-jewish-chornic-disease-hospital-study
183 Vernon, "Tuskegee Syphilis Study not Americas only Medical Scandal," 4.
184 Chester M. Southam, Alice E. Moore and Cornelius P. Rhoads, "Homotransplantation of Human Cell Lines," *Science* Volume 124, January 25, 1957, pp. 158-160.

SCIENCE, VOL. 125   25 JANUARY 1957

Homotransplantation of
Human Cell Lines

The development of human neoplastic cell lines that can be grown serially in tissue cultures (*1, 2*) and in heterologous hosts (*3*) has made necessary the investigation of the capacity of such cells to grow in a homologous (human) recipient. Such studies are of fundamental importance to our knowledge of tissue transplantation and host defense mechanisms. In addition, there is the possible danger of initiating neoplastic disease by accidental inoculation during laboratory investigation or by injection with such cells or cell products if they should be

Chester M. Southam
Alice E. Moore
Cornelius P. Rhoads
Division of Experimental Pathology,
Sloan-Kettering Institute for
Cancer Research, New York, New York

Southam et al. discovered the immune system's specific defense mechanism against cancer: properdin, a natural body-defense chemical occurring in the blood. Healthy individuals have good levels of this chemical and thus are able to ward off cancer. Cancer patients, he found, were deficient in this chemical.[185] Southam and other Sloan-Kettering scientists experimented with iatrogenic[186] immunosuppression, "conditioning" subjects for the experimental cancer implants by compromising the immune system via radiation and/or cortisone treatment.[187]

---

185 Chester M. Southam, "The Immunologic Status of Patients with Nonlymphomatous Cancer," *Cancer Research* 28 (July 1968): 1433-1440; Richard J.H. Johnston, "Cancer Defenses Found To Differ," *The New York Times* April 15, 1957; Chester Southam and L. Pillemer, "Serum Properdin Levels and Cancer Cell Homografts in Man," *Proceedings of the Society for Experimental Biology and Medicine* 96:3 (1957):596-601; Peter A. Herbut and William H. Kraemer, "The Possible Role of the Properdin System in Transplantable Cancer: The Effect of Zymosan on Transplantable Human Carcinoma," *Cancer Research* 16:11 (1956): 1048-1052.

186 Iatrogenic - relating to illness caused by medical examination or medical treatment.

187 For example Helene Wallace Toolan, "Transplantable Human Neoplasms Maintained in Cortisone-treated Laboratory Animals: H.S. #1; H.Ep. #1; H.Ep. #2; H.Ep. #3; and H.Emb.Rh. #1," *Cancer Research* 14:9 (1954): 660-666; idem, "Growth of human tumors in cortisone-treated laboratory animals: the

In May 1956 Sloan-Kettering partnered with that MKULTRA-institution, Ohio State University, to conduct cancer-injection experiments at Ohio State Penitentiary.[188] With the approval and assistance of Warden Ralph W. Alvis, inmates were injected with "cancer cells...grown in test tubes,"[189] i.e., live human cancer (HeLa) cells. This prison experiment was being carried out by the Division of Medical Research, College of Medicine, The Ohio State University, and the Sloan-Kettering Institute for Cancer Research, New York City. The experiment was led by Dr. Chester Southam with his partner Dr. Alice Moore and his mentor, Dr. Cornelius Rhoads.[190] The experiment continued for 12 years and eventually involved at

14 Convicts Injected With Live Cancer Cells

COLUMBUS, Ohio, June 14 (AP) — Fourteen Ohio penitentiary inmates were injected today with live cancer cells in a major study of the disease.

Warden Ralph W. Alvis said Dr. Alice Moore and Dr. Chester M. Southam of the Sloan-Kettering Institute in New York had administered the injections.

Some 134 inmates had volunteered to participate in the research program. Researchers from Ohio State University will examine the fourteen daily.

The cancer cells were grown in test tubes. A spokesman for the Cancer Foundation said any cancer injection that might take effect would spread slowly and remain in the area of the inoculation.

Physicians said the research program might provide information as to how the body reaction of the noncancerous individual killed off foreign cancer cells.

The fourteen inmates are between 25 and 55 years old.

The New York Times
Published: June 15, 1956
Copyright © The New York Times

least 396 inmates, almost half of them Black,[191] receiving injections of various types of cancer cells. Sloan-Kettering received between $300,000 and $500,000 (between $3 million and

---

possibility of obtaining permanently transplantable human tumors," *Cancer Research* 13:4 (1953): 389-394.

188 "Medicine: Volunteers for Cancer," *Time* June 4, 1956; "Cancer by the Needle," *Newsweek* June 4, 1956; "14 Convicts Injected With Live Cancer Cells," *The New York Times* June 15, 1956; "Medicine: Cancer Volunteers," *Time* February 25, 1957; Richard J.H. Johnston, "Cancer Defenses Found To Differ," *The New York Times* April 15, 1957; "Convicts Sought For Cancer Test," *The New York Times* August 1, 1957.

189 "14 Convicts Injected With Live Cancer Cells," *The New York Times* June 15, 1956.

190 Richard J.H. Johnston, "Cancer Defenses Found To Differ," *The New York Times* April 15, 1957.

191 Harriet A. Washington, "Tuskegee Experiment Was But One Medical Study That Exploited African-Americans Infamous Research," *The Baltimore Sun* March 18, 1995; "Medicine: Volunteers for Cancer," *Time* June 4, 1956;

$5 million in 2020 dollars) in federal funds from the National Cancer Institute and funding from the American Cancer Society for this project.[192]

In 1963, with funding from the United States Department of Public Health and the American Cancer Society, Southam and colleague Emanuel Mandel began a study to test Southam's hypothesis that chronically ill patients who were not suffering from cancer would be able to reject implanted cancer cells as rapidly as does patients who were not suffering from any disease and faster than those who were already cancer patients. This human experiment was conducted at the Jewish Hospital for Chronic Diseases (JHCD). Twenty-two unsuspecting non-cancerous *Black female* geriatric patients were injected with live cancer cells. Southam's JHCD experiment "was a continuation of cancer studies he had been doing for well over a decade," such as his work "in Africa injecting an assortment of rare and common viruses" into patients. [193]

Over more than a decade Southam implanted cancer cells in more than 600 persons, diseased and healthy.[194] These implanted cells *did* grow into cancerous tumors in some of the subjects and in some cases the implanted cancerous cells metastasized in the subjects.[195] But like his mentor before him, Dr. Cornelius Rhoads, "far from ostracized by his peers, Southam was elected president of the American Association for Cancer Research just a few years later [in 1968]. Obviously, breaching a code of medical ethics wasn't an impediment to career advancement in the 1960s."[196]

---

192 Vernon, "Tuskegee Syphilis Study not Americas only Medical Scandal," 6.
193 Allen M. Homblum, "NYC's forgotten cancer scandal," *New York Post* November 19, 2022.
194 Jay Katz, *Experimentation with Human Beings* (New York: Russel Sage Foundation, 1972) 11.
195 Elinor Langer, "Human Experimentation: Cancer Studies at Sloan-Kettering Stir Public Debate on Medical Ethics," *Science* 143 (February 7, 1964): 551-553.
196 Allen M. Homblum, "NYC's forgotten cancer scandal," *New York Post* November 19, 2022.

Southam here illustrates how he prepared the cancer injections used during his experiments.[197]

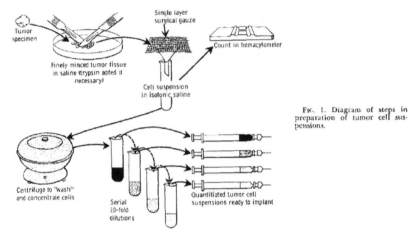

Fɪɢ. 1. Diagram of steps in preparation of tumor cell suspensions.

Southam's diagram illustrating how human cancer was transplanted from man-to-man.

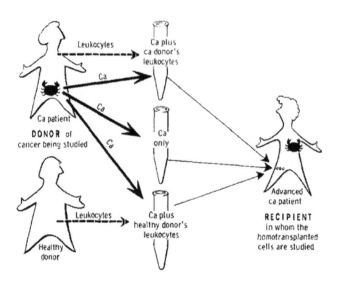

197 Chester M. Southam et al. "Effect of Leukocytes on Transplantability of Human Cancer," *Cancer* 19 (November 1966): 1743-1753.

III.   *SV40 and the Special Virus Cancer Program*

In 1959 Dr. Bernice Eddy of the National Institutes of Health (NIH) discovered a tumor-causing agent in the kidney cells of the monkeys used to make the polio vaccines of Dr. Jonas Stalk and Dr. Albert Sabin. The following year two scientists from the Merck laboratory in Pennsylvania, Dr. Maurice Hilleman and Dr. Ben Sweet, isolated that agent, a virus they named simian virus No. 40 (SV40). Tests found that SV40 contaminated both the Salk and Sabin polio vaccines that were administered to some 98 million Americans between 1955 and 1963. Since then, SV40 has been found in human bone cancers, brain cancers and lung cancers such as mesolthelioma.[198]

Once isolated, SV40 was experimented with on unsuspecting citizens. Between 1960 and 1962, nearly 1100 infants at the Cleveland Metropolitan General Hospital in Ohio were experimentally exposed to increasingly large amounts of polio virus within the Sabin vaccine while the researchers noted who got infected by the virus and from what dosage. "The majority were Negroes from the lower socioeconomic group," the researchers admit. Within three days of their birth these Black babies were inoculated with polio vaccine doses ranging up to *100 times the dosage recommended for adults.* On top of that, the experimental vaccines contained high titers of the cancer-causing SV40. So, while these black babies were still immunologically immature at 3 days old, they were experimentally exposed via

---

198 William Carlsen, "Rogue virus in the Vaccine/Early polio vaccine harbored virus now feared to cause cancer in humans," *San Francisco Chronicle* July 15, 2001: "For four decades, government officials have insisted that there is no evidence the simian virus called SV40 is harmful to humans. But in recent years, dozens of scientific studies have found the virus in a steadily increasing number of rare brain, bone and lung-related tumors - the same malignant cancer SV40 causes in lab animals." See further Debbie Bookchin and Jim Schumacher, The virus and the Vaccine: The True Story of a Cancer-Causing Monkey Virus, Contaminated Polio Vaccine, and the Millions Of Americans Exposed (New York : St. Martin's Press, 2004).

vaccines to high levels of polio virus as well as high levels of SV40.[199]

In 1960 J. Anthony Morris led a team of molecular biologist at the U.S. National Institutes of Health in a non-therapeutic clinical *in vivo* study of the carcinogenetic effects of SV40. Twenty-four federal prisoners were transferred to the NIH Clinical Center in Bethesda, Maryland, to serve as research subjects in an "intentional-infection experiment" for the NIH's National Institute of Allergy and Infectious Diseases (NIAID). With official blessing from the NIH human-subjects review board, Morris and his team intentionally infected the prisoners with SV40 in order to test "its potentialities as an infectious agent in man."[200] This study was conducted under the auspices of the NIH's in-house Prisoner Program. Established in 1959, this Prisoner Program was designed to "funnel healthy federal prisoner 'volunteers' to the Clinical Center for NIAID's intentional infection research."[201] By 1964 more than one thousand prisoners were bused in to Bethesda from sixteen penitentiaries across the country, places like the Atlanta Federal Penitentiary, to be used as human guinea pigs and be intentionally infected by a range of viruses like the ones that cause pneumonia, influenza, and the common cold (a

---

199 Martha Lipson Lepow et al., "Sabin Type I (LSc2ab) Oral Poliomyelitis Vaccine: Effect of Dose upon Response of Newborn Infants," *American Journal of Disease of Children* 104 (1962): 67-71; *Immunization Safety Review: SV40 Contamination of Polio Vaccine and Cancer*, ed. Kathleen Stratton, Donna A. Almario, and Marie C. McCormick (Washington D.C.: The National Academic Press, 2002) 44, 52-53.

200 J. A Morris, K. M. Johnson, C. G. Aulisio, R. M., Chanock, & V. Knight, (1961). "Clinical and serologic responses in volunteers given vacuolating virus (SV-40) by respiratory route," *Proceedings of the Society for Experimental Biology and Medicine. Society for Experimental Biology and Medicine* (New York, N.Y., 1961) 108, 56-59.

201 Laura Stark and Nancy D. Campbell, "Stowaways in the history of science: The case of simian virus 40 and clinical research on federal prisoners at the US National Institutes of Health, 1960," *Studies in History and Philosophy of Biological and Biomedical Sciences* 48 (2014): 218-230 (221).

coronavirus).[202] Morris and his team inoculated groups of prisoners with respiratory syncytial virus (RSV) and SV40.

In 1962, the National Cancer Institute (NCI) initiated *viral oncology programs* in which simians were inoculated with viruses in order to cause cancers. The aim of these programs was "to induce leukemia of human origin in an exceptional primate host and to recover the causative virus, establish laboratory strains of it, confirm its pathogenicity for humans through seroepidemiological studies, and develop an effective control measure for the disease."[203] In 1963 Hilary Koprowski and scientists from The Wistar Institute in Philadelphia experimentally injected a mixture of human cancer cells (HeLa) and SV40 in human subjects, inducing a sarcoma tumor.[204] When researchers began to systematically investigate the mechanism by which the monkey virus SV40 could be made to cause human tumors, they "found that by using the right mixture of human cancer cells and the SV40 virus...the SV40 monkey cancer virus could not only reproducibly cause tumors...in human subjects, but could also be retrieved in cells removed from induced cancer growths...eventually they found the SV40 monkey virus, when mixed and cultured properly, could produce human tumors (characterized as sarcomas) with comparable ease."[205]

In 1964 the National Cancer Institute (NCI) launched its Special Virus Cancer Program (SVCP) with a $10 million budget. Initially called the Special Virus Leukemia Program, one of SVCP's major goals was the finding and isolation of cancer-

202 Laura Stark, "Gaps in medical research ethics," *Los Angeles Times* October 8, 2010.
203 R.F. Kinard and H. Rabin, "Oncogenic Virus Studies in Nonhuman Primates under the Special Virus Cancer Program, *Medical Primatology 1972. Proceedings of the Third Conference on Experimental Medicine and Surgery in Primates, Lyons 1972*, Part I (Karger, Basel 1972): 115-119 (115).
204 Fred Jensen et al. "Autologous and Homologous Implantation of Human Cells Transformed *In Vitro* By Simian Virus 40," *Journal of the National Cancer Institute* 32 (1964): 917-937.
205 Leonard, *AIDS: The Perfect Disease*, 33-34.

causing viruses through the organization of experiments.[206] "Potential cancer-causing viruses were collected, grown in huge amounts, and distributed through the [S]VCP; thousands of animals were infected experimentally, and the aerosol distribution of carcinogenic viruses was studied."[207]

SVCP was an extramural research program of the NCI's Office of Viral Oncology, which means the SVCP outsourced it research to contractors. One major contractor was the Southwest Foundation for Research and Education Program in San Antonio, Texas, directed by Dr. S.S. Kalter at the time.[208] However, the SVCP's primary contractor was the Bionetics Research Laboratories of Litton Bionetics. This is how the SVCP became wedded to secret military biological research. Bionetics was a medical subsidiary of the mega-military weapons contractor Litton Industries, one of the nation's largest military contractors by 1968.[209]

> Litton is a conglomerate which has gotten rich primarily on contracts with various governments. Its Minnesota subsidiary has performed studies of delivery of biological weapons, and its Mississippi subsidiary produces nuclear submarines. Litton holds an $800 million contract with the Greek military junta for economic development of Western Peloponnesus and Crete.[210]

---

206 Nicholas Wade, "Special Virus Cancer Program: Travails of A Biological Moonshot," *Science* New Series 174: 4016 (December 24, 1971): 1306-1311.
207 Richard Hatch, "Cancer Warfare," *CovertAction* 39 (Winter 1991-92): 14-19 (15).
208 R.F. Kinard and H. Rabin, "Oncogenic Virus Studies in Nonhuman Primates under the Special Virus Cancer Program, *Medical Primatology 1972. Proceedings of the Third Conference on Experimental Medicine and Surgery in Primates, Lyons 1972*, Part I (Karger, Basel 1972): 115-119 (117).
209 Dennis McLellen, "Roy L. Ash, former OMB director, dies at 93," *The Washington Post* January 12, 2012. On Litton as Defense contractor see e.g. "Defense: Litton's Ships Come In," *Time* July 6, 1970; "Nation's 19th Largest Defense Contractor Barred From Pentagon Contracts," *Associated Press News* July 17, 1986;
210 Boston Science Teaching Collective, "Cancer: We Cause It! We Cure It!" *Science for the People* 3:3 (July 1971): 12.

In fact, "Congressional records showed Litton was among the most frequently contracted companies involved in [biological warfare] research and development between 1960 and 1970."[211]

> A major player in the military-industrial complex, the corporation worked extensively on the dispersion of BW agents from planes, and included U.S. Air Force contracts for "the supersonic delivery of dry biological agents." From 1966 to 1968, Bionetics Research Laboratories (which became Litton-Bionetics in 1973) held two contracts with the U.S. Army BW program. At the same time, it held major contracts with the NCI.[212]

This is the company that was the main contractor for the NCI's Special Virus Cancer Program. "One of Bionetics Research Laboratories' most important NCI contracts was a massive virus inoculation program that began in 1962 and ran until at least 1976, and used more than 2,000 monkeys."[213] In an effort to "find a transmissible cancer," "the monkeys were injected with everything from human cancer tissues to rare viruses and even sheep's blood....Many of these monkeys succumbed to immunosuppression after infection with the Mason-Pfizer monkey virus, the first known immunosuppressive retrovirus, a class of viruses that includes the human immunodeficiency virus."[214] SV40 was one of the viruses that Bionetics Research Laboratories conducted research on and research with as part of this NCI inoculation program.[215]

While the SVCP's main focus was the identification and production of oncogenic viruses, it also had a Chemical

---

211 Leonard G. Horowitz, *Emerging Viruses: AIDS and Ebola: nature, accident, or genocide?* (Rockport, MA: Tetrahedron, 1996) 76.
212 Hatch, "Cancer Warfare," 17.
213 Hatch, "Cancer Warfare," 17.
214 Hatch, "Cancer Warfare," 17.
215 Roy Kinard, "A Program For Inoculation of Primates with Potentially Oncogenic Viruses," and Stevan Sibinovic et al., "Maintenance of Juvenile Simians For Oncogenic Studies" in *Medical Primatology 1970. Proceedings of the Second Conference on Experimental Medicine and Surgery in Primates, New York, N.Y., September 1969*, ed. Edward I. Goldsmith and J. Moor-Jankowski (New York, 1970) 895-917, 912-917.

Carcinogenesis Area which investigated *chemical agents* as causes of cancer and as co-factors in viral carcinogenesis.[216] William Lijinsky, who was Director of the Chemical Carcinogenesis Area from 1976 to 1991, experimentally induced cancer in the laboratory successfully with a number of chemicals. He was an expert on the mechanisms of chemical carcinogenesis.[217]

IV.   *Not War* **On** *Cancer But War* **By** *Cancer*

In 1969, "for reasons of Machiavellian realpolitik,"[218] President Richard Nixon ordered a halt to offensive biological warfare research and weapons stockpiling by the United States. But the 1972 Biological Weapons Convention (BWC), to which the United States became a signatory, had a built-in loophole which the U.S. exploited: while the article prohibits the acquisition or use of biological agents for offensive or "hostile" purposes, it allows biological agent research for "prophylactic, protective or other peaceful purposes." As noted by Francis Boyle, drafter of the 1989 Biological Weapons Anti-Terrorism Act, "This became the proverbial exception that the United States government exploited in order to nullify the general rule of 'bios' prohibition found in BWC article I." Thus, "despite the President's order, the CIA continued to research and develop biological weapons."[219] *The*

---

216 *Special Virus-Cancer Program Progress Report #8 August 1971* (Bethesda, Maryland: National Institutes of Health, 1971) 27.
217 "William Lijinsky, 75," *The Washington Post* March 15, 2004; William Lijinsky, "Current Status of Experimental Chemical Carcinogenesis and its Application to Human Cancer Risk," *Cancer Research* 39 (1979): 2887-2890; W. Lijinsky, J.E. Saavedra and M.D. Reuber, "Induction of Carcinogenesis in Fischer Rats by Methylalkylnitrosamines," *Cancer Research* 41 (1981): 1288-1292; William Lijinsky, "Intestinal Cancer Induced by N-Nitroso Compounds," *Toxicologic Pathology* 16:2 (1988): 198-204.
218 Francis A. Boyle, *Biowarfare and Terrorism* (Atlanta: Clarity Press, Inc. 2005) 15.
219 Boyle, *Biowarfare and Terrorism* 16.

New York Times could still announce in 1982: "U.S. Continues Defensive Germ Warfare Research."

> The United States officially renounced biological warfare in 1969. But here, in a small corner of the military base where the American germ-weapon effort was located, Army scientists are still involved in what they call "medical defensive B.W. research"...

> Army officials are sensitive about describing their work, which has continued since 1969, when President Nixon renounced American use of biological weapons and ordered the destruction of existing arms. But he said that a defensive effort would continue, to guard against possible germ attacks by an enemy.

> "What we're doing is uniquely medical," said Col. Richard Barquist, the doctor who heads the Army Medical Institute of Infectious Diseases. "We're involved in medical defensive research."...

> Critics of the research at Fort Detrick have argued that there is little difference between "offensive" and "defensive" work. Colonel Barquist agreed. "As far as the research goes, there's no difference," he said. "But the U.S. is out of the B.W. business. What we don't do are mass cultures or deliverable weapons systems. It's all just medical research."[220]

"What we're doing is uniquely medical": this goes back to the "guise of legitimate medical work" that the CIA used since the 1950s to conduct its unethical "assassination cancer" research. In line with this "medical defensive B.W. research" ruse, President Nixon in 1971 ordered the conversion of the U.S. Army's BW center at Fort Detrick to civilian use. As a consequence, Fort Detrick was turned over to the NCI and renamed the Frederick Cancer Research Center. Instead of biowarfare, Nixon declared a "War on Cancer." Some of the scientific personnel of Fort Detrick transferred to the CIA and helped develop its clandestine biological apparatus for "defensive research."

In 1972 the NCI contracted Litton to operate the new Frederick Cancer Research Center at Fort Detrick - no surprise

---

220 "U.S. Continues Defensive Germ Warfare Research," *The New York Times* September 7, 1982.

here.[221] Litton Industries was one of the nation's largest military contractors by 1968, the year Litton president Roy Ash became advisor to U.S. President-elect Richard M. Nixon.[222] As chairman of President Nixon's Advisory Council on Executive Organizations, Ash oversaw all American industry during the Nixon administration beginning in 1969. He was also Assistant to the President of the United States and director of the Office of Management and Budget under Nixon. Litton was given $5 billion in military contracts during the first term of the Nixon Administration.

Nixon's "War *on* Cancer" was clearly a euphemism for the defense establishment's War *by* (means of) Cancer. Biowarfare research continued but under the guise of cancer research. According to official statements to the press, in the hands of Litton the Fort Detrick facilities would continue to research animal and human cancer viruses as well as "chemicals capable of causing cancer."[223] Virus will be "made" in large quantities for use. By 1972 the SVCP's budget climbed to $49 million and in 1973 the name was changed to the Virus Cancer Program (VCP). "The National Cancer Institute, while looking for a cure for cancer, spun off an intelligence agency «carve out» project under the Viral Cancer Project that researched military applications for cancer-causing biological agents."[224]

Ludwik Gross from the Cancer Research Unit of the Veterans Administration Hospital (Bronx, New York) warned in 1971: "Human cancer extracts, and also human cell suspensions, have been inoculated in recent years by several investigators into

221 Harold M. Schmeck Jr., "Litton to Run Cancer Research Lab," *The New York Times* June 25, 1972.
222 Dennis McLellen, "Roy L. Ash, former OMB director, dies at 93," *The Washington Post* January 12, 2012. On Litton as Defense contractor see e.g. "Defense: Litton's Ships Come In," *Time* July 6, 1970; "Nation's 19th Largest Defense Contractor Barred From Pentagon Contracts," *Associated Press News* July 17, 1986;
223 Harold M. Schmeck Jr., "Litton to Run Cancer Research Lab," *The New York Times* June 25, 1972.
224 Wayne Madsen, " 'Scientific Assassinations' Are Part of the CIA's Modus Operandi," *Global Research* March 12, 2013.

patients, including healthy volunteers, in experimental immunologic studies....*Inoculation of humans with live human cancer extracts may lead to the establishment of progressively growing tumors in the recipients and cause dissemination of a fatal disease.*"[225] The urgency of Gross's warning was heightened in 1975 when Dr. Seymour S. Kalter and colleagues from the Southwest Foundation for Research and Education in San Antonio, Texas – a major Virus Cancer Program (VCP) contractor - announced their successful engineering of a new, infectious cancer virus formed by combining elements of two different viruses: the outer coat of an infectious but non-cancerous baboon type C-RNA virus and the inner core of a noninfectious mouse sarcoma (cancer) virus. This is the creation of what scientists call a *pseudo-virus*. The murine/baboon pseudo-virus possessed extraordinary characteristics. It was shown to cause cancer in a wide range of *new* animal species, e.g., dogs, marmosets, monkeys, and chimpanzees. In addition, human cells growing in laboratory flasks were also transformed into a cancerous state when deliberately infected with the pseudo-virus.[226] This means a noninfectious cancer virus was combined with an infectious non-cancer virus resulting in an infectious cancer virus capable of infecting human cells![227] This makes Loeb and Tartof's 1976 warning acute: "it has been clearly demonstrated in all animal species that viruses manufactured in the laboratory can be oncogenic. It seems only reasonable to assume that humans may be similarly affected."[228]

By 1977 the VCP at Fort Detrick had produced 60,000 liters of cancer-causing and immunosuppressive viruses. Richard Hatch describes the situation well:

---

225 Ludwik Gross, "Transmission of Cancer In Man: Tentative Guidelines Referring to the Possible Effects of Inoculation of Homologous Cancer Extracts in Man," *Cancer* 28 (1971): 785-788.
226 Harold M. Schmeck Jr., "Joined Viruses Cause Cancer in Animals," *The New York Times* May 28, 1976.
227 Leonard, *How AIDS Was Invented*, 9.
228 Lawrence A. Loeb and Kenneth D. Tartof, "Construction of Human Tumor Viruses," *Science* Volume 193 Issue 4250, July 23, 1976, p. 272.

Research into viruses during the War on Cancer provided an ideal cover for continuing biological warfare research...the NCI project allowed the mass production of viruses, the development of means to enhance virulence, exploration of aerosol transmission, and the production of new recombinant disease agents. These 'civilian' projects ran concurrently with 'military' projects in many cases. When political expediency dictated an end to overt U.S. BW research, the Viral Cancer Program provided a means to continue experiments that would otherwise be difficult to justify.[229]

---

229 Hatch, "Cancer Warfare," 19.

Part 3

Assassination Cancer

Chapter Four

The Product and The Protocol

I.   *Medical "Manhattan Project" in New Orleans*

The idea was to try and get Castro ill, very ill, and eliminated through what seemed a natural cause. In this case, cancer. - Judyth Vary Baker, (Cancer Researcher, Mistress and Collaborator of Lee Harvey Oswald) in *The Men Who Killed Kennedy*, The History Chanel, November 17, 2003

Judith Baker, author of "Me and Lee - How I came to know, love, and lose Lee Harvey Oswald," presents an article at a symposium on Sat. Oct. 19, 2013 at Loyola University in New Orleans.

The first hand, autobiographical account of Judyth Vary Baker and the research of Edward Haslam and James Stewart

89

Campbell reveal a very important episode that occurred in the summer of 1963 in New Orleans.[230] Baker is a valuable witness to some critical events transpiring in New Orleans leading up to the assassination of President John Kennedy on November 22, 1963. She says she worked with Lee Harvey Oswald, the U.S. government agent, on the development of a biological weapon capable of killing anyone by injecting virulent cancer cells into them.

As a high school student in her hometown of Bradenton, Florida, Baker had a widely publicized reputation as a gifted student-prodigy. This is how she came to the attention of Dr. Alton Ochsner, the ex-president of the American Cancer Society and founder of the famed research hospital, the Ochsner Clinic. He invited her to New Orleans to be a technician in a cancer lab and to be a part of a project which she was made to understand had national security significance. For her service, Ochsner promised Baker advance admission to Tulane University Medical School, which was her dream. Baker would work under the direction of distinguished orthopedic doctor and cancer researcher Dr. Mary Sherman.

---

230 Judyth Vary Baker in *The Men Who Killed Kennedy. Episode 8: The Love Affair*. Directed by Nigel Turner. Aired on The History Chanel on November 17, 2003; Judyth Vary Baker, *Me & Lee: How I Came To Know, Love and Lose* (Walterville, OR: Trine Day, 2010); Edward T. Haslam, *Mary, Ferrie & the Monkey Virus: The Story of an Underground Medical Laboratory* (Albuquerque, N.M.: Wordsworth Communications, 1995); Edward T. Haslam, *Dr. Mary's Monkey: How the unsolved murder of a doctor, a secret laboratory in New Orleans and cancer-causing monkey viruses are linked to Lee Harvey Oswald, the JFK assassination and emerging global epidemics* (Waterville, OR: TrineDay, 2007); James Stewat Campbell, "The Project: Unethical Human Experiments, Carcinogenic Viruses, and Murder during the Cold War," *MEDesign* 2013 @ https://medesignman.com/MEDICINE/THE%20PROJECT/The%20Project%2 0-%20jcmd.html; "Dr. James Campbell speaking at the 2019 JFK Assassination Conference in Dallas, Texas" (November 21-24, 2019) @ https://www.youtube.com/watch?v=6iS-_O4x4Sw

Photo in *Herald-Tribune* (Bradenton, Florida) of high-school prodigy Judyth Vary in her cancer lab.

Judy Vary To Continue Research

FIRST FROM FLORIDA

SMOKED FOR FIRST TIME

Senior Attends National Meet With Scientists

ALSO AN ARTIST

Local news story of high school prodigy Judyth Vary

91

According to Baker, she was recruited by Dr. Alton Ochsner and Dr. Mary Sherman into a clandestine "get-Fidel Castro" project that had the backing of both the CIA and the New Orleans Mafia headed by Carlos Marcello. Called "The Project," it was a covert and clandestine effort to genetically alter cancer viruses to produce an "assassination cancer" to kill the Cuban leader. The Project was born on March 23, 1962, a week after US Attorney-General Robert Kennedy gave the green light to assassinate Castro. At least some of those involved in The Project understood the Attorney-General to have approved it.[231] On The History Chanel's *The Men Who Killed Kennedy*, in an episode dedicated to her story, Baker details this secret government medical assassination project.

> Dr. [Alton] Ochsner began to explain to me, and I had already been apprised a great deal more by Dr. David Ferrie, about the project that he had been working on for over a year and this clearly had to do working with the deadly cancer strains that he knew I was well adept at handling. The idea was to try and get Castro ill, very ill, and eliminated through what seemed a natural cause. In this case, cancer. The attractiveness of the plan that Dr. Ochsner and Dr. Sherman and David Ferrie were working on, is that up to now attempts to kill Castro had to involve some kind of violence that could be traced to some country or individual and that could lead to war - World War Three maybe, if Russia intervened. This was considered in my mind a noble experiment, a noble attempt to do away with Castro without anyone getting blamed or with only a few people being involved because it was biomedical. At any rate, at the end of the summer, he promised me that I would skip two years of school and go directly into medical school at Tulane medical school. Of course, uhmm, how could I say no?

> We were after a vicious cancer, a galloping cancer and all the tumor material that seemed to be the most vigorous was then placed in a blender and blended together so that they could recycle and not lose that virus and the other thing that we were doing was making tissue cell cultures from the most vigorous and deadly cancers.

231 Judyth Vary Baker, *David Ferrie: Mafia Pilot, Participation in Anti-Castro Bioweapon Plot, Friend of Lee Harvey Oswald and Key to the JFK Assassination* (Walterville, Oregon: Trine Day LLC, 2014) 184-185.

What Dr. Oshner and Dr. Mary Sherman and David Ferrie were doing was assembling various products that could be used by the CIA, perhaps by the Mafia, and they were involved with both, that could be used against Castro and against insurgents or mercenaries or groups that were communists that they felt were infiltrating Central and South America.

I convinced Dr. Ochsner and others that the real thing we need to do is pull down Castro's immune system by using several ploys and then when the cancer is introduced into his body it would be found in his blood system, they'd put him in front of the X-ray again and again and again. He'd be injected again and again. Supposedly he'd be getting treatments to kill the cancer when actually his immune system is getting destroyed. That could be done. In other words, Castro could be eliminated by using the X-ray and they'll think that it's the side effects from lung cancer... and that was my idea.[232]

Several important details are revealed here:

- The plan was to assassinate Castro but to make his death look as if it was of natural causes. It would be a "biomedical" assassination. Since Castro was known to be fond of smoking cigars, an artificially induced lung cancer would be the "natural cause."
- The assassination cancer would be "a galloping cancer" produced in a laboratory.
- Critical to the success of the "galloping" assassination cancer would be the target's deliberately compromised immune system (thus allowing the cancer to "take"). The Project thus required the plotters to "pull down Castro's immune system by using several ploys." For example, through the cooperation of medical persons connected to Castro he would be irradiated by being repeatedly put in front of an X-ray and then repeatedly injected with the cancer. Also, during treatment allegedly to treat the cancer, Castro's immune system would be "destroyed" to ensure that the injected cancer "takes" and does its job in eliminating the Cuban leader.

232 *The Men Who Killed Kennedy. Episode 8: The Love Affair.* Directed by Nigel Turner. Aired on The History Chanel on November 17, 2003.

- The "galloping" assassination cancer, once produced, could be used against others besides Castro: insurgents (read also: revolutionaries), mercenaries, and communist groups that were beginning to infiltrate Central and South America at the time.

According to Baker, Dr. Alton Ochsner directed the "Project," Dr. Mary Sherman supervised the secret research, David Ferry directed the secret labs and Lee Harvey Oswald was a runner. He acted as a go between for The Project members and ran supplies between a string of secret labs. The Project involved "a sophisticated network of laboratories strung across uptown New Orleans, each with different equipment and performing a different function, but all united by a common goal: to develop a cancer weapon and kill Fidel Castro."[233] One of those CIA laboratories was David Ferrie's apartment on Louisiana Parkway that doubled as a clandestine mouse laboratory. Baker worked there with 50-60 mice at a time, which had developed tumors due to cancer injections. Baker's job was to look for mice with the most aggressive tumor growth, terminate the mice and dissect them, and then remove, weigh and grind the tumors in a blender. Baker would then make tissue cell cultures from the most vigorous and deadly cancers. "Our goal was to find aggressive cancers that produced fast-growing tumors," Baker said. "The virus we were more concerned with was SV40."[234]

Baker compiled reports and delivered them and the tumor extracts to Dr. Mary Sherman for review. Dr. Sherman visualized the viral particles under an electron microscope at a clandestine lab on Prytania Street. She then exposed the strongest extracts to radiation at the U.S. Public Health Service Hospital.[235] The aim

233 Judyth Vary Baker, *Me & Lee: How I Came To Know, Love and Lose* (Walterville, OR: Trine Day, 2010) 207-208.
234 Baker, *Me & Lee*, 207-208, 210.
235 Haslam's research suggested Dr. Mary Sherman used a 5,000,000 volt linear particle accelerator that had been quietly built on the grounds of the U.S. Public Health Service Hospital in New Orleans, in the Infectious Disease Laboratory, to radiate cancer-causing monkey viruses.

was to alter the viruses' genetic components in order to enhance their potency. The strongest roasted viruses were then re-injected into mice and monkeys to determine which were "best" at producing tumors. This process was repeated until a cancer virus developed so potent that it could kill a human in a matter of days. The Project team succeeded in creating a "galloping cancer" believed at the time to be "the world's most aggressive cancer cells."[236] It was a radiation-altered SV40-derived cancer-causing virus. Haslam describes The Project as a New Orleans Medical "Manhattan Project"[237]

The new "galloping" SV40-virus was tested on several monkeys and it worked, killing them quickly. The Project team then tested the "galloping" assassination cancer on a human guinea pig: a prisoner(s) from Louisiana's Angola State Penitentiary. On August 29, 1963, Oswald and Ferrie reportedly drove with Clay Shaw to Clinton, Louisiana to intercept a prison van carrying the human guinea pig and follow it to Jackson State Mental Hospital in rural Louisiana. There the prisoner(s) was given a long exposure to X-Rays to cripple his immune system and then he was injected intravenously with the viral assassination cancer.[238] Two days later a special blood test was administered to see if the cancer was active. Kept at the Jackson facility for isolation and observation, the prisoner died of massive cancer metastasis in 28 days.[239]

---

236 Haslam, *Dr. Mary's Monkey*, 232
237 Edward T. Haslam, *Mary, Ferrie & the Monkey Virus: The Story of an Underground Medical Laboratory* (Albuquerque, N.M.: Wordsworth Communications, 1995); Edward T. Haslam, *Dr. Mary's Monkey: How the unsolved murder of a doctor, a secret laboratory in New Orleans and cancer-causing monkey viruses are linked to Lee Harvey Oswald, the JFK assassination and emerging global epidemics* (Waterville, OR: TrineDay, 2007).
238 Haslam, *Dr. Mary's Monkey*, 235.
239 Baker, *Me & Lee*, Chapter 23.

THE PROJECT TEAM

Dr. Alton Ochsner
"Director" of The Project

Dr. Mary Sherman.
"Medical Director" of
The Project

"Doctor" David Ferrie
"Laboratory Director" of The Project

Judyth Vary Baker
Laboratory Technician
and Literature Researcher
for The Project

Lee Harvey Oswald
Runner and Courier
for The Project

Along with the "galloping" assassination cancer, a protocol for its effective use on a healthy target was developed. "It must be accompanied by radiation and/or chemotherapy to be useful - and those adjunct forces could be manipulated," Baker says. "It was destruction of the immune system that would allow strengthened cancer cells to survive and reproduce in the victim's body."[240]

---

240 John Simkin, "Judyth Vary Baker," *Spartacus Educational* @ https://spartacus-educational.com/JFKbakerJ.htm

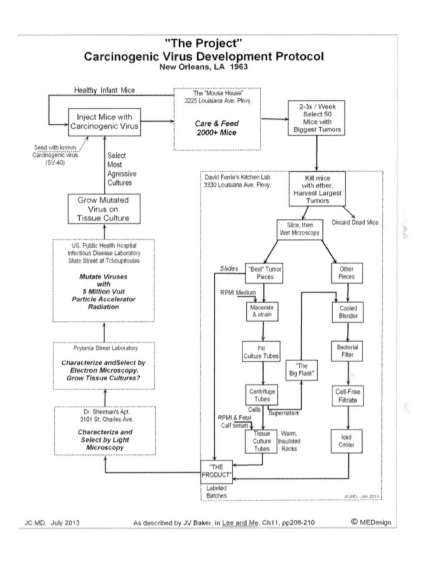

"The Project"
Carcinogenic Virus Development Protocol
New Orleans, LA 1963

Healthy Infant Mice

Inject Mice with Carcinogenic Virus

The "Mouse House" 3225 Louisiana Ave. Pkwy.
Care & Feed 2000+ Mice

2-3x / Week Select 50 Mice with Biggest Tumors

Seed with known Carcinogenic virus (SV-40)

Select Most Agressive Cultures

Grow Mutated Virus on Tissue Culture

David Ferrie's Kitchen Lab 3330 Louisiana Ave. Pkwy.

Kill mice with ether. Harvest Largest Tumors

Slice, then Wet Microscopy

Discard Dead Mice

U.S. Public Health Hospital Infectious Disease Laboratory State Street at Tchoupitoulas
Mutate Viruses with 5 Million Volt Particle Accelerator Radiation

Slides

"Best" Tumor Pieces

Other Pieces

RPMI Medium

Macerate & strain

Cooled Blender

Prytania Street Laboratory
Characterize and Select by Electron Microscopy. Grow Tissue Cultures?

Fill Culture Tubes

Bacterial Filter

"The Big Flask"

Centrifuge Tubes

Cell-Free Filtrate

Dr. Sherman's Apt. 3101 St. Charles Ave.
Characterize and Select by Light Microscopy

Cells

Supernatant

RPMI & Fetal Calf serum

Tissue Culture Tubes

Warm, Insulated Racks

Iced Cooler

"THE PRODUCT"

Labeled Batches

JC,MD, July 2013

JC,MD, July 2013   As described by JV Baker, in Lee and Me, Ch11, pp208-210   © MEDesign

97

"Development of the 'weapon' went like this: Newborn mice were injected with wild strain SV-40 virus to 'seed' a process loop to accelerate carcinogenic mutation. The weak immune system of these young mice could not fight off the virus, so some developed tumors. Several times a week, fifty mice with the biggest palpable tumors were selected. After killing these mice, the largest of the tumors were harvested, selected by microscopy, ground up, mixed with "RPMI" and other media, and centrifuged. The tumorous cells would settle to the bottom of the test tube to form the basis of tissue cultures to be grown elsewhere. Then the supernatant and the remainder of the tumor tissue were macerated in Ferrie's kitchen blender to form a 'tumor soup'...This dreadful 'soup' was then filtered to make a cell-free solution rich in carcinogenic viral particles, which, together with the centrifuged material for tissue culture and the microscope slides became 'The Product' of the lab. The Product was transferred to Dr. Sherman's apartment where she would further examine the tissues microscopically and take the best samples for examination by electron microscopy at the Prytania Street laboratory. Finally, the best and most aggressive tumor virus samples were taken back to the electron accelerator lab to be further mutated by radiation in secret late-night sessions. The irradiated viruses would then be grown on tissue cultures and the most aggressive colonies selected for injection into healthy newborn mice. The cycle would then begin again." James Stewart Campbell, "The Project: Unethical Human Experiments, Carcinogenic Viruses, and Murder during the Cold War" (2013)

98

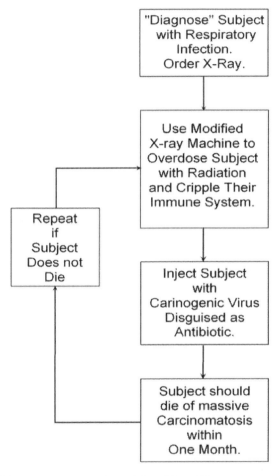

"The Project"
Protocol to Induce Metastatic Cancer in Humans
New Orleans, LA 1963

"Diagnose" Subject
with Respiratory
Infection.
Order X-Ray.

Use Modified
X-ray Machine to
Overdose Subject
with Radiation
and Cripple Their
Immune System.

Repeat
if
Subject
Does not
Die

Inject Subject
with
Carinogenic Virus
Disguised as
Antibiotic.

Subject should
die of massive
Carcinomatosis
within
One Month.

99

"Lethality to humans was a big problem...The mouse tumors were not transferring successfully into primates, due to their different and more powerful immune system. If healthy monkeys were not developing tumors from the injected mouse viruses, humans would probably react the same way. It was necessary to first irradiate the monkeys to hamper their immune systems so the tumor could survive. By mid-July the tumors were beginning to "take" in irradiated Marmoset monkeys. The virus was not only lethal to the injected monkeys, but also to the control group of irradiated monkeys that were housed with the injected animals. The virus had become contagious and transmissible... a protocol to induce cancer in an unsuspecting human was devised: The victim had to first be diagnosed falsely with "pneumonia," given a radiation overdose secretly during a bogus "chest X-ray," and then intravenously injected with the carcinogenic virus Product disguised as an antibiotic. Repeat as necessary until the victim dies of cancer." James Stewart Campbell, "The Project: Unethical Human Experiments, Carcinogenic Viruses, and Murder during the Cold War" (2013)

Now that the "galloping" assassination cancer proved effective on a human, it was ready for delivery to Cuba. In late September 1963 Oswald traveled to Mexico City with the bioweapon to hand it over to a contact - a medical technician who would then take the materials over to Cuba and hand it over to a member of Castro's medical team who was cooperating with the CIA. "Castro, who smoked cigars constantly, would seem to die of natural causes if the bioweapon worked".[241] The drop-off point in Mexico City was a souvenir shop, but the contact never showed. A hurricane was threatening Cuba and the CIA ordered Oswald back to Dallas for a debriefing, according to Baker. Thus, the 1963 "galloping" assassination cancer plot is one of the 638 failed or scrapped attempts to kill Fidel Castro.

II.   *Jack Ruby and Assassination Cancer*

Although the super virus bioweapon was never successfully deployed against Castro, it was used to kill others. To test how well the killer virus worked on humans, it was injected into several human guinea pigs. They were prisoners...Then it was used on Jack Ruby as he sat in his prison cell. He was expecting it, and he tried to warn authorities both before and after he was injected. Nobody listened. He died in a few weeks. - Edward T. Haslam, *Dr. Mary's Monkey (*2007)

Prior to his trial for murdering Lee Harvey Oswald, Jack Ruby repeatedly asked to speak to members of the Warren Commission and to be moved out of Dallas and to Washington D.C. because "I want to tell the truth, and I can't tell it here." He said, "My life is in danger here." The transfer of course neve occurred, so Ruby began talking. In March 1965, a year after his conviction, Jack Ruby conducted a brief televised news conference in which he stated:

Everything pertaining to what's happening has never come to the surface. The world will never know the true facts of what occurred, my motives.

---

241 Baker, *David Ferrie*, 276.

> The people who had so much to gain and had such an ulterior motive for putting me in the position I'm in, will never let the true facts come above board to the world.

When asked by a reporter, "Are these people in very high positions, Jack?" he responded "Yes."[242] Known as one of "[Lyndon] Johnson's boys,"[243] Ruby felt betrayed by the new President who did nothing to get him out of jail.[244] After being sentenced to life in prison, Ruby began to drop public seeds about what he knew of Johnson's involvement in the plot to kill his predecessor John F. Kennedy. "If [Adlai Stevenson] was Vice-President there would never have been an assassination of our beloved President Kennedy," Ruby said at a press conference, implicitly accusing Johnson of Kennedy's murder.[245] According to a *London Sunday Times* article (August 24, 1974) Ruby confided in psychiatrist Werner Teuter that the assassination of JFK was "an act of overthrowing the government," and that he knew "who had President Kennedy killed." Ruby claimed: "I am doomed. I do not want to die. But I am not insane. I was framed to kill Oswald."[246] He told Dallas Deputy Sheriff Al Maddox in a note that "it was a conspiracy" and "my role was to silence Oswald."

> I was part of the conspiracy in the assassination of [the] president, and I was used to silence Oswald. I walked into a trap the moment I walked down that ramp Sunday morning. This was the spot where they could frame the Jew, and that way, all of his people will be blamed as being Communists, this is what they were waiting for. They alone had planned the killing, by they I mean Johnson and others.[247]

---

242 "Jack Ruby Interview" on YouTube @ https://www.youtube.com/watch?v=NiPl2DNwJJk
243 According to former Nixon operative Roger Stone.
244 Guyénot, "Did Israel Kill the Kennedys?" On Ruby's statement see on YouTube, "Jack Ruby Talks."
245 Guyénot, *From Yahweh To Zion,* 220.
246 Jerry Carrier, *Hard Right Turn: The History and the Assassination of the American Left* (New York: Algora Publishing, 2015) 186.
247 Penn Jones Jr., *Forgive My Grief,* Vol. 1, 64-66.

In other words, Ruby was leaking all over the place. In October 1966 an appellate court overturned Ruby's March 1964 murder conviction. A retrial was granted, and it would be held in February or March 1967 outside of Dallas in Wichita Falls, Texas, "thus allowing him to speak freely if he so desired."[248] This was pleasing to Ruby, but very displeasing to those on whom Ruby had begun to subtly drop dimes. "There was every likelihood that within another month or two, Ruby would walk free, as his time in jail would be counted against a probable short prison term for murder without malice. He certainly would have been allowed to post bond and become accessible to the public."[249] However, only a few weeks after his grant of a new trial, in December 1966, Ruby was diagnosed with cancer. A month later, on January 3, 1967, Jack Ruby died of lung cancer. He never made it to a new trial to "speak freely."

248 Rod McPhee, "Was Lee Harvey Oswald's killer Jack Ruby injected with cancer to stop him revealing who really shot JFK?" *Mirror* January 6, 2017.
249 Jim Marrs, *Crossfire: The Plot That Killed Kennedy. Revised And Updated* (New York: Basic Books, 2013) 412-413.

Physical examinations and X-rays taken in 1963 and 1964 revealed no signs of cancer.[250] It was in October 1966, shortly after the grant of his new trial, that Ruby showed his first signs of illness. The prison doctors treated it as a cold or pneumonia and gave him frequent shots. Finally on December 9, 1966, Ruby was moved from the Dallas County Jail and admitted to Parkland Hospital. The next day end stage lung cancer was discovered in Ruby.

> When Jack Ruby was admitted to Parkland Hospital on December 9, his illness had been variously diagnosed as a "bad cold" (Jail Doctor John W. Callahan), "coronary occlusion" (Dr. J.M. Pickard, county health officer), and "pneumonia" (initial diagnosis of doctors at Parkland). Then doctors found malignant cells in a lymph node and in the lining of the lung. More than four quarts of mucous fluid were pumped from Ruby's chest the day after he was admitted. Less than a month later he was dead...Ruby's sister Eva and Texas editor Penn Jones Jr. implied that his cancer might conceivably have been induced...Callahan said Ruby first began coughing and vomiting at about the time his murder conviction was revered last October.[251]

An important witness is Dallas Deputy Sheriff Al Maddox, who frequently had contact with Ruby in the Dallas County Jail. He told both Baker and JFK researcher Jim Marrs that, after Ruby's "illness" developed in October, a doctor from Chicago came to Dallas and stayed until Ruby was transferred to Parkland. Then the doctor left. During his time in Dallas he gave Ruby repeated shots of "penicillin" for his "cold."[252]

Al Maddox and Jack Ruby.

250 UPI, "Ruby case Discussed: Doctors, Sheriff Deny Prisoner Was Neglected," *Reading Eagle* January 5, 1967.
251 David Welsh, "Jack Ruby and His Jail Doctors: A strange diagnosis, a familiar hospital, another death," *The Sunday Ramparts* January 15-21, 1967, p. 4.
252 Baker, *David Ferrie*, 385.

We had a phony doctor come in to [the Dallas County Jail] from Chicago, just as phony and as queer as a three-dollar bill. And he worked his way in through—I don't know, whoever supplied the county at that time with doctors....You could tell he was Ruby's doctor. He spent half his time up there talking with Ruby. And one day I went in and Ruby told me, he said, "Well, they injected me for a cold." He said it was cancer cells. That's what he told me, Ruby did. I said you don't believe that shit. He said, "I damn sure do!" I never said anything to [Dallas Sheriff Bill] Decker or anybody....[Then] one day when I started to leave, Ruby shook hands with me and I could feel a piece of paper in his palm....[In this note] he said it was a conspiracy and he said . . . if you will keep your eyes open and your mouth shut, you're gonna learn a lot. And that was the last letter I ever got from him. [253]

There is speculation that the "Doctor From Chicago" who gave Ruby these shots was infamous "CIA Doctor" Dr. Jolyon West. He was from Los Angeles, but he reportedly was engaged in Chicago at the time and could have traveled to Dallas from Chicago to carry out a requested medical assassination.[254] In any case, Ruby was sure that the injections he received from this mysterious doctor was not penicillin but cancer cells. In fact, the doctors reportedly *told him* this: "Jack Ruby was complaining of injections and said he was *told* it was cancer (this would make people think Ruby was paranoid, so it was just fine to tell him what he was getting - it would be undetectable, and Ruby would be laughed at and accused of being paranoid."[255] According to Baker, Ruby knew about the galloping assassination cancer that she worked on because she and David Ferrier discussed with Ruby The Project and its Product.[256] According to Gary Cartwright of *Texas Monthly* Ruby wrote a letter to Gordon McLendon, owner of radio station KLIF and

253 Marrs, *Crossfire*, 413-414; Rod McPhee, "Was Lee Harvey Oswald's killer Jack Ruby injected with cancer to stop him revealing who really shot JFK?" *Mirror* January 6, 2017.
254 Marrs, *Crossfire*, 414; Baker, *David Ferrie*, 386.
255 Baker, *David Ferrie*, 409.
256 Baker, *David Ferrie*, 386.

associate of Ruby's, claiming he was being poisoned by his jailers. [257] In addition, Marrs writes:

> Maddox was not the only law-enforcement officer to suspect that Ruby's death was not entirely natural. Policeman Tom Tilson told researchers, "It was the opinion of a number of other Dallas police officers that Ruby had received injections of cancer while he was incarcerated in the Dallas County Jail following the shooting of Lee Harvey Oswald.[258]

The presence of The Project's assassination cancer in this case is corroborated by Jack Ruby's handler's use (or abuse) of X-rays. One former Dallas law-enforcement officer told Jim Marrs: "Hell, it wasn't any big deal. They just took Ruby in for X-rays and had him wait in the X-ray room. While he sat there for fifteen or twenty minutes or more, they just left the X-ray machine on him."[259] Baker notes also, "One report said Ruby was in the x-ray room soon after admission (to the hospital) for 45 minutes."[260] According to James Campbell, "This indicates that the weaponized virus still required a compromised immune system to take hold. The Project had not been able to make a super-virulent tumorous virus that could infect a healthy human. But the virus was potent enough in Ruby's irradiated condition." [261]

It is also clear that Ruby's sudden cancer was indeed "galloping."[262] "An autopsy showed that he had traces of white cancerous tumors *coursing throughout his body*, with the greatest concentration in the right lung."[263] According to one press account, "Cancer has been found in the lining of Ruby's chest, in addition to the lymph node on his neck, where it was originally discovered. Both lungs are filled with suspicious looking nodules. The cancer

---

257 Gary Cartwright, "Who Was Jack Ruby?" *Texas Monthly* November 1975, pp. 82-86, 129-134 (129); idem, "Jack Ruby: Who Was He and Why Did He Do It?" *Village Voice* November 17, 1975, pp. 16-19 (18).
258 Marrs, *Crossfire*, 413-414.
259 Marrs, *Crossfire*, 414.
260 Baker, *David Ferrie*, 387.
261 Campbell, "The Project."
262 Baker, *David Ferrie*, 386. 384.
263 Campbell, "The Project."

spread to these areas; physicians are still looking for the place it started. The right lung was collapsed by the pressure of four quarts of fluid that were in his chest cavity when he was taken Friday from Dallas County Jail."[264] Joe Tonahill, one of the attorneys for Ruby during his trial, told Texas journalist Gary Cartwright in 1975 that the autopsy confirmed a "massive spread of cancer" and that "Ruby had *fifteen brain tumors*."[265] All of this developed rapidly. As was the case with the Angola State Penitentiary prisoner guinea pigs, Ruby died within 28 days after (presumably) being injected.[266]

District Attorney Jim Garrison believed also that Ruby was killed with "assassination cancer" that originated from the David Ferrie-Dr. Mary Sherman labs in New Orleans.[267]

[Former New Orleans District Attorney Jim] Garrison...said before his death in 1992: "Jack Ruby died of cancer a few weeks after his conviction for murder had been overruled in appeals court. He was ordered to stand trial outside of Dallas, thus allowing him to speak freely if he so desired. There was little hesitancy in killing Lee Harvey Oswald in order to prevent him from talking, so there is no reason to suspect that any more consideration would have been shown Jack Ruby if he had posed a threat to the architects of the conspiracy"... And Garrison believed he knew the potential source of the cancer cells. "David Ferrie had a rather curious hobby," he said. "He filled his apartment with white mice, at one point he had almost 2,000, and neighbours complained. "He wrote a medical treatise on the subject and worked with a number of New Orleans doctors on means of inducing cancer in mice. "After the assassination, one of these physicians, Dr Mary Sherman, was found hacked to death with a kitchen knife in her New Orleans apartment.[268]

---

264 Baker, *David Ferrie*, 386.
265 Gary Cartwright, "Who Was Jack Ruby?" *Texas Monthly* November 1975, pp. 82-86, 129-134 (129); idem, "Jack Ruby: Who Was He and Why Did He Do It?" *Village Voice* November 17, 1975, pp. 16-19 (17).
266 Baker, *David Ferrie*, 388.
267 Rod McPhee, "Was Lee Harvey Oswald's killer Jack Ruby injected with cancer to stop him revealing who really shot JFK?" *Mirror* January 6 2017.
268 Rod McPhee, "Was Lee Harvey Oswald's killer Jack Ruby injected with cancer to stop him revealing who really shot JFK?" *Mirror* January 6, 2017.

Finally, it appears that we have strong confirmation of Ruby's conviction and Garrison's belief that Ruby was biomedically with assassination cancer. CIA covert operations veteran Robert Trumbull Crowley, who retired from the CIA in 1980 as Assistant Deputy Director of Operations (ADDO), before his death on October 8, 2000, reportedly told journalist Gregory Douglas in a recorded conversation:

[Jack Ruby] knew all about keeping quiet, but he was ... very emotional - not stable....Certainly [we killed him]. Ruby died of rampant cancer. As you are aware, Gregory, we can give people fatal heart attacks and cancer is only a little more difficult and problematical. A medical examination, an injection with cells and so on. Ask a good oncologist. It is possible to do this. It takes more time but what did Ruby have? There was no immediate danger of him blabbing so we pacified him with stories of last minute rescues and let him die.[269]

---

269 Gregory Douglas, *Conversations with the Crow: The Final Coversations of Robert Trumbull Crowley – former Director of Clandestine Operations for the CIA* (Basilisk Press, 2001); Joel v.d. Reijden, "50 Years of CIA History With Top "Company" Man Robert Crowley: JFK, RFK, MLK, Guns, Drugs, Blackmail, Coups And All The Rest--A True Story Roman," *Institute for the Study of Globalization and Covert Politics* August 31, 2019

Chapter Five

Assassination M.O.s

I.   *Killing Castro 638 Ways*

Before he died in 2016, longtime Cuban leader El Comandante Fidel Castro was described as "the bearded bogeyman who haunted America's Cold War dreams."[270] In the words of Wayne Smith, former head of the US interests section in Havana: "Cuba seems to have the same effect on American administrations that a full moon has on a werewolf. We may not sprout hair and howl but we behave in the same way."[271] According to Fabian Escalante, the former head of Cuban Intelligence, the CIA made 638 assassination attempts against Castro, some of them very cunning.[272] According to the 1976 Church Committee (formally *the Select Committee to Study Governmental Operations with Respect to Intelligence Activities*), "The proposed assassination devices ran the gamut from high-powered rifles to poison pills, poison pens, deadly bacterial powders, and other devices which strain the imagination."[273] The

---

270 Darren Boyle, "Trained To Kill? Former Cuban accountant tells how the CIA instructed him to assassinate Fidel Castro using a gun hidden inside a camera," *Daily Mail* May 2, 2017.

271 Duncan Campbell, "Close but no cigar: how America failed to kill Fidel Castro," *The Guardian* November 26, 2016.

272 Fabián Escalante, *634 Ways To Kill Fidel* (New York: Seven Stories Press, 2021); *638 Ways To Kill Castro* 2006 documentary Directed Dollan Cannell and aired on Chanel 4; "How Castro survived 638 very cunning assassination attempts," *ABC* November 28 2016.

273 *United States. Congress. Senate. Select Committee to Study Governmental Operations with Respect to Intelligence Activities, Alleged Assassination Plots Involving Foreign Leaders: An Interim Report of the Select Committee to Study Governmental Operations with Respect to Intelligence Activities, United States*

Technical Services Division (TSD) of Sidney Gottlieb produced these weapons. The various weapons and *methods* of proposed assassination attempts against Castro throws light on the operations against Bob Marley.

- *Poisoned Shoes*: During a planned trip by Castro outside of Cuba, the CIA anticipated he would leave his shoes outside the door of his hotel room to be shinned. The Agency planned to dust his shoes with thallium salts, a strong depilatory that would, it was hoped, cause Castro's beard to fall out. Gottlieb's TSD (Technical Services Division = Technical Services Staff) procured the chemical, but Castro cancelled that trip.[274]

- *Poisoned Pen*: The TSD succeeded in converting a Paper-Mate ballpoint pen into a hypodermic syringe filled with the deadly insecticide Black leaf 40. The needle was so fine that "the victim would not notice its insertion." At most it would feel like the scratch from a shirt with too much starch.[275] This "straight out of 'James Bond'" plan to kill Castro involved a "highly placed Cuban official" who was in discussions with the CIA getting close enough to the Cuban leader to covertly inject him.[276]

- *Poisoned Food*: The Texas Department of Health and Human Services' "Botulism Fact Sheet" tells us that "Botulinum toxins may be aerosolized or used to sabotage food supplies."[277] Gottlieb is said to have liked Botulinum because it was more effective than cyanide and left no

---

Senate: Together with Additional, Supplemental, and Separate Views (, New York: Norton, 1976) 71.

Alleged Assassination Plots Involving Foreign Leaders, 72.

275 Escalante, *634 Ways To Kill Fidel*, 164-165.

276 Alexander Smith, "Fidel Castro: The CIA's 7 Most Bizarre Assassination Attempts," *NBC News* November 28, 2016; Dan Atkins, "Close, but no cigar," *Boston Herald* August 14, 2016.

277 Texas Department of Health and Human Services Botulism Fact Sheet @ https://www.dshs.texas.gov/foodborne-illness/botulism/botulism-fact-sheet

trace.[278] Just as he planned to liquidate Patrice Lumumba with botulism, Gottlieb also prepared botulism pills for Castro. El Comandante regularly patronized for lunch the Pekín Chinese Restaurant in the busy Vedado district, where the Mafia happened to have an asset. The Castro hit was a CIA-Mafia joint operation. The chef of Pekín was supposed to put the poison in Castro's food. This operation did not succeed. Similarly, the Mafia had three assets at the café and restaurant of Hotel Havana Libre. One of those assets was a maître d' in the restaurant, where Castro liked to frequent with foreign guests. Because Castro was known to enjoy ice cream, milk shakes in particular, in March 1963 the CIA/Mafia conspired to poison his chocolate milkshake with botulinum when he dined in the restaurant. A jar of poison pills was slipped to the asset but the asset left the poison in the freezer too long. The glass froze and broke.[279]

- *Poisoned Coffee*: The CIA prepared bacterial poisons to be placed in Castro's tea and coffee.[280] Castro's chief of staff Juan Orta Córdova owed a debt to mob boss Santo Trafficante because of kickbacks from gambling interests that Córdova received. He therefore owed Trafficante favors and could not refuse a request. Córdova was supposed to mix the CIA-supplied poison into one of Castro's many coffees that he consumed in his office. Córdova was removed from his position and thus lost access to Castro before he could accomplish his task.[281]

---

278 "The Assassination Plots: *Select Committee to Study Government Operations with Respect to Intelligence Activities*," in *The Cuba Reader: History, Culture, Politics*, ed. Aviva Chomsky, Pamela Maria Smorkaloff, Barry Carr, Robin Kirk and Orin Starn (*Durham, NC: Duke University Press* 2003) 552-556 (554).
279 Escalante, *634 Ways To Kill Fidel*, 132; 279 Atkins, "Close, but no cigar."
280 Duncan Campbell, "638 ways to kill Castro," *The Guardian* August 2, 2006.
281 Escalante, *634 Ways To Kill Fidel*, 78-79.

111

- *Poisoned Loves and Poisoned Gifts*: "Mr. [Sidney] Gottlieb...developed...an array of toxic gifts to be delivered to Fidel Castro."[282] Castro's enjoyment of cigars was well-known. In 1960 the Operations Division of the CIA's "Office of Medical Services" prepared "a box of Castro's favorite cigars" contaminated with "botulinum toxin so potent that a person would die after putting one in his mouth."[283] The CIA approached a New York City Police officer with an assassination plot: When Castro arrives in New York to speak at the 15th Session of the United Nations General Assembly, the officer would gift him with two boxes of the Cuban leaders favorite cigars, placed in his hotel room. One box would contain cigars laced with botulinum toxin and the other box would contain cigars packed with an explosive, "If and when [Castro] lit one...the cigar would explode and blow his head off."[284] We are told that the officer declined to participate in that plot.

Intelligence officials also thought they could use Castro's love of scuba-diving to topple him.[285] Knowing his fascination for scuba-diving off the coast of Cuba, the CIA invested in a large volume of Caribbean molluscs, with the aim of booby-trapping one seashell with explosives that would go off when the shell was picked up. The idea was to find a shell big enough to contain a lethal quantity of explosives, which would then be painted in colors lurid and bright enough to attract Castro's attention when he was

282 Tim Weiner, "Sidney Gottlieb, 80, Dies; Took LSD to C.I.A.," *The New York Times* March 10, 1999.
283 "The Assassination Plots: *Select Committee to Study Government Operations with Respect to Intelligence Activities*," in *The Cuba Reader: History, Culture, Politics*, ed. Aviva Chomsky, Pamela Maria Smorkaloff, Barry Carr, Robin Kirk and Orin Starn (*Durham, NC: Duke University Press* 2003) 552-556 (554).
284 Escalante, *634 Ways To Kill Fidel*, 64, 228.
285 Alexander Smith, "Fidel Castro: The CIA's 7 Most Bizarre Assassination Attempts," *NBC News* November 28, 2016.

underwater. The plan reportedly was abandoned because the CIA could not find a shell large enough to hold the explosives and still be "spectacular" enough to draw Castro's attention.[286]

- *A Gift of Tuberculosis*: Under the direction of Attorney General Robert Kennedy, lawyer James Donavan engaged in secret negotiations with Castro on behalf of the U.S. after the Cuba Missile Crisis in October 1962. Donavan was trying to secure the release of over 1,000 prisoners held in Cuba as a result of the failure of the Bag of Pigs Invasion, including three CIA agents. CIA Director John McCone designated a top Agency lawyer, Milan Miskovsky, to be Donavan's main handler in this process. However, a team of CIA officials from within the covert operations division saw an opportunity to use Donavan's unique access to Castro to assassinate the Cuban leader.[287] They devised a plan to kill Castro with Tuberculosis. Both Castro and Donavan were diving enthusiasts, and Donavan had already planned to gift Castro with a diving suit and diving watch as part of his negotiations to free the Americans. Donavan was prepared to deliver the gift to Castro during an April 1963 meeting. CIA officials from the covert operations division planned to secretly contaminate Donavan's gift divining suit with Madura foot fungus and the breathing apparatus with tuberculosis bacteria. However, CIA lawyer Miskovsky suspected that the covert ops guys were up to something and he advised Donavan to secure the diving suit so that it is not tampered with by the "executive action" side of the CIA. The plot was shelved and Donavan gifted Castro with an uncontaminated suit.[288]

---

286 Atkins, "Close, but no cigar"; Campbell, "638 ways to kill Castro."
287 "*National Security Archive* @ https://nsarchive.gwu.edu/briefing-book/cuba/2016-02-26/oscars-bridge-spies-sequel
288 "CIA tried to kill Castro by lacing diving suit with tuberculosis," *RT* February 27, 2016; Matt Novak, "The CIA Wanted to Kill Fidel Castro by

Fidel Castro and James Donovan at the Bay of Pigs. Castro is wearing the scuba-diving watch given to him by Donovan.

"Officially, the US has abandoned its attempt to kill its arch-enemy, but Cuban security are not taking any chances. Any gifts sent to the ailing leader as he lies ill this week will be carefully scrutinized, just as they were when those famous exploding cigars were being constructed by the CIA's technical services department in the early 60s."[289]

- *Kill Team Disguised as Camera Crew*: In December 1971 Castro planned a state visit to Chile led by the Socialist President Salvador Allende. David Atlee Phillips, head of the CIA's Chile Task Force and the agent in charge of all CIA Latin American operations, organized a plot to kill Castro during this state visit. The plot involved the CIA and Cuban exiles from the anti-Castro paramilitary organization Alpha 66. The Kill Team would pose as a press crew authorized to report on Castro's visit and accompany the press caravan traveling with him

Giving Him a Diving Suit Laced With Tuberculosis," *Gizmodo* February 26, 2016.

289 Duncan Campbell, "638 ways to kill Castro," *The Guardian* August 2, 2006.

throughout his stay in the country. Fake journalist credentials from Venevisión channel were secured. Two Cuban exiles arrived in Santiago de Chile "long before Castro was due to arrive" and began interviewing the Chilean government as if they were Venezuelan journalists. After scouting Castro's security arrangements, the next step "was [then] to convert the two [assassins] into Venevisión cameramen to subsequently infiltrate them into a press conference to be given by [Castro] in Santiago de Chile." The CIA's idea was to take advantage of the conference where 600 to 700 journalists would be present for the assassination. The Hit would be carried out using a gun camouflaged in a television camera: "by using a small weapon and hiding it in a certain section of the camera . . . the weapon wouldn't be detected."[290] This assassination attempt on Castro was planned as a False Flag operation: "As had been the case for the CIA since the 1960 plots with Johnny Rosselli and Santo Trafficante, the point for the Agency wasn't just to kill Fidel, but to do it in a way that someone else could be blamed besides the U.S. government and the CIA."[291] Unbeknownst to the two shooters, the plan was to kill them after they killed Castro. When the assassins were killed, the investigation would lead directly to the Venezuelan police archives where a file was fabricated and deposited within the Venezuelan Police Department that would "reveal" the two men as informers of Soviet intelligence. Doctored photos, fake passports, and fake diaries would link the two shooters to a couple of alleged KGB agents, so Fidel's murder could be blamed on the Soviets. Instructions supposedly received from the Soviets would be planted in the rooms of the patsies.[292] This operation failed when the assassins didn't show up.

---

290 Lamar Waldron, *Watergate: The Hidden History. Nixon, the Mafia, and the CIA* (Berkley, California: Counterpoint, 2012) 502.
291 Waldron, *Watergate*, 501.
292 Escalante, *634 Ways To Kill Fidel*, 185; Waldron, *Watergate*, 503.

II. *Did They Finally Get Castro With Cancer?*

> For good or ill, Mr. Castro is without a doubt the most important leader to emerge from Latin America since the wars of independence of the early 19th century, not only reshaping Cuban society but providing inspiration for leftists across Latin America and in other parts of the world... Mr. Castro's willingness to stand up to the United States and break free of American influence, even if it meant allying Cuba with another superpower, has been an inspiration to many Latin Americans, among them the new crop of left-leaning heads of state like Hugo Chavez of Venezuela, Evo Morales of Bolivia, and Luiz Inácio Lula da Silva of Brazil.[293]

When the South American trade block known as Mercosur (Spanish acronym for Common Market of the South) convened in Cordoba, Argentina on July 22, 2006, it was destined to be different than previous conventions. "The presence of Castro, Hugo Chavez of Venezuela and Evo Morales of Bolivia – Latin America's three most outspoken leftist leaders – added a jolt to Mercosur's normally staid summit," and their presence at the summit "underscored what appears to be a distinctly leftist tilt in the new Mercosur."[294] The three leftist leaders hosted a parallel "anti-imperialism" rally before tens of thousands of leftist sympathizers at a state university in Argentina, rallying against U.S.-backed policies that have enslaved the region.[295] "Castro's presence practically stole the show in Argentina."

After leaving the summit and returning to Cuba, Castro took an internal flight from Holguin to Havana on July 26, 2006. On the short flight Castro started bleeding and fell seriously ill. With no doctors aboard the plane it made an urgent landing. Castro suffered a mysterious "intestinal illness" that caused sustained bleeding, for which he underwent surgery. On July 31, 2006, he

---

293 James C. McKinley Jr., "Fidel Castro Resigns as Cuba's President," *The New York Times* February 20, 2008.
294 Patrick J. McDonnell, "Leftist Presidents Take Spotlight at Trade Summit," *Los Angeles Times* July 22, 2006.
295 The Associated Press, "Presidents rally against U.S.," *The Denver Post* July 22, 2006.

temporarily ceded power to his brother Raul Castro. Fidel lost 41 pounds in 34 days. According to reports he came close to death in July and then again in October 2006.

In March 2007 the head of the US interests section in Havana, Michael Parmly, sent a U.S. diplomatic cable that was later released by Wikileaks and published by the Spanish newspaper *El Pais*.[296] Marked CONFIDENTIAL, the cable reported detailed information about the July 26, 2006 flight incident and the subsequent "mystery ailment" that afflicted the Cuban leader. These details were based on a female source which the U.S. had on the ground in Cuba who was close to Castro and/or had access to his medical records. The source reported to U.S. diplomates in Havana. The source said Castro almost died after suffering a perforation of the large intestine that needed surgery, which he refused. Doctors found a fistula in his abdomen, which had the effect of blocking the digestion of food – resulting in the loss of 40lbs. Castro had to be fed IV serum, according to this Cuban source. In fact, this source seems to have had a surprising degree of knowledge of the malady that caused Castro's mystery illness. "This illness is not curable and will not, in her opinion, allow [Castro] to return to leading Cuba. *He won't die immediately, but he will progressively lose his faculties and become ever more debilitated until he dies*," the source's report concludes.[297]

By September 2006 the Western press was reporting that Castro's "mystery ailment" was an aggressive form of stomach cancer.[298] Cuban officials denied that he had stomach cancer.[299] However, this is consistent with the fact that the Cuban president's health was reserved as a state secret. Yet strangely U.S.

---

296 Mark Tran, "Wikileaks cables: Fidel Castro almost died in 2006," *The Guardian* December 16, 2010.
297 "US embassy cables: Could ailing Fidel Castro make a comeback in Cuba?" *The Guardian* December 16, 2010.
298 "Castro says he's getting better," *BBC Caribbean* September 5, 2006; "Castro says worst of illness behind him," *The Spokesman-Review* September 6, 2006; Leonard Doyle, "Cancer-ridden Castro may not live to see in new year," *Independent* December 8, 2006.
299 "Cuban VP denies Castro has stomach cancer," *Denver Post* August 6, 2006; "Cuba: Fidel Doesn't Have Cancer," *CBS* December 17, 2006.

government and defense officials were sure that Castro had cancer of the stomach, colon or pancreas, and that "the Cuban dictator is unlikely to live through 2007."[300]

> With chemotherapy, Castro may live up to 18 months, said the defense official. Without it, expected survival would drop to three months to eight months. American officials will not talk publicly about how they glean clues to Castro's health. But U.S. spy agencies include physicians who study pictures, video, public statements and other information coming out of Cuba.

The ailing Cuban President Fidel Castro is battling terminal cancer and could be dead by Christmas, senior Western diplomatic sources have said. Observers close to the Cuban regime have reported that the leader is suffering from an aggressive form of stomach cancer and has refused radiation therapy or any other form of treatment.

Castro's condition continued to degenerate, becoming "very serious" by January 2007 "after a series of three failed operations on his large intestine for diverticulitis, or inflamed bulge in the intestine, complicated by infection".[301]

> Diverticulitis is a condition in which pouch-like bulges in the wall of the intestine become inflamed or infected. In the first operation to remove part of Castro's large intestine, Cuban surgeons decided to connect the colon to the rectum to avoid a colostomy or opening in the abdomen to

300 The Associated Press, "U.S. officials believe Castro has terminal cancer," *NBC News* November 12, 2006.
301 Anthony Boadle, "Castro's prognosis 'very serious'," *Reuters* January 21, 2007.

get rid of stool, the newspaper said. But the short-cut failed, releasing faeces into the abdomen that caused another peritonitis, the report said. A second operation to clean and drain the infected area and perform a colostomy was also a failure, the paper said. Castro underwent a third operation to implant a Korean-made prosthesis, but it did not work and was replaced by one brought from Spain, according to El Pais.[302]

Despite the numerous operations Castro never fully recovered. He formally resigned as president of Cuba and commander-in-chief in February 2008, turning the reigns over to his brother Raul Castro and ending "one of the longest tenures as one of the most all-powerful communist heads of state in the world."[303] In an article published on Castro's 87th birthday in 2013 by the official newspaper of Cuba, *Granma*, the retired Cuban leader said he did not expect to survive the fatal stomach ailment that afflicted him in 2006 and live so long: "I was far from imagining that my life would extend for another seven years," he said.[304] Three years later on November 25, 2016, El Comandante Fidel Castro died. Was it natural causes or was it *pseudo*-natural causes? Did the CIA, on a 639th attempt to kill its nemesis, finally succeed? The assassination cancer that the CIA prepared specifically for Castro in 1963 but failed to deploy, was it ultimately perfected and deployed successfully in 2006 resulting in his death in 2016? These are questions.

302 Boadle, "Castro's prognosis 'very serious'."
303 James C. McKinley Jr., "Fidel Castro Resigns as Cuba's President," *The New York Times* February 20, 2008.
304 "Ex-Cuban leader Fidel Castro 'surprised' by survival," *BBC* August 15, 2013.

Chapter Six

The Case of Hugo Chavez

Venezuela's Chavez: did U.S. give Latin American leaders cancer?

By Daniel Wallis   4 MIN READ   f   ✦

CARACAS (Reuters) - Venezuelan President Hugo Chavez speculated on Wednesday that the United States might have developed a way to give Latin American leaders cancer, after Argentina's Cristina Fernandez joined the list of presidents diagnosed with the disease.

Venezuelan President Hugo Chavez speculated on Wednesday that the United States might have developed a way to give Latin American leaders cancer, after Argentina's Cristina Fernandez joined the list of presidents diagnosed with the disease....Chavez, Fernandez, Paraguay's Fernando Lugo, Brazil's Dilma Rousseff and former Brazilian leader Luiz Inacio Lula da Silva have all been diagnosed recently with cancer. All of them are leftists.[305]

      The South American country of Venezuela has the largest amount of oil reserves in the world, reserves which the American oil industry exploited in its own interests until the presidency of revolutionary socialist Hugo Chavez beginning in 1999. Chavez reasserted Venezuelan sovereignty over its oil

---

305 Daniel Wallis, "Venezuela's Chavez: did U.S. give Latin American leaders cancer?" *Reuters* December 28, 2011.

reserves, making him a hated Latin American head of state by the U.S. government, similar to his close friend Fidel Castro of Cuba. As the U.S. made as many as 638 assassination attempts against Castro, the "imperialist state of the North" also made many attempts on the life of President Chavez. As explained by Eva Golinger, an American attorney and journalist who was a legal advisor to the former Venezuelan president:

> Hugo Chavez defied the most powerful interests, and he refused to bow down....I believe there is a very strong possibility that President Chavez was assassinated....There were notorious and documented assassination attempts against him throughout his presidency. Most notable was the April 11, 2002 coup d'etat, during which he was kidnapped and set to be assassinated had it not been for the unprecedented uprising of the Venezuelan people and loyal military forces that rescued him and returned him to power within 48 hours. I was able to find irrefutable evidence using the US Freedom of Information Act (FOIA), that the CIA and other US agencies were behind that coup and supported, financially, militarily and politically, those involved....

> There was another, lesser-known plot against Chavez discovered in New York City during his visit to the United Nations General Assembly in September 2006. According to information provided by his security services, during standard security reconnaissance of an event where Chavez would address the US public at a local, renowned university, high levels of radiation were detected in the chair where he would have sat. The radiation was discovered by a Geiger detector, which is a handheld radiation detection device the presidential security used to ensure the President wasn't in danger of exposure to harmful rays. In this case, the chair was removed and subsequent tests showed it was emanating unusual amounts of radiation that could have resulted in significant harm to Chavez had it gone undiscovered. According to accounts by the presidential security at the event, an individual from the US who had been involved in the logistical support for the event and had provided the chair was shown to be acting with US intelligent agents.[306]

In June 2011, ahead of a bid for re-election in the 2012 presidential elections, Hugo Chavez was diagnosed with cancer

---

306 Mike Whitney with Eva Golinger, "The Strange Death of Hugo Chavez: Interview with Eva Golinger," *Venezuelanalysis* March 3, 2016.

detected in his pelvic region. On June 20 he underwent surgery in Havana to remove a "baseball-sized" malignant tumor. In October he declared himself cancer-free. Tests conducted in Havana showed no malignant cells following four cycles of chemotherapy.[307] There was mixed messages given in the press, however: "one Venezuelan doctor who has treated [Chavez] in the past was quoted this week as saying he only had two years maximum to live."[308] As it turns out, this anonymous Venezuelan doctor was spot-on.

On December 27, 2011, Chavez's colleague and fellow leftist leader, Argentine President Cristina de Kirchner, was diagnosed with thyroid cancer, prompting the Venezuelan leader to publicly suggest that the U.S. might have deliberately given her, himself, and other Latin American leaders cancer. In his December 28, 2011, end-of-year televised address to the Venezuelan military, Chavez said:

Would it be so strange that they've invented the technology to spread cancer and we won't know about it for 50 years?

I don't know but…it is very odd that we have seen (Paraguayan Fernando) Lugo affected by cancer, (Brazilian President) Dilma (Rousseff) when she was a candidate, me, going into an election year, not long ago Lula [=former Brazilian leader Luiz Inácio Lula da Silva] and now Cristina…It is very hard to explain, even with the law of probabilities, what has been happening to some leaders in Latin America. It's at the very least strange, very strange.

I repeat: I am not accusing anyone. I am simply taking advantage of my freedom to reflect and air my opinions faced with some very strange and hard to explain goings-on.

Fidel always told me, "Chavez take care. These people have developed technology. You are very careless. Take care what you eat, what they give you to eat…a little needle and they inject you with I don't know what."[309]

---

307 Mario Naranjo, "Venezuela's Chavez declares himself free of cancer," *Reuters* October 20, 2011.
308 Naranjo, "Venezuela's Chavez declares himself free of cancer."
309 Wallis, "Venezuela's Chavez.".

Added to this strange and growing list can be Bolivian president Evo Morales (nasal cancer).[310]

The fact that the "Venezuelan president suggests [a] spate of cancer among leftwing South American leaders may be inflicted by US technology"[311] certainly made headlines, and the U.S. predictably dismissed the charge as "absurd."[312] However, a number of writers have stood up to say: "Chavez is right."[313] For example, Keven Barrett's observation seems apt: "Strange indeed...so strange that if you think Venezuela's Hugo Chavez, Brazilian President Dilma Rousseff, Paraguayan Fernando Lugo, and former Brazilian leader Luiz Inácio Lula da Silva - Latin America's top anti-US empire leaders - all just happened to contract cancer around the same time by sheer chance, you must be some kind of crazy coincidence theorist."[314]   Likewise, American journalist Wayne Madsen pointed out: "The CIA pioneered in the use of cancer-causing agents that could infect their victims through injection; inhalation; skin contact through contaminated clothing, especially underwear – Chavez's formation of aggressive cancer in his pelvic region is germane in this respect; and contact with the digestive system through the use of contaminated food, drink, and even toothpaste."[315]

In May 2012, Dan Rather reported being informed by a source close to Chavez that the Venezuelan president had end stage

310 *Aislinn Laing* and *Daniel Ramos*, "Bolivian President Morales has emergency surgery for tumor," *Reuters* July 4, 2018.

311 Tom Phillips, "Hugo Chávez hints at US cancer plot," *The Guardian* December 29, 2011.

312 Rory Carroll, "US dismisses claims that CIA gave Chávez cancer as 'absurd'," *The Guardian* March 7, 2013.

313 For example Percy Alvarado, "Cáncer inducido, ¿un arma de la CIA?" ("Induced cancer, a CIA weapon?"), *Aporrea* December 30, 2011; Kevin Barrett, "Chavez: Another assassination victim, "*Mehr News* March 6, 2013.

314 Kevin Barrett, "Chavez: Another CIA assassinate victim," *Mehr News* March 6, 2013.

315 Wayne Madsen, "'Scientific Assassinations' Are Part of the CIA's Modus Operandi," *Global Research* March 12, 2013.

metastatic rhabdomyosarcoma, an aggressive cancer.[316] On March 5, 2013, President Hugo Chavez died. His successor, Venezuelan Vice President Nicolas Maduro, officially announced during a televised meeting of political and military leaders at the presidential palace that President Hugo Chavez was infected with cancer by Venezuela's "imperialist" enemies. "We have no doubt that commander Chavez was attacked with this illness...The old enemies of our fatherland looked for a way to harm his health," Maduro said, drawing a parallel to the illness and 2004 death of Palestinian leader Yasser Arafat.[317]

Vice President Maduro announced the expulsion from the country of two U.S. diplomats for allegedly trying to stir up a military plot against the Venezuelan government: U.S. Embassy Air Force attaché Colonel David delMonaco and Devlin Kostal. According to one report, delMonaco was accused of somehow assisting in the cancer "attack."[318] Maduro said that a special commission would investigate how the 58-year old Chavez ended up with the cancer "that months of chemotherapy and radiation and four surgeries failed to tame."[319] Venezuela will invite "the world's best scientists" to scientifically investigate whether Chavez had been poisoned, Maduro said.[320]

In the 1940s and 1950s, the United States and other countries had "scientific laboratories testing how to cause cancer," Maduro said. "Seventy years have passed. These kinds of laboratories of evil and death have not advanced?" Maduro stressed that he was not accusing the United States. "I am just saying something that is a truth, that is known," he said.[321]

---

316 Dan Rather, "Report: Chavez's cancer has 'entered the end stage'," *Yahoo! News* May 30, 2012.
317 Andrew Cawthorne and Daniel Wallis, "Venezuelan VP says Chavez was infected with cancer by foes," *Reuters* March 4, 2013.
318 J.K. Trotter, "Venezuelan VP Says This Attaché Is the Spy Who Gave Hugo Chavez Cancer," *The Atlantic* March 5, 2013.
319 "Venezuela VP: Chavez's cancer was an 'attack' by his enemies," *NBC News* March 5, 2013.
320 "Who Killed Hugo Chavez?" *Chicago Tribune* March 21, 2013.
321 Catherine E. Sholchet, "Scientists will study possible Chavez poisoning, Venezuelan leader says," *CNN* March 13, 2013.

Venezuela VP: Chavez's cancer was an 'attack' by his enemies

corazón
VENEZOLANO

Venezuelan Vice-President Nicolas Maduro (L) speaking at a meeting on Venezuela's political in Caracas on March 5, 2013.

Maduro told the government news agency *Telesur* "that details about Chavez's illness make officials 'almost certain' that there was foul play."[322] "We are almost certain based on the data we have," Maduro said. "He had an illness, a cancer that will be known in time, that broke with all the typical characteristics of this illness."

Venezuela will set up a formal inquiry into claims that deceased President Hugo Chavez's cancer was the result of poisoning by his enemies abroad, the government said... "We will seek the truth," Maduro told regional TV network Telesur. "We have the intuition that our commander Chavez was poisoned by dark forces that wanted him out of the way." Foreign scientists will be invited to join a state committee to probe the accusation, he said.

Maduro said it was too early to specifically point a finger over Chavez's cancer but noted that the United States had laboratories with experience in producing diseases. "He had a cancer that broke all norms," Maduro told Telesur. "Everything seems to indicate that they (enemies) affected

322 Sholchet, "Scientists will study possible Chavez poisoning."

126

his health using the most advanced techniques." Maduro has compared his suspicions over Chavez's death with allegations that Palestinian leader Yasser Arafat died in 2004 from poisoning by Israeli agents.[323]

Support for this investigation and the charges behind it came swiftly out of Russia. Gennady Zyuganov, the leader of Russia's Communist Party, declared that the death of Chavez from cancer "may have been part of a plot by the United States to infect its enemies in Latin America with the disease." In an interview with state television TV channel Russia 24, Zyuganov said: "How did it happen that six leaders of Latin American countries which had criticized U.S. policies and tried to create an influential alliance in order to be independent and sovereign states, fell ill simultaneously with the same disease, cancer?" "This is not a coincidence," Zyuganov said, "and it should be addressed, and international investigation regarding this issue is necessary."[324]

This sentiment was shared by several Latin American leaders as well. Bolivian President Evo Morales said he is "almost certain" Chavez was murdered.[325] Likewise, "(The new vice president of Venezuela) Aristóbulo Istúriz maintains that Hugo Chávez did not die naturally and that the cancer suffered by the former Venezuelan president was induced in order to put an end to his policy."[326]

[Istúriz] believes that the leader of the Bolivarian revolution, Hugo Chávez, was assassinated for wanting to end the "dictatorship of the dollar." According to Istúriz, the cancer that ended the life of the former head of state – who, for his part, had become the "fundamental target" and the "number one enemy of the world's great financial centers" – was induced. "Chávez is leaving us at the moment of greatest splendor of the

323 *Andrew Cawthorne*, "Venezuela to probe Chavez cancer poisoning accusation," *Reuters* March 12, 2013.
324 "Chavez Death Could Be US Plot – Russian Communist Leader," *Sputnik* March 6, 2013; "6 world leaders got cancer simultaneously," *Mehr News* March 7, 2013.
325 Keith Wagstaff, "3 conspiracy theories about Hugo Chavez's death," *The Week* January 8, 2015.
326 "The Venezuelan Vice President: Chávez was murdered for wanting to end the dictatorship of the dollar," *RT* May 18, 2016.

revolution," commented Istúriz in statements collected by 'El Universal'. "Chávez was carrying out the most important proposal of this process, which was the break with one of the ties of greatest domination of the peoples: the international monetary system, the dictatorship of the dollar," he added."[327]

It is not the case that Vice President Istúriz had no "definitive evidence that could support his theory." According to Venezuelan journalist Eleazar Díaz Rangel the government "learned that biopsy samples sent to specialized laboratories in Brazil, China, Russia, and with an assumed name, the USA, agreed that they were single cells, an extremely aggressive cancer, apparently unknown."[328] Thus, "The aggressive and unknown nature of President Chávez illness, in addition to the non-existence of a hereditary cancer in his family, clearly point to the real possibility that the leader of the Bolivarian Revolution has been assassinated."[329] Investigative journalist and attorney Eva Golinger says she has evidence that the U.S. induced Chavez's cancer.

While this all may sound very conspiracy theory-ish, these are facts that can be verified independently. It is also true, according to declassified secret US documents, that the US Army was developing an injectable radiation weapon to use for political assassinations of select enemies as far back as 1948. The Church Commission hearings into the Kennedy Assassination also uncovered the existence of an assassination weapon developed by CIA to induce heart attacks and soft-tissue cancers. Chavez died of an aggressive soft-tissue cancer. By the time it was detected it was too late. There is other information out there documenting the development of a "cancer virus" that was going to be weaponized and allegedly used to kill Fidel Castro in the 1960s...

In 2006, the US government formed a special Mission Manager for Venezuela and Cuba under the Directorate of National Intelligence. This elite intelligence unit was charged with expanding covert operations

327 "The Venezuelan Vice President: Chávez was murdered for wanting to end the dictatorship of the dollar," *RT* May 18, 2016.
328 Eleazar Díaz Rangel, "¿Cáncer inoculado?" ("Inoculated Cancer?"), *Última Noticias* March 18, 2013.
329 Eva Golinger, *¿Quién mató a Hugo Chávez? RT* April 6, 2013.

against Chavez and led clandestine missions out of an intelligence fusion center (CIA-DEA-DIA) in Colombia. Some of the pieces that have been coming together include the discovery of several close aides to Chavez who had private, unobstructed access to him over prolonged periods, who fled the country after his death and are collaborating with the US government. If he were assassinated by some kind of exposure to high levels of radiation, or otherwise inoculated or infected by a cancer-causing virus, it would have been done by someone with close access to him, whom he trusted.[330]

Two names have been most associated with a suspected murder plot against Chavez: Leamsy Villafaña Salazar and Claudia Díaz. Claudia Díaz joined Chavez's medical team in 2003 as a nurse and remained until 2011. Her husband, Adrian Velásquez was President Chávez's security chief.[331] Leamsy Villafaña Salazar was an ex-bodyguard of President Chavez, whom the latter considered to be "reliable, incorruptible, and professionally trained." However, in December 2014 Salazar defected to the United States after 13 months of secret negotiations with the Drug Enforcement Administration. He fled to the United States with assistance of the DEA's Special Operations Division and was placed in witness protection. Salazar provided bogus information to the U.S. implicating Diosdado Cabello, president of Venezuela's National Assembly, in drug trafficking.[332] Salazar's mother reportedly admitted that Salazar only begrudgingly remained a part of Chavez's presidential guard and he did so on behalf of some third party who was his true employer and who pressed him to stay on and faithfully execute his duties.[333] Eva Golinger explains further:

---

330 Mike Whitney with Eva Golinger, "The Strange Death of Hugo Chavez: Interview with Eva Golinger," *Venezuelanalysis* March 3, 2016.
331 Cody Jackson and Adriana Gomez Licon, "Hugo Chavez's ex-nurse-turned treasure extradited to US," *AP* May 13, 2022; Joshua Goodman, "How 250 gold bars allegedly wound up in the vault of Hugo Chávez's former nurse," *Los Angeles Times* August 4, 2020.
332 Lucas Koerner and Ricardo Vaz, "Media Continue to Push Misinformation About Venezuela and Drug Trafficking," *FAIR* September 24, 2019.
333 Nil Kikandrov, "The Murder of Chávez. The CIA and DEA Cover Their Tracks?" *Venezuela Analysis* March 16, 2016.

Leamsy Salazar was one of Chavez's closest aides for nearly seven years. He was a Lieutenant Colonel in the Venezuelan Navy...Salazar was both a bodyguard and an aide to Chavez, who would bring him coffee and meals, stand by his side, travel with him around the world and protect him during public events. I knew him and interacted with him many times. He was one of the familiar faces protecting Chavez for many years. He was a key member of Chavez's elite inner security  circle, with private access to Chavez and privileged and highly confidential knowledge of Chavez's comings and goings, daily routine, schedule and dealings.

After Chavez passed away in March 2013, because of his extended service and loyalty, Leamsy was transferred to the security detail of Diosdado Cabello, who was then president of Venezuela's National Assembly and considered one of the most powerful political and military figures in the country. Cabello was one of Chavez's closest allies. It should be noted that Leamsy remained with Chavez throughout most of his illness up to his death and had privileged access to him that few had, even from his security team.

Shockingly, in December 2014, news reports revealed that Leamsy had secretly been flown to the US from Spain, where he was allegedly on vacation with his family. The plane that flew him was said to be from the DEA. He was placed in witness protection and news reports have stated he is providing information to the US government about Venezuelan officials involved in a high level ring of drug trafficking. Opposition-owned media in Venezuela claim he gave details accusing Diosdado Cabello of being a drug-kingpin, but none of that information has been independently verified, nor have any court records or allegations been released, if they exist.

Another explanation for his going into the witness protection program in the US could include his involvement in the assassination of Chavez, possibly done as part of a CIA black op, or maybe even done under the auspices of CIA but carried out by corrupt elements within the Venezuelan government. Before the Panama Papers were released, I had accidentally discovered and was investigating a dangerous corrupt, high level individual within the government, who Chavez had previously dismissed, but who returned after his death and was placed in an even

130

more influential, powerful position. This individual also appears to be collaborating with the US government. People like that, who let greed obscure their conscience, and who are involved in lucrative criminal activity, could have also played a role in his death.

For example, the Panama Papers exposed another former Chavez aide, Army Captain Adrian Velasquez, who was in charge of security for Chavez's son Hugo. Captain Velasquez's wife, a former Navy Officer, Claudia Patricia Diaz Guillen, was Chavez's nurse for several years and  had private, unsupervised access to him. Furthermore, Claudia administered medicines, shots and other health and food-related materials to Chavez over a period of years. Just one month before his deadly illness was discovered in 2011, Chavez named Claudia as Treasurer of Venezuela, placing her in charge of the country's money. It's still unclear as to why she was named to this important position, considering she had previously been his nurse and had no similar experience. She was dismissed from the position right after Chavez passed away. Both Captain Velasquez and Claudia appeared in the Panama Papers as owning a shell company with millions of dollars. They also own property in an elite area in the Dominican Republic, Punta Cana, where properties cost in the millions, and they have resided there since at least June 2015. The documents show that right after Chavez passed away and Nicolas Maduro was elected president in April 2013, Captain Velasquez opened an off-shore company on April 18, 2013 through the Panamanian firm Mossack Fonesca, called Bleckner Associates Limited. A Swiss financial investment firm, V3 Capital Partners LLC, affirmed they manage the funds of Captain Velasquez, which number in the millions. It's impossible for an Army Captain to have earned that amount of money through legitimate means. Neither him nor his wife, Claudia, have returned to Venezuela since 2015.

Captain Velasquez was especially close with Leamsy Salazar...

Of course, it was highly suspicious that Salazar was flown out of Spain, where he was allegedly on vacation with his family, and taken to the United States on a DEA plane. There is no question that he was collaborating with the US government and betrayed his country. What remains to be seen is what his exact role was. Did he administer the murderous poison to Chavez, or was it one of his partners, such as Captain Velasquez or the nurse/treasurer Claudia?[334]

By 2022 governments were announcing the results of the Venezuelan scientific investigation into the death of Hugo Chavez. On August 4, 2022, in the midst of the Russian-Ukraine conflict, Lieutenant General Ígor Kirillov, Chief of the Radiological, Chemical and Biological Defense Troops of the Russian Armed Forces, issued a briefing at a press conference outlining threats related to the activities of US biological facilities in the region.[335] During this briefing he used slides to illustrate and support his information. At the conclusion of his briefing, Lt. Gen. Kirillov declared that the biological activity of the U.S. is linked to the death of former president Hugo Chávez; he was poisoned with a special carcinogenic substance.[336] Russia's Ministry of Defense representative stressed that the forensic examination evidenced the "atypical" course of the cancer and its resistance to the application of drugs, "corroborat[ing] the cause-effect relationship between the death of the former Venezuelan leader and developments in the field of biological weapons by Washington." [337] He said:

---

334 Whitney with Golinger, "The Strange Death of Hugo Chavez."
335 "Special operation drew world's attention to activity of US biolabs – Russian top brass," *TASS* (Russian News Agency) August 4, 2022; "Irina Yarovaya: we should not expect that the US reveal the truth about appearance of COVID, WHO should deal with secrets and the biological laboratories," *The State Duma* August 4, 2022.
336 Latin America News, "Russia claims Venezuela has evidence that Chavez was poisoned," *The Rio Times* August 4, 2022.
337 "El jefe de una rama del Ejército ruso vincula la actividad biológica de EE.UU. con la muerte de Hugo Chávez" ("The head of a branch of the Russian Army links US biological activity with the death of Hugo Chávez"), *RT* August 4, 2022.

On July 18, 2022, the President of the Republic of Venezuela, Nicolas Maduro, publicly declared the involvement of the United States in the assassination of former head of state Hugo Chávez.

According to information available to Venezuela, U.S. security services have been working since 2002 on possible ways to eliminate the Venezuelan leader, who has pursued an active anti-American policy. Numerous assassination attempts involving members of the US embassy in Caracas were uncovered and thwarted.

In violation of international law, the United States has been involved in the development of drugs that, when administered in the short term, cause chronic disease and develop various forms of cancer. According to the Venezuelan side, a similar drug was used to poison Chávez by Claudio Díaz, a member of the presidential entourage. She fled Venezuela with the assistance of US intelligence agencies and was subsequently removed to the US to avoid possible publicity about the details of her cooperation with US intelligence agencies.

A causal link between the Venezuelan leader's death and the development of biological weapons is confirmed by forensic evidence and the testimony of Cuban doctors who treated Chavez about the atypical course of the disease and its resistance to the use of medicines.[338]

338 Briefing by Lieutenant General Igor Kirillov, Head of Nuclear, Biological and Chemical Protection Troops of the Russian Armed Forces (Transcript), *Telegraph* (UK) August 4, 2022 @ https://telegra.ph/Briefing-by-Lieutenant-

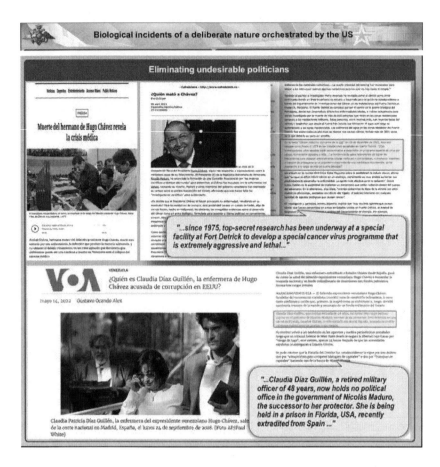

Some of Lieutenant General Kirillov's slides presented during his briefing

The details of the investigation and briefing were announced by the Russian Embassy on social media:

Russia in RSA 🔴 ✓
@EmbassyofRussia
🏛 Russia government organization

More from the US military bi010gical dossier. On July 18, 2022, the President of the Republic of Venezuela, Nicolas Maduro, publicly claimed the United States has been involved in the assassination of former head of state Hugo Chávez.

More 🔗 vk.cc/cfADVV

 MFA Russia 🔴 and 9 others

7:43 AM · Aug 5, 2022

🔴 Embassy of Russia in RSA   ➤

More from the US military biological dossier. On July 18, 2022, the President of the Republic of Venezuela, Nicolas Maduro, publicly claimed the United States has been involved in the assassination of former head of state Hugo Chávez.

According to Venezuela officials, U.S. security services have been working since 2002 on possible ways to eliminate the Venezuelan leader, who has pursued an active anti-American policy. Numerous assassination attempts involving members of the US embassy in Caracas were uncovered and thwarted.

In violation of international law, the United States has been developing drugs which, when administered in the short term, cause chronic disease and develop various forms of cancer.

A similar drug was used to poison Chávez by Claudia Díaz, a member of the presidential entourage, Venezuelan side claims. She fled Venezuela with the assistance of US intelligence agencies and was subsequently removed to the US to avoid possible publicity about the details of her cooperation with US intelligence agencies.

Source: Russian Defence Ministry report

t.me/RussianEmbassyZA/2347   130 👁

Michael Kosarev, edited Aug 5 at 07:12

135

It has been suggested that Chavez's cancer resulted from weaponized nanoparticles or a "nano poison" – *Pravda*, Russia's state-run newspaper, has reported this possibility, for example.[339] North Korea also accuses the U.S. of possessing and deploying a "nano poison." According to a May 5, 2017, report by KCNA (the North Korean state news agency), a CIA and South Korean Intelligence Service (IS) terrorist group conspired to assassinate President Kim Jong Un using "biochemical substances including radioactive substance and nano poisonous substance."[340] The Ministry of State Security announced that the CIA "ideologically corrupted and bribed a DPRK citizen surnamed Kim," a then-worker of the timber industrial branch in the Khabarovsk Territory of Russia in June 2014, "and turned him into a terrorist full of repugnance and revenge." The U.S. and South Korea then provided Kim with "20,000 U.S. dollars on two occasions and a satellite transmitter-receiver" along with some kind of delayed-action biochemical weapon supplied by the CIA "that does not require access to the target (as) their lethal results will appear after six or 12 months".[341] The would-be assassin was supposed to deploy the weapon after he returned home to North Korea. As *Defense Mirror.com* reports: "There was no official denial from the US or South Korea to the North [Korea] allegations about the assassination plot."[342]

339 "US nano weapon killed Venezuela's Hugo Chavez, scientists say," *Pravada.Ru* (English) June 6, 2016; Antonio José Herrada Ávila, "On September 15, 2005, the North American Empire inoculated Commander Chávez with cancer," *Aporra* September 14, 2016.

340Louis A. Del Monte, "North Korea Accuses US/South Korea of 'Nano Poison' Plot to Kill Kim Jong Un," *HuffPost* May 5, 2017.

341 Eric Levitz, "North Korea Accuses U.S. of Assassination Attempt Against Kim Jong-un," *New York Magazine* May 5, 2017; Ewen MacAskill, "The CIA has a long history of helping to kill leaders around the world," *The Guardian* May 5, 2017.

342 "CIA Used 'Nano-poisonous' Radioactive Substance in Kim Assassination Attempt: North Korea," *Defense Mirror.com* May 6, 2017.

Why nano-poison? Louis A. Del Monte writing in *HuffPost* provides an answer to this question:

> Nanoweapons are any military technology that exploits the power of nanotechnology...You may wonder, Why would someone use nano poisons? The size of nanoparticles, the components of a nano poison, allows living tissue to absorb them more readily than other known toxins. Nanoparticles are able to cross biological membranes and access cells, tissues and organs that their larger counterparts cannot. Therefore, nano poisons are more deadly than their bulk counterparts are...Unlike nuclear, chemical, and biological weapons, no international treaties limit the development and deployment of nanoweapons or their use in warfare.[343]

343Louis A. Del Monte, "North Korea Accuses US/South Korea of 'Nano Poison' Plot to Kill Kim Jong Un," *HuffPost* May 5, 2017.

CONCLUSION

Professor Fred Zindi said regarding the possibility that Bob Marley was assassinated with cancer:

> To our mind, it is absolutely plausible and extremely likely that cancer can be artificially induced in a specific target...The only thing you have to entertain is whether you think it is possible; whether the technological understanding exists; whether the malice exists to give someone cancer and whether you think it was possible to do those things in the 1970s.[344]

We have overwhelmingly shown that both the technological understanding and capability to artifiically induce cancer in a traget and the *malice to do so* absolutely existed at the time of Bob Marley's death. The assassination apparatuses of the U.S. and of Israel have perfected the science and the techniques of "death by natural causes," the "silent" or "low-signature" kill operation that ensures plausible deniablity.

In 1952 the U.S. Army Chemical Corps' Special Operations Division partnered with the Technical Services Staff of the CIA in a joint project called MKNAOMI, the aim of which was the development of biological agents and their delivery systems for operational use. One of the very first biological agents MKNOAMI scientists began to weaponize was cancer. As one declassified 1952 CIA memorandum asks: "How [to] knock off key guys [?]" Answer: "Natural Causes." Method: "Produce cancer."

> "How knock off key guys ... Natural Causes.
>
> "Method produce cancer. ·.
>
> "Heart techniques ...

---

344 Fred Zindi, "How Did Bob Marley Die?" *The Herald* (Zimbabwe) October 4, 2015.

For the whole of twenty years before Bob Marley was diagnosed with cancer in his right big toe in 1977 the U.S. had labored to master the techniques of both chemical carcinogenesis and viral oncogenesis. MKNAOMI intially focused on cancer-causing chemicals such as beryllium and methylcholanthrene. Soon, the Agency concentrated on oncogenic viruses. By 1965 MKNAOMI was studying the aerosol transmission of cancer-causing viruses. During this time, over 600 patients and prisoners – over half of them Black – were deliberatley injected with cancer cells with the aim of inducing various forms of cancer in these human guinea pigs. These cancer injection experiments were funded by the U.S. government.

When the U.S. Army's biowarfare center at Fort Detrick, Maryland was converted in 1971-1972 to the civilian Frederick Cancer Research Center, biowarfare research was conducted under the guise of cancer research. In 1975 government-funded scientists succeeded in combining the outer coat of an infectious but non-cancerous baboon virus with the inner core of a noninfectious but cancerous mouse virus, thus producing an infectious pseudo-virus with extrordinry characteristics, such as the ability to cause cancer in a wide range of previous nonsusceptible animal species, as well as in human cells. This murine-baboon hybrid was nothing less than a "super cancer" virus of its day. By 1977 the Virus Cancer Project at Fort Detrick was producing 60,000 liters of various cancer-causing viruses and immunosupressive viruses.

Wayne Madsen thus reported correctly:

Since the 1970s, the bio-warfare capabilities of the United States, including the covert introduction of cancer-causing pathogens into targeted persons has mushroomed in cost and effectiveness. The use of nano-technology and micro-mechanical flying and crawling insects, coupled with bio-toxin payloads, is no longer in the realm of science fiction but is scientific fact. Not only are cancer-causing biological toxins used for cancer weapons but inorganic elements are also employed. Only a few micrograms of beryllium and polonium-210 are required to cause the development of fibrotic tumors that result in lung cancer.[345]

Most significantly for our focus, the CIA succeeded in 1963 in creating an *assassination cancer* – an SV40 cancer virus mutated by radiation which, when injected into a target, he will over the course of time devlope a "galloping cancer" and die. A Protocol on the effective use of this assassination cancer was developed and successfully deployed against Jack Ruby, who died of a "galloping cancer" in 1967. Israel was by the 1970s killing her enemies with a chemical weapon that the Mossad called the "Potion of the Gods." It created a leukemia-like condition in the target. His autopsy will say he died of a blood cancer.

By Bob Marley's day, the CIA had developed a special delivery mechanism for this assassination cancer: a "nondiscernable microbioinoculator." That is: a tiny ("micro") inoculator or syringe that will inoculate or inject a "bio" or biological agent into a target in a "nondiscernable" manner. The target would not know that he was just injected with cancer. This "micro-syringe" with its cancerous payload can be launched from a specialized dart-gun, assasulting the target from a safe distance, or it can be hidden in a specialized PaperMate pen, to nondiscernably inject the target up close. Or, it can be made as a small wire hidden in a gift pair of shoes, waiting for the target's foot to slide in to inject the payload into his toe.

Enter Bob Marley.

---

345 "Special Report: CIA Cancer Warfare. Not Just Chavez but Neto and Thompson – Victims of CIA Cancer Weapons?" *Wayne Madsen Report* March 11-12, 2013.

Part 4

Who Shot The Sheriff
(And Gave Him Cancer)?

Chapter Seven

The CIA and the Death of Bob Marley

We had been operating a damned Murder Inc. in the Caribbean.
Former President Lyndon B. Johnson (1973)

Journalist: "Do you know who shot you?"
Bob Marley: "Yeah, but dat top secret. Really top secret."[346]

I.   *Casualty of The Cold War*

After 453 yeas as a colony, first of Spain and then of the British Empire, the Caribbean Island of Jamaica gained independence in 1962. Jamaica's first independent government was led by the conservative Jamaica Labor Party (JLP). This pleased the United States, who felt that under JLP rule this island on its doorstep was a safe and ideologically aligned ally, *contra* that "other" Caribbean island (i.e., Cuba). This all changed in 1972 when Michael Manley and his Left-leaning People's National

---

346 Don Taylor with Mike Henry, *Marley And Me: The Real Bob Marley Story* (Fort Less, New Jersey: Barricade Books, 1994) 169.

Party (PNP) won the election. Jamaica suddenly became a Cold War battleground, and it appears that Bob Marley may have been its most famous casualty.

When Manley's PNP was elected in 1972, some of his closest advisers at the time were members of Jamaica's white oligarchy, the so-called "Twenty-one Families" (more on them below). It was in 1974 that Manley really stirred the hornets' nest by announcing a policy of *democratic socialism*. "The inevitable consequence of this change was a 'destabilization' of the oligarchy."[347] Also inevitable was the reaction of the U.S. "The American eagle hovered fiercely over Jamaica's doomed experiment in democratic socialism and eventually routed it with the same methods the State Department and the Central Intelligence Agency had used elsewhere."[348] Jamaica's Manley developed a relationship with Cuba's Castro, and he supported Angola's nationalist movement, the Popular Movement for the Liberation of Angola (MPLA), against whom the U.S. covertly fought.[349] This placed Jamaica firmly in the crosshairs of American covert operations. Manley's election in 1972 was destined to turn Jamaica into one of the primary Cold War battlegrounds.

> On the doorstep of the US, and with the JLP holding political power since independence, Jamaica had come to be thought of (in the U.S.) as a safe and ideologically aligned US ally. All this changed with the election of Michael Manley and his People's National Party administration in 1972...So it was that Edward Seaga emerged as a reactionary right-wing figure to steer Jamaica on a more US-friendly course.[350]

---

347 Ellen Ray, "CIA and Local Gunmen Plan Jamaican Coup," *CounterSpy* 3:2 (December 1976): 36-41 (37)
348 Laurie Gunst, *Born Fi' Dead: A Journey Through the Jamaican Posse Underground* (New York: Henry Holt and Company) xvii-xviii.
349 UPI, "Cilby: No American In Angola Fighting," *Washington Post* December 13, 1975; Henry Kissinger, "CIA's Secret War in Angola," *Intelligence Report* 1:1 (1975): 1-12; Stephen R. Weissman, "CIA Covert Action in Zaire ad Angola: Patterns and Consequences," *Political Science Quarterly* 94:2 (Summer 1979): 263-286.
350 Kevin Edmonds, "Guns, gangs and garrison communities in the politics of Jamaica," *Race & Class* 57:4 (2016): 54-74 (61).

As historian Laurie Gunst notes: "The United States embraced Seaga with predictable fervor"[351]

In December 1975 U.S. Secretary of State Henry Kissinger traveled to Jamaica to deliver an ultimatum to Prime Minister Manley: abandon his policies of socialism and break off relations with Angola's MPLA and with Castro's Cuba. In return, Kissinger promised U.S. A.I.D. and economic relief to Jamaica, to the tune of $100 million.[352] Manley refused and Kissinger grimaced. After Manley reiterated his backing of Castro and the MPLA, the U.S. Secretary of State issued a backhanded warning, as Manley later recounts: "He then assured me I should not worry about CIA activities in Jamaica."[353] By the end of that very month a new CIA station chief arrived in Jamaica: Norman Descoteaux, an expert on destabilization campaigns in South America. Thus began the CIA's notorious and bloody destabilization campaign in Jamaica to oust the Manley government.[354]

---

351 Laurie Gunst, *Born Fi' Dead: A Journey Through the Jamaican Posse Underground* (New York: Henry Holt and Company) xvii-xviii.
352 William Blum, *Killing Hope: U.S. Military and CIA Interventions Since World War II* (London: Zed Books, 2003) 263-267.
353 Saul Landau, "A Tale Of Two Extraditions," *Transnational Institute* July 19, 2010.
354 "Kissinger's Operations To Destabilize The Governments of Guyana And Jamaica," *Executive Intelligence Review* 3:10 (March 9, 1976): 18-20;

Prior to Michael Manley's administration Jamaica was not open to the Nation of Islam. Prime Minister Hugh Sheare (1967-1972) rejected the Honorable Elijah Muhammad and his delegation when his plane landed in Jamaica. Under his government Nation of Islam meetings were banned, as was the newspaper *Muhammad Speaks*. Michael Manley's election opened Jamaica's doors to the Nation. In December 1974 Prime Minister Manley hosted a Muhammad Ali Day, and NOI National Representative Minister Louis Farrakhan delivered the keynote address to 25,000 people at the national stadium.

Former CIA Agent Philip Agee, who stunned the American intelligence community with his 1975 tell-all, *Inside The Company: CIA Diary*, in September 1976 was invited by the Jamaica Council for Human Rights, a local civil rights organization, to come to the island where he held a press conference at the Social Action Center in St. Andrew Parish, north of Kingston. During the press conference Agee released the names of nine CIA officers associated with the CIA Jamaica station who were operating out of the U.S. embassy in Kingston, including identifying the embassy attaché Norman Descoteaux as the CIA station chief. Agee noted that he worked with Descoteaux while he was a case officer in Guayaquil, Ecuador. Agee provided the names, addresses and telephone numbers of these CIA

146

employees.[355] Documents captured by Jamaican Security Forces in 1976 exposed a plot by local forces with the help of the CIA to violently overthrow the government of Michael Manley, a plot referred to in the documents as *Operation Werewolf*.[356]

In 1977 Ernst Volkman of *Newsday* and John Cummings of *Penthouse* collaborated in a groundbreaking article which detailed a CIA covert program to undermine Jamaica economically, politically and socially.[357] Citing "several senior American intelligence sources," the authors report that this covert program was initiated after Prime Minister Manley refused U.S. Secretary of State Kissinger's Decemb er 1975 ultimatum and was drawn up by CIA station chief in Jamaica Norman Descoteaux. The CIA approved three plots to assassinate Manley, though all were aborted. Kissinger ordered and directed these assassination schemes. This destabilization program contained the following elements:

1.) Covert shipments of arms and other equipment to opposition forces (Seaga's JLP). "The CIA quickly sought to organize and expand the violence: shipments of guns and sophisticated communications equipment began to be smuggled into the island. In one shipment alone, which was grabbed by Manley's security forces, there were 500 submachine guns."
2.) Extensive labor unrest
3.) Economic destabilization
4.) Covert financial support for the opposition (Seaga's JLP)
5.) Mobilization of the middle class into CIA-created anti-government organizations to carry out well-publicized demonstrations

---

355 Jonathan Stevenson, *A Drop of Treason: Philip Agee and His Exposure of the CIA* (Chicago: University of Chicago Press, 2021) 95-96.
356 Ellen Ray, "CIA and Local Gunmen Plan Jamaican Coup," *CounterSpy* 3:2 (December 1976): 36-41.
357 Ernst Volkman and John Cummings, "Murder As Usual," *Penthouse* December 1977.

6.) Infiltration of security services and armed forces to turn them against the government. "With liberal bribes, the CIA turned many security personnel into paid informants for the agency."

Breaking with its tradition of non-response, the CIA went public to "strenuously deny" the reporting of this article.[358] This is how we know the article hit the bullseye. For example, the revelation by Volkman and Cummings that the CIA provided covert shipments of arms and other equipment to the JLP has been confirmed.

> An arsenal of automatic weapons somehow found their way to Jamaica...Huge consignments of guns and advanced communications gear were smuggled onto the island. One such shipment was intercepted by Manley's security patrols—a caché of 500 man-eating submachine guns. The firearms were shipped to the island from Miami by the Jamaica Freedom League, a right-wing paramilitary faction with roots in the CIA, financed largely by drugs. Peter Whittington, the group's second in command, was convicted of drug trafficking in Dade County. The funds were laundered by the League at Miami's Bank of Perrine, the key American subsidiary of Castle Bank, then the CIA's financial base in Latin America. The bank was owned and operated by Paul Helliwell, bagman for the Bay of Pigs invasion, accused even by the conservative Wall Street Journal of involvement in the global narcotics trade.[359]

On July 2, 1980, Louis Wolf, editor of *Covert Action Information Bulletin*, gave a press conference in Kingston and announced that after an "extensive and exhaustive investigation" he confirmed that the CIA Jamaica station increased from 9 to 15, and Wolf identified the new chief of station: first secretary of the embassy Richard Kinsman. This made the Jamaican station the largest in the Caribbean. According to Wolf, this station was engaged in "unlawful interference in the internal affairs of Jamaica." "They are seeking to disrupt the society to the point

---

358 "Report of Plot Against Jamaica Denied by CIA," *The Washington Post* November 3, 1977.
359 Alex Constantine, *The Covert War Against Rock* (Port Townsend, Washington: Feral House, 2000) 138.

where it will be impossible for Manley to rule the country," he said.[360] Wolf's revelations were supported by former CIA Agent John Stockwell, who affirmed in a May 1982 interview on *Alterative Views* that the 15-person CIA station in Jamaica was "huge" for such a small area (an island population of two million), and this was typical of the CIA having a big operation under way, specifically a "massive" destabilization operation.[361]

The JLP's relationship to the CIA was known in the ghetto streets of Jamaica and Edward Seaga's nickname, CIAga, was painted on gulley walls, as above.

The most obvious, and dastardly, fruit of this destabilization campaign was the sudden paroxysm of political violence leading up to the 1976 Jamaican elections pitting the incumbent Manley of the PNP against the U.S.-supported Seaga and the JLP. Jamaicans and the world were shocked by the level of indiscriminate violence that marked 1976: a wave of shootings and arsons swept the island, terrorizing the population and leaving hundreds dead or maimed. Prime Minister Manley even lamented:

---

360 Ellen Ray and Bill Schaap, "Chile All Over Again? Massive Destabilization in Jamaica," *CovertAction* Number 10 (August September 1980): 7-17; "Jamaica: US Diplomats named as 'CIA operatives'," *Latin News* July 11, 1980; "'Destabilizing' Jamaica," *The Washington Post* July 28, 1980; "Naming the CIA's Names," *The Washington Post* July 30, 1980.
361 https://www.youtube.com/watch?v=Vf2MQC4v9ts

"We have witnessed a type and scale of violence unique in our history, terrorist activities previously unknown to us."[362] He rightly suspected that the CIA was behind this new terroristic violence. Former CIA agent Philip Agee affirmed a causal link between the arrival of the new members of the CIA Jamaica station in December 1975 and the initiation of violence in the island in 1976. In a September 17, 1976, press release he said: "I would like to call the attention of the Jamaican press and people to the fact that the current [CIA] chief of station here [Norman Descoteaux], and two of the operations officers arrived in Kingston during the middle and latter part of last year prior to the initiation of violence." Agee said further: "the CIA was using the JLP as its instrument in the campaign against the Michael Manley government. I'd say most of the violence was coming from the JLP, and behind them was the CIA in terms of getting weapons in and getting money in." Kevin Edmonds reminds us, "starting in the mid-1970s, the CIA conducted lengthy destabilisation campaigns in Jamaica, consisting of the steady provision of financial support and covert arms shipments to supporters of ...Edward Seaga's pro-US Jamaican Labour Party (JLP)...the JLP did receive covert shipments of arms from the CIA, in addition to other social control tactical equipment"[363]

Out of this CIA-JLP alliance came the notorious Jamaican gang called the *Shower Posse*.

> One organization that has been linked to Edward Seaga was the deadly Shower Posse that wreaked murder, violence and drug running in the Caribbean, North America and Europe. The historical record now attests to the fact that this organization was integrated into the networks of the Central Intelligence Agency (CIA) of the United States when the USA moved to destabilize Jamaican society in the 1970's.[364]

---

362 "Jamaica: Jah Kingdom Goes To Waste," *Time* June 28, 1976.
363 Edmonds, "Guns, gangs and garrison communities," 55, 62.
364 Horace G. Campbell, "Edward Seaga and the Institutionalization of Thuggery, Violence and Dehumanization in Jamaica," *Counterpunch* June 14, 2019.

Casey Gane-McCalla has also shown the role that the U.S. government and the CIA played in training, arming and empowering the Shower Posse. "In its efforts to destabilize the Jamaican government in the 1970s, the CIA created a group of drug-dealing, gun running, political criminals. Through the cocaine trade, these criminals would eventually become more powerful than the politicians they were connected to. The CIA destabilization program did not only destabilize Jamaica in the 70s, but it destabilized Jamaica for the next 40 years."[365]

Members of the Shower Posse have confirmed this connection to the CIA. One member told the *South Florida Sun Sentinel*: "We received several shipments of guns from the CIA. The guns were sent to the JLP by plane. The planes were then reloaded with ganja (marijuana) for the return flight to America."[366] According to what a former Jamaican government official told the *Sun Sentinel*, the CIA also gave the JLP's Posse members training. One of the founders of the Shower Posse, Lester "Jim Brown" Coke, father of the notorious Christopher "Dukes" Coke, was one of Edward Seaga's bodyguards and political enforcers. Jim Brown's associate Cecil Connor, aka Charles "Lil Nut" Miller, revealed that he and the Shower Posse received "secret U.S. training" to fight political wars for the JLP, including the "murder [of] leftist opponents of Edward Seaga". Miller confirmed that "CIA agents taught him how to kill with as little as the springs of a wristwatch."[367] "The United States made me what I am," he boasted.

365 Casey Gane-McCalla, "How The CIA Created The Jamaican Shower Posse," *Newsone* June 3, 2010.
366 Roger M. Richards, "The Posse Wars," *South Florida Sun Sentinel* March 11, 1989.
367 David Adams, "Threat to Kill Americans: a dilemma for St. Kitts," *Tampa Bay Times* August 15, 1998.

II.   *Enter Bob Marley*

The second half of the 1970s, the period when Bob Marley began to reap the rewards of his long apprenticeship as a musician, was a time of turbulence not only in Jamaica but around the globe. The Cold War was at its most intense; proxy wars were being waged between East and West in developing-world countries; anticolonial wars were still being fought in Africa; there were anti-imperialist struggles taking place in South America. Jamaica was on the brink of all-out civil war as the opposition, aided and abetted by the CIA, sought to wrest power from Michael Manley's democratic socialist government. Bob Marley almost lost his life during that conflict. His music is resonant of that period; it reflects the zeitgeist. At the apotheosis of his career, he had become a kind of Che Guevara of popular culture.[368]

Bob's international success made him a symbol of a troubled island's hopes. He now found himself in the unenviable position of being the prize of a tug-of-war between the island's two political parties. As the material for his album Exodus began to brew in 1976, the island was convulsed with lethal political agitation, and Bob's star status did not confer immunity - rather, it was the reverse. "People see him as a big man now, gone international," as his boyhood friend Mikey Smith explains. "Everyone want Bob Marley deh 'pon their team."[369]

I do not defend Marxism nor capitalism. We are strictly Rasta – Bob Marley in a television interview.[370]

By the time of the 1976 elections Bob Marley's music propelled him to the status of a "folk hero in Jamaica" of considerable *power*.[371]   As *The New York Times* reported: "By 1976, he had become such an important figure in Jamaica that his popularity *rivaled and, quite likely, eclipsed that of the Government*."[372] Bob Marley scholar Roger Steffens expounds:

368 Linton Kwesi Johnson, "The People Speak," in Roger Steffens, *So Much Things To Say: The Oral History of Bob Marley* (New York: W.W. Norton & Company, 2017) xiii.
369 Vivien Goldman, "Dread, beat and blood," *The Guardian* July 16, 2006.
370 Anthony Turner, "Who shot Bob Marley?" *The Gleaner* May 10, 2020.
371 Prestholdt, "Rebel Music," 83.
372 Robert Palmer, "Bob Marley, in the Key of Peace," *The New York Times* June 16, 1978.

Marley was so important that, whether he could or not, he was perceived as being able to sway a national election. He was without question the most popular person that Jamaica has produced, at least since Marcus Garvey, and he was at the same time a very fearful figure to a lot of people because he could change things if he wanted to.[373]

But Marley's power and influence was not limited to the small island of Jamaica. In 1977 and 1978 *The New York Times* described him as "a hero" to "the 'downpressed' of the third world" and "an international pop star of considerable power."[374] In fact, Marley had become a lodestar for armed struggle across the globe.[375] In the late 1970s Nicaraguan Marxist-Leninist insurgents, the Sandinista National Liberation Front (Frente Sandinista de Liberación Nacional), reportedly listened to Marley's music before going into combat, singing his *Road Block* "while battling the US-funded Contras in Nicaragua".[376]

As the Cold War drew to a close, Bob Marley remained a primary vehicle for sociopolitical critique. He also continued to be a lodestar for armed movements from Southeast Asia to the Pacific and West Africa. For example, among those resisting the 1975 Indonesian military occupation of East Timor, Marley became an inspirational icon of "just rebellion", alongside Che Guevara and Nelson Mandela. Specifically, Marley's image became associated with support for the Timorese rebels, Armed Forces for the National Liberation of East Timor (Forças Armadas da Libertação Nacional de Timor-Leste, or Falintil). Marley's calls for

---

373 Quoted in "What'cha Gonna Do? ... The Deaths of Bob Marley and Peter Tosh," in Alex Constantine, *The Covert War Against Rock* (Port Townsend, Washington: Feral House, 2000) 131.

374 Robert Palmer, "Bob Marley, in the Key of Peace," *The New York Times* June 16, 1978.

375 Jeremy Prestholdt, "Between Revolution and the Market: Bob Marley and the Cultural Politics of the Youth Icon," in B. van der Steen and T. Verburgh (eds) *Researching Subcultures, Myth and Memory*. Palgrave Studies in the History of Subcultures and Popular Music (Cham: Palgrave Macmillan, 2020) 171-194 (188).

376 Gregory Stephens, *On Racial Frontiers: The New Culture of Frederick Douglass, Ralph Ellison, and Bob Marley* (Cambridge University Press, 1999) 214; Jeremy Prestholdt, "Rebel Music: Bob Marley and the Cultural Politics of Liberation," in idem, *Icons of Dissent: The Global Resonance of Che, Marley, Tupac and Bin Laden* (Oxford University Press, 2019) 70.

neocolonial liberation were attractive to Falintil supporters, but affinities also went beyond his message. Since many saw parallels between Bob Marley's hairstyle and that of Falintil guerrillas, Marley's personal style also acted as a bridge. Marley became so synonymous with hyper-masculine concepts of rebelliousness in East Timor that even street gangs in Dili began using his image as an emblem.[377]

Marley's songs were listened to with reverence on transistor wireless radio in the guerilla camps in Mozambique.[378] During the final months of the Zimbabwe War of Liberation, Marley's 1979 track "Zimbabwe," which praised Marxist-Leninist and Maoist guerrillas fighting to end white minority rule in Rhodesia, lifted the militants' morale.[379] "Zimbabwe" portrays what Marley biographer Timothy White called an "apocalyptic battle" against Babylon in southern Africa in the person of the minority government of Ian Smith.[380] It encourages armed struggle ("So arm in arms, with arms, we'll fight this little struggle"). "In Zimbabwe, popular songs were central to the century-long fight to end the colonial system, and Marley's claim that music was 'the biggest gun because the oppressed cannot afford weapons' was nowhere more resonant.'[381]

"During the years of Chimurenga (chiShona for uprising), Bob Marley's music had been adopted by the guerrilla forces of the Patriotic Front; indeed, there were stories of ZANLA troops playing Marley cassettes in the bush," says [University of Zimbabwe Professor Fred] Zindi. "Certainly, Marley's music has potency and a commitment which goes far beyond simple entertainment. He now enjoys a special place in Third World culture; an artist who directly identifies with the black African struggle. Thus, he was the only outside artist asked to participate in Zimbabwe's independence celebrations."

---

377 Prestholdt, "Rebel Music," 94.
378 Percy Zvomuya, "Soon we'll find out who is the real revolutionary: Marley and the birth of Zimbabwe," *Mail & Guardian* April 16, 2020.
379 Prestholdt, "Rebel Music," 70.
380 Prestholdt, "Rebel Music," 80.
381 Anakwa Dwamena, "Zimbabwe's Powerful Music of Struggle," *New Yorker Magazine* March 20, 2018.

"His songs were the food that people in liberation movements, particularly the armed wings, were swallowing," says Shadrack Gutto, a Unisa professor and constitutional law expert in South Africa, who was to teach law in Zimbabwe for 12 years.[382]

By the time the war ended in 1980 and Bob Marley arrived in Africa in April to headline the independence celebrations that would see Rhodesia become Zimbabwe, Marley's homage to the liberation struggle had become so popular that *Survival* (the album featuring the song) was Zimbabwe's top-selling record.[383] While in Africa Marley had a stopover in Kenya, where he reportedly "spurned an audience with Prince Charles." The English Prince was on his way to Salisbury as the representative of the Queen. Learning that Marley and his band were waiting in a transit lounge in Nairobi, Prince Charles sent an emissary with an invitation to Marley to pay his respects while the Prince was in the VIP suite. "In typical fashion, Marley told the emissary that if the royal wanted to meet him, he instead should come to where he and his band were seated."[384] This one incident was a powerful symbolic rebuke, not just of Prince Charles, but of the entire legacy of white colonial rule in Africa.

Marley explained in a 1979 interview that he imagined himself a revolutionary without weapons or political influence, but fighting "single-handed, with music."[385] The last vestiges of white colonial rule in Africa saw and treated Marley's revolutionary music as a threat. For example, because his music was so closely associated with the politics of liberation and resistance, the Apartheid government of South Africa banned many of Marley's songs. Romantic love songs such as "Is This Love?" and "She's Gone" were allowed uncensored, but Marley's "subversive" music, such as "Zimbabwe," was officially classified as

---

382 Thobile Hans, "Remembering Bob Marley At The Birth of Zimbabwe," *Forbes Africa* April 2, 2015.
383 Prestholdt, "Rebel Music," 80; Dwamena, "Zimbabwe's Powerful Music of Struggle."
384 Percy Zvomuya, "Soon we'll find out who is the real revolutionary: Marley and the birth of Zimbabwe," *Mail & Guardian* April 16, 2020.
385 Prestholdt, "Rebel Music," 76.

"undesirable" under the South African Publications Act of 1974. To restrict access to such subversive tracks, the Apartheid government blacked out lyrics on Marley's record sleeves and censored specific tracks by scoring them. "Nevertheless, Marley's political messages circulated widely in South Africa as uncensored records were smuggled in from neighboring nations, including Zimbabwe." "Only in 1992, as the Apartheid system collapsed, did the South African government officially reclassify Survival as 'not undesirable'."[386]

Jeremy Prestholdt makes an important observation: "Bob Marley was not only emblematic of a wider structure of feeling in the late Cold War era. He also gave form and voice to the transnational cultural politics of the left. As a symbol of Third World liberation, Bob Marley was an artistic and spiritual *parallel to Che Guevara*."[387] Linton Kwesi Johnson makes a similar observation: "[Marley's] music is resonant of that period; it reflects the zeitgeist. At the apotheosis of his career, he had become *a kind of Che Guevara of popular culture*."[388] We now know that the U.S. government assassinated Che Guevara.[389]

---

386 Jeremy Prestholdt, "Between Revolution and the Market: Bob Marley and the Cultural Politics of the Youth Icon," in B. van der Steen and T. Verburgh (eds) *Researching Subcultures, Myth and Memory*. Palgrave Studies in the History of Subcultures and Popular Music (Cham: Palgrave Macmillan, 2020) 171-194 (188); Prestholdt, "Rebel Music," 90.
387 Prestholdt, "Rebel Music," 71.
388 Linton Kwesi Johnson, "The People Speak," in Roger Steffens, *So Much Things To Say: The Oral History of Bob Marley* (New York: W.W. Norton & Company, 2017) xiii.
389 On October 9th, 1967, Ernesto "Che" Guevara was put to death by Bolivian soldiers, trained, equipped and guided by U.S. Green Beret and CIA operatives. See *Peter Kornbluh, "*The Death of Che Guevara Declassified," *The Nation* October 10, 2017; Michèle Ray, "In Cold Blood: The Execution of Che by the CIA," Ramparts Magazine (March 1968): 21–37; Will Grant, "CIA man recounts Che Guevara's death," BBC News 8 October 8, 2007.

III.   *When Peace is an Operational Threat*

The U.S. spent 1975 trying to destabilize Jamaica and remove the Cuba-friendly government of Michael Manley in the 1976 elections. The CIA made the island convulse with lethal political agitation. The effort failed. Manley was re-elected overwhelmingly, and the U.S. government intensified its efforts. The International Monetary Fund made the people more destitute,[390] and the CIA raised the level of political violence and terrorism on the streets. The aim was to turn the populace against the Manley government and secure the election of Seaga's JLP in 1980. Thus, from 1974 to 1980 Jamaica was rife with political violence as the island's two parties, the PNP and the JLP, were locked in an urban paramilitary conflict that killed, injured, and displaced thousands of people. This violent civil war between the PNP and the JLP, sparked and fueled by the Agency, was operationally crucial to the CIA destabilization plan. Bob Marley, the effective ambassador of peace, was a bonafide threat to this plan.

Bob Marley was politically neutral and his home/studio at 56 Hope Road was always a neutral turf where murderous rivals

---

390 Abbie Bakan, "How the IMF wrecked Jamaica," *Socialist Worker Issue 2059*
July 10, 2007; Karen DeYoung, "Manley's Rift With the IMF Dominates Jamaican Economics," *The Washington Post* September 6, 1980.

from both warring factions could come and socialize in peace. This contributed to Bob's image as Jamaica's prince of peace. Once the rivals left Bob's place, however, the fighting continued. The civil war between the two parties took such a toll on both sides that representatives from each faction were compelled to try to end it, and they turned to the one man who they felt could make peace possible: Bob Marley. In January 1978 two rivals, PNP triggerman Buckie Marshall and his JLP counterpart, Claudie Massop, together led an all-night candle-lit vigil in the streets of the ghetto and the next day announced an effective truce. "Bob's message of peace was so seductive," Vivien Goldman tells us, "he was changing peoples' hearts and minds as he did with somebody like Claudie Massop. And that is why Bob was such a threat." [391] The truce triggered mass revelry throughout Jamaica's ghettos. "A young reggae performer, Jacob Miller, immediately broadcast the news by cutting a single, set to the tune of When Johnny Comes Marching Home Again, called The Peace Treaty Special. Another reggae song, The War Is Over, quickly rose to No. 4 on the Kingston hit parade. Peace had come to West Kingston."[392]

A Peace Committee was formed and it planned to hold a Peace concert to promote love and unity, and they turned to Jamaica's Ambassador of Peace – who was in self-exile in London – to headline it and cement the truce. Buckie and Claudie together travelled to London to recruit Bob Marley. Billed as the "Third World Woodstock," the One Love Peace Concert was held on April 22, 1978, and attracted 30,000 people to the National Stadium in Kingston. Present, for political purposes, were both Prime Minister Michael Manley and opposition leader Edward Seaga. Unexpectedly, Marley summoned both politicians to the stage who eventually, reluctantly, acquiesced.

At Marley's prompting, the two politicians—long-sworn enemies—were seen clasping hands sheepishly. Marley's mission was accomplished. The ghetto's most famous citizen, whose inflammatory

---

391 Vivien Goldman in *ReMastered: Who Shot the Sheriff? A Bob Marley Story* (2018). Directed by Kief Davidson.
392 Adele Freedman, "Fairer wind for Jamaica," *MacLeans* May 29, 1978.

protest songs had advertised the plight of Kingston's poor to the entire world, had forced two political enemies into symbolic accord. It was an example of what the people, singing the people's music and preaching the people's philosophy, could accomplish—if they tried.[393]

Seaga's presence at the Peace Concert was certainly not about peace, and the concert itself was highjacked by the CIA to promote its program of Jamaican destabilization through civil war. As historian Gunst reports

> Marley didn't know it that night, but his One Love Peace Concert had been used as a cover for Seaga's forces to smuggle guns into the country. They were hidden inside a shipment of lighting equipment used for the show. "Those guns came in right under the noses of the custom people," Trevor [Phillips, chairman of the Peace Council] said. "And I was so naïve and gullible that I had no idea of what was going on."
>   On the night of the show, Chris Blackwell (owner Marley's label Island Records)...sent someone to the stadium to tell Trevor that this equipment was on the wharf waiting for clearance...Trevor made an urgent call to Dudley Thompson, the minister of national security, to clear the containers. It was not until a few days later that Trevor found out about the guns at a post-concert meeting of the Central Peace Council. Byah Mitchell, the gunman from (Seaga's) Tivoli Gardens, threw him the warning: "Mr. Chairman," Byah growled at Trevor, "is not peace we dealin' with. Is pieces (i.e. guns)."[394]

A "Whole heep o' guns come down in the equipment," it was revealed. As a result, "The 'peace' brought about by the One Love Peace Concert was somewhat illusory: in 1978, almost four hundred people were killed in Jamaica,"[395] with the help of guns that came in during and by means of the Peace Concert. Because the civil war was operationally necessary to the CIA's objectives in Jamaica, a genuine peace movement was a threat to these objectives, particularly on the eve of the 1980 elections. Consequently, the grass roots leaders who were involved with the peace movement were summarily killed. As Vivien Goldman remarks, "For some people, peace doesn't pay, and many of the

393 Freedman, "Fairer wind for Jamaica."
394 Gunst, *Born Fi' Dead*, 196-197.
395 Salewicz, *Bob Marley*, 341.

prime movers of the peace were killed in a very short time thereafter."[396] JLP gunman Massop was the first to pay, as Laurie Gunst notes: "Claudie Massop's participation in The Downtown Truce sealed Massop's fate. Massop became a liability and so did all of the gang leaders who participated in that truce."[397] "Massop crossed the CIA by agreeing to the peace concert with the PNP's Buckie Marshall. For this he was shot, dead."[398] "Within a year, by 1979, every one of the rankings involved with the truce was dead."[399]

> Within three years some of the leading players in the show died. Massop was controversially killed by police in Kingston in February 1979. He was only 30 years old. Miller died in an auto accident in March 1980 at age 27; and Marley succumbed to cancer in May 1981 at age 36. Tosh was murdered at his home in Kingston in September 1987. He was 42. The gang violence the concert was held to suppress still continued to rage leading up to the general election in October 1980, won in landslide fashion by Seaga and the JLP. More than 800 persons were murdered that year.[400]

Where the CIA failed in 1976 it succeeded in 1980. The lethal political agitation swept Manley out of office and Seaga/CIAga in. With the U.S. now firmly in control of the Jamaican government, "Jamaica became a node in this Dark Alliance of the CIA, Contras and Cocaine during the period when the Seaga administration was in power, 1980-1989."[401]

---

396 Vivien Goldman in *ReMastered: Who Shot the Sheriff? A Bob Marley Story* (2018). Directed by Kief Davidson.

397 Laurie Gunst in *ReMastered: Who Shot the Sheriff? A Bob Marley Story* (2018). Directed by Kief Davidson.

398 Horace G. Campbell, "Edward Seaga and the Institutionalization of Thuggery, Violence and Dehumanization in Jamaica," *Counterpunch* June 14, 2019.

399 Gunst, *Born Fi' Dead*, 199.

400 Howard Campbell, "The One Love Peace Concert," *Jamaica Observer* July 30, 2022.

401 Horace G. Campbell, "Edward Seaga and the Institutionalization of Thuggery, Violence and Dehumanization in Jamaica," *Counterpunch* June 14, 2019.

The 1980 election was one of the bloodiest in the history of Jamaica, with hundreds dead and thousands dispersed. This counter revolutionary phase in the Caribbean reached new levels as the CIA supported the Contras in Nicaragua, the militarists in El Salvador and the conservative military forces throughout the Caribbean. It was in this period that Walter Rodney was assassinated in Guyana and Archbishop Romero was assassinated in San Salvador. Manley was defeated in the elections of 1980. In 1980 when Edward Seaga became the Prime Minister of Jamaica the society was deployed at the service of the US counter revolution in the region. It was not by chance that the Prime Minister of Jamaica was at the forefront of those giving military, diplomatic and political cover for the US invasion of Grenada in 1983.[402]

This is all the background to and the context of the events that transpired on the night of December 3, 1976, at 56 Hope Road. President Kennedy wanted détente between the U.S. and Russia, and he was killed for it by Cold Warriors within his own government. The détente that got Kennedy shot on November 22, 1963, likely also got Bob Marley shot on December 3, 1976.

IV.   *The CIA and the Ambush in the Night*

Bob Marley also became a victim of the indiscriminate violence in 1976 when he offered a free concert in the midst of the CIA inspired violence and killings in Jamaica.[403]

You might wonder why the CIA would find [Bob Marley] particularly threatening. But documents released under the US Freedom of Information Act have shown that the CIA and other US government agencies did have files on the singer and took more than a passing interest in his career.[404]

---

402 Horace Campbell, "The Region: Gangsters, politicians, cocaine and bankers," *Starbroek News* August 31, 2010.
403 Campbell, "The Region."
404 Ian Shircore, *Conspiracy: 49 Reasons to Doubt, 50 Reasons To Believe* (New York: John Blake Pub., 2012) Chapter 41.

The CIA particularly worried about Marley helping a socialist prime minister win re-election against the candidate they backed.... Evidence supports that the CIA acted on increasing concerns about Bob Marley.[405]

Bob Marley wanted to give a benefit concert for the people of Jamaica. Called "Smile Jamaica" and scheduled for December 5, 1976, at the National Heroes Park in Kingston, Jamaica. This was the *first* "Peace Concert"; its aim was to promote unity and peace and counter the political violence that had recently erupted on the island. Desiring to use the upcoming concert to his political advantage, Prime Minister Michael Manley decided, to Bob Marley's chagrin, to schedule the national elections for December 15, making it appear that the December 5 concert was in support of Manley's PNP campaign. This enflamed Seaga and the JLP. Bob Marley was warned not to show up at the concert. "JLP operatives around Bob—Claudie Massop, Tommy Cowan, Harry J and Tek Life—all warned him that their party did not want his free concert. Claudie, who was then in prison, sent Bob an urgent message to this effect. The JLP saw the concert as an endorsement of Michael Manley and his socialist policies and took it as a slap in the face."[406]

In the week leading up to the Smile Jamaica concert, an "unsettling" incident occurred. During rehearsals at 56 Hope Road a "white bwai" (white boy), as Bob described him, came to the property and warned the Reggae star to tone down his lyrics and to stop aiming at a white audience in the USA; if he didn't, Bob would find his visa to enter America taken away and "me can't go to America again." The "white bwai" approached Bob even though he was surrounded by his men with their guns. "I told him tek yu blood claat out of my yard, before me lick yu up," Bob told his

405 John Potash, *The FBI War on Tupac Shakur and Black Leaders* (Baltimore: Progressive Left press, 2007) 563, 565. See also idem, *Drugs as Weapons Against Us: The CIA's Murderous Targeting of SDS, Panthers, Hendrix, Lennon, Cobain, Tupac, and Other Activists* (Waterville, OR: Trine Day, LLC, 2015) Chapter Eighteen, "Drugs and the Murder of Jamaica's Bob Marley."
406 Don Taylor with Mike Henry, *Marley and Me: The Real Bob Marley* (Fort Lee, New Jersey: Barricade Books,) 141.

manager Don Taylor.[407] As British music journalist Chris Salewicz recounts:

> Then the man left, as suddenly as he had arrived. Whoever this was, he would appear to have been acting under instructions from the US Embassy, if not from the CIA. Don Taylor was convinced it was a message from the CIA, who at that time had a close relationship with the JLP; this was part of a strategy of relentlessly undermining Michael Manley's policy of allying with other Third World nations, notably communist Cuba. Effectively, Jamaica was in a state of covert civil.[408]

DECEMBER 3, 1976

Marley is a powerful political voice in Jamaica and it is, perhaps, this along with his criticisms of his country that instigated 'the incident' last December. - The New York Times August 14, 1977

There were early signs that something was brooding on December 3, 1976, two days before the planned Smile Jamaica concert. In the previous days some gangsters who were extorting Bob Marley came every Friday to pick up the money. On December 3, they never showed.[409] As threats against Marley's life had become frequent following the announcement of the concert, protection had been arranged. The Echo Squad, a loose confederation of gang members of both political parties JLP and PNP including men that Prime Minister Michael Manley sent over to guard Marley, stood twenty-four-armed guard with automatic

407 Taylor, *Marley and Me*, 143.
408 Chris Salewicz, *Bob Marley: The Untold Story* (London: HarperCollins, 2009) 297.
409 Timothy White, *Catch a Fire: The Life of Bob Marley* Revised and Enlarged (New York: Henry Holt, 2006) 288.

rifles at 56 Hope Road and allowed only members of Bob's band on or off the property without permission.[410]

Marley associates Neville Garrick and Jody Mowatt left Tuff Gong, the studio at 56 Hope Road, at 8:30 PM and drove through the front gate, clearing the Echo Squad guards. Seecho Patterson, who was at the studio, happened to look out the front porch at 8:45 as the sun was setting and noticed that there were (now) no members of the Echo Squad on the front grounds.[411] "They [mysteriously] disappeared from Hope Road shortly before the attack occurred" and "they just disappeared from their posts and they left the home unguarded."[412] The two plainclothes cops who had been stationed outside the house during the rehearsals mysteriously disappeared as well.[413] According to Garrick, the Protective Services guards that were assigned to Marley by the PNP disappeared on the night of the shooting.[414] On cue Bob Marley's entire protective forces abandoned him. "Suddenly, two white Datsuns barreled through the iron gates into a concrete yard mysteriously emptied of guards."[415]

> The gunmen were peppering the house with a barrage of rifle and pistol fire, shattering windows and splintering plaster and woodwork on the first floor. Four of the gunmen surrounded the house, while two others guarded the front yard.
>
> Rita [Bob Marley's wife] was shot by one of the two men in the front yard as she ran out of the house with the five Marley children and a

410 Steffens, *So Much Things To Say*, 223; White, *Catch a Fire,* 287; Brad Schreiber, *Music Is Power: Popular Songs, Social Justice, and the Will to Change* (New Brunswick: Rutgers University Press, 2020) 248.
411 White, *Catch a Fire*, 288.
412 Roger Steffens, "The Night Bob Marley Got Shot," *Rolling Stone* July 10, 2017; Steffens, *So Much Things To Say*, 223, 225; Roger Steffens on *ReMastered*; Ann Brown, "10 Things To Know About The Assassination Attempt On Bob Marley," *The Moguldom Nation* August 31, 2020.
413 Vivien Goldman, "Dread, beat and blood," *The Guardian* July 16, 2006.
414 *ReMastered: Who Shot the Sheriff? A Bob Marley Story* (2018). Directed by Kief Davidson.
415 Sherryl Connelly, "Bob Marley hired Gambino mobsters for protection in New York, new book claims," *Daily News* July 8, 2017.

reporter from the Jamaica Daily News. The bullet caught her in the head, lifting her off her feet as it burrowed between the scalp and skull.

Meanwhile, a man with an automatic rifle had burst through the back door off the kitchen pantry, pushing past a fleeing Seeco Patterson to aim beyond Don Taylor at Bob Marley....The gunman got off eight shots. One bullet hit a counter, another buried itself in the sagging ceiling, and five tore into Don Taylor. The last creased Marley's breast below his heart and drilled deep inside his arm.[416]

The assassination attempt was carried out by enforcers from the CIA-backed Jamaican Labor Party. "Eyewitnesses identified one of the shooters as Lester Coke, a.k.a. 'Jim Brown.' He had been Edward Seaga's bodyguard and was head of the so-called Shower Posse, a pro-JLP gang involved in the trafficking of heroin and cocaine."[417] The seven-man hit squad was said to have been led by Jim Brown and Carl 'Bryah' Mitchell.[418] JLP gunman Mitchell reportedly was contracted by the CIA to organize the hit on Marley.[419] Journalist Timothy White, former editor-in-chief of *Billboard* and author of the classic, definitive, richly detailed biography of Bob Marley, reports:

One of the last men slain in revenge for the assassination attempt on Marley was Carl 'Byah' Mitchell, a JLP goon active in the burgeoning new West Kingston cocaine trade (Byah was purportedly force-fed the drug until it stopped his heart). According to in—depth confidential discussions this writer has had over the last decade with key members of the JLP and PNP, former U.S. Information Service agents stationed in Jamaica in 1976 and New York law—enforcement officials currently active in U.S. prosecution of Jamaican drug posses under the Federal Racketeer Influenced and Corrupt Organizations Act (RICO), Byah Mitchell was generally believed to have been contracted by the CIA to plant and instruct some of the gunmen who staged the murderous assault on Marley's house. Byah's involvement was seen to be a facet of the

---

416 White, *Catch A Fire*, 288-289.
417 Schreiber, *Music Is Power*, 248.
418 Ian Shircore, *Conspiracy: 49 Reasons to Doubt, 50 Reasons To Believe* (New York: John Blake Pub., 2012) Chapter 41.
419 Ann Brown, "10 Things To Know About The Assassination Attempt On Bob Marley," *The Moguldom Nation* August 31, 2020

CIA—JLP destabilization campaign that Michael Manley had long been railing against in the press.

Byah's accomplice in the Marley shooting, the enforcer who actually helped lead the charge on Hope Road, was a Seaga—loyal lieutenant named Lester "Jim Brown" Coke, one of the founders of the Shower Posse.[420]

In the summer of 1977 Marley's label head, "a Jewish Jamaican entrepreneur named Chris Blackwell,"[421] was summoned to the U.S. Embassy in Kingston. According to Blackwell, because "people in positions of authority feared the power [Bob Marley] wielded over his audience," the U.S. ambassador warned Blackwell that the intelligence community had its eye on Bob. "They saw him as dangerous and subversive," Blackwell says, as "someone who was capable of destabilizing politics and inciting young people." Therefore, the CIA kept a file on Marley "as though he were some sort of malign influence," Blackwell discovered.[422] According to declassified CIA documents, Marley was indeed deemed "subversive" by the Agency.[423] Around the same time in the summer of 1977 Prime Minister Michael Manley visited London while Marley was staying there and requested Bob and his manager Don Taylor meet him at the Jamaican Embassy in Kensington Gore, central London. Manley told Bob and Don that he knew "for certain that responsibility for the shooting lay directly with the CIA" who wanted to oust him (Michael Manley) from power.[424] The Prime Minister said he was sure that Bob Marley would want to know the true cause and reason behind the shooting.[425] Nevertheless, Manley argued that it was important for Bob's sake that he return

---

420 White, *Catch a Fire*, 456.
421 Jon Stratton, "Chris Blackwell and 'My Boy Lollipop': Ska, Race, and British Popular Music," *Journal of Popular Music Studies* 22:4 (2010): 436-465 (465).
422 Blackwell, *Islander*, 225; Salewicz, *Bob Marley*, 325.
423 Goldman, *Book of Exodus*, 119.
424 Salewicz, *Bob Marley*, 325.
425 Taylor, *Marley and Me*, 157-158.

to Jamaica. Bob refused for understandable reasons. "After the assassination attempt, a rumor circulated that the CIA was going to finish Marley off. The source of the rumor was the agency itself. The Wailers had set out on a world tour, and CIA agents informed Marley that should he return to Jamaica before the election, he would be murdered."[426]

Marley was finally persuaded to return to Jamaica for the One Love Peace Concert in April 1978. On a Wednesday afternoon the summer after the Peace Concert Bob and Don Taylor were taken by JLP thug Earl 'Tek Life' Wadley to McGregor Gully, a neighborhood in Kingston, where Bob and Don witnessed a Ghetto Court in session and Ghetto Justice executed against some of those said to be involved in the December 3, 1976, shooting at 56 Hope Road. Don Taylor, who took the bulk of the gunshots on that fateful night, gives the details of this experience in his book, *Marley and Me*.

> The ghetto, meanwhile, having apparently cracked the mystery of the assassination attempt, called on us, one Wednesday afternoon in June 1978, to be witnesses for the prosecution. One of Claudie's (Massop) right-hand men led us to a lonely spot near the MacGregor Gully. When asked in May 1977, "Do you know who shot you?" Bob had replied, "Yeah, but dat top secret. Really top secret." Having faced the gunmen, he had probably known or suspected more than I did. Perhaps he was even referring to the secret message sent to him from prison by Claudie. I did not know until then that the Jamaican underworld was so well organized. Here was the proof: the underworld had cracked a case the police claimed they could not solve. To give the police the benefit of the doubt, however, their investigations may well have been hampered by the alleged CIA involvement and their fear of the US government.

> Three young men were tied and bound in the gully when we arrived. One, a young man I knew only as Leggo Beast, told the ghetto court that four of them had been trained by the CIA and given guns and unlimited supplies of cocaine to do the assassination. Claiming that they had been caught up in a situation over which they had no control, the prisoners tried to explain their involvement while pleading with me and Bob for mercy. But ghetto justice had to prevail.

---

426 Alex Constantine, "Chanting Down Babylon: The CIA & the Death of Bob Marley," *High Times* February 2002

The court, as constituted, listened to every plea and then passed sentence on the three accused, who confirmed that four men had been involved in the shooting.

Two of the accused were hanged and one shot in the head sometime between 5 and 6 p.m. on that Wednesday afternoon. The fourth man, I later learned, went insane over the attempted assassination and died afterwards of a cocaine overdose.

Before shooting the last victim, the ghetto generals offered the gun to Bob, saying, "Skip, yuh waan shoot the blood claat here?" As I watched, Bob refused without emotion. He was, I realized then, entering a different phase.

The grisly events of that day are still vivid in my memory: the noose being wrapped around the neck of one of the men, who was dragged away out of our sight to be hanged; the condemned men screaming and begging for mercy.

But the ghetto judges were unmoved. They had wanted Bob to see for himself that they had had nothing to do with the shooting. I was present not just as an observer—but because I, as Bob's right-hand man, had myself also been shot.

We got in the car and drove back to Hope Road. We didn't talk about what we had witnessed.

We never mentioned that day again.

It was as if that judgment Wednesday had never happened.[427]

V.   *Jamaica's Jews, Chris Blackwell, and the Ambush at Hope Road*

Jewish people played an undeniable role in plantation slavery in Jamaica. Ironically, Jewish exiles in the strange lands of the so-called 'New World' were complicit in the process of enslaving Africans...The Jewish exile in the Caribbean enabled the transatlantic trade in enslaved

427 Taylor, *Marley and Me*, 168-170.

Africans and the migration of waves of indentured labourers from Europe and Asia.[428]

Central to the Jewish slavocracy in Jamaica was the Lindo Family.[429] An old Sephardic Jewish family that originated in Medieval Spain, they fled the Inquisition and pretended conversion to Catholicism, becoming New Christians or *conversos*. When the family emigrated to Portugal, Venice, London and Amsterdam, they openly practiced their Judaism again. Alexandre Lindo brought his family to Jamaica in 1765. In 1775 he entered the lucrative slave trade and owned two trans-Atlantic vessels. By 1793 Lindo & Lake was the largest slave factoring company in Jamaica and Alexandre Lindo was the largest slave-trader in British Jamaica.[430] "Between 1786 and 1788, Alexandre Lindo, the leading broker in Kingston, brought in 7,873 Africans and sold 7,510 as slaves, with 4,780 (73.6 per cent) re-exported."[431] He made a great fortune which he invested in sugar plantations, ships and urban properties in Jamaica.

In 1803 Alexandre Lindo moved to London and in 1805 he was elected a *parnas* (the president or the trustee) of the Bevis Marks synagogue. According to Trevor Burnard, "Alexandre Lindo, the most substantial slave trader in Kingston, was so wealthy that he could arrange to lend the amazing sum of £500,000 to Napoleon for his campaign in Haiti in 1802 and 1803."[432] When Napoleon's government defaulted on its debt, Alexandre Lindo lost nearly everything. His grandson Frederick recouped the family fortunes by investing in banana plantations in Costa Rica. Frederick's son Percival married his cousin Hilda Violet Lindo in

---

428 Carolyn Cooper, "Jews and plantation slavery in the Caribbean," *The Gleaner* (Jamaica) July 8, 2012.
429 The Nation of Islam, *The Secret Relationship Between Blacks & Jews* Volume 1: *The Jewish Role in the Enslavement of the African* (Chicago: Latimer Associates, 2017) 74.
430 Jackie Ranston, *The Lindo Legacy* (London: Toucan Books, 2000) 144.
431 Trevor Burnard, "Slaves and Slavery in Kingston, 1770-1815," *IRSH* 65 (2020): 39-65 (50-51)
432 Burnard, "Slaves and Slavery in Kingston, 1770-1815," 56.

1910. Their daughter was Blanche Lindo and their grandson was Christopher Blackwell.[433]

BLANCHE BLACKWELL AND THE TWENTY-ONE FAMILIES

Blanche Blackwell in her youth in Jamaica

Daughter of Hilda (nee Lindo) and Percy Lindo, cousins who married, she was born into a wealthy Jamaican family, descended from Sephardic Jews from western Europe who had settled in Kingston in the mid-18th century and came to control much of the island's commerce.[434]

In 1936 Blanche Lindo married the Anglo-Irish soldier and businessman Middleton Joseph Blackwell of the *Crosse & Blackwell* fortune. They had a single child, *Christopher*. The couple divorced in 1949. Middleton moved to the U.S. and Chris Blackwell stayed with his mother in Jamaica. London's *The Telegraph* tells us Blanche was "one of the last survivors from the age when some 20 families ran Jamaica."[435]

433 Edgar Samuel, "Review: The Lindo Legacy by Jackie Ranston," *Jewish Historical Studies* 36 (1999-2001):174-176 (175).
434 Ian Thomson, "Blanche Blackwell obituary," *The Guardian* August 29, 2017.
435 "Blanche Blackwell, Ian Fleming's mistress – obituary," *The Telegraph* (UK) August 10, 2017; "Chris Blackwell's mom, Blanche passes at 104," *Jamaica Observer* August 13, 2017.

Her family, the Lindos, were Sephardic Jews from Portugal who had arrived in Jamaica in 1743 to make their money from sugar, rum, coconuts and cattle."[436]

And slaves.

In the mid-1970s a team at The University of the West Indies headed by Professor Stanley Reid collated firm economic research showing the high concentration of ownership and corporate power in a small group near the top of the social structure in Jamaica. Reid's published study was entitled "An Introductory Approach to the Concentration of Power in the Jamaican Corporate Economy and Notes on its Origin." It became popularly known as the "Twenty-One Families Study" because it demonstrated that "the concentration of economic power and control in Jamaica lies in the hands of minority ethnic elites and is mainly dispersed through 21 families and their interest groups."[437] The study illustrated "the dynamic and evolutionary relationship between power and colour and the plantation economy"; it "provided powerful first-time insights into the workings of corporate power in terms of overlapping memberships on boards of directors, inter-marriages, social interaction in the area of sports and recreational clubs, and voluntary advisory services to political directorates in return for protection from the State."[438]

This corporate power in Jamaica was disproportionately Jewish. Reid documented that, "Of the minority ethnic elites, Jews have one of the longest unbroken traditions of occupying important economic and political roles in the Jamaican political economy."[439] According to Carol Holzberg's parallel research,

---

436 "Blanche Blackwell, Ian Fleming's mistress – obituary."
437 Stanley Reid, "Economic Elites in Jamaica: A Study of Monistic Relationship," *Athropologies* 22 (1980): 25-44 (26, 27); Stanley Reid, "An Introductory Approach to the Concentration of Power in the Jamaican Corporate Economy and Notes on its Origin," in Carl Stone and Aggrey Brown (edd.) *Essays on Power and Change in Jamaica* (Kingston: Jamaica Publishing House, 1977) 15-44.
438 Everton Pryce, "The grip of corporate power," *Jamaica Observer* May 24, 2013.
439 Reid, "Economic Elites in Jamaica," 26, 27.

"The Jews in Jamaica were a powerful minority, disproportionately represented in the upper echelons of the country's big business sector. They enjoyed a high standard of living relative to the black majority."[440] By the 1970s Jews constituted 1 percent of the island's total population but 25 percent "of the personnel involved in the upper level organization, direction, and finance of those companies quoted on the Jamaica Stock Exchange."[441] The Jews' "superordinate position" was particularly noticeable among the oligarchy of the Twenty-One Families.

> Economic purists of the '70s said the lumpen proletariat were forever enslaved by the economic chains of 'The Twenty-One Families', whose primary concern was preserving their wealth while leaving the masses to fight for "money jingling in their pockets". Who were these 'Twenty-One Families'? Some of us are old enough to remember names that included Ashenheim, Issa, Henriques, Matalon, Hart, DaCosta, Mahfood, Hendrickson, Melhado, Clarke – to name a few. They achieved this economic branding based mainly on interlocutory corporate brand membership and intermarriage. It is clear that many of these reflected a heavy concentration of old Jewish families or descended from the plantocracy.[442]

This is the oligarchy that the election of Michael Manley in 1972 "destabilized." "Once in power, Manley began to alter the economic and social structure of Jamaica," *The New York Times* reported in 1976.

> Chinese and Jewish businessmen have traditionally dominated the Jamaican economy, and the [Michael Manley] Government's economic and agricultural reforms have cut deeply into the businessman's ability to make large profits. In March the nation had only two week's worth of valid foreign exchange reserves, and the Government was implementing

---

440 Carol S. Holzberg, "Strategies and Problems among Economic Elites in Jamaica: The Evolution of a Research," *Anthropologica* New Series 22:1 (1980): 5-23

441 Holzberg, "Strategies and Problems among Economic Elites in Jamaica," 7.

442 Lennie Little-White, "Money talks, wealth whispers," *The Gleaner* December 22, 2019.

new austerity measures, higher taxes and tighter import restrictions on a weekly basis. The result is a continuing brain-drain migration of the middle class and anybody — black or white — with the resources to leave the country. According to one businessman, "The rich and the middle class have been protected in Jamaica for literally hundreds of years. They always have been able to buy or influence their way around inconveniences, customs regulations, tax laws. But now Manley is closing up their loopholes. All my friends are in panic. Everybody wants to run."[443]

And run they did, particularly the Jews. "The result was that a lot of Jamaica's real wealth fled." [444]

The Jamaican Jewish community thrived during the 18th and early 19th centuries. Under British rule, Jews flourished by selling sugar, vanilla, tobacco, gold, rum, and other products. But by the early 20th century, the economy began a slow decline, and many Jamaican Jews emigrated to the United States, England and Australia...Several Jamaican Jews rose to political prominence in the mid-20th century. Neville Ashenheim (of the Twenty-One Families) served as the first ambassador to the United States after Jamaica won its independence from Britain in 1962, serving in the post until 1967. (Ashenheim's great-grandfather, Lewis Ashenheim, was the editor of the first Jewish newspaper in the West Indies.) Mayer Matalon was one of the most important advisors to the Jamaican government in the 1970s and owned many businesses, especially in construction. Matalon's brother, Eli Matalon, served in several government posts, including mayor of Kingston, minister of education, and minister of national security and justice. But the 1970s saw a particularly drastic exodus of Jamaican Jews after then Prime Minister Michael Manley — seen by some as a leader in the style of Fidel Castro — moved the country toward socialism and flirted with revolution. Under Manley's rule, much of the Jamaican elite left the country. When the 1980 election brought Edward Seaga to power, significant numbers of those elites returned. But many others did not, including many of the leaders of the Jewish community. Though the community today is but a fraction of its former size, its impact on Jamaica endures.[445]

443 Stephen Davis, "Fear in Paradise," *The New York Times* July 15, 1976.
444 Little-White, "Money talks, wealth whispers."
445 Dana Evan Kaplan, "The Jewish Community of Jamaica," *My Jewish Learning* @ https://www.myjewishlearning.com/article/the-jewish-community-of-jamaica/

Mayer Matalon's son, Paul Matalon, who became Vice President of the United Congregation of Israelites, expounds

> We've had members of our congregation at the highest levels of government in Jamaica, both under British rule and since independence. We've had representatives in the parliament. My father was the Deputy Prime Minister of Jamaica, Minister of Security, Minister of Education, Mayor of Kingston. He was very political. We've had ambassadors to Washington, ambassadors to London. Unfortunately, in the 70s, when we had that socialist experiment in Jamaica, the Jews were the first to go. Under Michael Manley, we were almost communists. His allegiance grew so tight to Castro that all the Jews left. They nationalized our businesses, and it was just uncomfortable.[446]

According to Matalon, as the Manley-led Jamaican Government embraced democratic socialism, the Jews of Jamaica grew nervous, "So they left. They went to England, Panama, Canada, the United States... mostly North America."[447]

BLACKWELL AND THE LINDO LEGACY

Chris Blackwell (right) with Junior Marvin, Bob Marley, and Jacob Miller (from left), en route to Brazil, 1980

---

446 Zoe Katz, "The Disappearing Jews of Jamaica," *Curating Zoe* @ http://dpshowcase.cdvl.agnesscott.org/zoekatz/writing/the-disappearing-jews-of-jamaica/index.html
447 Katz, "The Disappearing Jews of Jamaica."

Blanche (Lindo) Blackwell, mother of Bob Marley's label head Chris Blackwell, was "one of the last survivors from the age when some 20 families ran Jamaica."[448] Chris Blackwell can be considered a legacy of the Lindo Slave Holding Family in Jamaica. In his autobiographical *The Islander*, Blackwell boasts: "There's no two ways about it: I am a member of the Lucky Sperm Club. I was born into wealth and position, albeit of a particularly mixed sort endemic to Jamaica. I am Jamaican, but I am also English, Irish, Portuguese, Spanish, Jewish, and Catholic."[449] Blackwell reveals a significant personal and family incident, albeit in a self-rescuing way.

> In 1838, all Black people in Jamaica had been emancipated from slavery. This, however, did not do much to improve their lot under British rule, where they lived as politically disenfranchised second-class citizens. One day, I witnessed something that shattered the illusion of the English as kind, genteel employers. My mother had been asked by her brothers Roy and Cecil to help manage the Lindo family's banana plantation. I was sometimes taken on horse and buggy to visit them. On this particular occasion, I saw a dead Black field worker casually slung over the shoulders of a foreman. The worker had been caught trying to steal some bananas for himself and then tried to make a getaway. He was shot as he ran-killed for the sake of a few bananas. It was a terribly sight, an abrupt whip-crack of reality. To the Lindos, this seemed a normal form of punishment, a routine way of maintaining order.[450]

This Lindo family ethos was never too far from Blackwell and Bob Marley, as illustrated by 56 Hope Road, a family property that Blackwell made available to Marley, selling it to him in 1975. *Jackie Ranston*, a biographer of the Lindo Family, reveals an interesting detail about this property:

---

448 "Blanche Blackwell, Ian Fleming's mistress – obituary," *The Telegraph* (UK) August 10, 2017; "Chris Blackwell's mom, Blanche passes at 104," *Jamaica Observer* August 13, 2017.
449 Chris Blackwell with Paul Morley, *The Islander: My Life In Music and Beyond* (New York: Gallery Books, 2022) 13.
450 Blackwell, *Islander*, 18.

Blanche's son, Chris Blackwell, initially set his own wheel of fortune spinning for his country and himself, promoting Jamaican music with Bob Marley among one of his early recording artistes. Some may argue that Blackwell and Marley were destined to meet. Marley's success with Blackwell's Island Records was crowned with a move from Trench Town – a government housing scheme – to a more palatial residence at 56 Hope Road, now a major Kingston tourist attraction. The entrance columns bear name plates telling visitors that this is now the Bob Marley Museum. They hide the original name of the house – Odnil – an inversion of Lindo, whose family home it once was. "In this great future," Bob Marley reminds us in 'Trench Town Roc', "you cannot forget your past.""[451]

56 Hope Road is where Bob Marley was ambushed at night and shot.

It turns out that the horrifying Jewish treatment of Black Jamaicans witnessed by the young Blackwell on the Lindo banana plantation was not isolated or restricted to the Lindos or to the distant past. An exact incident was witnessed decades later by American historian Lauri Gunst.

After winning the election in 1980 with the bloody assistance of the CIA, Jamaica under Edward Seaga became a node in the CIA drug trafficking operation.[452] Seaga entered into a

---

451 *Jackie Ranston, Belisario: Sketches of Character. A Historical Biography of a Jamaican Artist* (Kingston, Jamaica: Mills Press, 2008)

452 Campbell, "Gangsters": "In 1980 when Edward Seaga became the Prime Minister of Jamaica the society was deployed at the service of the US counter revolution in the region. It was not by chance that the Prime Minister of Jamaica was at the forefront of those giving military, diplomatic and political cover for the US invasion of Grenada in 1983. In this period when the CIA was fighting against the Contras, the export of cocaine from Colombia was one means of providing the financial resources for the campaign of destabilisation... Jamaica became central to this dark alliance during the period when the JLP government was in power, 1980-1989." See further idem, "Edward Seaga and the Institutionalization of Thuggery, Violence and Dehumanization in Jamaica," *Counterpunch* June 14, 2019; Daurius Figueira, *Cocaine and Heroin Trafficking in the Caribbean: The Case of Trinidad and Tobago, Jamaica and Guyana* (Lincoln, NE: iUniverse, 2004); Gary Webb, *Dark Alliance: The CIA, The Contras, and the Crack Cocaine Explosion* (New York: Seven Stories Press, 1999).

partnership with notorious Israeli mobster Eli Tisona, who was convicted in 1999 of conspiracy and money laundering for disguising US $43 million in Colombian drug cash for the Cali Cartel. In the early 1980s he was in Jamaica running Seaga's "Spring Plains Argo 21," which was a high-tech Israeli agribusiness project. While ostensibly the project grew and sold winter vegetables to the US market, in reality the planes leased to fly vegetables to the U.S. brought cocaine into Jamaica from Columbia.[453] As Professor Horace Campbell explains:

> It turned out that this was just another front for the transfer of cocaine from Colombia to the United States through Jamaica. During the Seaga period, the planes that were leased to fly out the winter vegetables flew from Colombia before collecting the 'vegetables' from Jamaica. At this period International Lease Financing Corp (ILFC), the Los Angeles-based aircraft leasing division of AIG, was the biggest force in the leasing of planes. AIG worked closely with the US intelligence services to the point where the CEO of AIG was once under consideration to become the director of the CIA.

> After the end of the Cold war and the defeat of Edward Seaga, Tisona was arrested and jailed in the United States on charges of fraud and money laundering. In 1997, an Israeli Knesset committee report named Eli Tisona and his brother, Ezra, as being the country's two most powerful drug lords. Tisona was jailed in the US in 1999.[454]

On 550 acres of farmland in Clarendon, Spring Plains was ran by a group of Israelis like a quasi-slave plantation, similar to those run by the Lindos and visited by the young Chris Blackwell. 1600 poor Black Jamaican laborers worked the land at Spring Plains, oversaw by 32 Israelis (described as agricultural experts).[455] Lauri Gunst was invited by one of the Israelis to tour Spring Plains. She recounts:

---

453 Mark Wignall, "Seaga cannot have it both ways," *Jamaica Observer* June 20, 2010.
454 Horace Campbell, "The Region: Gangsters, politicians, cocaine and bankers," *Starbroek News* August 31, 2010.
455 Joseph B. Treaster, "Making an Island Bloom: Israelis Help in Jamaica," *The New York Times* August 25, 1984.

These farms were high-technology plantations with the state-of-the-art machinery and a barefooted workforce of laborers who migrated from one rural parish to another in search of jobs. I met a young Israeli at a party in Kingston who was an overseer at Spring Plain, an agrofarm in the parish of Clarendon, and he invited me on a tour of the place. Hebrew-speaking masters roared across irrigated fields in fancy jeeps, yelling at ragged laborers and complaining to me in English about a dearth of a work ethic among Jamaicans. Guards patrolled the fields and shipping areas with high-powered weapons; a few weeks after I was there, a worker was shot to death for allegedly pilfering produce.[456]

The more things change, the more they stay the same – at least when it comes to the Black-Jewish relationship in Jamaica. Bob Marley and Chris Blackwell were a Black-Jewish relationship in Jamaica.

The founding members of the Wailers were Bob Marley, Peter Tosh, and Bunny Wailer. In 1972 they signed with Chris Blackwell's Island Records. The group soon broke up. According to Wailer's producer Lee "Scratch" Perry, the Wailers "worked like brothers 'til Chris Blackwell saw it was something great and came like a big hawk and grab Bob Marley up."[457] The first to leave the group was Bunny Wailer. He explains:

After the spring tour of 1973 in the UK, we went to Chris to discuss where the tour would be going next in the United States. We were looking forward now to larger venues, getting exposed to bigger markets because we had proved ourselves. If we continue to play these little gigs we wouldn't be making money. So I said, "Chris, what kind of thing you have planned for us going to America now-where are we going to, play?" He said, "Freak clubs.'" So me say, "What you mean by freak clubs?" Him say, "Well, you know, clubs where gay guys and gals, gals meet gals and guys meet guys and freak out. Drug business, all kind of stuff-freak." We say, "What the blood-claat?" So me say, "Chris, you know I & I is Rasta. How you want to take us all in that direction? Why you want draw us down in dem kind of things? After you know say we is Rasta, we no stand for dem things. Why don't you get us cultural centers and even the polytechnic college what we just do? We stay on a trend now and we sing for children now. We no care to go sing for no freaks."

456 Gunst, *Born Fi' Dead*, 35.
457 Steffens, *So Much Things To Say*, 126.

Chris said, "If you don't do these clubs you are nobody." Just like that. So me just say, "Listen, Chris, 'body' is buried. I am a living being, a living soul. I'm not a body. And if where you have in mind for the Wailers is where bodies go, I won't be going. And one monkey don't spoil no show."[458]

Bunny left the group. Peter Tosh was gone soon thereafter. In one incident in Jamaica, during talks between Blackwell and Tosh, the latter became infuriated, left the room, and returned with a machete to confront Blackwell, who left immediately.[459] Roger Steffens tells us:

According to his biographer John Masouri, Peter believed Bob had betrayed the Wailers by siding with Chris Blackwell, and it happened because Bob was half-white. "There was an old saying that, 'If you're white, you're all right. If you're brown stay around. But if you're black, stay back.' Well that's what it had come to. It felt like he and Bunny were too black for the group now they were at the threshold of success, despite having worked long and hard in building the Wailers' reputation. Bob had sold them out right at the point they were supposed to stand firm, although Peter felt it was time to strike out on his own in to any case. 'I did not come on earth to be a only background singer.'" Peter confirmed to me that they were given only a hundred pounds each at the conclusion of the tour, which dropped its twelve final dates due to Peter's bronchitis. Years later his anger was still at fever pitch.[460]

Attorney-at-law Maxine Stowe, who served as Bunny Wailer's manger, says the Wailers were deliberately fragmented by Blackwell, whose "pre-meditated false marketing" of the group aimed at "black erasure" of Peter Tosh and Bunny Wailer.[461] She, along with Tosh and Bunny, said Blackwell favored Bob because he was half-white (and half-Jewish[462]). Rastafarian attorney

---

458 Bunny Wailer in Steffens, *So Much Things To Say*, 166.
459 Steffens, *So Much Things To Say*, 167-168.
460 Steffens, *So Much Things To Say*, 167-168.
461 Claudia Gardner, "Maxine Stowe Calls Out Chris Blackwell's "White Knight Storyline," *Dancehall Magazine* June 1, 2022.
462 Bob's father, Norval Marley, was the son of Ellen Broomfield, a white Jewish Syrian Jamaican. Adam Chandler, "Bob Marley's Jewish Father," *Tablet Magazine* February 6, 2013.

Miguel Lorne, who was Bunny Wailer's lawyer, recently blamed Blackwell of the same at a Peter Tosh Symposium at The University of The West Indies. He accused Blackwell of breaking up the trio because Blackwell "found it easier to package and promote Bob to a European market". In a 2016 interview Blackwell admitted that Bob Marley and the Wailers "were trying to reach the African-American market. I could see that they had a better chance of reaching white college kids."[463] But that meant erasing the darker Tosh and Bunny, according to Lorne.

> The break-up of The Wailers in the sense of division between Bob, Peter and Bunny, really hurt Peter Tosh. And he saw through Blackwell's tricks. Blackwell helped to break up the group on the basis that Blackwell felt that he could market Bob Marley to the World, but when he said the World he meant the White World. And so, he wanted more or less that if Peter and Bunny stayed around, they would more or less be appendages to sorta prop up Bob. Naturally they couldn't accept that type of status. They continued as brothers. So, when Peter Tosh referred to Blackwell as 'Whitewell', it wasn't just another joke. It wasn't just a matter of changing the name – or 'Whiteworst' – Peter saw through the racism that Blackwell was now introducing into the music genre. In other words, Blackwell really felt that Bob being of that colour, was much more easier to package especially to the North American and European market, than having these two other black persons there.[464]

According to Sebastian Clarke, who was working with the Wailers at the time, Blackwell's Island Records also dealt with the group in an underhanded way to rob them of their royalties. "After waiting several months to get some funds we were confronted with a pile of papers so high, telling us that we owed Island Records forty-two thousand pounds as tour expenses. And yet before we made the tour there was an agreement that Island Records would cover all the expenses."[465]

---

463 Steffens, *So Much Things To Say*, 150.
464 Claudia Gardner, "Blackwell Addresses Perceived Favoritism Towards Bob Marley At The Expense Of Peter Tosh, Bunny Wailer," *Dancehall Magazine* May 30, 2022.
465 Steffens, *So Much Things To Say*, 167-168.

Blackwell's anti-Black marketing plan worked – for Blackwell.

> Chris Blackwell was reaping the benefits of Bob's ever-increasing success as Bob took control of producing his own product-on which, nevertheless, Blackwell was still taking a production override royalty. He himself has said that he and Bob were never friends, just work associates. Yet he found it expedient to use his perceived closeness to the burgeoning superstar Marley to gain entry into the highest levels of international society. To his credit, it is generally agreed that Bob might have never reached his unprecedented level of success were it not for skillful promotion by Blackwell, who was actually taken aback at how big Bob had become.[466]

But this marketing plan wasn't working for Bob, who coveted the Black American audience. In 1980, on the eve of Marley's death, he was finally fed up and was leaving Island Records. Danny Sims negotiated a new label deal with two major companies and huge advances. As Steffen notes, "[Bob] was about to separate from Chris Blackwell and Island Records, saying all they could do was to bring white college kids to him. Blackwell was losing his biggest money-maker."[467] Less than a year later Bob Marley was dead.

VI. *The CIA's Cancer?*

It is claimed that the CIA artificially induced cancer into Bob Marley's toe. Surviving a failed attempt on his life by a wellarmed death squad at his 56 Hope Road home in Kingston, Jamaica, Bob was later given a 'gift' of a new pair of boots by Carl Colby, son of the late CIA director, William Colby. When the unsuspecting Marley put them on, something pricked his foot. He then reached into one of the boots and pulled a piece of copper wire. Coincidently, that same toe later became the source of malignant cancer that spread throughout his body, killing him. Many of his closest friends suspected that the wire contained some carcinogenic

---

466 Steffens, *So Much Things To Say*, 277.
467 Steffens, *So Much Things To Say*, 387.

substance, since Marley contracted cancer shortly thereafter. - Professor
Fred Zindi of the University of Zimbabwe (2015)[468]

After surviving the CIA-orchestrated ambush on December
3, 1976, Bob Marley triumphantly mounted the stage at the Smile
Jamaica on December 5. On the night of the Ambush, Chris
Blackwell was supposed to be at the rehearsal at 56 Hope Road.
He was scheduled to meet a documentary crew there that he hired
from New York to film the Smile Jamaica concert.[469] On his way
to the studio Blackwell made a detour to Lee Scratch Perry's
studio. He says:

> I was due at Bob's to watch hm rehearse for the Smile Jamaica concert,
> *right at what turned out to be the time of the attack.* Beforehand, I had
> gone to visit Lee Perry at his Black Ark Studios, where he was recording
> a track called "Dreadlocks in Moonlight," which he had written for Bob
> to Sing. Lee sang it for me in his tiny studio's tiny control room, mad
> even smaller by its wall coverings of red, green, and black fake fur.
> Hearing anything by Lee at the time was like suddenly dropping through
> a trapdoor into woozy outer space. His voice was so tender and frail, I
> couldn't imagine even Bob improving upon Lee's performance.
> Watching the wired, wiry Lee at work in his cap and shorts was a
> privilege in itself, like watching Picasso bring a painting to life. Instead
> of driving over to Hope Road for the rehearsal, I hung around late while
> Lee finished up; surely Bob wouldn't mind. This change of plan may
> have saved my life, as I was still at Black Ark when the shooting
> started...[470]

When Blackwell asked Scratch to mix the tape, he was informed
that the process would take the producer a few minutes, at most
about thirty minutes. However, according to what Blackwell
claimed later, "technical hitches" made the promised few minutes
stretch into an hour to two hours – long enough for Blackwell to
miss being at 56 Hope Road when the gunmen invaded. "Had not
Scratch's tune been so good, he might have arrived at Hope Road

468 Fred Zindi, "How Did Bob Marley Die?" *The Herald* (Zimbabwe) October
4, 2015.
469 Salewicz, *Bob Marley*, 301.
470 Blackwell, *Islander*, 219.

at exactly the time the bullets were flying."[471] Good fortune or pre-planning?

Blackwell did visit Bob and the other victims in the hospital that night. Then "Chris Blackwell and Dickie Jobson hastily chartered a private jet and left the island" that same night.[472] After Bob left the hospital that evening, he was taken into hiding at Strawberry Hill, Blackwell's secluded retreat in the peaks of the Blue Mountains overlooking Kingston. Only a select few of Marley's most trusted comrades knew his location.[473] The next day (Saturday) the film crew from New York hired by Blackwell arrived at Strawberry Hill. Marley's manager Don Taylor, who was in the hospital with several gunshot wounds, had previously been sent to New York to recruit the crew for the concert.[474] Don Taylor recalled later:

> As Bob was undeterred and still resolved to hold the concert, I wired my standby crew in America, confirming the arrangements I had made with them in New York...I would later find out that among the crew hired to come to Jamaica was the son of a prominent CIA official *who had traveled under an alias*. This information convinced me that the CIA had been behind the plot to kill Bob Marley because of his possible influence on Jamaican politics and on the wider world.[475]

CARL COLBY AND HIS CIA DAD

That film crew member who was a "son of a prominent CIA official" who had traveled to Jamaica under an alias was Carl Colby, son of former CIA Director William Colby (1972-1975/1976). In intelligence, there is an ideal type of spy known as the "Gray Man" who can blend in anywhere and hide in plain sight;

---

471 Salewicz, *Bob Marley*, 301.
472 White, *Catch a Fire*, 290.
473 Steffens, *So Much Things To Say*, 231.
474 Don Taylor with Mike Henry, *Marley and Me: The Real Bob Marley* (Fort Lee, New Jersey: Barricade Books,) 142.
475 Taylor, *Marley and Me*, 143, 149.

183

who is "so inconspicuous that he can never catch the waiter's eye in a restaurant." While he's really an alpha-dog operator, to protect operational security the Gray Man becomes a "soft-looking, unassuming 'snowflake'" who is easily overlooked and eminently ignorable.[476] Bill Colby was the quintessential "Gray Man."[477] The operations he carried out were "gray" that way too. Bill Colby's operational moto was: "If it's done right, you will never know who did it or why."[478]

After his time in the Office of Strategic Services (OSS) in 1947, Bill Colby joined the Manhattan law firm, Donovan, Leisure, Newton, Lombard & Irvine, run by OSS founder William "Wild Bill" Donovan. From there, he was recruited by a former OSS colleague into the CIA in 1951. He was assigned as the CIA station in the U.S. Embassy in Rome. There Colby was sent to help build up the "Operation Gladio" network of clandestine "stay-behind" armies throughout Western Europe. "Our aim was the creation of an Italian nationalism capable of halting the slide to the

476 Greg Schneider, "Covert Operator: 10 Signs You Might Be A Gray Man," *Skillset Magazine* July 13, 2021.
477 Evan Thomas, "The Gray Man," *The New York Times* May 3, 2013.
478 According to Senator John DeCamp in a 2011 interview by Ted Gunderson.

left," he says.[479] Halting a nation's slide to the Left was Colby's personal religious crusade.[480] Building up local fascist nationalisms to counter the Left became Colby's expertise.

Director of Central Intelligence William Colby, 1973-1975/1976

Colby was CIA station chief in Saigon from 1959 to 1962 and then was appointed head of the CIA's East Asian division. In Indonesia Colby oversaw an operation aimed at the Communist Party which resulted in a million Indonesian deaths, according to Amnesty International.[481] From Indonesia Colby turned his attention to Viet Nam. "From 1968 to 1971, under the aegis of the Agency for International Development, Mr. Colby had run

479 Gaither Stewart, "Gladio: The Story of a Conspiracy," *CounterPunch* December 20, 2019.
480 Tim Weiner, "William E. Colby, 76, Head of the C.I.A. in a Time of Upheaval," *The New York Times* May 7, 1996: "Mr. Colby spent most of his adult life as a cold warrior in his country's clandestine service, a 'soldier priest'...on a covert crusade."
481 Rhodri Jeffreys-Jones, "Murder By Index Card: William Colby and the American Tradition of Atrocity," *Diplomatic History* 28 (2004): 805-808.

programs that included Operation Phoenix."[482] Over 20,000 alleged members of the Viet Cong were eliminated by the CIA during this operation. Human rights activists have described the program as a "U.S.-backed assassination program" and former U.S. Army soldiers who were a part of Operation Phoenix said it was a "sterile, depersonalized murder program" run by the CIA.[483] Bill Colby ran it.

Colby has been called "The well-known architect of many of the Agency's dirtiest tricks" and "the man who pioneered U.S. counterinsurgency warfare." "Colby developed the strategy of training and arming local troops to assist with counterinsurgency during the Vietnam War -- the same tactic in use today by U.S. and NATO forces..."[484] – including in Jamaica during the 1970s. Before he was made Director of Central Intelligence (DCI) in 1973, Colby directed the Agency's covert operations.[485]

And Colby proved himself master of the CIA operation called "Limited Hangout."[486] Famous (or infamous) for allegedly "giving away the CIA's Family Jewels," i.e., a list of Agency misdeeds in a 693-page "Family Jewels" document given to Congressional investigators, Colby later basically admitted that this was a cover-up, noting that "for an intelligence agency operating for 25 years at the height of the cold war, this list of

---

482 Weiner, "William E. Colby."
483 Mary McGrory, "Phoenix Program Details: 'Sterile, Depersonalized Murder' Plan," *The Washington Post* August 3, 1971.
484 Christina Wilkie, "Former CIA Director's Death Raises Questions, Divides Family," *HuffPost* December 5, 2011.
485 Weiner, "William E. Colby."
486 "Limited hangout" is intelligence jargon for a form of propaganda in which a selected portion of a scandal, criminal act, sensitive or classified information, etc. is revealed or leaked, without telling the whole story. The intention may be to establish credibility as a critic of something or somebody by engaging in criticism of them while in fact covering up for them by omitting many details; to distance oneself publicly from something using innocuous or vague criticism even when one's own sympathies are privately with them; or to divert public attention away from a more heinous act by leaking information about something less heinous. This is a common tactic used by government intelligence agencies caught in scandals.

misdeeds was 'surprising mild.'"[487] As his eldest son, Jonathan Colby, said: "the release of the family jewels was the only way he knew to save the agency, in effect showing Congress, 'Look, this is all we did, nothing more!'"[488]

An important moment for our discussion occurred during the Church Committee Hearing on September 16, 1975, when at Colby's instruction his assistant produced a top-secret CIA weapon from out of a bag on the floor, the infamous "non-discernable microbioinoculator," and handed it to Senator Church. As we saw above, this micro+bio+inoculator is capable of firing a special "non-discernable" dart at a target that could either cause an instant heart attack or cause cancer (if coated with a carcinogenic substance). It was Bill Colby who presented this weapon to Congress in 1975 and explained it to them.

DCI William Colby explaining the Agency's secret "heart-attack and cancer" gun to Frank Church, chairman of the Senate Committee on Intelligence and Senator John G. Tower of Texas on September 16, 1975

As a result of this "Limited Hangout" – and likely as a part of the overall cover-up – President Gerald Ford replaced Bill Colby as DCI in November 1975, though Colby stayed on until

---

487 Evan Thomas, "The Gray Man," *The New York Times* May 3, 2013.
488 Christina Wilkie, "Former CIA Director's Death Raises Questions, Divides Family," *HuffPost* December 5, 2011.

January 1976.[489] Jonathan Colby, Bill's oldest son, "recalls his father neither bitter nor broken-up when Ford replaced him with future president George H.W. Bush. 'He actually stayed on for three months after Ford canned him, unlike [then-Defense Secretary James] Schlesinger, who was fired the same day as my father was, and who walked out right away'."[490]

"Once CIA always CIA," the motto goes. The motto certainly applied to Bill Colby. In 1978 Colby was still having lunch with "the old boys" of the CIA and he served on a board for former intelligence officers.[491] Both his successor as CIA Director, George Bush, and subsequent CIA Director Admiral Stansfield Turner called Colby back to speak at the CIA training course. Colby admitted in 1978: "I've seen them (Director Bush and Director Turner) for little chats; they've picked my brain."[492] Understatement is the "Gray Man's" special skill.

William E. Colby, right, with another former director of central intelligence, George H. W. Bush, in 1978.
George Tames/The New York Times

489 Weiner, "William E. Colby"; Thomas, "The Gray Man."
490 Wilkie, "Former CIA Director's Death Raises Questions, Divides Family."
491 Paul Hendrickson, "Cooling Off With William Colby," *The Washington Post* May 24, 1978.
492 "Playboy Interview: William Colby," *Playboy* July 1978, p.70.

Bill Colby continued to have strong links to the intelligence community. Recall that after his time in the OSS in 1947 and before he was recruited to the CIA in 1951, Colby joined the Manhattan law firm of OSS founder William "Wild Bill" Donovan, Donovan, Leisure, Newton, Lombard & Irvine. These "white-shoe firms" founded by intelligence personnel serve as "cut-outs" for the intelligence community and engage in covert operations. Donovan, Leisure, Newton & Lombard is a great illustration.

When Walt Disney set out to establish the Disney World Theme Park in Florida in the 1960s, Disney formed an alliance with the CIA and with Donovan, Leisure, Newton & Lombard. This alliance ultimately made it possible for Disney to legally operate *outside of federal and state authority*. This story is revealed by investigative journalist Timothy D. Allman.[493] Disney benefited from two key intelligence contacts. One is senior clandestine operative Paul Helliwell who helped launch the CIA's secret war in Indochina. He then moved to Miami to coordinate the Agency's dirty tricks against Castro. Helliwell served as Disney's principle legal strategist. Helliwell advised Disney in a CIA strategy employed in foreign countries: set up a puppet government and then use that regime to do your bidding. Thus, Disney was advised by Helliwell to establish two "phantom cities" populated by handpicked Disney loyalists. Those two phantom cities became the Disney World Theme Park cites of Bay Lake and Lake Buena Vista, Florida. Disney's other essential intelligence contact was William "Wild Bill" Donovan, himself. His law firm, Donovan, Leisure, Newton, Lombard & Irvine, engaged in clandestine activity on Disney's behalf: his attorneys provided fake identities for Disney agents; they set up a secret communications center and orchestrated a disinformation campaign for Disney. Teams of Disney lawyers worked with Donovan's intelligence-based law firm to draft legislation establishing the two pseudo-cities.

---

493 T.D. Allman, *Finding Florida: The True History of the Sunshine State* (New York: Grove Press, 2013.

Law firms established by intelligence operatives are cut-outs that engage in covert activity for the intelligence community. After Bill Colby retired from the CIA in 1976, he too founded a "white shoe" D.C. law firm, called Colby, Miller & Hanes. From his law firm Colby continued to walk to the exclusive Federal City Club during lunch. Founded in 1963 by Washington's elite,[494] the Federal City Club was where the "good old boys" gathered for martini lunches in smoke-filled rooms to engage in business "done in a very low-key way,"[495] i.e., clandestinely. These lunches were "off-the-record events" where the "movers and shakers of D.C." convened and formed alliances and talked public policy,[496] and also no doubt "off the books" clandestine intelligence activities. William Colby continued engaging in these "low-key" policy meetings after he officially resigned as CIA Director.[497] Then, in 1987 Colby rejoined "Wild Bill" Donovan's intelligence cut-out law firm, Donovan, Leisure, Newton & Irvine.[498] That same year Donovan, Leisure, Newton & Irvine merged with Rogovin, Huge & Schiller, the Washington law firm headed by Mitchell Rogovin, former assistant attorney general, chief counsel to the IRS and special counsel to the CIA.[499] In other words, Bill Colby never left the world of clandestine and covert operations.

---

494 Founding members include founded the Club, including Congressman James W. Symington (D-Mo.), who was a member of the House from 1969 to 1977; Sen. Edward M. Kennedy (D-Mass.), Franklin D. Roosevelt Jr., Robert S. McNamara, Carl T. Rowan, David Brinkley, Hugh Sidey, C. Wyatt Dickerson Jr., Arthur Schlesinger Jr. and George Stevens Jr. President Kennedy offered to host the Club's off-the-record lunches on the third floor of the White House. Instead, they were held for a long time at Sheraton Carlton Hotel. See Roxanne Roberts, "Will It Clique?" *The Washington Post* June 14, 2004.

495 Roxanne Roberts, "Will It Clique?" *The Washington Post* June 14, 2004.

496 Anne Hull, "Venerable Federal City Club Has Had Its Last Policy Lunch," *The Washington Post* January 19, 2006.

497 Paul Hendrickson, "Cooling Off With William Colby," *The Washington Post* May 24, 1978.

498 "Former CIA Chief Joins Law Firm," *AP Press* August 3, 1987.

499 Robert Thomason, "D.C. Law Firm Agrees To Merger With N.Y. Lawyers," *The Washington Post* November 20, 1989.

And "Gray Man" Bill Colby's son showed up under an alias at Strawberry Hill where Bob Marley was hiding out a day after the ambush and CIA-supported attempt on his life; at a time when the CIA was running a massive destabilization operation in Jamaica, an operation which Bob Marley's "peace activism" threatened. It is impossible to consider Carl Colby's presence as a coincidence.

Carl Colby and the film crew reportedly had been at Strawberry Hill all day that Saturday (December 4), filming the wounded Marley and his entourage.[500] Carl Colby admits that they "did a whole interview on film" with Marley on that day.[501] The film, directed by Jeff Walker, was never given an official release.[502] According to Roger Steffens "In June 1977 [Chris] Blackwell had insisted he did not want any of [the film or footage] to be released publicly because it was 'too political'."[503] We have good reason to suspect that there is more to it than this. The next day Sunday, December 5, Carl Colby returned to Strawberry Hill with Island Records' Jeff Walker but reportedly *without a camera* (Carl Coby was the crew's cameraman), according to journalist Timothy White. "One of the 'Smile Jamaica' film crew had also found his way up to the camp-minus his camera. The Rastas had no inkling of it, but the cameraman was Carl Colby, son of CIA director William Colby."[504] In an interview with Roger Steffens Carl Colby gives some important background information (emphasis mine).

I was never recruited by the CIA. No, I would be the worst possible person to be. I'm the son of the CIA director, they already know, they'd

---

500 Salewicz, *Bob Marley*, 305; Carl Colby in 500 Steffens, *So Much Things To Say*, 236-239.
501 Steffens, *So Much Things To Say*, 239.
502 Salewicz, *Bob Marley*, 305.
503 Steffens, *So Much Things To Say*, 236.
504 White, *Catch a Fire*, 291.

think that I was anyway. l wouldn't be a good agent. I wasn't interested in that. I studied philosophy, I was a filmmaker, I'd started making documentary films when I was at Georgetown. I was also very interested in art and all of the interest that I had in politics was sort of dissipated and I became very interested in journalism and particularly documentary filmmaking. So I started making films about artists. I had a good friend at the time who was the sister of Peter Frank, a Harvard-educated wild man in New York, who had started a company called the Video Lab with two other characters, and I joined forces with them probably in October '76, and I moved up to New York. I met Chris Blackwell and we'd all go roller-blading out in Brooklyn at this roller emporium, which was really crazy. Yeah, Blackwell was out there with his girlfriend at the time. Anyway, he was a great guy, very relaxed, and we all went to this Ray Barretto concert at the Village Gate. I remember very well because I met Perry Henzell for the first time and I had always loved his movie *The Harder They Come*, because obviously I loved filmmaking. I'd probably seen it five or six times. Anyway, I liked Perry right away. You could see he was of the same ilk as Chris Blackwell, they're both white Jamaicans and sort of landed gentry, but at the same time incredibly aware of what the culture was like there. They started talking about reggae and about this reggae concert coming up, Smile Jamaica, with this Bob Marley person. I thought well, this is the most incredible thing of all, I've got to be involved in this.[505]

Two points deserve comment here. First, Colby Jr.'s disclaimer that he was never recruited to the CIA because it was known that he was the former DCI's son and therefore "wouldn't be a good agent" is disingenuous. Carl Colby could be an Agency *asset* rather than an actual CIA *agent*. Carl Colby likely operated as an asset in Jamaica in 1976. Second, it is very significant that in October 1976, two months before the CIA-supported assassination attempt on Bob Marley, the son of master "Gray Man" William Colby began hanging out *with Chris Blackwell,* Marley's Jewish label-head.

On Sunday, December 5 Carl Colby, under an alias, went up to Strawberry Hill. This time, according to a number of persons present that day, "he came bearing a gift."[506] The gift that Colby

505 Steffens, *So Much Things To Say*, 227-229.
506 Constantine, *Covert War Against Rock*, 135-136; Ian Shircore, *Conspiracy: 49 Reasons to Doubt, 50 Reasons To Believe* (New York: John Blake Pub., 2012) Chapter 41.

Jr. reportedly presented was a pair of soccer boots – Marley's obsession with the sport was well-known (as was Castro's obsession with cigars and scuba diving). Many people were at the property on that night, including former Black Panther Lee Lew-Lee, who was a cinematographer (the Oscar-winning documentary *The Panama Deception*, 1992) and a director (*All Power to the People*, 1997). He was also close friends with members of the Wailers. Lew-Lee was interviewed by author Alex Constantine in Los Angeles on October 30, 1997, and told him:

> LEE: People came by his house. There were always people going in and out. Someone gave Bob a pair of boots. He put his foot in and said "Ow! A friend got in there" - you know how Jamaicans are. He said, "let's get in here" - in the boot, and he pulled a piece of copper wire out. It was embedded in the boot.
>
> A.C.: Do you believe it was radioactive?
>
> LEE: I didn't think so at the time, but I've always had my suspicions because Marley later broke his toe playing soccer, and when the bone wouldn't mend, the doctors found that the toe had cancer. The cancer metastasized throughout his body...[507]

"Had the wire been treated chemically with a carcinogenic toxin?" Constantine asks. "The appearance of [Carl] Colby at Marley's compound was certainly provocative..."[508] Lew-Lee believes that Marley's cancer can be traced to the soccer boots Carl Colby gave him before the Smile Jamaica Concert. "The argument is that the [ambush] assailants were hired by the CIA and when they failed to finish the job, the agency opted for a 'quieter' mode of assassination; artificially-induced cancer."[509] When Roger Steffens presented Carl Colby in an interview with Lew-Lee's account and Constantine's theory of Colby's cancer-causing pair

507 Constantine, *The Covert War Against Rock*, 135-136, 140-141.
508 Constantine, *Covert War Against Rock*, 135-136.
509 "The Dark Cloud Surrounding Bob Marley's Death," *BobMarleyLove.org* May 10, 2019.

of gift soccer boots, the son of CIA Master Spy expectedly denied the charge:

Carl Colby with a copy of *The Beat's* cover story 'The Night They Shot Bob Marley," Los Angeles, December 2001. From Steffens, 2017.

Frankly, I'm outraged that anyone would accuse me of doing anything to harm, much less lead to the death of, the incomparable Bob Marley, whom I consider to be one of the greatest musicians and artists since the birth of the cool in the 1950s. First of all, the truth is that I was a professional documentary filmmaker, brought down to Jamaica from New York by Chris Blackwell and Perry Henzell. To address this false and extremely inflammatory accusation directly, I was up at Chris Blackwell's house in the mountains above Kingston as part of this filmmaking effort. I was accompanied by Island Records publicist Jeff Walker. We felt that we had been commissioned by Chris Blackwell to make a film of the Smile Jamaica concert and about Bob, so we simply wanted to follow through and do our jobs. I had plenty of experience with unusual and somewhat unstable situations as a young boy, including living for three and a half years in Saigon, so the thought of going up to talk to a famous reggae musician like Bob, whom I admired greatly, was not something to be feared. I was excited. I was going to meet Bob Marley and it was my job to shoot a film about him-so I went. And, by the way, no one there knew who my father was-and by that time, December 5, 1976, my father had resigned from the CIA. He had been fired by President Gerald Ford. So, my word to this Alex Constantine is, please check your facts first-and your sources; simply shoddy, piss-poor journalism in my opinion and an outrageous defamation of my character.

The story about a boot being delivered is pure nonsense. I never saw or heard about any boot being delivered to Bob. And anyone who was there would know that Bob was in no mood for hijinks or in any way interested in boots. He was recuperating from some serious injuries and yet he was gracious enough to talk to Jeff and me about his music, about Jamaica, about the politics, and about himself - his hopes and dreams for Jamaica and for his people. He was not that accessible when we first got there. Yes, there were a few machete-wielding guys guarding the compound when we got there, but Jeff simply said we were from Island Records and the door was opened. Again, remember Island Records was Marley's record company-we were welcome. It took a couple of hours just hanging around to get to the point of approaching Bob and getting him to talk. Remember, he'd been shot-and he was recuperating, and he was exhausted.[510]

Some remarks are warranted. First, Carl Colby acknowledges that it was Chris Blackwell who brought him to Jamaica. Second, Carl Colby's statement is true but deceptive: "by that time, December 5, 1976, my father had resigned from the CIA. He had been fired by President Gerald Ford. So, my word to this Alex Constantine is, please check your facts first-and your sources; simply shoddy, piss-poor journalism..." While President Ford did *officially* replace Bill Colby as DCI with George Bush in December 1975, Bill Colby epitomized the motto, "Once CIA always CIA." He remained involved with the intelligence community and (likely) its operations long after his retirement from the Agency, as we saw. Still in 1978, over a year after the CIA-operation that targeted Marley at 56 Hope Road, Bill Colby was brought back to the CIA to help train the agents and to have his "brain picked" by CIA directors George Bush and Admiral Stansfield Turner. In one of those "little chats" I'm sure he offered the services of his son Carl Colby as an operational asset. "Some people believe that Carl Colby dispatched the gunmen who opened fire on Marley's home in 1976".[511] Carl Colby denies the allegation. There are reports that while on the island Carl Colby proclaimed that he could have an army of U.S. troops in Jamaica

510 Steffens, *So Much Things To Say*, 260-261.
511 Hua Hsu, "Manufacturing Bob Marley," *The New Yorker* July 17, 2017.

in twenty-fours with one call. He denies these reports also, of course.[512]

Third: While Carl Colby claims that "The story about a boot being delivered is pure nonsense" and that he "never saw or heard about any boot being delivered to Bob," Ian Shircore writes that "*Several* of Marley's friends, including film-maker and former Black Panther activist Lee Lew-Lee, claim to have seen him try on the boots and jab his toe."[513] An extremely important second witness is Bob Marley's own personal physician Dr. Carlton "Pee Wee" Fraser, who was reportedly a "trusted physician of Marley."[514] Dr. Fraser, who was present at Strawberry Hill on the occasion,[515] "supports an allegation that the reggae king was deliberately injected with cancer cells through a needle placed in a pair of shoes that was given to him."[516] We will return to Dr. Fraser below.

It's important to remember what Bill Colby's operational expertise was:

- As director of the CIA's covert operations, he pioneered U.S. counterinsurgency warfare and was the architect of many of the Agency's "dirtiest tricks."
- His religious crusade was halting a nation's slide to the left. To do this, he specialized in building up within that nation a fascist nationalism to counter the leftward movement. The election of Michael Manley as Prime Minister of Jamaica in 1972 moved the island toward the Left and with his public embrace of Democratic Socialism the CIA initiated a destabilization operation to bring down the

---

512 Steffens, *So Much Things To Say*, 262-263.
513 Ian Shircore, *Conspiracy: 49 Reasons to Doubt, 50 Reasons To Believe* (New York: John Blake Pub., 2012) Chapter 41.
514 Brian Bonitto, "'Skill' hails 'Pee Wee' Fraser," *Daily Observer* (Jamaica) November 22, 2021.
515 Goldman, *Book of Exodus*, 119; Salewicz, *Bob Marley*, 303-304.
516 Richard Johnson, "Doctor in Bob's house," *Jamaica Observer* May 11, 2021

196

Manley government, an operation that involved supporting the allegedly "fascist" politics of Edward Seaga and the training and arming of his supporters for "counterinsurgency" activities, i.e., killing Manley supporters or non-political civilians. This Jamaican blueprint was Bill Colby's.

- While stationed in East Asia Bill Colby was operationally responsible for the deaths of one million Indonesians and over 20,000 Vietnamese.
- It was Bill Colby who presented to the Senate Select Committee Hearing the CIA's secret "cancer-causing" and heart attack-inducing micro-bio-inoculator.

The whole Jamaican operation has the contours of Bill Colby's profile. In addition, the suggested "Murder-by-Cancer" operation against Bob Marley is operationally consistent with several CIA assassination plots against Castro during Bill Colby's time.

- *Toxic Gifts* – The CIA tried to exploit Castro's known indulgences with poisoned gifts. "Mr. [Sidney] Gottlieb...developed...an array of toxic gifts to be delivered to Fidel Castro."[517] The Agency wanted to kill the Cuban leader trough his love of cigars, so they prepared boxes of his favorite brand packed with explosives and laced with botulinum toxin. The weaponized cigars were to be given to Castro as gifts by a cooperating New York Police officer who was responsible for the leader's security while he visited the city. The Agency also wanted to kill Castro through his love of scuba diving, so they plotted to poison him with a diving suit that would be presented to him as gift. The suit would be contaminated with Madura foot fugus and with tuberculosis.

---

517 Tim Weiner, "Sidney Gottlieb, 80, Dies; Took LSD to C.I.A.," *The New York Times* March 10, 1999.

It is well-known that Bob Marley's two passions were music and football (soccer). Whenever he was not doing one, he was doing the other. Those close to him "couldn't figure out which Bob loved more music or football."[518] Throughout the 1970s Bob's tour manager was one of Jamaica's most renowned soccer players, Alan "Skill" Cole.[519] Thus,  the circumstance that the CIA exploited Marley's love for soccer to kill him with a trojan horse gift of football sneakers that were contaminated in some way with a toxin is standard Agency *modus operandi*. Weaponizing a target's shoes is also Agency *MO*. The CIA planned to dust Castro's shoes with the toxin thallium when he put them outside his hotel room door to be shinned. As Charles Kongo Soo observes, "There is an eerie similarity between Marley and Castro involving poisoned shoes....In the case of Marley, the CIA allegedly used cancer in his shoes, for Castro they placed the highly toxic poison thallium salts in his shoes."[520]

- *Micro-bio-inoculators* – According to witnesses, when Bob put his right foot into the football boot gifted him by Carl Colby, son of master "Gray Man" Bill Colby, there

---

518 Words of prominent Jamaican soccer figure and Marley associate Carl Brown. In Jeff Gorra, "Bob Marley's True Passion: Football," *Artist Wave* May 11, 2016

519 On Marley and soccer see *Rhythm of the Game*, Episode 4 of the 12-part documentary series, *Legacy* Directed by Marcus McDougald.

520 Charles Kongo Soo, "Cancer the secret weapon?" *Trinidad & Tobago Guardian* February 26, 2012.

was a small copper wire hidden in there that is believed to have been treated chemically with a carcinogenic toxin. The wire served as a *micro-bio-inoculator,* inoculating Bob's foot with a biological substance. This is the theory, and it is consistent with CIA *MO.* The Paper-Mate ballpoint pen prepared by the CIA for a "Castro job" was outfitted with a tiny needle, a makeshift hypodermic syringe that, with a "non-discernable" poke, can deliver the toxin Black leaf 40 into its victim. The hidden needle is a micro-bio-inoculator. Most famous of course is the dart gun presented to the Church Committee by Bill Colby himself. The ammunition was a poison frozen into a tiny, quarter inch dart the width of a human hair. This dart is a non-discernable flying syringe, a micro-bio-inoculator that can deliver a carcinogenic toxin.

- *Kill Team Disguised as Film Crew* – The claim is that the film crew from New York hired by Chris Blackwell to film the Smile Jamaica concert actually consisted of a Kill Team led by Carl Colby, son of the architect the CIA's "dirtiest tricks" Bill Colby. Posing as a camera crew, the assassins were able to get close to the target to deliver the poisoned gift of football sneakers. This is consistent with the CIA operation five years earlier in Chile to kill Socialist President Salvador Allende. The assassins posed as a film crew equipped with counterfeit press credentials, allowing them to infiltrate a press conference with camera's containing a camouflaged gun to kill the Chilean president.

All of this indicates that the proposed "murder-by-cancer" operation that targeted Marley on Sunday December 5, 1976, possessed all of the hallmarks of a traditional CIA operation: the Kill Team disguised as a film crew; exploiting the target's known love (soccer) with a trojan horse gift (soccer cleats); the use of a micro-bio-inoculator (copper wire) in the gifted shoes to deliver the lethal toxin (a carcinogenic substance). These events of

199

Sunday, December 5 at Strawberry Hill must be seen in the context of the events of Friday December 3 at 56 Hope Road: the CIA-supported shooting of Bob Marley. The CIA's known involvement in Friday's *failed* assassination attempt makes the charge of a second CIA-involved assassination attempt on Sunday – a *biological* assassination attempt – eminently credible.

VII. *Bob Marley's Galloping Cancer*

But The Product – the active carcinogenic virus – what happened to it? If stored at the temperature of liquid nitrogen it could be kept indefinitely, and could be brought back into tissue cultures and animals at any time, as potent as ever...It is quite possible the carcinogenic virus strain has been kept frozen but alive in some secret laboratory to this day - James Stewat Campbell, "The Project: Unethical Human Experiments, Carcinogenic Viruses, and Murder during the Cold War" (2013)

As an avid soccer player Bob suffered occasional foot injuries throughout the years, including an injury to his right toe that was pricked by the copper wire in the CIA-gifted soccer boots. These prior injuries always healed on their own.[521] After the prick at Strawberry Hill, things took a different turn. While on tour in France in the spring of 1977, Bob and the Wailers played football games. In a May 13, 1977, soccer game in Paris against French journalists Bob injured his right big toe again. The hotel doctor removed the toenail and bandaged the toe. This time the wound deteriorated. Later that summer while in London Bob visited a doctor who was shocked at the ugly appearance of the toe, as if it was "eating away."[522] A skin biopsy was done from the toe and malignant melanoma (skin cancer) was diagnosed. Instead of amputating the toe, Marley opted for a surgical excision to cut away the cancerous tissue and do a skin graft. This was done at

---

521 Steffens, *So Much Things To Say*, 282-283.
522 Dr. Cleland Gooding, "A Death by Skin Cancer? The Bob Marley Story," *Repeating Islands* April 15, 2011.

Cedars of Lebanon Hospital (now University of Miami Hospital) by Dr. William Bacon, a renowned Black orthopedic surgeon. Dr. Bacon was reportedly one of the ten top orthopedic surgeons in the world, but he was also in the military for twenty years and the orthopedic doctor for the U.S. Army before he turned to private practice in Miami. The surgery was reported as a tremendous success. His personal physician Dr. Fraser said, "we cured Bob as the cancer in his toe had not spread, and everything was fine."[523]

> **Cindy Breakspear** (Bob Marley's girlfriend and baby mother): "And I mean that healed beautifully. It healed really, really beautifully, and he used to take good care of it and everything. It really healed well and he wouldn't allow it to get injured in any way. The skin over it of course was very tender, having been taken from the leg, the upper thigh area. So it wasn't quite like the skin that would be on the toe. It was softer. It wasn't hardened or calloused. So one needed to be careful, what shoes you wore and everything, so nothing irritated it and rubbed on it too much, but it healed beautifully."[524]

> **Gilly Gilbert** (Bob Marley's road manager): "The skin graft was in early '78 in Miami, or late '77. He thought it was cured at that point, 'cause it healed. They gave him a cap to put over it if he was going to play soccer. He played after, he played hard soccer. It was like a sponge thing. He never talked about it over the next two and a half years. At the start of the U.S. leg of the '80 tour he had an exam that he passed. To this day I just can't understand. Bob played soccer in Australia, Zimbabwe, everywhere we go and he was playing like a champion. Even before we went on the U.S. tour in '80, we had a send-off soccer game in southwest Miami here against a Haitian team, Am-Jam United, my team in Miami. He was running well like anybody else, he was kicking the ball like a bullet. If Bob was feeling pain I would have seen it while he was playing.[525]

But everything was not fine, and therein lies a great mystery. By the summer of 1980 the cancer was metastasizing through Bob's body. "The surgical excision done and the skin graft

---

523 Richard Johnson, "Doctor in Bob's house," *Jamaica Observer* May 11, 2021
524 Steffens, *So Much Things To Say*, 285.
525 Steffens, *So Much Things To Say*, 285-286.

was ineffective or simply too late."[526] In September 1980, Bob began a nationwide tour across the US, starting in Boston and followed by New York, even though he clearly wasn't in the best health condition for such a strenuous tour. "According to sources, he did not feel well and saw a doctor who gives him clearance to go on tour!"[527] This may be the doctor who "passed" Bob's medical exam as mentioned by Gilly Gilbert. During the Madison Square Garden performance on September 19 Bob Marley fell ill and almost fainted, causing him to cut short the show.

The next morning while jogging through Central Park Bob Marley suffered a stroke and collapsed with a seizure. His team rushed him to the Sloan-Kettering Cancer Center in Manhattan, New York City. Tests disclosed the cancer was now aggressively spreading to his vital organs, his liver, lungs, and brain. According to Marley's manager at the time Danny Sims, a doctor at Sloan Kettering said Bob had "more cancer in him than I've seen with a live human being."[528] The reggae legend was suffering from *a galloping cancer*! Neurologists at the hospital advised him that, given his brain cancer, he had about a month to live. Bob received a few radiation treatments but checked himself out of the New York hospital.

An obvious question is how Bob went from a successful surgical excision and healed toe in 1977 to a galloping cancer spread to his lungs, liver, and brain in 1980? We can understand Gilly Gilbert's exacerbation: "At the start of the U.S. leg of the '80 tour he had an exam that he passed. To this day I just can't understand." It cannot be ruled out that any number of the doctors who treated Marley over the years were recruited into the medical conspiracy against him. Prominent Bahamian doctor Dr. Philip Thompson of the University of The West Indies, who treated Bob Marley at some point, reportedly believed that Bob was murdered. He said some highly-connected people tried to coerce him (Dr.

---

526 Gooding, "A Death by Skin Cancer?"
527 Gooding, "A Death by Skin Cancer?"
528 Hua Hsu, "Manufacturing Bob Marley," *The New Yorker* July 17, 2017.

Thompson) into ceasing Marley's treatment. Dr. Thompson says he refused to succumb to their pressure.[529]

Bob's physician Dr. Fraser is sure he knows the answer to this riddle. He gave an interview with *Jamaica Observer* in 2021.

Dr. Fraser

Bob Marley died of acral lentiginous melanoma on May 11, 1981, after being diagnosed in 1977. At the time of his death and for many years after, many fans believed that he was purposefully injected with cancer. It's a theory that many fervent fans still believe. A recent interview that his personal physician, Dr. Carlton "Pee Wee" Fraser, had with Jamaica Observer may lend some credence to their theory. He believes that Bob Marley may have been injected with the disease a little while after the assassination attempt at Hope Road. In fact, he added that he believed he is aware of the method of delivery. Most people believe that Marley's woes started after a football injury but Dr Fraser believes differently. He believes that Marley's troubles all started with the gift of a pair of sneakers.[530]

Dr. Fraser thought the surgical excision by Dr. Bacon cured Bob of the melanoma. When he was told the cancer metastasized, Fraser was incredulous. "How could this be?" he questioned. "There were no medical factors to show how this manifested. We had done all the technical scans and X-rays to make sure there was no evidence of cancer in his toe." Then Dr. Fraser says with certainty, "They definitely know what they did."[531]

What did "they" do?

---

529 "The Dark Cloud Surrounding Bob Marley's Death," *BobMarleyLove.org* May 10, 2019.
530 Shirvan Williams, "Bob Marley 40 Years After Death Personal Doctor Suspects Foul Play," *Urban Islandz* May 11, 2021.
531 Richard Johnson, "Doctor in Bob's house," *Jamaica Observer* May 11, 2021

Sometime after the surgical excision in 1977 and Bob resumed touring he began to have "strange maladies" which included nose bleeds and headaches. According to Dr. Fraser, what "they" did was deliberately infect Bob *with cancer a second time,* during his tour to promote the Uprising album.[532] The promotional tour was May 30-July 13, 1980, in Europe and September 1980 in the U.S.

VIII. *Black Messiah and the Nazi Doctor*

Around the world, Bob Marley is seen as the Redeemer figure returning to lead this planet out of confusion. Some will come out and say it directly: that Bob Marley is the reincarnation of Jesus Christ long waited by much of the world. In such an interpretation of his life, the cancer that killed him is inevitably described as a modern version of a crucifixion.[533]

Being distrustful of traditional Western medicine which had declared of Bob in New York, "He is dead, he's a dead man walking,"[534] Bob Marley tried the alternative medicine of Dr. Josef Issels, a "holistic comprehensive immunotherapist" who had a clinic in Rottach-Egern, a small village in Bavaria, Germany. In November 1980 Marley travelled there with his physician Dr. Carlton 'Pee Wee' Frazier, his manager Alan "Skill" Cole, and his cook Glenford 'Early Bird' Phipps and checked into Issels' clinic. According to Cole, "no one close to Marley knew about Issels' ties to the Nazis."[535]

During WWII, it seems, Dr. Issels could be found plying his "research" skills in Poland, at the Auschwitz concentration camp, working aside Dr.

---

532 Shirvan Williams, "Bob Marley 40 Years After Death Personal Doctor Suspects Foul Play," *Urban Islandz* May 11, 2021.

533 Hakeem Babalola, "Remembering A True Prophet, Bob Marley," *Sahara Reports* February 6, 2012.

534 A Sloan-Kettering doctor said this to Danny Sims, Bob's manager. Steffens, *So Much Things To Say*, 387.

535 Howard Campbell, "Dr. Josef Issels: A man of mystery," *Daily Observer* (Jamaica) April 6, 2021.

Joseph Mengele, no less, according to several of the Wailers who have investigated the German "alternative" practitioner's past. Bob Marley, the "dangerous" racial enemy of fascists everywhere, had placed his life in the hands of a Nazi doctor, Mengele's protegé, an accomplice of the "Angel of Death" in horrific medical atrocities committed against racial "subhumans."[536]

The first encounter between the prophet from Jamaica and the doctor from Nazi Germany was revealing. Bob's mother, who spent considerable time in Bavaria and got to know the Nazi doctor up close, tells us:

> I wasn't present when Nesta [=Bob Marley] first came to Issels, but someone who was there told me that Issels looked Nesta up and down and said, "I hear you're one of the most dangerous black men in the world." Nesta was at this time completely bald from the chemotherapy he'd received in New York. He looked gaunt and sickly..."But you don't look so dangerous to me," Issels added, eyeing the pitifully sick figure standing before him. Knowing that wretch as I now do, I can imagine the scorn he must have put into that look, those hard-hearted words.[537]

"I hear you're one of the most dangerous black men in the world. But you don't look so dangerous to me" – said the former Nazi

---

536 Constantine, *Covert War Against Rock*, 141.
537 Booker, *Bob Marley, My Son*, 191.

doctor to the ailing Black "prophet." According to Constantine's research, Issels told Bob that the person who alerted Issels to the fact that Bob was such a dangerous Black man advised Issels not to treat him.[538] Issels began treating Bob Marley, to notable benefit, but then Issels' reportedly turned to torturing him and hastening his agonizing death, according to Marley's close associates.[539] Lew-Lee recalls that Marley

> was getting all of this crazy, crazy medical treatment in Bavaria. I know this because Ray von Evans, who played in Marley's group, we were very close friends, [told me] Bob was receiving these medical treatments, and Ray would come by every two or three months, 1979–80, and told me: "Yeah, mon, they're killing Bob. They are KILLING Bob." I said, "What do you mean 'they are killing Bob?'" "No, no, mon," he said. "Dis Dr. Issels, he's a Nazi!" We found out later that Dr. Issels was a Nazi doctor. And he had worked with Dr. Mengele.[540]

Cedella Booker, Bob's Mom, shares as well:

> I myself witnessed Issels' rough treatment of Nesta. One time I went with Nesta to the clinic, and we settled down in a treatment room. Issels came in and announced to Nesta, 'I'm going to give you a needle.' Then, as he prepared his needle, he said over his shoulder to me, 'Mother, you better go out.' 'No,' I replied, 'I ain't going nowhere.' Issels shrugged as if he didn't care. He gave me a long hard look, then he went to stand over Nesta, who was lying on the examination table. He rolled over the waist of Nesta's pants, lifted up his shirt, and plunged the needle straight into Nesta's navel right down to the syringe. Nesta grunted and winced. He could only lie there helplessly, writhing on the table, trying his best to hide his pain. 'Jesus Christ,' I heard myself muttering. Issels pulled out the needle. Then he left the room with a swish. 'Imagine, Mamma,' Nesta

---

538 Fred Zindi, "How Did Bob Marley Die?" *The Herald* (Zimbabwe) October 4, 2015.

539 Constantine, *Covert War Against Rock*, 142: "Marley, unaware of his physician's past, was placed on a regimen of exercise, vaccines (some illegal), ozone injections, vitamin and trace minerals, and other treatments. In time, Dr. Issels also introduced torture. Long needles were plunged through Marley's stomach to the spine. The patient-victim was told that this was part of his "treatment." The torture continued until Marley foundered on the threshold of death."

540 Constantine, *Covert War Against Rock*, 141.

groaned, 'de man push de needle right inna me navel. Right down to me belly!' He was nearly in tears.[541]

I made three visits to be with Nesta during the six months in Germany...With every visit I found him smaller, frailer, thinner. As the months of dying dragged past, the suffering was etched all over his face. He would fall into fits of shaking, when he would lose all control and shiver from head to toe like a coconut leaf in a breeze. His eyes would turn in his head, rolling in their sockets until even the white jelly was quivering.[542]

Cedella Booker and Bob Marley with Dr. Josef Issels

Marley's torment was aggravated by forced starvation, which must have *devastated his immune system* and rushed his demise.[543] Cedella booker tells us

---

541 Booker, *Bob Marley, My Son*, 191.
542 Cedella Marley Booker with Anthony C. Winkler, *Bob Marley, My Son* (London: Taylor Trade Publishing, 2003)179.
543 Constantine, *Covert War Against Rock*, 142-143.

Part of Issels' treatment required putting Nesta on a strict on-and-off diet. For a whole week sometimes Nesta would be allowed no nourishment other than what he got intravenously. Constantly hungry, even starving, he wasted away to a skeleton. To watch my first-born shrivel up to skin and bone ripped at my mother's heart. Moreover, with no solid food in his stomach, Nesta's tripe knotted up and became blocked. Issels had to cut open his belly to clear it.[544]

"Less than 70 pounds, he was too weak to lift the guitar he hardly left alone for 20 years," recounts friend Isaac Fergusson.[545] "It is believed that Issels injected Marley with poison." [546] "His hair had fallen out from the radiation treatment, leaving him completely bald," Cedella Booker tells us. "He was looking thin, haggard and gaunt. He tired easily, his body being full of the poison of cancer added to Issels' medicine."[547] "It would drag on so, for one long painful month after the other, and every day would be a knife that death stabbed and twisted anew in an already open, bleeding wound."

Like Jesus, in Bob Marley's last days he was surrounded by all women – his male comrades had left and given him up to die in Germany, according to his mother.

With death tiptoeing towards Nesta's (Bob's) bed, all his male friends, his so-called *pasayros* (buddies), had left him. There were only women now left behind in the rented house to care for Nesta: me, Diane Jobson and Denise Mills. We had gone from a full house ringing with the chatter, bustle and liveliness of Jamaican men and women to an empty, quite house with three solitary, mournful women.[548]

With Bob Marley completely emaciated, weak, and in agony, Issels' kicked him out of his clinic. Cedealla Booker recounts:

---

544 Booker, *Bob Marley, My Son*, 180.
545 Isaac Fergusson, " 'So Much Things To Say': The Journey of Bob Marley," *Village Voice* May 18, 1982, p. 146.
546 Fred Zindi, "How Did Bob Marley Die?" *The Herald* (Zimbabwe) October 4, 2015.
547 Booker, *Bob Marley, My Son*, 181.
548 Booker, *Bob Marley, My Son*, 206.

On the Wednesday of that same week, Dr. Issels returned from holiday and came to examine Nesta in the hospital. He stomped into the room without knocking and went to stand over Nesta's bed. I was in a chair, reading. Diane was also present, keeping vigil. Finally, after rummaging over Nesta and completing his examination, Issles glanced up at me and said bluntly, 'He's not going to live.' 'What?' I cried. 'It suits him to go home,' Issels said calmly. 'He can leave tomorrow.' I began to cry. Issels glanced stonily at me. 'Dr. Issels,' I asked through my tears, 'don't you think it would be wise for a doctor to go with Nesta on de plane?' 'He don't need that,' he said gruffly. 'But is a ten-hour flight. And we'll be up dere in the breeze with nobody to look after him if something happen.' He stared at me. 'I'll get a nurse to go with you,' he finally said. Then he walked out the room without a backward look.[549]

After six months in Germany, Bob boarded a plane home to *Jamaica*. However, on the flight his condition worsened, and the plane was diverted to Miami where he was rushed to Cedars Lebanon Hospital. On May 11, 1981, Bob Marley died. He was 36 years old.

Dion Wilson, a friend of Marley's when he stayed in Delaware with his mother in 1966, tells a telling story. While sitting in a tree one day with a young Nesta and another friend, Ibis Pitts, Nesta started talking to them about Jesus Christ and how his mission began at age thirty-three. Then young Marley said: "Me gwan die at t'irty-six, jus' like Christ."[550]

549 Booker, *Bob Marley, My Son*, 206-207.
550 White, *Catch a Fire*, 298.

Book II

Killing The King of Pop

Part 5

Murder Was The (Real) Case

Chapter Eight

Introductory Summary

syn•ec•do•che – a figure of speech in which a part of something is made
to represent the whole or vice versa.

Michael Jackson's life and his death can be described as a
synecdoche for all of Black America, especially Black men in
America. The manner in which he was killed – we say murdered –
has become the trendy cause of death of scores of young Black
men and women. Hip Hop has been used to normalize this cause
of death: Death By Polypharmacy.

There is compelling evidence that the death of Michael
Jackson on June 25, 2009 was no accident – it was not the result
of negligence but of deliberate decision-making. Michael Jackson
was murdered. Prosecuting Attorney during the Michael Jackson
manslaughter trial David Walgren said: "It was a pharmaceutical
experiment on Michael Jackson. It was an obscene experiment in
2009…" It was not propofol that killed Michael, but a chemical
cocktail only one ingredient of which was propofol. There are very
good reasons why some of the other chemicals of that fatal cocktail
totally disappeared from the conversation. In fact, just as Dr.
Conrad Murray was clearly the *fall guy* in a much bigger
conspiracy, so too was propofol the *fall drug* of that much bigger
chemical cocktail that killed Michael Jackson. Michael had a
premonition that he would die like Elvis Presley died, and he did.
The evidence is strong that Elvis's death was a Mafia hit by means
of a so-called *syringe job*: death by chemical ingestion or injection.
The Mafia likewise put a contract out on Michael Jackson's life,
and along with the structural parallels between Elvis's and
Michael's death, there are also important *personnel* connections
between Elvis Presley's demise and Michael Jackson's demise.
This is not pure speculation. These charges are sustained by a
tremendous amount of evidence, including most importantly the

215

explosive testimony of a government witness who was a high-level investigator out of the State Attorney General's office as well as the detailed revelations of *a whistleblower – one involved in the plot who spilled a whole lot of beans!*

Michael Jackson was likely neither gay nor a child molester. Rather, he was vindictively framed by a circle of gay child molesters. And then, he was murdered. Hollywood's "Jewish Gay Mafia" with its pedophile ring *targeted* Michael Jackson with a slanderous media and legal campaign falsely charging him *with their own crime*: gay pedophilia. And then after sinking Michael in tremendous debt, a "Rich Entertainment Conglomerate" organized a "comeback concert" which, according to a key whistleblower, was only a cover for a murder that was planned: the murder of Michael Jackson and the hijacking of his tremendously valuable asset, the Beatles catalogue.

Hollywood has for a very long time had a very dark underbelly: organized pedophilia. This organized pedophilia intersected with gay prostitution networks. Powerful Hollywood figures lorded over these networks and rings. Some of these Hollywood figures and their "Pedophile Agenda" targeted Michael Jackson as far back as 1986. In that year the pro-pedophilia group NAMbLA (North American Man/boy Love Association) met in Hollywood and, taking note of Michael Jackson's very public though very innocent relationship with children, NAMbLA members discussed Michael Jackson as a potential celebrity poster-boy for *their cause* to normalize pedophilia in society. One of the attendees was Chilean free-lance journalist Victor Gutierrez. Gutierrez left that meeting in 1986 with his life's mission defined: to "out" Michael Jackson as a gay pedophile. Not only was Gutierrez an agent of NAMbLA's in this cause: he also worked undercover for the Los Angeles Police Department and he collaborated with the FBI in targeting Michael Jackson. This contributed to the false tagging of Jackson as a pedophile. All three agencies were invested in "converting" Michael into a gay pedophile in the public eye. Victor Gutierrez - with NAMbLa, the LAPD, and the FBI with him – is the one man who is most responsible for the false "Michael Jackson is a child molester" narrative. His fingerprint is all over the false narrative that was constructed around Michael Jackson.

While at some distance a "Pedophile Agenda" was targeting Michael Jackson, closer to home a "Gay Agenda" was also literally targeting him. By 1990 Michael Jackson had befriended and surrounded himself with prominent figures who were reputedly members of Hollywood's "Gay Mafia": David Geffen, its putative head, was Michael's financial advisor; Sandy Gallin was his manager; Steven Spielberg was the fullfiller of his movie dreams; Arnold Klein was his dermatologist. These Jewish and allegedly gay "best friends" of Michael turned on him, becoming his toxic frenemies. According to one account, the rupture occurred because the alleged head of the "Gay Mafia" David Geffen attempted to kiss and seduce Michael, who rejected the sexual advance. From that point on, the Gay Mafia reputedly worked clandestinely to ruin Michael: financially, socially, even physically.

All of these various hostile forces converged during that fateful year of 1993: the year of conspiracy and of trauma for Michael. Michael was unnecessarily but no doubt deliberately made a drug addict by doctors who served interests that were not Michael's: Michael Jackson was literally *chemically assaulted*. Michael was falsely accused of child molestation; he was forced to cancel the last leg of his *Dangerous* tour, thereby incurring great financial loss and debt. In many ways 1993 laid the foundation for the rest of Michael Jackson's career, his life, and his death. Almost everything that happened to Michael subsequently was anchored in the events of 1993 and their consequences. The Pedophile Agenda, the Gay Mafia, corrupt LAPD, greedy Hollywood Jews, Sony execs, all of these forces converged and were behind the scenes pulling the strings of Michael Jackson's life drama of 1993.

But really, Michael's demise was probably set in 1985, when he showed himself to be one of if not *the best* business minds in the industry when he purchased for $47.5 million the company that housed the prized music catalogue of the Beatles, ATV. This genius move nevertheless made Michael probably the most *marked man* in Hollywood. Everybody wanted this asset after he

217

acquired it. Ultimately, a "Rich Entertainment Conglomerate" consisting of Italian and Jewish Mafia figures, Gay Mafia figures, AEG Live executives, and Sony Music executives, all had a hand in separating Michael Jackson from his $1 – $2 billion asset.

Due to the financial damage which the 1993 False Charges and Chemical Assault did to Michael, Sony was able to acquire half of Michael's catalogue in 1995. Sony wanted it all, and conspired behind Michael's back to own it all. Behind the scenes of the very public dispute in 2002 between Michael Jackson and Tommy Mottola, CEO of Sony Music, Mottola was on company conference calls threatening to ruin Michael Jackson in order to seize Michael's catalogue. Michael believed that Sony deliberately sabotaged the success of his *Invincible* album in 2001. Sony *did* have something to gain by Michael's career failing: they hoped he would have to sell the remaining half of his catalogue to them and at a low price. A 2003 private investigation commissioned by Michael Jackson turned up a scheme by Michael's lawyer, John Branca, and Michael's nemesis Tommy Mottola to defraud Michael and divert his money into offshore accounts in the Caribbean. Michael fired Branca and declared that he is to never have anything to do with him again. Within a year Mottola was terminated at Sony. Mottola was a longtime ally of David Geffen. Mottola, Branca, Geffen: these became very formidable enemies of Michael Jackson. Michael had good reason to suspect that they were working behind the scenes during the 2005 child molestation case, a case built on false charges. Michael won the court case and was acquitted and exonerated of these charges.

And then, 2009. The Beginning of the End. In January Michael Jackson was approached by Randy Phillips, the Jewish CEO of AEG Live CEO, about a series of concerts in London. Michael had reportedly already rebuffed such an offer in the past. But this time was different. AEG, the parent company of AEG Live, is headed by Jewish billionaire Phillip Anschutz, who is good friends with Tom Barrack. Barrack owns Colony Capital, which bought the $23 million loan on Michael's Jackson's Neverland Ranch in 2008, saving it from foreclosure. As part of the terms of the rescue, Michael would agree to allow Barrack's friend, Phillip

Anschutz and AEG, to stage Michael's comeback with a number of concerts at AEG's newly renovated O2 Arena in London. This is how the "This Is It" tour came about. But the AEG Live executives used hook and crook, lies and deception to actually get Michael to sign on the dotted line. They had a transparent disdain for Michael Jackson as a person.

Tom Barrack also co-owned Sunrise Colony, which owned the mortgage on the $1.2 million mansion of one Dr. Conrad Murray in the Red Rock Section of Las Vegas. Murray was over $100,000 behind in mortgage payments and Barrack and Sunrise Colony were foreclosing on the property. This is how Dr. Murray ended up as Michael Jackson's physician for the Tour, and this is why Dr. Murray was compelled to serve AEG's interests, not Michael Jackson's interests. Because Murray was indebted to Tom Barrack, Murray was made beholden to Barrack's friend, Phillip Anschutz and AEG.

While the contract bound Michael to 10 shows and AEG backdoored 50 shows, the plan was *never* to do *any* London concerts. This is why AEG did not bother to get Conrad Murray licensed in England. This we learn from Dr. Arnold Klein, the Whistleblower. The contract that Michael's treacherous lawyers signed with AEG had a clause in it that, if the concerts are cancelled because Michael is incapable of performing, AEG could assume ownership of Michael Jackson's chief asset which he put up as collateral: his catalogue. AEG Live thus allegedly secured Arnold Klein to drug Michael with Demerol, "the pharmacological equivalent of heroin" and secured Conrad Murray allegedly to drug Michael with the hypnotic drug propofol. Michael was a healthy, non-drug abuser in January of 2009. By June AEG Live (through Dr. Arnold Klein and Dr. Conrad Murray) had made Michael Jackson a desperately ill drug addled victim. The plan, according to the Whistleblower, was to chemically maintain Michael Jackson in a state of continuous confusion and compliance and to take advantage of his reduced mental capacity. The incapacitation made Michael incompetent to make rational decisions. This is allegedly how AEG Live got Michael to re-sign his enemy John Branca as his lawyer. AEG Live reportedly kept

219

Michael drugged in order to physically incapacitate him as well. By making Michael unable to perform at rehearsals, AEG could use that as a [false] pretext to "pull the plug" on the show, charge Michael with anticipatory breach of contract, and take possession of his assets, particularly the catalogue as well as the insurance payout.

The chemical concoction used to control Michael included a very dark drug: Midazolam, also called Versed. This drug is used as a part of lethal injection executions in some states; it is also used as a date rape drug because it forces compliance ("patient control") and then amnesia. Midazolam/Versed was also the "preferred drug" during the CIA's torture and drug experimentation program called Project Medication, launched immediately after the events of 9/11. One of the purposes of Project Medication was to use Midazolam/Versed to induce in a prisoner the state of "learned helplessness," a condition in which a person suffers from a sense of powerlessness. AEG-hired doctors (Murray and Klein) induced in Michael Jackson a state of learned helplessness and the same "preferred drug" of the CIA was used to do it. It appears that the death of Michael Jackson on June 25 was caused by a potent injection of Demerol which may have fatally reacted with the Midazolam already present in Michael's system. While Dr. Murray was eventually convicted of involuntary manslaughter, his conduct that resulted in the death of Michael seems to fit the requirements of second-degree murder, specifically the State of California's Depraved Heart Murder.

June 19, 2009, can be considered the day that marked the beginning of the end for Michael Jackson. Kenny Ortega, the show director for the *This Is It* tour, and Randy Phillips decided on that day to "pull the plug" on the show and on Michael Jackson. On that day all financial support to Michael was cut off. On June 23rd, AEG Live contacted Lloyd's of London to try to push through the new insurance policy covering the 50 shows. The first policy covering the 10 shows went through because the then-healthy, non-drug abusing Michael Jackson passed the initial physical exam "with flying colors." However, Lloyd's of London required a second, more extensive physical exam in order to extend the policy to cover the additional shows, and now Michael was a very sick, drug addled mess. He would have never passed that second physical exam, and failure would have dashed ALL of AEG Live's dreams of a mega insurance payout or *any* payout. Lloyd's of London scheduled that certain-doom physical exam for June 26, 2009. This is why Michael Jackson was dead on June 25. The initial insurance policy that AEG Live negotiated had a drug overdose provision, allowing AEG Live to collect the insurance if Michael Jackson died of a non-illicit drug overdose. Only hours after Michael Jackson was killed by a drug cocktail by AEG Live's employee Dr. Conrad Murray, AEG Live filed its insurance claim.

Chapter Nine

"Die Like Elvis"

I.   *"You aren't going to kill the artist, are you?"*

Despite a very rough week of being sick, emaciated, and suffering from alternating cold and hot spells such that he had to be sent home from rehearsal at the Staples Center on June 19th, on Michael Jackson's last night on earth Wednesday, June 24, 2009 during what would be his final rehearsal for his planned London concert run ("This Is It"), the King of Pop experienced a burst of energy and had his best performance in months, according to witnesses. "He came on stage and he was electric. It was like he had been holding back and suddenly he was performing as one remembered him in the past," recalled lighting director Patrick Woodroffe.[551] Michael might have found a reason to "just beam with gladness" as he did what he did best on that stage,[552] but unbeknownst to him a darkness was playing out behind the scenes that night.

According to Michael Jackson's son Prince, while Michael was remarkably "bursting with enthusiasm" on stage at the Staples Center that night, Randy Phillips, CEO of the concert promoter AEG Live was at Michael's Los Angeles home. Young Prince saw Phillips engaged in a "heated conversation" with Dr. Conrad Murray, the physician who would administer the drugs that would kill Michael Jackson by lunchtime the next day. According to Prince, the AEG Live executive "looked aggressive," even

---

551 Anita Singh, "Video: Michael Jackson's weird and wonderful life," *Telegraph* June 26, 2009.
552 Chris Lee and Harriet Ryan, "Michael Jackson's last rehearsal: 'just beaming with gladness'," *Los Angeles Times* June 27, 2009.

grabbing Murray's elbow. What were they arguing about? Why all of the aggression and, apparently, coercion? Was Phillips demanding something from Dr. Murray that evening which Dr. Murray was resisting? When Prince called his dad on the phone and informed him Phillips was there, Michael instructed his son to ask if Phillips wanted anything to eat or drink.[553] A kind gesture, despite the fact that at times when Michael was home Prince often saw his father on the phone with AEG Live executives and witnessed conversations that frequently ended with Michael in tears; Prince would overhear Michael say after such calls: "They're going to kill me, they're going to kill me."[554] On Michael's last night alive, sometime after Phillips' aggressive and heated conversation with Dr. Murray, who was *Phillips'* employee rather than Michael's,[555] Dr. Murray began administering to Michael the fatal chemical cocktail that would hours later rob the world of much more than the "king" of popular music. Rather, what was killed on June 25, 2009, was "the Archangel of sound, song, and dance" and a "herald of the Messiah," in the revealing words of Michael Jackson's close friend and confidant, The Honorable Minister Louis Farrakhan.[556]

The words that Prince overheard from his father, "They're going to kill me, they're going to kill me," were neither rhetorical nor rare. The plot to kill Michael was a preoccupation of his. Following his death there was talk of "post-it notes" scattered around Michael's room. The L.A. detectives working on (*sic*) the

---

553 Marc Hogan, "Michael Jackson Feared for His Life Before the End, Son Testifies," *Spin* June 27, 2013; "'Sorry kids…Dad's dead': Prince Jackson reveals how Conrad Murray broke news of King of Pop's passing," *Daily Mail* June 26, 2013; "Michael Jackson's son Prince says father feared concert promoter," *India Today* June 27, 2013.
554 Hogan, "Michael Jackson Feared for His Life."
555 Steve Knopper, "Why AEG Live Won the Michael Jackson Lawsuit," *Rolling Stone* October 4, 2013.
556 The Honorable Minister Farrakhan, "The Crucifixion of Michael Jackson and All Responsible Black Leadership," Mosque Maryam July 26, 2009 @ https://www.youtube.com/watch?v=JnoOa_A45dg; Richard Muhammad, "Farrakhan reveals truth about attacks on Michael Jackson, Black leadership," *The Final Call* July 28, 2009.

case presented these notes as quite benign: "There were post-it notes, or pieces of paper taped all over the room and mirrors and doors with little slogans or phrases. I don't know if they were lyrics or thoughts. Some of them seemed like poems," claimed Detective Orlando Martinez.[557] But motivating statements like "I am so grateful that I am a magnet for miracles," were accompanied by much darker notes with pleas like "help get these people out of my life" and warnings like "They are trying to murder me."[558]

The nature of these notes was illustrated by the collection of letters and notes passed by Michael weeks before his death to German businessman and, reportedly, friend Michael Jacobshagen, who shared them with journalist Daphne Barak. The messages on these notes included: "the system wants to kill me for my catalogue"; "I'm scared about my life" because of AEG; "I'm afraid someone is trying to murder me."[559] Journalist Ian Halperin reports that members of Michael Jackson's circle told him "[Michael] had nightmares about being murdered" and "when he did sleep, he had nightmares that he was going to be murdered...He said he thought he'd die before doing the London concerts."[560] He did. According to emails revealed during the wrongful-death trial against AEG Live brought by mother Katherine Jackson and Michael's children, Michael even asked producers at one of the rehearsals, "You aren't going to kill the artist, are you?"[561] This was June 19th, six days before the artist was indeed killed.

557 Tyler McDanold, "'Killing Michael Jackson' Reveals Scene Of Death Contained Pictures Of Babies And A Child's Doll," *The Inquisitr* June 20, 2019.
558 Sean Michaels, "Michael Jackson was murdered, says his sister La Toya," *The Guardian* June 23, 2011.
559 James Beal, "Plot To Kill Jacko: Michael Jackson feared he would be murdered in notes written just weeks before his death," *The Sun* June 27, 2017; Jack Shepherd, "Michael Jackson predicted he would be murdered just before his death," *Independent* May 7, 2017.
560 Ian Halperin, "'I'm better off dead. I'm done': Michael Jackson's fateful prediction just a week before his death," *Daily Mail* June 29 2009.
561 Nancy Dillion, "Michael Jackson feared for his safety during 'This Is It' tour, emails reveal," *New York Daily News* May 30, 2013. Dillion is wrong when she says: "[Jon] Hougdahl (who sent the email) said he assumed the comment was a passing reference to the pyrotechnics" that were a part of the show. In

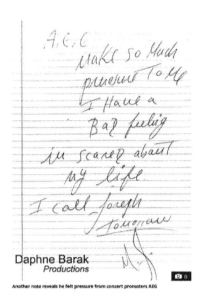

Another note reveals he felt pressure from concert promoters AEG

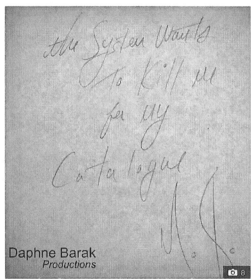

The late singer claimed 'the system wanted to kill him for his catalogue'

fact, Hougdahl says just *the opposite* of the that in his email, that Michael "didn't appear to be referring to the fireworks." "AEG Live CEO Randy Phillips Testifies About Emails on Michael Jackson's Condition," *Billboard* June 7, 2013.

226

Michael's fears *before his death* are now *after his death* the conviction of those closest to him, his family in particular.

Jackson family patriarch Joe Jackson appeared on *Larry King Live* just hours after Dr. Conrad Murray was arraigned on involuntary manslaughter charges stemming from the death of Michael Jackson and revealed his belief that Murray was part of a conspiracy to murder the King of Pop — and that the real individuals responsible have yet to be charged. "To me, he's just a fall guy," Jackson said of Murray, according to CNN. "There's other people, I think, involved with this whole thing. But I think that [if Murray's] interrogated — he would come clean and tell everything he knows."[562]

Michael Jackson's sister La Toya has said there was a conspiracy to murder her brother. "People come into your life, wiggle their way in, control you, manipulate, control your funds, your finances, everything that you have," she told Piers Morgan on CNN this week. She said her brother knew he was going to be killed, and claimed he told her shortly before his death: "La Toya, I'm going to be murdered for my music publishing catalogue and my estate" ... "Michael told me that they were going to murder him," she told Morgan. "He was afraid. He was afraid for his life." She added: "I believe that when Michael walked in that house that night, whatever it was that greeted him, he knew that his end was upon him. And as soon as he had passed, some of the very people he had expressed suspicions about now controlled his estate" ... Although Michael's private physician, Conrad Murray, is due to stand trial for the singer's death, La Toya suggests he was far from the centre of the conspiracy. "I truly feel Dr Murray was simply the fall guy," she told the US TV show Extra. "I think it's too easy to blame him. I think the investigation needs to go ... further."[563]

"[Dr. Conrad Murray] did not act alone. I, all feel, myself, Randy, LaToya, all of us feel that he's the fall guy. And knowing how this whole thing works and knowing it's higher up than just the doctor." - Jermaine Jackson with Larry King, *CNN* June 25, 2010.

---

562 Daniel Kreps, "Joe Jackson Hints at Michael Jackson Murder Conspiracy, Calls Murray 'Fall Guy,'" *Rolling Stone* February 9, 2010.
563 Sean Michaels, "Michael Jackson was murdered, says his sister La Toya," *The Guardian* June 23, 2011; Katie Hodge, "Michael Jackson murdered for hit catalogue, claims LaToya," *Independent* June 24, 2010; Chris McGreal, "After the tributes, the twist: was Michael Jackson's death murder?" *The Guardian* July 15, 2009.

Paris Jackson has claimed her father Michael Jackson was murdered and insisted everyone in her family is aware of it. The late singer's only daughter, who is now 18, suggested Jackson's death was a "set-up" and "all arrows" back up her belief that he was murdered. In her first ever in-depth interview, Paris said her father would hint people were after him and at one point even feared they might end up killing him. "He would drop hints about people being out to get him. And at some point he was like, 'They're gonna kill me one day'," she told *Rolling Stone*. Paris said she was certain her father was murdered and argued it was "obvious". "All arrows point to that. It sounds like a total conspiracy theory and it sounds like bullshit, but all real fans and everybody in the family knows it. It was a setup. It was bullshit." When pressed about who would want the late singer dead, she said "a lot of people" but did not specify who. She said she was still seeking justice for the death. "It's a chess game. And I am trying to play the chess game the right way. And that's all I can say about that right now."[564]

Michael not only knew that he would ultimately be murdered and why, but apparently, he knew (or had a premonition) of *how he would be murdered*. While on Oprah Winfrey's show in 2010 Michael's ex-wife Lisa Marie Presley revealed that during a conversation in 2005 Michael told her that he was afraid for his life: "The final part of the conversation was him telling me that he felt that someone was going to try to kill him to get a hold of his catalogue and his estate." According to Lisa Marie-Presley, Michael gave her names which she preferred not to disclose. But there is more: the day of Michael's death the daughter of Elvis Presley posted on MySpace:

Years ago Michael and I were having a deep conversation about life in general. I can't recall the exact subject matter but he may have been questioning me about the circumstances of my father's death.

At some point he paused, he stared at me very intensely and he stated with an almost calm certainty: "I am afraid that I am going to end up like him, the way he did". I promptly tried to deter him from the idea, at which point he just shrugged his shoulders and nodded, almost matter of fact, as if to let me know he knew what he knew and that was kind of

---

564 Maya Oppenheim, "Michael Jackson 'was murdered,' claim's singer's 18-year-old daughter Paris," *Independent* January 25, 2017; Brian Hiatt, "Paris Jackson: Life After Neverland," *Rolling Stone* January 26, 2017.

that. Four years later I am sitting here watching on the news an ambulance leaving the driveway of his home, the big gates, the crowds outside the gates, the coverage, the crowds outside the hospital, *the cause of death* and *what may have led up to it* and the memory of this conversation hit me, as did the unstoppable tears. A predicted ending by him, by loved ones and by me, but what I didn't predict was how much it was going to hurt when it finally happened.[565]

If Michael "knew" he would "die like Elvis Presley," and according to Lisa-Marie Presley *he did die like Elvis*, how did Elvis Presley die?

II. *Killing The King of Rock N Roll*

The so-called "King of Rock n Roll" died of a drug overdose in his bathroom on August 16, 1977. There were signs that a cover-up immediately began. "The King's bedroom and bathroom were wiped clean of any drugs by his aunt and his staff before the police arrived."[566] Elvis's "best friend" (sic) Joe Esposito admitted to finding Elvis's dead body in the bathroom and sanitizing the death scene by removing the rug and disposing of a bunch of pill bottles.[567] Six hours after Elvis died the Memphis police closed the case. No real investigation into his death was conducted.[568] The trauma team that worked on Elvis at the Baptist Memorial Hospital threw the stomach contents away before the autopsy and without being analyzed. "The medical examiner's notes, toxicology report, and photos, disappeared from official files."[569]

---

565 "Michael Jackson feared he would die like Elvis Presley," *Telegraph* June 26, 2009.
566 Alice Vincent, "Touring, hamburgers and drugs that didn't work: the mystery of Elvis Presley's last days," *The Telegraph* April 11, 2018.
567 "What Really Killed Elvis? New Bombshell Discovery Exposes Truth Behind Singer's Death," *Radar Online* July 26, 2017.
568 Who killed Elvis Presley? A special investigation | 60 Minutes Australia, 1979 @ https://www.youtube.com/watch?v=8hOJFqawlPU&t=92s
569 David Comfort, "The King & the Cover-ups," *The Wrap* August 14, 2009.

Before an autopsy was even concluded the cause of death was officially announced as "fatal heart arrythmia" – a heart attack. The post-mortem report is secret until 2027. But independent tissue analysis showed something different which stunned the toxicologists. "Never before" had they "seen a more alarming case". They figured the yet unidentified subject they examined "must have been gobbling up prescription drugs like a kid at a candy store".[570] The independent toxicology reports that were released showed fourteen different drugs in Elvis's system. The expert at the trial of his personal physician Dr. George Nichopoulos said that "he had never seen such a massive concentration of depressants."[571] Elvis's was thus a "death by polypharmacy."[572] "Polypharmacy" refers to the combined reaction of several prescription drugs. The physician Dr. Nichopoulos was acquitted of charges he overprescribed Elvis. Of the 14 drugs in Elvis's system only 4 were Dr. Nichopoulos's prescriptions.

Dr. George Nichopoulos treated Elvis for insomnia[573] (just as Dr. Conrad Murray treated Michael Jackson for insomnia). Among the drugs in Elvis's system was Demerol,[574] as he had a Demerol addiction,[575] (as Michael Jackson had a Demerol addiction). But the most toxic of this "chemical cocktail" was the codeine, which was present in Elvis's body *at 10 times the accepted level of toxicity*.[576] Elvis surely would never have popped such a massive amount or *any amount* of codeine pills recreationally or medicinally because "he knew he was dangerously allergic" to the drug.[577] Those around him knew it

---

570 James P. Cole and Charles C. Thompson, "The Death of Elvis," *Memphis Magazine* January 1991.
571 Pamela Murphy, "Fourteen different drugs –including 10 times the normal…" *UPI* October 19, 1981.
572 Cole and Thompson, "Death of Elvis."
573 Adam Higginbotham, "Doctor Feelgood," *The Guardian* August 10, 2002.
574 Murphy, "Fourteen different drugs."
575 Higginbotham, "Doctor Feelgood."
576 Murphy, "Fourteen different drugs."
577 David Comfort, "The King & the Cover-ups," *The Wrap* August 14, 2009.

too. What or who is the source of all of the codeine found in Elvis's system *and how did it get there*?

The morning prior to his death Elvis visited his dentist Dr. Lester Hofman for a procedure. *Radar Online* announced that their investigation revealed that Elvis "was really killed by a fatal decision made by the dentist, who prescribed him prescription drugs in which he knew Elvis was allergic," i.e. the painkiller codeine, *even though the fact that Elvis was highly allergic was clearly marked on his medical charts and hospital records.*[578] The codeine prescription that Dr. Hofman wrote for Elvis was filled by one of his security personnel, presumably Ricky Stanley who was on duty that night and got Elvis's prescriptions filled at Baptist Memorial Hospital. Rickey Stanley had two brothers: David and Billy. The three of them are Elvis's stepbrothers who worked for him. David Stanley has been described as chief of security for Elvis.

On *Current Affair* in November of 1990 Dr. Nichopoulos revealed that someone close to Elvis confessed to several persons that he had killed the rock-n-roll singer.[579] During the episode Dr. Nichopoulos said the name of the confessed killer a few times, but "for legal reasons" *Current Affair* bleeped the name out. However, from other interviews with Dr. Nichopoulos we learn the identity of the alleged confessor: David Stanley,[580] Rickey's brother. According to Dr. Nichopoulos's account on national television, David Stanley confessed to having killed Elvis. How might that have happened? The "karate kick" theory is not convincing. On the other hand, David's brother Rickey was on duty at Graceland (the mansion of Elvis) that final night and, according to the account of Elvis's last hours as given by his fiancé Ginger Alden and by Rickey himself, it was Rickey who secured the drugs (went to the

---

578 "What Really Killed Elvis? New Bombshell Discovery Exposes Truth Behind Singer's Death," *Radar Online* July 26, 2017.
579 Elvis Was Murdered. Dr Nick. Current Affair November 11, 1990 @ https://www.youtube.com/watch?v=PT0pxsWzX2w
580 "Dr. Nick talks to EIN about his new book and what really happened three decades ago! Interview by Nigel Patterson," *Elvis Information Network* Feb 2010 @ https://www.elvisinfonet.com/interview_drnick_2010.htm.

Baptist Memorial Hospital pharmacy and filled the prescriptions) that night for Elvis and handed them to him before Elvis went into the bathroom and was killed by a mysterious "polypharmacy of drugs," including the extreme amount of codeine, to which Elvis was highly allergic and thus would never have knowingly ingested it.[581]

But who would have wanted Elvis dead? All three stepbrothers hated Elvis so they had their own personal motives, but there was a bigger fish with a stronger reason to want Elvis Presley dead.

On August 16, 1977 – the very day of Elvis Presley's death – he and his father Vernon Presley were scheduled to appear in front of a grand jury to give evidence against the Italian Mafia as part of an extensive FBI investigation called Operation Fountain Pen. What most people don't know is: Elvis Presley was a badge-carrying narc. On December 21, 1970, when Elvis Presley met with President Nixon in the Oval Office, Elvis pledged his help in fighting America's drug problem by infiltrating and influencing the hippie anti-war movement, the SDS, and the Black Panthers.[582] In return, Nixon gave Presley a Federal Bureau of Narcotics and Dangerous Drugs badge, credentialing him as a narc. Reportedly Elvis worked as an undercover agent and drug informant for the FBI while doing his tour in Las Vegas and while staying at Mafia-owned casinos. He provided cover as bass players and backup singers in his band for FBI agents investigating the Mob in Las Vegas.[583] This can't be good.

---

581 Who killed Elvis Presley? A special investigation | 60 Minutes Australia, 1979 @ https://www.youtube.com/watch?v=8hOJFqawlPU&t=92s
582 Joanna Connors, "When Elvis Met Nixon: The true story behind the gun, the badge, and the movie," *Cleveland.com* Aril 2016; "Elvis Presley Died Working As A Federal Agent," *Radar Online* January 16, 2017.
583 Stephen B. Ubaney, *Who Murdered Elvis? 5thEdition* (Los Angeles: Writers Guild of America, West Inc., 2018).

And then…

On August 15 the FBI prepared arrest warrants for seven men in various cities around the world in connection with the Operation Fountain Pen scam. All of the men were located and were ready to be apprehended the following day when the unthinkable happened.

Suddenly, on August 16th 1977, every television set around the world flashed the incredible news that Elvis Presley, the FBI's key witness, was mysteriously found dead. You would be the biggest fool in the world if you thought this was mere coincidence.[584]

"The King" was dead. The Elvis "hit" was likely carried out via what is referred to by organized crime investigators as *a syringe job*: the victim was made to ingest a drug or drugs or the drug(s)

---

584 Ubaney, *Who Murdered Elvis?*; John Parker, *Elvis Murdered By the Mob* (London: Random House, 1994).

was injected into the victim. There is considerable evidence that Michael Jackson's murder was contracted by the Mafia and, as we shall show, everything about his murder fits the profile of a syringe job as well.

Not only are there remarkable parallels (as we shall see) between the deaths of Elvis Presley and of Michael Jackson, but there are also *direct connections*. The co-CEO of AEG Live, whom Michael feared was trying to kill him, was Paul Gongaware. "Gongaware was specifically involved in AEG Live trying to secure Michael Jackson for the O2 shows." [585] Gongaware's career

Paul Gongaware

as a concert promoter began with Elvis Presley's last tours. He worked advance promotion on Elvis Presley's tours under the direction of Colonel Tom Parker, Presley's tour manager.[586] "In fact, Gongaware was working alongside Colonel Tom Parker, Presley's manager, when Elvis died in 1977 in a case coincidentally also related to prescription drugs, this time given to Presley by *his* doctor, Dr. Nick."[587] It was Gongaware himself who confessed the direct connection between the two deaths that he was directly connected to. On July 5, 2009, two weeks after Michael's death, Gongaware emailed responses to condolence messages, stating: "I was working on the Elvis tour when he died so I kind of knew what to expect. Still quite a shock."[588] *He expected Michael to die like Elvis*. Michael's fear that he would "die like Elvis" was thus not isolated. In fact, Gongaware was with Presley's manager

585 Richards and Langthorne, *83 Minutes*, 120.
586 Alan Duke, "What killed Elvis? It's a question at Michael Jackson's death trial," *CNN* June 2, 2013.
587 Richards and Langthorne, *83 Minutes*, 120.
588 Duke, "What killed Elvis?"

Colonel Tom Parker when he first met Jackson in Las Vegas.[589] This is extremely important because

> many suspicions were focused on Colonel Parker…Parker had a lot to gain from Elvis's death – only a day after the death, he had persuaded the singer's father to sign over to him 50 percent of The King's posthumous earnings.[590]

Gongaware, as an understudy of Colonel Tom Park, therefore got good training, as we shall see.

Colonel Tom Park reportedly had many connections with the Mafia, connections which some investigators believe aided the plot to murder Elvis Presley. Michael Jackson apparently was very frightened because of his debt owed to Italian Mafia figures like Al Malnik (see below). Audio recordings from 2003 retrieved from the answering machine of associates of Michael attest to this fact.

> The tapes reveal a man that was heavily paranoid and fearing for his life. He referred to the Italian mafia in the tapes and his fear that they would kill him. He also referred to being stalked on the tapes. On the tapes there are frequent requests for "150" to be placed into his account which meant $150,000.[591]

> In the first message he says: "It is Michael calling. It is very important, I want that 150 in that account for me, because... I am very concerned about my life." He then goes on to express fears that someone is trying to "sabotage" him and that he wants to be in a place where "they"- who he doesn't specify – can't find him. Then in a barely audible voice he repeats "help me" three times before ending: "We are brothers."

> In another message left at 4.30am, Jackson returns, again in a slurring voice, to the theme of money. "I am very concerned. I don't trust that man. We think he's bad, we think he is Italian Mafia. Please... we must be smarter than him. So please, help me with this. I need to get that, those

---

589 Alab Duke, "Promoter: 'I kind of knew what was going to happen' to Michael Jackson," *CNN* May 28, 2013.
590 Suzanna Leigh, "Why I'm convinced the Mob killed my soulmate Elvis," *Daily Mail* September 30, 2011.
591 Peter Kent, "Anthony Fiato Tapes Reveal Mafia Loan Debts Terrified Michael Jackson," *Constantine Report* July 12, 2010

funds so I can do that, I wanna be away... I don't want to be in Neverland right now." The singer leaves a separate message saying he needs to talk about a "very top, top secret matter" and that he needs access to a German or Swiss bank. Shortly after he leaves another message using the words 'Sun Screen' which appears to be a code word, possibly relating to protection money. "I am very embarrassed. But, um, there should be that I have some finance that's coming up January, February 2nd, and um... that's why I, we need to have on Sun Screen to the account 150. Please don't be mad at me for ... [inaudible]."[592]

In June of 2005 Michael Jackson was telling Dick Gregory "They're trying to kill me," and he would not eat because "They're trying to poison me."[593]

The "they" involved in this conspiracy against Michael Jackson were not, according to him, just Italians. The conspiring "they" also included elements of the *Jewish* Mafia, as another set of recorded phone calls also from the year 2003 reveals. Michael describes a "conspiracy" of Jewish "leeches" that have conspired to leave him "penniless": "They suck. I'm so tired of it...It's a conspiracy. Jews do it on purpose."[594]

We will document in this Report that the death of Michael Jackson was *not* an accident; that the guilty parties include Dr. Conrad Murray but go way beyond Murray. He was an employee; a patsy, if you will. The interests which converged resulting in the death of Michael Jackson on June 25, 2009, included AEG LIVE, Sony Music, the Italian Mafia, the Jewish Mafia, and a "Gay Mafia." Los Angeles law enforcement agencies and likely government agencies as well were involved, certainly at the level of the cover-up. This is not pure speculation. These charges are sustained by a tremendous amount of evidence, including most importantly the explosive testimony of a government witness who

---

592 Carol Driver, "'Top Secret' messages reveal Michael Jackson's troubled mind 'due to medication addiction' SIX years before he died," *Daily Mail* May 13, 2010.
593 Claire Hoffman, "The Last Days of Michael Jackson," *Rolling Stone* August 4, 2009.
594 Gary Young, "Jackson in trouble after anti-semitic phone rant," *The Guardian* November 24, 2005; Nathan Guttman, "Michael Jackson calls Jews 'leeches'," *The Jerusalem Post* November 24, 2005.

was a high-level investigator out of the State Attorney General's office as well as the detailed revelations of *a whistleblower – one involved in the plot who spilled a whole lot of beans!*

The Gay Mafia with its Hollywood pedophile ring *targeted Michael Jackson* with a slanderous media and legal campaign falsely charging him with *their own crime*: gay pedophilia. Michael Jackson was neither gay nor a child molester. Rather, he was vindictively framed by a circle of gay child molesters.

Part 6

Michael's Enemies

Chapter Ten

The Jewish Gay Mafia

I.   *The Enemies List*

The *New York Post* reported in 2003,

> [Steven] Spielberg and [David] Geffen were two of 25 people on [Michael] Jackson's "enemies list," [*Vanity Fair*] reported.[595] Jackson reportedly hates Geffen for being a part of what he calls Hollywood's "Gay Mafia," which he believes sank his career.[596]

According to Michael Jackson's former manager Dieter Wiesner, Michael dictated to him a list of "enemies," persons who sought to destroy Michael. This list was to be shared with Michael's closest associates in order to "protect him."[597] On the list, according to Wiesner, were Israeli illusionist Uri Geller who (fatefully) introduced Michael to Martin Bashir; Rabbi Schmuley Boteach, Michael's one-time "spiritual advisor"; Feminist attorney Gloria Allred; Sony head Tommy Mottola; Janet Arvizo, who falsely accused Michael of molesting her son; as well as Santa Barbara, California, District Attorney Tom Sneddon, who led the charge against Michael during the 1993 and 2005 child molestation cases.

However, according to Maureen Orth of *Vanity Fair*, Michael's Enemies List was topped by none other than music and

---

595 Maureen Orth, "Michael Jackson: You Cannot Make this Stuff Up. New details on the boys, the business, the bizarre blood rituals," *Vanity Fair* April 2003.
596 Bill Hoffmann, "Jacko's Voodoo Curses," *New York Post* March 4, 2003.
597 "Uri Geller, Shmuley Boteach Are on Michael Jackson's 'List of enemies'," *Haaretz* September 18, 2009.

movie mogul David Geffen and Steven Spielberg.[598] It was this "Gay Mafia" that ruined Michael's career, he believed. In 1995, Michael was still proclaiming "My three best friends are Jewish – David Geffen, Jeffrey Katzenberg and Steven Spielberg."[599] This was despite the fact that the three of them had already turned against Michael. The evidence is clear in hindsight. First, Spielberg dashed Michael's dreams when he abruptly dropped the "Peter Pan" movie project starring Michael Jackson in 1990 and replaced it with the "Hook" project starring Robin Williams released in 1991. It is reported that this deeply hurt Michael. The betrayal continued when those three - Geffen, Katzenberg and Spielberg – formed DreamWorks in 1994 and not only locked Michael out of the deal that he was supposed to be a part of, *but they also were accused of stealing his logo as well* (the boy on the moon). In addition, the tremendous controversy over Michael Jackson's "They Don't Care About Us" lyrics in 1995 was *all started* by a leak to and misrepresentation by Geffen's pal at *The New York Times*, Bernard Weinraub.[600] In 1995, Michael apparently didn't see what was going on with the people around him. Geffen, Katzenberg and Spielberg, while maybe "best friends" through the Eighties, had already morphed to "worst frenemies" by the Nineties. What happened? We may have at least part of an answer, and it's quite startling.

II.   *The Jewish Gay Mafia Is Real*

In 2012 Hollywood icon John Travolta was sued by a masseur who claimed the star attempted to coerce him into unwanted sexual acts in a California hotel. Travolta denied the

---

598 Maureen Orth, "Losing His Grip," *Vanity Fair* April 1, 2003.

599 Bernard Weinraub, "In New Lyrics, Jackson Uses Slurs," *The New York Times* June 15, 1995.

600 Weinraub, "In New Lyrics, Jackson Uses Slurs"; "Industry Standards," *LA Magazine* 49 (March 2004): 44-50 (48): "Some said he was way too close to Geffen and Walt Disney Motion Pictures chairman Joe Ruth."

allegations and the lawsuit was later dismissed by the court. But there is an interesting detail buried in the initial complaint for damages document filed with the United States District Court for the District of California:

> Defendant (Travolta) began screaming at Plaintiff, telling Plaintiff how selfish he was; that Defendant got to where he is now due to sexual favors he had performed when he was in his *Welcome Back, Kotter* days; and that *Hollywood is controlled by homosexual Jewish men* who expect favors in return for sexual activity. Defendant then went on to say how he had done things in his past that would make most people throw up.[601]

Charges of Anti-Semitism went flying in the press, of course, and Travolta did deny making such statements. But the claim of a Jewish homosexual cabal in Hollywood – a Jewish Gay Mafia, if you will - has deep resonance.

In 1992 Laureen Hobbs informed us in *Spy Magazine* of a "powerful gay tong" of Hollywood that included, among others, industry powerhouses Barry Diller, David Geffen, Sandy Gallin and Howard Rosenman.[602] A "tong" is a Chinese concept that refers to a secret association, society, or sworn brotherhood that is frequently associated with criminal activity. The four

Adam Carolla: The Gay Mafia Is Real

members of this gay tong identified by Hobbs happened also to be Jewish. Writing for the *Baltimore Sun* in 1995 and attempting to dismiss the rumors of a "Velvet Mafia," a "nasty, vindictive, homosexual cabal that supposedly rules the entertainment world

---

601 Renee Ghert-Zand, "Travolta Sex Abuse Case Takes Anti-Semitic Turn," *The Schmooze* May 8, 2012; "Travolta Says Hollywood Run By Gay Jews Lawsuit Claims," *The Jewish Voice* May 16, 2012.
602 Laureen Habbs, "Diller's Crossing," *Spy Magazine* Vol. 6 May 1992, pp. 18-19.

with an iron swish," Gabriel Rotello nevertheless correctly observed: "it hardly seems coincidental that most members of this latest alleged cabal are, in fact, both gay and Jewish."[603] Celebrity crime investigative journalist and *New York Times* bestselling author Mark Ebner affirmed:

> Despite numerous denials, the Gay Mafia *does* exist, in hierarchical factions…Behind that [pink] curtain is a power so far-reaching it's mind-boggling (emphasis original).[604]

Reputed members of Hollywood's "Gay Mafia": Sandy Gallin, Calvin Klein, David Geffen (in jeans), Barry Diller, and unidentified friends.

Ebner identifies billionaire music and movie mogul David Geffen as the leader of the Gay Mafia ("sitting pretty at the helm"). "In the upper echelons of this 'family,' there exist men like David Geffen, who can end a career with a phone call."[605] It is the case, according to Alan Citron, "Geffen is surrounded by a core group of high-powered friends with an almost familial loyalty."[606] Comedian Andrew Dice Clay, who was signed to Geffen Records, said:

---

603 Gabriel Rotello, "The velvet slur," *The Baltimore Sun* April 19, 1995.
604 Mark Ebner, "The Gay Mafia," *Spy Magazine* Vol. 9 May/June 1995, pp. 42-49.
605 Ebner, "Gay Mafia," 44.
606 Alan Citron, "David Geffen…" *Los Angeles Times* March 7, 1993.

I'd been around long enough to know that [Sandy] Gallin was part of what was known as the Gay Mafia. Along with his close friends David Geffen...and Barry Diller...he was part of an out-of-the-closet Hollywood powerhouse.[607]

David Geffen   Sandy Gallin

In a very *mafioso* way the "best friends" Geffen, Diller, Gallin and Calvin Klein speak of their larger group as *family*, but in the "socialist state" type of way. As Matthew Trynauer writes in *Vanity Fair*:

[Sandy] Gallin, it is very well known, has familial ties apart from the Queen of Country. He is a member of a group of people whose longtime association makes Bloomsbury look dull and unindustrious. "Barry Diller, Diane Von Furstenberg, Calvin and Kelly Klein, David Geffen, and Fran Lebowitz are like an extended family," Gallin acknowledges with a good deal of pride. "There are a lot of other people in and out of the family, too . . . but over the last 20 years that's the core." This glamorous, *rich* crowd goes on vacations together, as they did last Christmas, to Harbour Island in the Bahamas. And everyone calls everyone else—especially Geffen, Diller, and Gallin, who are all Malibu neighbors—with great frequency. "Cradle to grave, just like a good socialist state" is how Barry Diller describes the loyalty and support of his group of close friends. Gallin confirms this: "Just like any family, [we] go through periods of fighting with each other, being disappointed

607 Andrew Dice Clay with David Ritz, *The Filthy Truth* (New York: Touchstone, 2014) 174.

with each other—and that's why it's like a family, because it has lasted for 20 to 30 years."[608]

Gallin admits that keeping quiet about their dark activities is a code of this "family":

> Gallin admits that because of his place in this family he has been an eyewitness to some remarkable events in show-business and pop history. At one point he muses aloud about the bestseller he may write one day. "You're going to ask a question—why don't I write a book about all my friends and the things I've done? "My answer is: *Where would I live?*""[609]

It was David Geffen who introduced Gallin to Michael Jackson.[610]

Another important member of this extended family known as the (Jewish) Gay Mafia is Dr. Arnold Klein, "Dermatologists of the Stars" whose regular patients included, of course, Geffen, Gallin, and Diller, but also Michael Jackson.

> Jackson didn't become a Klein patient until his landmark appearance at the Pasadena Civic Auditorium, on the 25th anniversary of Motown, March 25, 1983, when he unleashed the Moonwalk. Among the cheering multitude in the audience was Arnie Klein. "I was blown away," he told me. "A week later *I was sitting in David Geffen's driveway and in comes Michael Jackson*. He is sitting in the back of a Lincoln Town Car and he looked very lonely. Within a week, *David brought Michael to me*.[611]

As Michael met Sandy Gallin through Geffen, he also met Arnold Klein through Geffen. This is not an insignificant fact.

---

608 Matthew Trynauer, "Sandy's Castle," *Vanity Fair* April 1996.
609 Trynauer, "Sandy's Castle."
610 Trynauer, "Sandy's Castle."
611 Mark Seal, "The Ugly world of Dr. Arnie Klein, Beverly Hills' King of Botox," *Vanity Fair* February 2, 2012.

Klein was Jewish, the son of a Rabbi. He liked to brag of his great, great uncle being Albert Einstein.[612] Klein was a dermatology student of Dr. Albert Kligman – *connect the dots!*[613]

> "He was one of my best students and I truly think he deserves the fame," said Dr. Albert Kligman, who discovered the acne-treating substance Retin-A and was one of Klein's medical school professors. "He's very good with his hands and head. Dr. Klein is an intellectual and not just a technician, even though he chose to go out to California, the home of all the fruits and nuts in the world."[614]

When he arrived in California Klein became "immensely wealthy and well connected."[615] One of those connections was with David Geffen. "In 1984, in the living room of his Los Angeles home, Dr. Klein, along with David Geffen, Dr. Mathilde Krim, and others founded the American Foundation for AIDS Research (amfAR)."[616] Klein became "an eminence in Los Angeles."

---

612 Seal, "The Ugly world of Dr. Arnie Klein."
613 See Wesley Muhammad, *The Pot Plot: Marijuana, Hip Hop and the Scientific Assault on Black America* (Atlanta: A-Team Publishing, 2020) 115-126.
614 Lisa Boren, "Kelin," (sic) *Los Angeles Business Journal* July 12, 1999.
615 Sullivan, *Untouchable*.
616 "Contributor: Dr. Arnold Klein," *HuffPost* @ https://www.huffpost.com/author/arnold-william-klein; Lisa Boren, "Kelin," (sic) *Los Angeles Business Journal* July 12, 1999.

He demonstrated how willing he was to fight any accusations made against him during a lawsuit filed in 2004 by Irena Medavoy, wife of former TriStar Pictures chairman Morris Mike Medavoy, who accused the doctor of giving her Botox treatments that brought on crippling migraine headaches. Klein won the case even in the face of evidence that demonstrated how dependent his medical practice was on injection treatments, and that he had collected a good deal of money from Botox manufacturer Allergan. He was by then an eminence in Los Angeles, a confounder with his friend Rose Tarlow (LA's most prominent interior designer) of the Breast Cancer Foundation at UCLA and a philanthropist credited with raising more than $300 million for HIV research. He was among Southern California's leading art collectors and delighted in mentioning that one of his patients had offered to name a new building at UCLA's School of Medicine for him, but that he had modestly declined, accepting an Arnold Klein teaching chair instead.[617]

Klein was Professor of Medicine and Dermatology at UCLA's David Geffen School of Medicine, so named after David Geffen donated $200 million in 2001 to UCLA's School of Medicine. In 2004, having been "a valuable member of the UCLA faculty for 25 years,"[618] the UCLA Division of Dermatology at the David Geffen School of Medicine named an endowed chair to honor Klein: The Arnold Klein, MD Chair in Dermatology. This was five years before the murder of Michael Jackson.

With Geffen, Gallin, Diller, and Calvin Klein, among others, Arnold Klein was an eminent member of the Jewish Gay Mafia. He was part of a community of overweight gay men called "Bears," an assortment of gay men weighing 250-350-plus pounds.[619] According to his former office manager Jason Pfeiffer in a lawsuit filed against him, Klein constantly prowled the internet and the streets for male sex partners, even homeless men.

In legal documents, Pfeiffer details the duties he says he agreed to perform for Klein: "Prepare him for sexual encounters with masseurs, paid escorts, and prostitutes [and] administer Klein's Cialis, Viagra, and similar prescription drugs. In Palm Springs, Klein dispatched Pfeiffer

617 Sullivan, *Untouchable*.
618 Rachel Champeau, "UCLA Announces New Endowed Chair: The Arnold Klein, M.D., Chair in Dermatology," *UCLA News* July 23, 2004.
619 Seal, "The Ugly world of Dr. Arnie Klein."

and another employee to find a man with whom Klein could have sex. Pfeiffer and the other employee returned with a large-bodied homeless man for Klein Dr. Klein repeatedly subjected Pfeiffer to unwelcomed, unwanted, offensive sexual conduct."[620]

Why Being "Gay in the '70s in New York and L.A. Was Magic" — and How Hollywood Has Changed (Guest Column)

6:45 AM PDT 5/3/2019 by Howard Rosenman

Courtesy of Howard Rosenman
Rosenman (right) with David Geffen.

While he doesn't use any of the noted designations, the reality of the Velvet Underground or Gay Mafia was all but explicitly confirmed by one of the members of Laureen Hobbs' "Hollywood's powerful gay tong." In 2019, Howard Rosenman wrote a guest column for *Hollywood Reporter* entitled: "Why Being 'Gay in the '70s in New York and L.A. Was Magic' – and How Hollywood Has Changed." Rosenman was born in Brooklyn, New York to Ashkenazi Jews from Palestine. He fought for the Israeli Defense forces during the Six-Day War in 1967. In the column he recounts meeting that same year (1967) Barry Diller, David Geffen, and Sandy Gallin during a brunch in New York, "I was the luckiest gay Jew in the world," Rosenman says. He goes on to describe Hollywood's gay tong:

---

620 Seal, "The Ugly world of Dr. Arnie Klein."

The most wonderful thing about those days was that *the gay folks in power* lent a hand to young gay people trying to get a foothold in the business. There was *a powerful network* of older successful gay men … who introduced younger gay men to successful showbiz types…You see, all the cognoscenti knew about each other and it wasn't secretive or shameful, *but there was a code that no one spoke publicly about it*. It wasn't being "out" as we know it today — *the press never wrote about it*. My very first feature film that I produced happened because of this gay network…If I wasn't gay, I never would have had the career that I have.[621]

1981 photograph of what *New York Magazine* (October 5, 2015) called "the Ultimate Power Nap" aboard the chartered yacht *Midnight Saga*: Barry Diller, then chairman of Paramount Pictures; Calvin Klein, fashion designer; David Geffen, music and movie mogul; and Sandy Gallin, Hollywood talent manager. Names who have been associated with the "Gay Mafia" include but are not limited to: David Geffen, Barry Diller, Sandy Gallin, Howard Rosenman, Jeffrey Katzenberg, Calvin Klein, Steve Tisch, Steven Spielberg, Ray Stark, Aaron Spelling, etc.

---

621 Howard Rosenman, "Why Being 'Gay in the '70s in New York and L.A. Was Magic' – and How Hollywood Has Changed," *Hollywood Reporter* May 3, 2019.

Hollywood is like the Balkans. "There are duchesses and dukes and a court of sychophants"…And David [Geffen] is one of the emperors. There's Mike Ortiz and there's David. Two emperors."[622]

And then there was one.

His mother would call him "King David" after the biblical prophet. "Geffen's parents, Abraham and Batya, were east European Jews who met in Palestine and immigrated to the United States."[623] Geffen's "journey from middle-class Jewish boy from Brooklyn to masterful music and movie mogul,"[624] was a journey filled with waging and wining wars against Geffen's rivals and enemies, real and perceived.

Geffen wasn't tall or good-looking, and he certainly hadn't played football. Indeed, his fanatical drive to succeed was fueled by his considerable insecurities. With chutzpah, David figured he could beat just about anyone at the entertainment game. The key, though, was to earn the trust of an inner circle of artists and *then wage war on everybody else*…"That was the beginning of the end of the love groove in American music," [Paul] Rothchild says. "To me, that's the moment. When David Geffen enters the California waters as a manager, the sharks have entered the lagoon."[625]

Before "King David" was the "King of Hollywood," that title was held by super-agent and Hollywood dealmaker Michael Ovitz, born of Romanian Jewish parents in Chicago. "Ovitz happens to be a close friend of the younger [Edgar] Bronfman."[626] For 20 years through the 1980s and 1990s Ovitz was hailed as the

---

622 Bernard Weinraub, "David Geffen, Still Hungry," *The New York Times Magazine* May 2, 1993.
623 "David Geffen reinvented himself as a somebody," *CJ News* November 15, 2012.
624 Danielle Berrin, "Deconstructing David Geffen," *Jewish Journal* September 11, 2012.
625 Barney Hoskyns, "Sex, drugs and the billion-dollar rise of David Geffen," *Independent* Friday 18, November 2005.
626 "Bronfman Clout Felt in L.a. by Movie and Jewish Worlds," *Jewish Telegraphic Agency* May 29, 1995.

"Most Powerful Man in Hollywood." By 2002 he was dethroned by David Geffen. In the August 2002 edition of *Vanity Fair*, an emotionally wrecked and thus candid Ovitz blamed his demise on a "shadowy Hollywood cabal" which he explicitly identifies as "The Gay Mafia."[627] This Gay Mafia, led by David Geffen and his pal *New York Times* Los Angeles correspondent Bernard Weinraub, "stabbed him in his back" and engineered his downfall, according to Ovitz.[628]

As a result, Hollywood had a new king: David Geffen. The ensuing controversy over his remarks forced Ovitz to later apologize for using the "stupid" and "offensive" language "gay mafia,"[629] but there can be no doubt that the "shadowy Hollywood cabal" of gay Jews that brought about his ruination was real.

627 Ryan Burrough, "Ovitz Agonistes," *Vanity Fair* August 2002.
628 Rick Lyman, "Ovitz Bitterly Bares Soul, and Film Industry Reacts," *The New York Times* July 3, 2002; Paul Tharp, "Ovitz: Felled By 'Gay Mafia,'" *New York Post* July 2, 2002.
629 Steven Gorman, "Ex-Hollywood Superagent OVITZ Regrets 'Gay Mafia' Remark," *Reuters* July 3, 2002; Rebecca Keegan, "Michael Ovitz Still Can't Help Himself," *Vanity Fair* October 5, 2018.

Geffen has been described as "a ruthless schemer."[630] Even one of Geffen's closest friends describes him thusly:

> And David sort of sits there in the darkness. Very quiet. You don't know what he's doing *except controlling and manipulating.* Sort of like the original-cast album cover of 'My Fair Lady.' That's David." [631]

This is reportedly Geffen's *modus operandi*: he controls the people who control the people.

Geffen has been described in the press as "Hollywood's premier manipulator."[632] "He's such a Machiavellian character," it is said. And his methods are ruthless.

---

630 Barney Hoskyns, "Sex, drugs and the billion-dollar rise of David Geffen," *Independent* Friday 18, November 2005.
631 Weinraub, "David Geffen, Still Hungry."
632 James Bates and Elaine Dutka, "Tom King, 39; Wall Street Journal Columnist Wrote Geffen Bestseller," *Los Angeles Times* April 15, 2003.

But David Geffen has trafficked in fictions all his life. The Operator (as he is called) could have easily been called The Liar...He'd advise clients to lie to get what they wanted; *he'd spread lies about people with whom he was feuding...*[633]

Geffen seems at points to realize that his best traits are undermined by his worst traits—greed and *a vengeful spirit*—but seems at a loss to change his behavior...The richer Geffen became, the more good he did, but it is confounding that he hurt so many people in the process. Geffen's most disturbing trait as relayed in this book is *his willingness to sabotage the careers of others by manufacturing toxic and unfounded rumors.*[634]

Before Geffen sank Ovitz, his subtle methods of vengeance such as rumors and press leaks hastened the downfall of his longtime nemesis CBS Records president Walter Yetnikoff in 1990, sending a clear message: "any of Geffen's other putative rivals might take a moment to reflect on the fact that the last person to take a shot publicly at David Geffen was Walter Yetnikoff. And nobody's quite sure what he's doing these days."[635] Geffen became "one of the most feared and loathed players in his field," "a slender man so puckish-looking that at 47 he could still be called the enfant terrible of the entertainment business."[636] But the enfant terrible is now "the industry godfather."[637] "Geffen lives an awful lot like a sultan."[638]

But both Yetnikoff and Orvitz apparently got off easy compared to *Wall Street Journal* journalist Tom King, who wrote the only (originally authorized) biography about Geffen called *The*

633 David Handelman, "How David Geffen Got Ahead: Lies, Loot and a Little Luck," *Observer* March 13, 2000.
634 Tom King, *The Operator: David Geffen Builds, Buys, and Sells The New Hollywood* (New York: Broadway Books, 2000).
635 Fred Goodman, "Who's the biggest Hollywood? Sizing Up David Geffen, the Toughest, Richest Impressario in show Business," *Spy Magazine* April 1997: 36-43 (42); Dannen, *Hit Men* 336-343.
636 Goodman, "Who's the biggest Hollywood?"
637 John Seabrook, "The many Lives of David Geffen," *The New Yorker* February 23, 1998; Danielle Berrin, "Deconstructing David Geffen," *Jewish Journal* September 11, 2012.
638 Weinraub, "David Geffen, Still Hungry."

Operator. King was given by Geffen unique access to his life, including permission to interview many of Geffen's famous friends. King is gay like Geffen, who hoped King would immortalize him in print. However, the truthful portrait that was developing under King's pen was not to Geffen's liking. He felt King betrayed him. When the book was released in 2000 it is "said to have caused a panic not seen in America's entertainment capital since the revelations of the prostitute Heidi Fleiss."[639] The book infuriated Geffen. And then

> Typically, Geffen has vowed that King will come to regret his betrayal. At the very least, he has told friends, King will never write another book in this town again. That might be wishful thinking. Last week, before a single book appeared in stores, *The Operator* had already climbed to No. 20 on the Amazon list. King, who sets out on his book tour this week, is back to work at the *Journal,* writing a weekly column about Hollywood. *So far, being Geffen's No. 1 enemy hasn't hindered his job.* "If anything, I get my calls returned faster," he says. "At the end of the day," says one of King's colleagues, "Who cares what David Geffen thinks of him? He's a reporter at the *Wall Street Journal.* What's the worst thing that could happen to Tom? He won't get a contract at DreamWorks?"[640]

This optimism in these words from Lisa DePaulo of *New York Magazine*, written in 2000, proved premature and tragic. Three years after the book's publication while on vacation the healthy, 39-year old King complained of a headache, collapsed on the floor and died of a brain hemorrhage. The managing editor of the *Wall Street Journal* Paul Steiger noted that King "was in apparently excellent health and fine spirits." Joanne Lipman, a deputy managing editor, said also: "He was in perfect physical health. He was always very boyish," she said. "Even though he was young, he looked even younger."[641] The message that went throughout the industry was clear. When *The Daily Beast* reporter Nicole LaPorte

---

639 "Hollywood mogul Geffen savaged in new biography," *The Guardian* February 25, 2000.
640 Lisa DePaulo, "Whose Life Is It, Anyway?" *New York Magazine* March 13, 2000.
641 Nicole Laporte, "WSJ H'w'd columnist Tom King dies at 39 Journal staffers 'devasted and shocked'," *Variety* April 13, 2003.

asked one of Geffen's friends to speak on the record in 2010 (!), the friend replied: "The last person who wrote a book about David Geffen is dead! And he was young. And healthy. And now he's dead! Click."[642] Geffen became "the most feared and powerful man in Hollywood."[643] Tom King had been lauded: "He was courageous *to take on a sacred cow of the industry.*"[644] But it cost him his life, according to the word on Hollywood's Palm tree lined streets. As Geffen's friend and fellow "Gay Mafia" member Howard Rosenman said: "David will do anything for you if you're his friend. But if you're his enemy, well, you might as well kill yourself."[645]

By 2007, David Geffen had been crowned the most powerful gay man in America by *Out*.[646] In 2016 he reportedly had a fortune of $6.5 billion.[647] And he transparently had a "gay agenda." The *Los Angeles Times* described him as "a gay man with a liberal social agenda"[648]

> Geffen's been a consistent support of progressive causes over the years. But the continuing battle over the gays in the military offers the best insights into *the behind-the-scenes manner* in which he now intends to use his considerable influence. [649]

As a "movie-music kingpin,"[650] Geffen is "the only man in the history of American cultural capitalism who has succeeded in three

---

642 Nicole LaPorte, "The Spectacular Rise and Fall of DreamWorks," *The Telegraph* June 9, 2010.

643 Lisa DePaulo, "Whose Life Is It, Anyway?" *New York Magazine* March 13, 2000.

644 James Bates and Elaine Dutka, "Tom King, 39; Wall Street Journal Columnist Wrote Geffen Bestseller," *Los Angeles Times* April 15, 2003.

645 Weinraub, "David Geffen, Still Hungry."

646 "The Power 50," *OUT* April 3, 2007.

647 Laura M. Holson, "The Boy From Brooklyn: David Geffen Comes Home, With Cash to Spare," *The New York Times* February 20, 2016.

648 Citron, "David Geffen…"

649 Citron, "David Geffen…"

650 Paul Tharp, "Bronfman Adrift From Diller, Geffen," *New York Post* March 6, 2000.

different industries-popular music, Broadway, and Hollywood."[651] His fingerprint is all over the cultural industry.

> Geffen has played the architect, in his case refashioning the movie and music industries so substantially he's compared to Hollywood's founding fathers. As actor Tom Hanks plainly puts it… "He defined this culture. He built it.[652]

IV.   *Michael's False Accusers: Hollywood's Pedophile Ring*

Hollywood's Gay Mafia and its associates have been linked to what has been descried as "Hollywood's 'big secret'": it's "pedophilia crisis." In May of 2016 former child actor Elijah Wood ("Frodo Baggins" of *The Lord of the Rings*) told Britain's **Sunday Times** that "Hollywood is in the grip of a child sexual abuse epidemic, with rich and powerful industry figures abusing child actors with impunity."[653] Wood descried the "darkness in the underbelly" of the industry as a "major," "organized" phenomenon in which "vipers" prey on young people and are protected by top Hollywood figures.   According to Wood, Hollywood parties are the setting for this child abuse.

651 John Seabrook, "The Many Lives of David Geffen," *The New Yorker* February 23, 1998.
652 Danielle Berrin, "Deconstructing David Geffen," *Jewish Journal* September 11, 2012.
653 Tom Sykes, "Elijah Wood Calls Out Hollywood's Pedophile Problem," *The Daily Beast* April 13, 2017.

Wood is not alone. Former child actor Corey Feldman of the Eighties smashes *The Goonies* and *Stand By Me* "has made it his personal crusade to expose the ring of elite pedophiles" in Hollywood "that he says has been tormenting young actors for decades."[654] Feldman, who was himself a victim, told ABC News in 2011:

> I can tell you that the No. 1 problem in Hollywood was and is and always will be pedophilia... I was surrounded by [pedophiles] when I was 14 years old... They were everywhere... There was a circle of older men... around this group of kids. And they all had either their own power or connections to great power in the entertainment industry... There are people... who have gotten away with it for so long that they feel they're above the law.

According to Feldman, this network of pedophiles is a circle of "some of the richest, most powerful people" in the business.[655]

---

654 Yuliya Talmazan, "Corey Feldman Vows to Expose Hollywood Pedophile Ring," *NBC News* October 27, 2017.
655 *An Open Secret* 2014 Documentary by Amy Berg @ https://vimeo.com/142444429.

"And all of these men were all friends."[656] The "sick network targeted boys aged ten to 16, meeting them at awards shows and glitzy parties then *grooming them*." [657] According to a number of lawsuits filed by alleged victims, Hollywood is in the grip of a cabal of predators who plie young boys and teens with hard drugs and alcohol before sexually assaulting them.[658] A favorite pastime of Hollywood's Gay Mafia is evidently throwing big orgy parties.

> It's this group of young, really good-looking guys that travel around everywhere, from coast to coast, and cater to the big orgy parties. They fly these guys out en masse, and they just party, party, party…so far out that no one would hear the screams.[659]

David Geffen's biographer, Tom King, who was also gay, describes first meeting Geffen at such a party, "You know, one of these parties that are mobbed by the middle-aged – it's *charitable* to call them that – but the middle-aged moguls and the pretty mail-room boys who want to be producers."[660] Some of these were reportedly "nude wrestling parties" involving underage boys.[661] David Geffen's association with Digital Entertainment Network (DEN), an online video streaming service (pre-YouTube and Netflix), directly connects him with a notorious pedophile ring in Hollywood.

In 2014 award-winning and Oscar-nominated director Amy Berg premiered the documentary *An Open Secret* which exposes a child sex ring that was operating in the heart of Los

---

656 Grant Rollings, "The child sex scandal that could tear Hollywood apart: Lost Boys star Corey Feldman lifts lid on darkest movie secret," *The Sun* May 27, 2016.

657 Rollings, "The child sex scandal."

658 Michelle Malkin, "Hollywood's Sexual Predator Problem Explodes," *NewsBusters* May 6, 2014.

659 Ebner, "Gay Mafia," 46.

660 Lisa DePaulo, "Whose Life Is I, Anyway?" *New York Magazine* March 13, 2000.

661 Howard Rosenman, "Why Being 'Gay in the '70s in New York and L.A. Was Magic' – and How Hollywood Has Changed," *Hollywood Reporter* May 3, 2019.

Angeles in the late-Nineties. Because no distributer would touch the explosive film – "the film Hollywood doesn't want you to see," says film producer Gabe Hoffman – *An Open Secret* was released for free on Vimeo.[662] The documentary centers on DEN, the 1998 precursor to modern streaming platforms. DEN provided original content staring child actors. But now we know that it was a front for a child abuse ring.   DEN was founded by convicted child predator Marc Collins-Rector, his young victim/boyfriend Chad Shackley (Shackley was 15 and Collins-Rector was 31 when their relationship began) and Brock Peirce, the former child actor from "Mighty Ducks" (1992).

Marc Collins-Rector, Chad Shackley and Brock Peirce

Collins-Rector's idea for DEN was to produce TV shows and movies for 14-to-24-year-olds *with an emphasis on stories for gay teens and distribute them online.*[663] By 1999 DEN succeeded in raising $72 million in investment before opening.   And the list of investors is shocking. Except, it is not…not really.

662 *An Open Secret* 2014 Documentary by Amy Berg @ https://vimeo.com/142444429; Jenna Marotta, "Hollywood's Underage Sexual Abuse Problem: 5 Shocking Injustices From 'An Open Secret', *Indie Wire* Oct 26, 2017.
663 Alex French and Maximillian Potter, " 'Nobody Is Going to Believe You'," *The Atlantic* March 2019

An SEC filing obtained by Hollywood periodical *Radar Online* reveals that DEN's investors included a shocking number of big name personalities such as media executives Garth Ancier and David Geffen, former Yahoo CEO Terry Semel, film producers Gary Goddard and Bryan Singer, Wall Street czar Mitchell Blutt, A&M Records head Gilbert Friesen (now deceased), former Disney executive David Neuman, manager and label executive Gary Gersh, investor Jeffrey Sachs, former Congressman Michael Huffington, actors Ben and Fred Savage, and tech companies such as Microsoft and Dell. *The lack of apparent revenue raises questions about what investors in DEN were expecting in return* (emphasis added – WM).[664]

  Collins-Rector and Shackley moved to Los Angeles in the mid-Nineties and chose as their residence the $4.2 million Spanish colonial mansion previously owned by Death Row Records C.E.O. Suge Knight. The digital pioneer and confessed child molester Collins-Rector immediately got "well-connected" in L.A. "Among their new acquaintances in Los Angeles were such industry heavies as David Geffen, uber-manager Sandy Gallin, then–NBC Entertainment president Garth Ancier, and *Usual Suspects* director Bryan Singer."[665] Bryan Singer invested $50,000 and David Geffen invested $250,000 in the company. In a letter written by Collins-Rector he speaks of "my *friend* Bryan Singer [who] introduced us to a young actor named Brock Pierce."[666] In addition, "David Geffen...socializ[ed] at the estate with other investors".[667]

  The estate is the infamous palatial estate in Encino called the "M&C Estate" for "Marc & Chad." There, the three founders of DEN

---

664 Elizabeth Vos, "Tech Figure In Dot-Com Child Sex Scandal Was A Clinton Global Initiative Member," *Disobedient Media* January 25, 2017.
665 John Gorenfeld and Patrick Runkle, "Fast Company: A high-flying Web start-up, DEN imploded among allegations of drug use, guns, and pedophilia," *Radar Magazine* November 5, 2007.
666 *An Open Secret* 2014 Documentary by Amy Berg @ https://vimeo.com/142444429.
667 Robert Kolker, "What Happens When You Accuse a Major Hollywood Director of Rape?" *Vulture* September 7, 2014.

hosted lavish parties attended by Hollywood's gay A-list. Their guests included relative newcomer Bryan Singer, now the director of the *X-Men* movies, and legendary media mogul David Geffen, both of whom were investors in DEN. It was at those parties that Collins-Rector and others allegedly sexually assaulted half a dozen teenage boys, according to two sets of civil lawsuits…[668]

The pool parties at the M&C Estate were all the rave in L.A. "The Encino mansion…was home to the wild gay sex parties where Hollywood bigwigs allegedly preyed on underage boys."[669] According to reports, including lawsuits,

> Hollywood's rich and powerful men enjoyed a secret party [at the M&C Estate] that would go on late into the night. Behind its high walls were a group of young wannabes all desperate to make it in the movies. *They were all boys — no girls were allowed — carefully selected for the entertainment of the group of predatory paedophiles.* These wide-eyed hopefuls were plied with drugs and alcohol and told anyone using the hot tub had to strip naked.[670]

> According to online reports, the revelrous, sexually-fueled pool parties…are one of Hollywood's worst kept secrets, with a guest list often consisting of older show biz power brokers and youngish teenage boys culled from a time-tested selection process that starts on the nightclub circuit in West Hollywood and Hollywood each Thursday. At the 18-and-up parties, collaborators get the phone numbers of the youngish looking attendees, who are subsequently invited to weekend parties where sex is common, behind closed doors or in full display of the others.[671]

---

668 Ellie Hall, Nicolás Medina Mora and David Noriega, "Found: The Elusive Man At The Heart Of The Hollywood Sex Abuse Scandal," *Buzzfeed* June 26, 2014.
669 Tracie Egan Morrissey, "Inside the Hollywood Sex Ring Mansion From the Bryan Singer Lawsuit," *Jezebel* April 25, 2014.
670 Grant Rollings, "The child sex scandal that could tear Hollywood apart: Lost Boys star Corey Feldman lifts lid on darkest movie secret," *The Sun* May 27, 2016.
671 "Hollywood's Worst Kept Secret – 'Sexually-Fueled Pool Parties': The Latest Developments in Bryan Singer Teen Abuse Lawsuit," *Radar Online* April 18, 2014.

The reckoning did come. Days before DEN's planned $75 million IPO (initial public offering) in October 1999 a young man filed a lawsuit claiming he'd been molested by Collins-Rector for three years, beginning when he was 13. Collins-Rector quickly paid a settlement. The IPO was withdrawn. A number of DEN employees eventually filed lawsuits alleging they were raped and/or sexually abused at the M&C Estate by the three cofounders and guests. Allegedly drugs were used to carry out the attacks:[672] Valium, Vicodin, Xanax, Percocet, ecstasy, roofies, cocaine, marijuana. "Young actors who attended parties remember troves of prescription drugs and alcohol, plus Collins-Rector's gun collection. One man recalled when, as a minor, Collins-Rector threatened his career if he did not sleep in his bed. Although the actor refused and camped out on the couch, he nonetheless awoke in Collins-Rector's bed, convinced that a laced drink had led to abuse."[673] The victims claimed DEN was but "a front for a sex ring which operated in 1999."[674]

> One early, senior-level DEN employee remembers asking why so many teenage boys were on the payroll and being told that they did computer work. The employee also recalls attending a company party and seeing teenage boys filing into a movie theater in the Encino mansion. The employee tried to go inside but was stopped by a bodyguard, who said: "Kids only." The employee asked a colleague what was going on. "[He] said that he had seen some of it, and that it was definitely porn ... [The kids] were all laughing and eating candy. But we were totally not allowed into that room.[675]

---

672 John Gorenfeld and Patrick Runkle, "Fast Company: A high-flying Web start-up, DEN imploded among allegations of drug use, guns, and pedophilia," *Radar Magazine* November 5, 2007.
673 Jenna Marotta, "Hollywood's Underage Sexual Abuse Problem: 5 Shocking Injustices From 'An Open Secret'," *Indie Wire* Oct 26, 2017.
674 Grant Rollings, "The child sex scandal that could tear Hollywood apart: Lost Boys star Corey Feldman lifts lid on darkest movie secret," *The Sun* May 27, 2016.
675 Alex French and Maximillian Potter, " 'Nobody Is Going to Believe You'," *The Atlantic* March 2019

But what about the "bigwig" investors in Collins-Rector's company? "Were Singer, Ancier, Goddard and Neuman really blind to where their money was going and what kind of behavior it was funding?" asked *Radar Online*.[676] Daniel Cheren, the attorney who represented the DEN employees, says no, telling a reporter: "Some of these investors received in addition to their stock, *a piece of a male brothel for their money*"; "Anyone who had a dinner at that estate or went to a party there, had to know what was going on."[677] *Radar Magazine* tells us that, in its heyday, "a Who's Who of gay Hollywood flocked to notorious all-night bashes at the M&C estate".[678] Topping that "Who's Who" list were "the likes of record boss David Geffen, film producer Michael Huffington and X-Men director Bryan Singer. Those three men allegedly attended the parties…"[679] According to his attorney, however "Geffen was not accused of any misconduct in the suits nor named as a defendant." [680] The same could not be said of Geffen's protégé Bryan Singer, a fellow gay Jew who is from West Windsor, New Jersey.[681]

---

676 "Bryan Singer & Other Hollywood Sex Ring Defendants Exposed As Investors in Shady Company Run By Pedophile," *Radar Online* April 24, 2014.
677 "Bryan Singer & Other Hollywood Sex Ring Defendants Exposed As Investors in Shady Company Run By Pedophile," *Radar Online* April 24, 2014.
678 John Gorenfeld and Patrick Runkle, "Fast Company: A high-flying Web start-up, DEN imploded among allegations of drug use, guns, and pedophilia," *Radar Magazine* November 5, 2007.
679 Grant Rollings, "The child sex scandal that could tear Hollywood apart: Lost Boys star Corey Feldman lifts lid on darkest movie secret," *The Sun* May 27, 2016.
680 Ellie Hall, Nicolás Medina Mora and David Noriega, "Found: The Elusive Man At The Heart Of The Hollywood Sex Abuse Scandal," *Buzzfeed* June 26, 2014.
681 Alex French and Maximillian Potter, " 'Nobody Is Going to Believe You'," *The Atlantic* March 2019

A-list Hollywood director Bryan Singer, friend of Marc Collins-Rector and reputed protégé of David Geffen, pictured with one of his infamous "twinks." *Twink* is a gay slang term describing a young or young-looking slender male with little or no body hair or facial hair. In addition, "At its most pejorative, the term describes a uniquely disposable kind of young gay man: Hairless, guileless, witless. The term's namesake is Twinkie, a junk food containing shiny packaging, a sweet taste, and zero nutritional value." Scott Bixby, "Inside Hollywood's 'Twink' Pool Parties," *The Daily Beast* July 12, 2017.

"Singer and Collins-Rector were close friends, and according to at least five sources, Singer was a regular at the M&C Estate." [682] It was Singer who introduced Collins-Rector to Brock Pierce, the third of the three founders of DEN. And even more than Collins-Rector, *Singer is known for his own Hollywood gay parties.*

What is not in dispute is that, since launching his career with 1995's *The Usual Suspects* and becoming a blockbuster filmmaker with 2000's *X-Men*, Singer has been a fixture in the gay Hollywood party scene, hosting and attending gatherings at homes in Los Angeles that have drawn

---

682 French and Potter, "'Nobody Is Going to Believe You'."

anywhere between a few dozen to 1,200 revelers, most of them very young men.[683]

By the late '90s, Singer also had a reputation on the gay Hollywood scene—in part for the pool parties he threw at a house he lived in on Butler Avenue, in the Mar Vista neighborhood. A friend of Singer's recalls attending one of these parties when he was in his early 20s (and Singer was in his early 30s) and being shocked by how young many of the guests looked. "It felt like a high-school party," the friend says. He remembers wondering: *How did all these boys get here? Where are their parents?* (emphasis original).[684]

The Emmerich/Singer party on June 15, 2009

The *American Psycho* author Brett Easton Ellis said he knew about Bryan Singer's "underage (sex) parties" where fake ID's were important because he dated two participants of those parties.[685] Director Roland Emmerich (*Independence Day* and *2012*) co-

---

683 Adam B. Vary, "Inside Bryan Singer's Wild Hollywood World," *BuzzFeed* April 23, 2014.
684 French and Potter, " 'Nobody Is Going to Believe You'."
685 "Bryan Singer Sex Abuse Suit: Bret Easton Ellis Says He Dated Two People Who 'Went Through World of Underage Parties' (Audio)," *Hollywood Reporter* April 29, 2014.

hosted with Singer parties over Pride weekend at Emmerich's L.A. home, such as the one pictured above from June 15, 2009.[686] Reportedly "the Hollywood Elite [flocked] to his parties," and these parties are said to be an entire production involving modeling agencies, club promoters, and studio executives.[687] The party drug Molly often fueled the gay bacchanals. [688]

> Singer's pool parties have been a topic of discussion in gay entertainment circles for years. Some parties, co-hosted with fellow out director Roland Emmerich, have featured more than a thousand celebrants. Emmerich told *The Advocate*, "when [Singer] makes a New Year's party, there's like 600, 700 twinks running around and he's hiding in his room. That's quite typical." Emmerich estimates that the last party they hosted, in 2009, drew 1,200 guests... "I don't recall anyone bringing a bathing suit," says [party attendant Jason] Dottley. "It was a healthy mixture of underwear and no underwear." He pauses. "Mostly no underwear, to be honest."[689]

Singer was known for his own "Twink Parties" and he was also a fixture at the "pedophile sex den,"[690] the "male brothel,"[691] i.e. the M&C Estate of Collins-Rector. Subsequently, a number of lawsuits alleging rape and/or sexual abuse were directed at the bigwig investors and party-goers. The accusers "named prominent members of the gay Hollywood elite,"[692] including Hollywood's A-list director Bryan Singer but also David Neuman (former Disney executive), Garth Ancier (president of NBC), and Hollywood producer Garry Goddard.

---

686 "Friends In High Places: Bryan Singer and the Hollywood Elite Flocking to his Parties," *ONTD* October 31, 2017.
687 "Friends In High Places."
688 French and Potter, " 'Nobody Is Going to Believe You'."
689 Scott Bixby, "Inside Hollywood's 'Twink' Pool Parties," *The Daily Beast* July 12, 2017.
690 Robert Kolker, "What Happens When You Accuse a Major Hollywood Director of Rape?" *Vulture* September 7, 2014.
691 "Bryan Singer & Other Hollywood Sex Ring Defendants Exposed As Investors in Shady Company Run By Pedophile," *Radar Online* April 24, 2014.
692 Kolker, "What Happens."

In 2019 after a 12-month investigation with over 50 sources spoken to *The Atlantic* published a blockbuster investigative report detailing decades of sexual abuse allegations against Bryan Singer.[693]

> Almost from the moment his star began to rise, Singer, who is now 53, has been trailed by allegations of sexual misconduct. These allegations were so well known that 4,000 students, faculty members, and alumni at the University of Southern California had signed a petition asking the school to take Singer's name off one of its programs, the Bryan Singer Division of Cinema and Media Studies—which the school did immediately after Sanchez-Guzman filed his suit. As one prominent actor told us, "After the Harvey Weinstein news came out, everyone thought Bryan Singer would be next."[694]

The Atlantic report built "a powerful case that friends, associates and ultimately his industry aided and abetted Singer."[695] It was common knowledge in Hollywood

> the filmmaker's private world of gay Hollywood parties and the friends who scout young men to go to them... BuzzFeed has spoken with six people who have gone to them...These sources provided a stark portrait of an entrenched system, facilitated by these scouts, who bring Singer into regular orbit with 18- to 20-year-olds at parties sustained by large amounts of alcohol and drugs — edging precariously close to the line between legality and illegality...To scout for attractive young men to attend his parties, Singer has relied on a network of friends, according to multiple sources.[696]

Some of the lawsuits against the Hollywood bigwigs began to unravel, no doubt due to the power of the Hollywood elite to fight and protect themselves.[697] Nevertheless, Bryan Singer agreed

---

693 French and Potter, "'Nobody Is Going to Believe You'."
694 French and Potter, "'Nobody Is Going to Believe You'."
695 Marina Hyde, "R Kelly, Michael Jackson and Bryan Singer. Who Knew? Everyone," *The Guardian* January 31, 2019.
696 Adam B. Vary, "Inside Bryan Singer's Wild Hollywood World," *BuzzFeed* April 23, 2014.
697 French and Potter, "'Nobody Is Going to Believe You'."

to an out of court settlement,[698] and others such as Garry Goddard soon faced further pedophilia charges.[699]

> If Singer's alleged predatory behavior was able to continue unabated, it's because people in the industry protected him, and they did so because he made them lots and lots of money.[700]

Reports are that Singer is David Geffen's acolyte, his "chosen replacement," and as such it is Geffen who has been Singer's "protector."[701]

After *Star Treck: Discovery* star Anthony Rapp came out with an accusation against Kevin Spacey of sexual misconduct when Rapp was 14 years old – Spacey and Singer are pals, by the way[702] - Rose McGowan, one of the most outspoken accusers of Harvey Weinstein who accused him of raping her in 1997, offered her support in tweets that cryptically allude to David Geffen, Bryan Singer and the alleged Hollywood pedophile ring.[703]

---

698 Tim Teeman, "Bryan Singer Agreed to Settle Sex Abuse Lawsuit for $100,000, but Insists He's Innocent," *The Daily Beast* April 14, 2017; Becky Freeth, "Director Bryan Singer agrees to pay $150,000 to settle rape case," *Metro* Jun 13, 2019.
699 Gus Garcia-Roberts, "Hollywood producer Gary Goddard accused of sexual misconduct by 8 former child actors," *Los Angeles Times* December 20, 2017.
700 Steven Blum, "Will the Industry Continue to Embrace Director Bryan Singer?" *Los Angeles Magazine* January 25, 2019.
701 codyave, "The Mogul, according to CDAN," *Medium* August 26, 2019.
702 Rae Alexandra, "It's Not Hard to Connect the Dots in Hollywood's Culture of Abuse," *KQED* November 7, 2017.
703 Max Mundan, "Rose McGown Asks 'Are They Trying To Silence Me?' To News of Virginia Arrest Warrant," *Inquisitr* October 31, 2017.

But Singer's sins seem to be surpassing even Geffen's protective shadow. 20th Century Fox fired Singer in December 2017, just two weeks before completion of the filming of Singer's blockbuster project *Bohemian Rhapsody*. Coincidently, also in December, news of another sexual abuse lawsuit against the director broke, a Seattle man charging Singer had raped him when he was 17. [704] When the movie *Bohemian Rhapsody* won two Golden Globes in January 2019, Singer was conspicuously absent from the ceremony.

Shortly after the M&C Estate sexual assault allegations surfaced in 2000, Collins-Rector, Shackley and Pierce fled the

---

704 French and Potter, "'Nobody Is Going to Believe You'."

country and lived undetected for two years in Spain before Interpol picked them up. Authorities discovered a cache of weapons and 8,000 images of child pornography in the villa where Collins-Rector's lived. In June 2004 Collins-Rector pled guilty to transporting minors across state lines for the purpose of sex. However, there is a deeper angel to this story.

According to court documents, Collins-Rector left the country, not because (or not *only* because) of the charges that were filed against him. Rather, he fled *out of fear that David Geffen was out to destroy him.*[705] In 2003 Brock Pierce testified under oath that Geffen, no longer satisfied with being a minority partner in DEN, tried multiple times to buy DEN outright from Collins-Rector. When Collins-Rector refused to sell, Geffen reportedly said, "I'm going to take your business, whether you like it or not."[706] According to Pierce's testimony, Collins-Rector believed and feared that Geffen *and the "Gay Mafia" were intending to kill him*! These are the words found in the court records: Gay Mafia.[707] Indeed, ultimately the Gay Mafia ran things at the M&C Estate. As John Connolly, former NYPD detective-turned-investigative reporter said in *An Open Secret*: "Hollywood is a company town. Marc Rector joined that company and that town. And they get away with murder, or in this case they get away with being pedophiles."[708] As a company man you get away with murder and with pedophilia – until you run afoul with the company. According to one of the alleged victims of the M&C Estate sexual abuses, Bryan Singer told him, "We control Hollywood. We can eliminate

---

705 Deposition of Brock Pierce, October 21, 2003, Circuit Court of the Eleventh Judicial Circuit in and for Miami-Dade County, Florida, Case No. 02-3317 CA-20; Ellie Hall, Nicolás Medina Mora and David Noriega, "Found: The Elusive Man At The Heart Of The Hollywood Sex Abuse Scandal," *Buzzfeed* June 26, 2014.
706 Hall, Mora and Noriega, "Found: The Elusive Man."
707 Deposition of Brock Pierce, October 21, 2003, Circuit Court of the Eleventh Judicial Circuit in and for Miami-Dade County, Florida, Case No. 02-3317 CA-20.
708 *An Open Secret* 2014 Documentary by Amy Berg @ https://vimeo.com/142444429.

271

you; we *will* eliminate you."[709] That "we" is likely Hollywood's Gay Mafia. Collins-Rector knew their power. For this reason Collins-Rector, Shackley, and Peirce hastily charted a jet and flew to Spain where they hid from Geffen and the Gay Mafia for two years until Interpol caught up with Collins-Rector in Spain in 2002. This, according to testimony under oath.

Fear of David Geffen seems to be part of the very landscape of Hollywood. In 2015 a gay porn star and male prostitute, Justin Griggs, who appeared as a government witness in an extortion trial of a fellow porn actor and escort, told the court of his ties to David Geffen, and admitted that he feared disclosing the details of this relationship with the "very powerful" billionaire out of fear for his safety.[710]

> A gay porn star who moonlighted as a paid escort recently told FBI agents that he did not want to discuss details of his relationship with David Geffen because the billionaire was very powerful, adding that his hesitance grew out of fear for his own safety, according to a court transcript.[711]

---

709 "Bryan Singer's Accuser Claims He 'Was Like A Piece Of Meat' To The 'X-Men' Producer; Says Sex Ring Boasted 'We Control Hollywood…We Can Eliminate You'," *Radar Online* April 17, 2014; Tim Teeman, " 'I Considered Suicide,' Alleged Sex Abuse Victim of Bryan Singer Tells The Daily Beast," *The Daily Beast* April 17, 2014.

710 Snejana Farberov, "Gay porn actor reveals his ties to David Geffen and says he 'fears for his safety' - as his male escort friend is found guilty of $1.4m extortion plot," *Daily Mail* July 10, 2015; "Male Escort Told FBI He Feared David Geffen," *the smoking gun* July 9, 2015.

711 Farberov, "Gay porn actor reveals"; "Male Escort Told FBI He Feared David Geffen," *the smoking gun* July 9, 2015.

Thus, Rea Alexandra wisely pointed out:

> If you spend even a small amount of time researching the rumors about and charges against Hollywood's pedophiles (both convicted and alleged), it doesn't take long to see the dots connecting and one large circle forming. As fresh tales of abuse continue to emerge over the next few weeks and months, that circle is bound to get larger. One can only guess at its final enormity.[712]

The dots certainly connect: David Geffen • Sandy Gallin • Bryan Singer • Marc Collins-Rector • The Gay Mafia • Jewish Hollywood • Edgar Bronfman Jr. • Michael Jackson's enemies

---

712 Rae Alexandra, "It's Not Hard to Connect the Dots in Hollywood's Culture of Abuse," *KQED* November 7, 2017.

While Dr. Conrad Murray *has* undoubtedly told fictions regarding Michael Jackson, I do believe this part of his testimony.

> [Michael Jackson] liked skinny [female] brunettes. He told me his whole life gay men had tried it on with him. 'He was uncomfortable with a lot of it. He said it was part of being in showbusiness. I don't think he was homophobic but I know he'd had some terrible experiences.[713]

One of those "terrible experiences" allegedly involved David Geffen.

Shana Mangatal was the receptionist for Gallin Morey Associates for 7 years during the time Sandy Gallin was managing Michael Jackson (1990-1996). Gallin is Geffen's close pal. Like Geffen, he is gay and a Jew from New York. It was Geffen who had Michael Jackson accept Gallin as his manager. Shana Mangatal was front and center at Gallin's office during these years and allegedly had some kind of relationship with Michael Jackson. Mangatal was friends with her boss Sandy Gallin while he was managing Michael and she thus gives us something of an insider's view in her book, *Michael and Me: The Untold Story of Michael Jackson's Secret Romance.*[714] Mangatal shares with us a vitally important nugget and clue to understanding so many of the unfortunate events that had occurred in Michael's life. She relates:

---

713 Caroline Graham, "NO, I didn't kill Michael. He did it himself…with a massive overdose using his own stash," *Daily Mail* November 24, 2013.
714 Shana Mangatal, *Michael and Me: The Untold Story of Michael Jackson's Secret Romance* (Chicago: Chicago Review Press, Inc., 2016).

Gallin Morey Associates was one of the hottest music and talent management companies of the '90s. … for seven years, I was front and center in this exclusive enclave of dream makers…

The Untold Story of
MICHAEL JACKSON'S
Secret Romance
Shana Mangatal

Sandy Gallin was a flamboyant and charming Hollywood power player. His best friend was billionaire David Geffen. Together they knew everybody. They were a part of the so-called Velvet Mafia, which consisted of some of the most powerful gay executives in town…

My desk was the calm in the middle of the storm and often I acted as a therapist, encouraging the assistants to hang in there. Some of those assistants were the young, gay, handsome boys Sandy met at his famous weekly pool parties, which were held at his sprawling mansion in Beverly Hills or his beach home in Malibu. Most of these boys were fresh off the bus from small towns across the country. They harbored dreams of becoming rich or famous – or both. I chuckled every time a new one stepped off the elevator for his first day on the job. They were so fresh-faced and eager. That excitement never lasted long…

My first month on the job, I was invited to one of Sandy's famous parties. They were a thing of legend something you only read about in magazines. Think The Great Gatsby. This would be my first real Hollywood party…The bash was being thrown in honor of Sandy's boyfriend, Tom. It was his birthday…Sandy's best friend, David Geffen, was also there. At that moment, he was the richest, most powerful man in town...David and Sandy were both in their late forties but in incredible shape, able to attract any young, hot guy they desired. Everyone wanted to know David, and, at this time, Michael Jackson was no different. David and Michael had become fast friends, and David introduced Michael to Sandy. That's how Michael became Sandy's client…Years later, I asked Michael about David and why they were no longer close

275

friends (Michael managed to fall out with most of his friends every few years). I don't know how true it is, because Michael was known to exaggerate on occasion, but he said that David had tried to seduce him, attempting to kiss him, and, according to Michael, he refused. Their friendship was strained after that.

David Geffen made a homosexual advance at Michael Jackson and he rebuffed it; he *rejected* Geffen's sexual advance. This is deep. According to Mangatal's recounting, Michael understood *this* moment as the moment he and Geffen's relationship "strained." Michael would come to know to what extent Geffen was insulted and how David Geffen handles being insulted. As David Handelman and Tom King reported: "The Operator (David Geffen) could have easily been called The Liar… he'd spread lies about people with whom he was feuding…"[715]; "Geffen's most disturbing trait…is his willingness to sabotage the careers of others by manufacturing toxic and unfounded rumors.[716]

---

715 David Handelman, "How David Geffen Got Ahead: Lies, Loot and a Little Luck," *Observer* March 13, 2000.
716 Tom King, *The Operator: David Geffen Builds, Buys, and Sells The New Hollywood* (New York: Broadway Books, 2000).

Part 7

Plotting Against The King

Chapter Eleven

Medical Abuse

I.   *Deliberately Making Michael Jackson an Addict. 1993*

For Michael Jackson 1993 was a watershed year – a year of trauma and of conspiracy. In this year Michael was *made* into an addict and also this year Michael was first framed for a crime he never committed and for which he was never even indicted. Yet the false chargers changed the course of his career and likely of his life permanently.

After Michael's hair caught on fire during the filming of a Pepsi commercial in 1984, an accident that severely burned his scalp, the resulting surgeries introduced Michael to painkilling drugs. But by all accounts, Michael did not develop a dependency until the fateful year of 1993, and this dependency did not develop because Michael Jackson was a *drug seeker*. He was not. According to David Fournier, the certified nurse anesthetist who worked for Michael for 10 years (1993-2003), "Jackson never asked for specific drugs"[717] and he "didn't exhibit any drug-seeking behavior or signs that he was doctor-shopping."[718] Nor was Michael's drug dependency that did develop in 1993 the unfortunate but entirely conceivable consequence of all of the medical procedures he underwent during which anesthetics were required. Rather, Michael's first battle with drug addiction came as a consequence of an addiction that was *wholly unnecessary* and

---

717 Alan Duke, "Michael Jackson's drug use explored in trial," *CNN* July 26, 2013.
718 Associated Press, "Michael Jackson's Drug History Scrutinized in Court," *Billboard* July 26, 2013.

very likely *deliberately* induced in him by a yet unrecognized *frenemy* – unrecognized by Michael.

1993 was the year Michael Jackson became addicted to a specific drug: Demerol.[719] Demerol is a synthetic (man-made) opioid, described as "the pharmacological equivalent of heroin."[720] Thus, Michael's 1997 song *Morphine* is a haunting reflection on addiction to Demerol. His friend and personal assistant Frank Cascio said that while Michael first encountered Demerol in 1984 after the hair fire, it was only in 1993 during the *Dangerous* tour that he first noticed Michael taking the drug.[721] Cascio remembers being concerned later with the great amount of Demerol Michael was being given and voiced his concern. Michael then called the doctor that was injecting him with the drug and, on speaker phone, "asked him to verify that the quantity of Demerol he was taking was safe and appropriate."[722] Who was this "Demerol Doctor"? It was Dr. Arnold Klein.

Dr. Stuart Finkelstein, the tour doctor who travelled with Michael Jackson during the *Dangerous* tour, recalled that in Thailand, before he could "administer pain relief to Jackson" Dr. Finkelstein called "the singer's Los Angeles doctor on the phone and agreed to give him pain medication to help the singer cope with a severe headache."[723] Michael's Los Angeles doctor was Dr. Klein and the drug that Dr. Finkelstein went on to administer was Demerol. Reportedly, Michael was "given 'two to four' 10mg doses of Demerol *each day for the length of the tour*."[724] Dr. Klein was not on the tour, but on his behalf his nurse assistant since 1977

---

719 "'Michael Jackson was drug addict in 1993' – doctor," *Newshub* September 7, 2013.
720 Colin Vickery, "Michael Jackson should have died earlier, autopsy report reveals," *News Corp Australia* June 25, 2014.
721 The Associated Press, "Manager: Michael Jackson took drugs before performing," *Newsday* November 12, 2011.
722 Mark Seal, "The Doctor Will Sue You Now," *Vanity Fair* February 2, 2012
723 "'Michael Jackson was drug addict in 1993' – doctor," *Newshub* September 7, 2013.
724 Toyin Owoseje, "Michael Jackson Doctor: Star's Infected Buttocks Revealed Drug Addition," *IB Times* July 1, 2014.

Debbi Rowe was. Karen Faye, Michael's make-up artist and hair-dresser, testified in 2013 that

> nurse Debbie Rowe, who would later become Jackson's second wife and the mother of his two oldest children, would travel with them on the "Dangerous" tour in 1992 with "a little bag" of medications.
>
> "Debbie Rowe asked me to learn how to give injections," [Karen Faye] said. "I thought about it and said 'No.' I am not qualified to handle any kind of medications."
>
> When the tour was on its way to Bangkok, Thailand, Faye was asked to carry a package she was told contained medicine patches for Jackson's pain, she testified. She refused to travel with it, she said.
>
> Faye testified that the tour doctor, Dr. Stuart Finkelstein, later told her "I'm glad you weren't carrying it. It has vials and syringes. If you had brought this in, you might not be here." The implication was she could have been arrested for smuggling drugs.
>
> [Paul] Gongaware, now the Co-CEO of AEG Live, was in charge of logistics for the "Dangerous" tour and was involved in the incident, Faye said.[725]

While Faye might have rejected Rowe's request that she help by learning herself how to administer the Demerol injections to Michael, according to Dr. Finkelstein Faye did give Michael two ampules of Demerol that were for Jackson's injections. Dr. Finkelstein also recalled Michael wearing a Duragesic patch, which contained another opiate which is absorbed through the skin.[726]

Michael Jackson may even have been drugged against his will in order to *get him to Thailand*.[727] On August 18, 1993, attorneys told Michael that a criminal investigation into child

---

725 Alan Duke, "Witness: Michael Jackson was paranoid, talking to himself in last days," *CNN* May 9, 2013
726 "'Michael Jackson was drug addict in 1993' – doctor," *Newshub* September 7, 2013.
727 Stefan Kyriazis, "Michael Jackson child abuse case: New shock revelations from his lawyer and manager," *Express* June 22, 2016.

molestation allegations had begun. Michael was scheduled to fly to Bangkok in the next three days. The news killed Michael's spirit or desire to complete the tour. He "no longer felt like hitting the road."[728] Sandy Gallin was Michael's manager at the time.

> Bert Fields (Michael's lawyer), fearing Michael would be arrested, called Michael's manager Sandy Gallin and told him they needed to get Michael out of the country as soon as possible. "Bert told me that if they didn't get him out of the country, Michael would be arrested," Gallin recalls. "And then the whole tour would have been cancelled at a huge financial loss...Michael did not want to go on the tour, but somehow, Anthony Pellicano got him on the plane. How, I don't know. He went to his apartment in Century City; he may have drugged him, tied him up, or talked him into going quietly."[729]

Anthony Pellicano was Bert Fields' Private Investigator. The *Los Angeles Times* exposed Pellicano's Mafia ties in 1993.[730]

Britain's *The Sun* (July 24, 2009) reported seeing proof that Michael Jackson's "first major battle with drug addiction occurred shortly after [Dr. Arnold Klein] treated him [in 1993] with *four times* the daily maximum recommended amount of the drug."[731] Dr. Steven Hoefflin, Michael's long-time plastic surgeon, examined Michael's medical records in 1993 per Michael's request and discovered "the insane amount of Demerol" that Dr. Klein was *unnecessarily* administering to Michael for minor dermatological procedures. "The maximum amount you should give a patient of his weight and build in severe surgical pain is 200mg a day. Michael was being given 800mg a day," for minor procedures such as acne treatment.

---

728 Michael "may have been drugged to get him out of the country before the county police could arrest him in 1993": Stefan Kyriazis, "Michael Jackson child abuse allegations: His first lawyer believed he was Innocent," *Express* May 7, 2019.
729 Stefan Kyriazis, "Michael Jackson child abuse allegations: His first lawyer believed he was Innocent," *Express* May 7, 2019.
730 Ken Auletta, "Hollywood Ending," *The New Yorker* July 17, 2006.
731 Mark Seal, "The Ugly world of Dr. Arnie Klein, Beverly Hills' King of Botox," *Vanity Fair* February 2, 2012

"I was shocked to see the huge amount of narcotics … and other medications that both Dr. Klein and Debbie Rowe were injecting into Michael," Hoefflin states.

For example, Klein and Rowe, who worked as a nurse for Klein, injected as much as 1,850 mg of Demerol into Jackson during a three-day period in August 1993, according to Hoefflin's declaration.[732]

This is a massive and totally unnecessary amount. Dr. Hoefflin thus charged Dr. Klein: "You caused his Demerol and other prescription pain medicine addiction. You instructed Debbie Rowe to inject large quantities of Demerol while she was alone in his home."[733] Debbie Rowe herself testified that Dr. Klein "regularly loaded up Jackson with Demerol and Percocet…"[734] and, as his nurse assistant, she "provided the painkiller Demerol and Propofol for many of the hundreds of treatments Jackson received over 20 years."[735] Dr. Klein himself admitted to Harvey Levin of TMZ Live in November 2009 that *Michael Jackson never requested Demerol* from him and *never wanted it!*[736] Why, then, was Michael pumped with such an extreme amount of this "pharmacological equivalent of heroin"? Rowe reveals of Dr. Klein: he "*was not doing what was best for Michael.*"[737] Then whose interests was he serving? If Michael Jackson's best interest *was not* Dr. Klein's

---

732 "Lawyers For 'Dermatologist' to the Stars' Argue Against Defamation Case," *Waven Newspapers* June 16, 2011.
733 Seal, "The Ugly world of Dr. Arnie Klein."
734 Richard Johnson, "They didn't care about him: Michael Jackson's ex-wife rips doctors in star's death," *New York Post* August 15, 2013
735 "Michael Jackson trial: Debbie Rowe cries during testimony," *ABC7* August 14, 2013.
736 November 5, 2009, Interview (90 minutes):

Harvey Levin	Did [Michael] ever ask you for Demerol?
Arnold Klein	No.
Harvey Levin	He never said, "I want Demerol"?
Arnold Klein	No, because I wouldn't give him what he wanted. You don't give a person what they want.

737 Jeff Gottlieb, "Debbie Rowe: Michael Jackson's doctors competed to give pain eds," *Los Angeles Times* August 14, 2013.

concern, what was his objective in 1993 in treating Michael Jackson with *four times the daily maximum recommended amount of the drug?*

On November 11, 1993 the remainder of Michael Jackson's *Dangerous* tour was abruptly cancelled. According to Michael's attorney Bert Fields the cancellation was the consequence of a painkiller addiction which Michael developed "in recent weeks"[738] - an addiction caused by Dr. Arnold Klein. This is why Dr. Hoefflin charged: "You [Dr. Klein] prevented [Michael] from continuing his Dangerous Tour."[739] Michael was flown to England where he spent time in a drug rehabilitation program which, according to Dr. Klein's admission, was successful. Michael Jackson came home clean.[740] He had won this first battle with drug addiction which was induced by one of the many enemies around him that posed as friends.

II.   *How Michael Was Made "White"*

I'm a Black American. I am proud to be a Black American. I am proud of my race, and I am proud of who I am. I have a lot of pride and dignity of who I am. - Michael Jackson on Oprah Winfrey, 1993.

Dr. Steve Hoefflin informs us of another very important fact: "Dr. Klein is the one who made [Michael Jackson's] face white by using Benoquin, a permanent bleaching agent".[741]

---

738 Jessica Seigel, "Ailing Michael Jackson Not 'hiding Out', His Lawyer Says," *Chicago Tribune* November 16, 1993.
739 Seal, "The Ugly world of Dr. Arnie Klein."
740 Harvey Levin, TMZ Live Interview, November 5, 2009.
741 "Former Jackson Doctor Claims Michael 'Had Lethal Amounts of Demerol & Propofol'," *Access Hollywood* July 23, 2009.

Michael had the skin condition called vitiligo which produces loss of skin color in blotches due to the death or dysfunction of pigment producing cells. Michael never wanted to go "white." He first used a special make up to cover up (darken) the light blotches. Vitiligo can be treated with corticosteroids and oral medicine combined with ultraviolet light therapies to restore pigment to the skin. This available phototherapy treatment for vitiligo is called Narrowband UVB. I don't know if Michael ever tried this treatment (though Dr Klein below suggests that it may have been considered). However, Michael *did* try to medically darken the blotches, i.e. *re*-pigmentize his skin. Dr. Richard Strick, one of the doctors appointed by the Santa Barbara District Attorney who performed the body search on Michael Jackson during the 1993 case reviewed Michael's medical records and testified:

> Michael had a disease vitiligo in which the pigment is lost and *attempts had been made to bring that pigment back* which had been unsuccessful so he tried to bleach it out so it would be one color.[742]

But it categorically *was not* Michael Jackson who "tried to bleach it out."

> it was decided [in 1990] by his dermatologist, none other than Dr Arnold Klein, that the easiest way to treat the condition, rather than

---

742 https://www.youtube.com/watch?v=RTuvCalcgPw.

drugs and ultraviolet light treatments, was by using creams to make the darker spots fade so the pigments could be evened out across the body. The cream that Klein used on Jackson was Benoquin...[743]

And as Dr. Klein admitted on Larry King Live, it was never Michael's decision to go white.

KING: So let's clear up something. [Michael] was not someone desirous of being white?

KLEIN: No. Michael was black. He was very proud of his black heritage. He changed the world for black people. We now have a black president.

KING: So how do you treat vitiligo?

KLEIN: Well, I mean there's certain treatments. *You have one choice where you can use certain drugs called* (INAUDIBLE) *and ultraviolet light treatments to try to make the white spots turn dark* or — his became so severe, that the easier way is to use certain creams that will make the dark spots turn light so you can even out the pigments totally.

KING: So *your* decision there was he would go light?

KLEIN: *Well, yes*, that's ultimately what the decision had to be, because there was too much vitiligo to deal with and...
.....

KING: How did you treat the vitiligo?

KLEIN: Well, we basically used creams that would even out the same color and *we destroyed the remaining pigment cells.*

KING: And did his color change a lot over the years?

KLEIN: No, because once we got — we got it more uniform, it remained stable. But you still had to treat it because once in a while — and he had to also be extraordinary careful with sun exposure because of a lot of things. And that's why he had the umbrellas all the time (INAUDIBLE) skin now.[744]

---

743 Richards and Langthorne, *83 Minutes,* 114.
744 https://www.youtube.com/watch?v=2foESMQDBAY.

Dr. Klein has been known to lie on Michael Jackson many times and even admitted to it (as we shall see), yet we unfortunately are forced to take his word here that Michael's vitiligo was so severe that the only real option was to go light rather than even out the dark skin. The "bleaching cream" that *Dr. Klein* put Michael on, Benoquin, not only lightens skin but *permanently removes pigment* and thus leaves the person "extremely sensitive to the sun."[745] Thus Michael Jackson said in his 1996 VH1 interview: "I am totally completely allergic to the sun."[746] A Black God *made* totally allergic to the sun?! Michael was *made allergic to the Life-Giving Sun by the same frenemy who drugged him unnecessarily and got him – no doubt deliberately – addicted.* If, as Debbie Rowe admitted, Dr. Klein "*was not* doing what was best for Michael" when he was drugging him, do we think Dr. Klein was doing what was best *for Michael* when he (Dr. Klein) was bleaching Michael white by *permanently destroying his pigment cells* (melanin = The Black God Molecule) and making Michael allergic to the sun? Hardly.

We have reason to believe that Michael Jackson regretted what was done to his appearance, including this skin whitening. Teddy Riley travelled with Michael on the *Dangerous* tour and said in *Rolling Stone* that during the tour Michael spoke a lot about what was done to his face and his skin and Riley suggested that Michael indeed had regrets, saying: "I'm quite sure if Michael could have done it all over again, *he would not have done that.* But there's no turning back. Once you change your description, you can't turn back. You can't get your own face or your own skin back again."[747]

---

745 Madison Park, "In life of mysteries, Jackson's changed color baffled public," *CNN* July 8, 2009.
746 https://www.youtube.com/watch?v=E-YuS3UiDK4.
747 Michael Goldberg, "Michael Jackson: The Making of 'The King of Pop'," *Rolling Stone* January 9, 1992.

Chapter Twelve

The Plot To Frame Michael Jackson

I.   *The Pedophile Agenda Targets Michael Jackson*

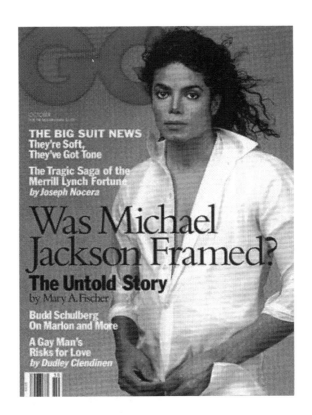

In August 1993 while Michael Jackson was in London fighting his addiction to Dr. Klein's Demerol, back home in California the world woke up to *startling* news: an investigation has been launched of child molestation allegations against Michael Jackson. But the evidence is now clear and overwhelming that

289

Michael Jackson was not guilty of those charges but was *framed* in 1993. Mary Fisher, senior writer at *GQ*, wrote a game-changing article in 1994 entitled, "Was Michael Jackson Framed?" She concludes

> It is, of course, impossible to prove a negative—that is, prove that something didn't happen. But it is possible to take an in-depth look at the people who made the allegations against Jackson and thus gain insight into their character and motives. What emerges from such an examination, based on court documents, business records and scores of interviews, is a persuasive argument that Jackson molested no one and that he himself may have been the victim of a well-conceived plan to extract money from him.[748]

Who framed Michael Jackson? And *why*? We can actually go a long way in answering these critical questions.

Victor Gutierrez is a man who was *central* to the Set Up and Framing of Michael Jackson on bogus child molestation charges, both in 1993 and in 2005. Gutierrez is said to be the one man who has influenced the media reporting and probably the formation of the allegations against Michael more than anyone else. According to anti-Michael Jackson journalist Maureen Orth of *Vanity Fair* the 2005 prosecution's case against Michael relied on Gutierrez's salacious and fraudulent 1996 book, *Michael Jackson Was My Lover: the secret diary of Jordy Chandler.* "Many of the witnesses who testified for the prosecution at Jackson's 2005 trial, and on whom the prosecution's 'prior bad acts' case was mostly built, were people who had contact with Victor Gutierrez prior to selling their stories to the tabloids for money."[749] Gutierrez features in almost every single allegation against Michael: "Every witness was through him, every victim was someone he had met at some point." Victor Gutierrez was

---

748 Mary A. Fisher, "Was Michael Jackson Framed: The Untold Story That Brought Down A Superstar" (The Original *GQ* Article) (2003) 1.
749 Linda-Raven woods, "The New Lynching of Michael Jackson: Dan Reed's *Leaving Neverland*, In Fact, Leave Blood on Many Hands," *Medium* February 27, 2019.

deeply involved in crafting the pedophile narrative around Michael Jackson.

A free-lance journalist from Santiago, Chile, Gutierrez in his crusade against Michael Jackson actually served at least three different organizations who had targeted the singer: NAMBLA,

Victor Gutierrez

the Los Angeles Police Department, and the F.B.I. NAMBLA is the North American Man/Boy Love Association, a *pro-pedophilia* organization which "advocates sex between men and boys and cites ancient Greece to justify the practice."[750] According to the F.B.I., at NAMBLA's "secret" conferences there takes place "networking for illicit activities" such as "trips abroad to abuse children."[751] During November 7-9, 1986 NAMBLA held their conference (The 10th International Membership Conference) in Los Angeles. By Gutierrez's own admission he was in attendance.[752]

According to Gutierrez it was at this 1986 NAMBLA conference that his mission came to him. He reports on discussions among the conference pedophiles about Michael Jackson. Michael's very public love of and surrounding by children, all very *innocent*, nevertheless gave those NAMBLA members hope *and an idea*: use a perverted caricature of Michael Jackson to *normalize their cause*. By "outing" Michael Jackson as, i.e. "converting" him into, a *pedophile* – a sexual lover of young boys – NAMBLA would have a celebrity poster-boy for their cause. *"At the conference Gutierrez hears for the first time: 'Michael is one of us.' A pedophile. 'Jackson was treated like an idol there,* as a

---

750 Onell R. Soto, "FBI Targets Pedophilia Advocates. Little-Known Group Promotes 'Benevolent' Sex," *San Diego Union-Tribune* February 18, 2005.
751 Soto, "FBI Targets Pedophilia Advocates."
752 Robert Sandall, "Michael Jackson Was My Lover" *GQ Magazine* September 2006; Henning Kober, "Es war Liebe!" *Die Tageszeitung*, April 5, 2005 @
http://www.taz.de/1/archiv/?id=archivseite&dig=2005/04/05/a0170

hope for social acceptance.'"[753] Gutierrez and his fellow pedophiles thought that, with the help of Michael Jackson's celebrity, "In a hundred years maybe such relationships will be socially accepted."

Gutierrez admits leaving that meeting with his mission clear: to "out" Michael Jackson as, not a "child molester" but a *pedophile* (pedophiles draw a strong distinction) like Gutierrez's fellow pedophiles at NAMBLA. For the next five years Gutierrez targeted Michael Jackson's Latin employees, ingratiating himself on them and planting seeds in their minds. He "Interviews" boys who had been around Michael. As is clear from his book, Gutierrez's modus operandi was to approach persons and *give them the idea* that Michael had these relations with boys and then invites the person to "add to" his information.

In this NAMBLA-inspired mission against Michael Jackson Gutierrez had some relationship with the LAPD as far back as 1986 and that relationship would be critical for the 1993 Set Up and "investigation" of the false charges. In his coverage of Victor Gutierrez for *GQ Magazine* in 2006 Robert Sandall makes the important revelation (mostly mis-read by Michael Jackson Fan commentators): "Gutierrez began his investigation [of Michael Jackson] in 1986 *when he went undercover with the LAPD.*"[754] Gutierrez would thus send investigative reports to the LAPD, he admits.[755] The LAPD would supply Gutierrez with legal documents, and the LAPD admitted to relying on Gutierrez's "original manuscript," which he sent them, after the Chandler allegations were publicized in 1993.[756] This is why in his book, along with NAMBLA, Gutierrez thanks for their assistance "detectives of the Sheriff's Department of Santa Barbara" and "officials and detectives of the Child Abuse Unit of the LAPD." Gutierrez also thanked the F.B.I. How did they assist? Paulina

---

753 Robert Sandall, "Michael Jackson Was My Lover" *GQ Magazine* September 2006.
754 Sandall, "Michael Jackson Was My Lover."
755 Sandall, "Michael Jackson Was My Lover." He says he provided a copy of his book "after the first phase of his research."
756 Sandall, "Michael Jackson Was My Lover."

Toro writing in the Spanish language periodical *El Universal* affirmed in 2005: "When no one imagined that Michael Jackson could have deviant sexual relations with boys, FBI agents gave journalist Victor Gutierrez a list of famous pedophiles in Los Angeles. Among them was Jackson's name."[757] LAPD documents further suggest a relationship between the F.B.I. and Gutierrez. So these three institutions – NAMBLA, the LAPD and the FBI – all demonstrated an interest as far back as 1986 in (falsely) tagging Michael Jackson as a pedophile and they all relied upon this man Victor Gutierrez to deliver.

We know that NAMBLA's interest was in using a fabricated "pedophile Michael Jackson" in their cause to normalize pedophilia. Victor Gutierrez's book, *Michael Jackson Was My Lover*, presents the false sexual relationship between Michael Jackson and the first accuser, the 13-year old Jordan Chandler, as a consensual, loving, sexual relationship. And as Linda-Raven Woods writing for *Medium* pointed out:

> [The book] was, as it turned out, little more than a piece of NAMBLA propaganda, written with the intent of promoting man/boy love, with the added spice of throwing in the name Michael Jackson. What was even more disturbing was the fact that Gutierrez and the boy's father, Evan Chandler, obviously collaborated on the project...[758]

In April 2005 Victor Gutierrez was interviewed by the German pro-pedophilia periodical *Tageszeitung*. The name of the article is "Es War Liebe!" "It Was Love!", referring to the alleged relationship between Michael Jackson and Jordan Chandler.[759]

What was the LAPD and the FBI's interest in fabricating a "pedophile" Michael Jackson? We don't know, but we have good grounds to speculate: a fabricated and falsely charged "pedophile

---

757 Paulina Toro, "Victor Gutierrez, Bashir advisor," *El Universal* March 19, 2005.
758 Linda-Raven woods, "The New Lynching of Michael Jackson: Dan Reed's *Leaving Neverland*, In Fact, Leave Blood on Many Hands," *Medium* February 27, 2019.
759 Henning Kober, "Es war Liebe!" *Die Tageszeitung*, April 5, 2005 @
  http://www.taz.de/1/archiv/?id=archivseite&dig=2005/04/05/a0170

Michael Jackson" could be used to *distract attention from Hollywood's true pedophiles* who were *protected by the LAPD.* For example, Hollywood gay pornography figure-turned-celebrity sleuth who (like Victor Gutierrez) made money selling celebrity dirt to tabloids, Paul Barresi, once assisted the LAPD (as did Gutierrez) uncover a male prostitution ring. The investigation was derailed because, according to Barresi, "they [the LAPD] didn't want to touch [a high-ranking member of the Velvet Mafia, Hollywood's cadre of gay moguls]."[760] That derailed investigation was likely the one that involved David Forest, a pal of David Geffen, who was arrested in November 1993 for running a male prostitution ring in Los Angeles.[761] According to Barresi – who assisted the LAPD in this case - Detective Keith Haight affirmed that Geffen's name was on the client list of Forest's escort service. Haight reportedly told Barresi that Geffen's name will not be used as evidence during any trial because "We don't wanna touch Geffen."[762] According to Geffen's mysteriously deceased biographer Tom King, Geffen frequently engaged male prostitutes.[763] Paul Barresi has been associated with John Travolta and David Geffen.[764] According to Mark Ebner Barresi was once David Geffen's personal trainer.[765] This male prostitution ring that was uncovered by the LAPD and was linked to David Geffen through his pal David Forest came to light in 1993 and was derailed. 1993 was the year the first false charges of child sexual abuse were leveled against Michael Jackson.

---

760 Breitbart and Ebner, *Hollywood, Interrupted,* 172
761 See "David Forest Obituary" *Los Angeles Times* @ https://www.legacy.com/obituaries/latimes/obituary.aspx?n=david-forest&pid=175753794&fhid=20193.
762 See "David Forest Obituary" *Los Angeles Times* @ https://www.legacy.com/obituaries/latimes/obituary.aspx?n=david-forest&pid=175753794&fhid=20193.
763 King, *The Operator,* 321.
764 Andrew Breitbart and Mark Ebner, *Hollywood, Interrupted. Insanity Chic in Babylon-The Case Against Celebrity* (New Jersey: John Wiley & Sons, Inc., 2004) 170.
765 Ebner, "The Gay Mafia," 48.

II.   *"Let's Get Rid of Michael Jackson"*

[Evan] Chandler: "it could be a massacre if I don't get what I want...

"once I make that phone call, this guy's just going to destroy everybody in sight in any devious, nasty, cruel way that he can do it. And I've given him full authority to do that...

"If I go through with this, I win big time. There's no way that I lose. I've checked that out inside out...I will get everything I want, and they will be totally — they will be destroyed forever. They will be destroyed. June is gonna lose Jordy. She will have no right to ever see him again...Michael's career will be over.

[David] Schwartz: "And does that help Jordy?"

Chandler: "It's irrelevant to me."

...

Chandler: "Michael Jackson — Michael Jackson's career, Dave. This man is gonna be humiliated beyond belief. You'll not believe it. He will not believe what's going to happen to him...Beyond his worst nightmares. [tape irregularity] not sell one more record...

Schwartz: "I would do anything for Jordy. I would lose everything. I would die for Jordy. That's the bottom line.

Chandler: "Then why don't you just back me up right now and let's get rid of Michael Jackson."

These various excerpts are from three secretly taped phone calls between Evan Chandler, the father of the first Michael Jackson accuser in 1993, and David Schwartz, the accuser's stepfather. These calls were recorded on July 8, 1993. At this time the 13-year old accuser, Jordan Chandler, had denied that any sexual relationship existed between he and Michael Jackson and Evan Chandler himself in these very calls admits to having no knowledge of such abuse or activity.

Schwartz: I mean, do you think that he's fucking him?
Chandler: I don't know. I have no idea.

Why would this man want to "get rid of Michael Jackson" so much that he would frame him and set him up with false charges of molesting his son, while the potential damage that this could do (and did do) to his son was "irrelevant" to him? Two words: jealousy and money. And when you add to that the manipulations of Victor Gutierrez and the Pedophile Agenda, you have the recipe for one of the greatest social, legal, and cultural crimes of the century: the false child molestation allegations against Michael Jackson and his consequent cultural lynching or, better, crucifixion.

Evan Chandler was born Evan Robert Charmatz in the Bronx to Jewish parents. He changed his name from Charmatz to Chandler because he thought Charmatz was "too Jewish-sounding". He had been divorced from his son Jordan's mother, June, since 1985 and she had remarried David Schwartz. In 1993, however, June and David were estranged and living separately. Evan and David seem to have had some sort of comradery at the time, even while Evan and June were in the middle of a bitter custody dispute over Jordan. By the time Michael entered their lives in May 1992 Evan owed June nearly $70,000 in back child support. And, reportedly, Evan was bipolar. Michael had no idea of the level of family and human dysfunction he was stepping into.

At first Evan was proud of his son's friendship with the biggest superstar on the planet, Michael Jackson. He bragged to his colleagues. But as the media got wind of Michael's new friends, trouble started. When the *National Enquirer* in May 1993 presented June, Jordan and David's daughter Lili as Michael Jackson's "secret family" and humiliated David, things changed. When Evan started "acting weird" and *entitled* to Michael, apparently Michael "fell back" from Evan Chandler and Evan clearly felt some type of way.

> **Chandler to Schwartz:** "I had a good communication with Michael. We were friends. I liked him and I respected him and everything else for what he is. There was no reason why he had to stop calling me."

296

Michael Jackson has developed a bizarre obsession with a woman and her two children — and turned them into his secret family!

The superstar has grown incredibly attached to June Chandler Schwartz, her 13-year-old son Jordie and 3-year-old daughter Lily. Since meeting the mom and her children early this year, Michael has:

• Brought them to his ranch nearly every weekend.
• Phoned them as many as four times each day.
• Shared a suite with them during a Las Vegas vacation.
• Spent $1,500 on Jordie during one trip to Toys 'R' Us.

"I consider you my own family," he told June. "And I'll look after you as if you were."

June, 40, is the wife of Dave Schwartz, who went from rags to riches by starting Rent A Wreck and turning it into a $3.66 million a year car rental company.

Michael "adopted" June and her two children soon after he first met them at a Los Angeles Rent A Wreck office, said an insider.

"Michael rents cars from Rent A Wreck to make himself less conspicuous. He was in the office when June stopped by with her kids so they could see their dad.

"Michael struck up a conversation with Jordie and the family was so close she over the encounter."

After that meeting, Michael began calling the family every day and the insider.

"He had long conversations with Jordie and became fascinated by June, a beautiful Oriental woman.

"Michael was calling three

Michael Jackson's secret family — a millionaire's wife and her two kids

He was smiling like a proud papa

or four times a day."

June and the children made their first trip to the Neverland Valley ranch a few months ago.

The group had such a good time that Michael, in disguise, took the family to Disneyland several times.

"The more they enjoyed it, the more I did — and the closer we became," he told the insider.

Added the insider, "Michael began hosting them at Neverland nearly every weekend.

took Jordie and Lily to the "Beginner & Soy" show.

"When Michael walked back to his villa holding their hands, he was smiling like a proud papa," said an eyewitness.

The day after that, Michael and Jordie ate dinner at the Mirage's Chinese restaurant.

"They talked in whispers and laughed like a father and son," said waiter Chad John, who served them.

Later that night, the two went to the hotel's circus-type show, called Cirque Du Soleil.

"They sat in section 246, row CC," said the eyewitness. "When the show was over, Michael bought the boy a Cirque Du Soleil sweatshirt.

"When the group left Las Vegas, they headed to Michael's

'We have so much fun it's ecstasy'

ranch, said the insider.

Since then, the singer has also taken "his family" on excursions to Disney World in Florida. And last week they all went to Monte Carlo, where Michael attended the World Music Awards.

"He's infatuated and obsessed with June, Jordie and Lily," said the insider. "He has adopted this family as his own.

"Michael told me, 'I'm enjoying having June, Jordie and Lily with me.

'The four of us are like a little family. We all have so much fun together that it's ecstasy.'"

— BARBARA STRINGS and DAVID DUFFY

PLUM RIDE: Michael Jackson plays father to Jordie Schwartz (left) and his sister Lily at Florida's Disney World. June Schwartz, the children's mother sits behind them, beside an unidentified man.

His special treat was to take the hotel's dolphin pool, said the children to Toys 'R' Us on the source.

"One morning, he bought shopping again and Michael Jordie $1,500 worth of toys!"

Michael recently took June and the children on a five-day vacation to Las Vegas, where they all stayed in his private three-bedroom villa at The Mirage hotel, said a source.

"When they arrived, Michael gave the children and their monkey a tour of the place. The next day he took them shopping then to the hotel arcade."

John Mikle, who runs the arcade, said Michael couldn't stay long "because too many kids crowded around him." That night, Michael and Jordie swam with dolphins in

The next day, they went shopping again and Michael

A MASKED Michael carries Lily Schwartz from a flight in Monte Carlo, where they all went to attend the World Music Awards.

DAVE Schwartz (left), the man who started Rent A Wreck. Michael met Dave's wife June (right) and her kids when he was renting a car there.

Add to this Evan's ambition and his expectations from his son's superstar friend. Evan Chandler was a Hollywood dentist with celebrity patients such a Carrie Fisher. He hated being a dentist, however, and had a big dream of being a Hollywood screenwriter. He expected Michael Jackson to finance his career as a Hollywood screenwriter. Michael Jackson had a film production company "Lost Boys Production" that Sony invested $40 million in. Evan Chandler, having known Michael himself for only a short while, expected Michael to make him a partner in the company, worth $20 million. As the *Los Angeles Times* reported: "Film industry sources have said that the boy's father sought a $20-million movie production and financing deal with Jackson."[766] This is

---

766 Charles P. Wallace and Jim Newton, "Jackson Back n Stage; Inquiry Continues: Investigation: Singer resumes Bangkok concerts after two-day

corroborated by painter David Nordahl, who revealed in his 2010 interview with Deborah L. Kunesh:

> I was working on sketches for his film production company, called "Lost Boys Productions"....Sony had given him (Michael) $40 million to start this production company and that little boy's dad (Evan Chandler), who considered himself to be show business material, because he had written part of a script....after that he considered himself a Hollywood screenwriter, and being friends with Michael and his son being friends with Michael, this guy had assumed that Michael was going to make him a partner in this film production company and that's where the $20 million figure came from. He wanted ½ of that Sony money. It was proven. It was an extortion.[767]

Evan Chandler and his attorney attempted to force Michael Jackson to set him up with four film projects, $5 million per year for four years or he will go public with child molestation allegations, even though "The boy repeatedly denied that anything had happened."[768] When Michael's team refused, Evan Chandler was furious.

> Instead of making any report to the police for what supposedly happened to his son, [Evan Chandler] arranged a meeting with Michael and his attorneys to discuss movie deals. The father initially asked for funding for four movies, at $5 million each, a total of $20 million. This was refused by the Jackson camp and a counter-offer of $350,000 for one movie was made. After considering it, Chandler refused...According to [Private Investigator Anthony] Pellicano, the one picture deal was refused because it wasn't enough for Chandler to shut down his dental practice and focus on writing screenplays full time.[769]

This is what Evan meant in his secretly recorded phone conversation with David Schwartz on July 8th: "it could be a

---

absence. Officials here are now looking into extortion claims," *Los Angeles Times* August 28, 1993.
767 Deborah L. Kunesh, "Friendship & A Paintbrush," (2010) http://www.reflectionsonthedance.com/interviewwithdavidnordahl.html
768 Mary A. Fisher, "Was Michael Jackson Framed: The Untold Story That Brought Down A Superstar" (The Original *GQ* Article) (2003) 13.
769 Campbell, *Michael Jackson*, 55.

massacre if I don't get *what I want*." But the plan to set up and frame Michael Jackson actually was *not Evan's*. He was a player, but he said: "I've been told what to do and I have to do it."

Chandler to Schwartz: "There are other people involved that are waiting for my phone call that are intentionally going to be in certain positions – [tape irregularity]. I paid them to do it. They're doing their job. I gotta just go ahead and follow through on the time zone. I mean the time set out. Everything is going *according to a certain plan that isn't just mine. There's other people involved*."

"*My instructions* were to kill and destroy [tape irregularity], I'm telling you. I mean, and by killing and destroying, I'm going to torture them, Dave...

"It's going to be bigger than all of us put together. The whole thing is going to crash down on everybody and destroy everybody in sight. It will be a massacre if I don't get what I want."

Clearly, by his own admission Evan Chandler's plot to frame and extort Michael Jackson involved other people higher up than him. Of course, a key figure here is the one whom Evan described as "the nastiest son of a bitch"; the guy who, on Evan's and the "other people's" behalf planned to "destroy everybody in site in any devious, nasty, cruel way that he can do it." That one is Attorney Barry K. Rothman. A New York Jew who graduated from UCLA and practiced entertainment law in Hollywood, there is no way this "nastiest son of a bitch" did not cross paths with David Geffen and his circle. Rothman had a buddy, a dental anesthesiologist named Mark Torbiner (= a Jewish surname). Rothman, who on at least eight occasions had been given a general anesthetic by Torbiner during hair-transplant procedures, introduced him to Evan Chandler in 1991.[770] These three were allegedly the nucleus of the operationalization of the plot to frame Michael Jackson.

---

770 Fisher, "Was Michael Jackson Framed," 16.

Barry Rothman   Evan Chandler   Mark Torbiner

During Rothman's involvement in the Chandler case Geraldine Hughes was Rothman's sole legal secretary. She literally was *witness* to the conspiracy as it unfolded *in her attorney's office.*[771] She reports the attorney's *coaching* the 13-year old boy secretly in his office.

> I really believe that the whole thing was plotted and planned and the words were given to him [Jordan Chandler] to say because I actually witnessed the 13 year old in my attorney's office without any supervision of his parents and he was kind of snuck in there, it was like no one in the office knew he was in there. He was behind closed doors with my attorney for several hours, and I kind of believe that is where he was being told what to say... everything that they were doing was part of a plan. It was already mapped out, it was planned out. They even mapped out the part about how it was going to be reported...The way they plotted it was that he was supposed to go talk to a psychiatrist and that's where he would tell the psychiatrist the different things that he told him, and the psychiatrist would be the one that reported it because he's a credible cohort. He's somebody that nobody is going to question and he's a mandated reporter.
>
> I typed the letter to the father where the attorney was telling him how to report it using a third party. I remember typing the short letter. He typed him a letter and he sent him some information on child molestation being reported through a psychiatrist, so he was informing the father how to go about it and that was his plan. So he was literally just making him feel

---

771 Geraldine Hughes, *Redemption: The Truth Behind the Michael Jackson Child Molestation Allegations* (Radford, VA: Branch & Vine Publishers, LLC, 2004).

comfortable, making him so he felt okay with it, giving him some articles, we sent him some newspapers, something we sent along with it. But I remember when I typed that letter, I said, "Why are you writing him telling him?" I said if anybody has got a suspicion of child molestation, all he has to do is pick up the telephone. You don't have to plot and plan and take him to a psychiatrist because nobody else has the credibility to report it.[772]

III.   *"There's Other People Involved": The Pedophiles Approach*

From the three secretly recorded calls between Evan Chandler and Dave Schwartz on July 8, 1993, it is clear that Evan Chandler *had no suspicions whatsoever* regarding the (legal) appropriateness of Michael and Jordan's relationship. As he admitted, he had "no idea" of any sexual activity. June Chandler, who always accompanied Jordan and Michael, insisted there was nothing inappropriate taking place (until she later flipped for money). But there were *outside* people who, after the tabloids shinned a light on the family and their relationship to Michael Jackson, approached Evan and *convinced him* that there was something sexual going on in the Michael Jackson-Jordan Chandler relationship. Evan said he resisted their suggestions (because he knew better), but ultimately they "opened his eyes." These people planted seeds into Evan's already troubled mind about Michael and they manipulated his thinking about his son's relationship with the star.

Chandler: Everybody agrees with that. I mean, they — *it's their opinions that have convinced me to not stay away*. You know, I'm not confrontational. I've got an [tape irregularity] inclination to do what you do, say, "Okay. Go fuck yourself. Go do what you want to do, and, you

---

772 Deborah L. Kunesh, "A Witness To Extortion…: An Exclusive, In-Depth Interview with author Geraldine Hughes, sharing the truth behind the Michael Jackson 1993 Child Molestation Allegations," @ http://www.reflectionsonthedance.com/Interview-with-Geraldine-Hughes.html.

know, call me some day. I'll see you then. I got a [tape irregularity]," but I've been so convinced by professional opinions that I have been negligent in not stepping in sooner that now it's made me insane. Now I actually feel [tape irregularity] –

...

Chandler: In fact, in their opinion I have been negligent not to put a stop to [tape irregularity] opinion. *I happen to agree with them now. I didn't agree with them at first…I didn't even want to know about it…*I kept saying, "No, this is okay. There's nothing wrong. This is great." It took experts to convince me [tape irregularity] that by not taking action my son was going to be irreparably damaged for the rest of his life [tape irregularity]. That was what I heard.

Schwartz: Because his friend is older, or because of all the seduction?

Chandler: Well, you know, *age in and of itself is not a harmful thing.*

Schwartz: Yeah.

Chandler: But it could have been used to advantage, and in some ways Michael is using his age and experience and his money and his power to great advantage to Jordy. The problem is he's also harming him, greatly harming him, for his own selfish reasons. He's not the altruistic, kind human being that he appears to be…

Chandler: — and that's not my opinion. I mean, I happen to be believe it now because my eyes have been opened but I'm not the one that first [tape irregularity], so what I'm saying to you is that I'm acting because [tape irregularity] I'm going to cause him great harm, and you tell me if maybe it's gonna cause him harm right now. I think he'll be harmed much greater if I do nothing, and besides now I'm convinced that if I do nothing I'm going to be, from doing nothing, causing him harm, and I couldn't…I'm just trying to do what I have been led to believe is the right action to take so that he's not harmed.

Who are these people, these "professionals" and "experts" who opened Evan's eyes to the true nature of his 13-year old son's relationship with Michael Jackson? They certainly are not psychiatric professionals because, according to Evan's loyal brother Raymond Chandler in his book (*All That Glitters*, co-authored by Evan) it is stated that, at this point Evan *had not* contacted any psychologist, psychiatrist or therapist. On the other

302

hand, at least one of the "professionals" who approached Evan during this period was certainly Victor Gutierrez. And it was no doubt Gutierrez who planted the seed in Evan's mind of a "sexual relationship." Gutierrez admits that the Chandlers were given his attention when they began appearing in the media, around April and May 1993.

> It is known fact that Gutierrez actually knew and consulted with Evan Chandler, at just about the same time that Chandler was growing disgruntled with Jackson's lack of "cooperation" in funding his projects and had grown increasingly jealous of Jackson's relationship with his ex-wife June, son Jordan, and daughter Lily.[773]

Evan's view was that his son's relationship with Michael "was great" and there was "nothing wrong." But we see in April the effects of the seeds that were dropped in Evan's mind even though he didn't meet Michael Jackson himself for the first time until May 20, 1993. Evan Chandler knew that one of his celebrity patients, Carrie Fisher ("Princess Leah" of *Star Wars*) was close friends with Dr. Arnold Klein. According to Evan Chandler on April 16, while he was giving Carrie Fisher a ride home Evan had her call Arnold Klein on his car phone and ask him about Michael Jackson's sexuality. Dr. Klein affirmed that Michael is "perfectly straight," "absolutely heterosexual."[774] Dr. Klein and Victor Gutierrez had clearly not yet been in sync. Evan did not stop there, because I'm sure his "handlers" did not allow him to stop at Dr. Klein's testimony. So something very evil took place, as reported by both Randy/Evan Chandler and Victor Gutierrez.

Evan Chandler met Michael Jackson for the first time on May 20th. On May 21th he claims to have confronted Michael with the question: "Are you fucking my son in the ass?" Notice the

---

773 Linda-Raven woods, "The New Lynching of Michael Jackson: Dan Reed's *Leaving Neverland*, In Fact, Leave Blood on Many Hands," *Medium* February 27, 2019.

774 Diane Dimond, *Be Careful Who You Love: Inside the Michael Jackson Case* (New York: Atria, 2005) 51; J. Randy Taraborrelli, *Michael Jackson: The Magic, The Madness, The Whole Story, 1958-2009* (Grand Central Publishing, 2009) 465-467.

wording?! Not, "are you sexually abusing my child?" Evan's language reflects the perspective *of the pedophiles*! This is further confirmed by what allegedly happened next, on May 28th while Michael and Jordan were visiting Evan for Memorial Day weekend. Evan said to his son: "Hey Jordie, are you and Michael doin' it?" Jordan responded: "That's disgusting! I'm not into that!" To which Evan replied: "Just kidding."[775] This is remarkable, if true. Again, Evan does not in any way frame his question in the context of sexual abuse, for example "Is Michael molesting you?!" or "Is Michael touching you?" etc. Rather, Evan's language reflects his thoughts of possible sexual relations between a grown man and his 13-year old son *as consensual*: "Are you and Michael doin' it?" Wow. This is *strong* evidence of the influence of the pedophile's perspective, like that of NAMBLA and Victor Gutierrez. According to Evan, Jordan was "repulsed" by his father's suggestion.

Still not satisfied, Evan Chandler takes his inquisition to a devilish low. The next day, May 29th, Michael complained about a headache. According to the account of Evan's brother Raymond, Evan

called Mark Torbiner for advice. The anesthesiologist suggested an injection of Toradol, a non-narcotic equivalent to Demerol, and offered to pick some up at Evan's office and bring it to his house.

Evan injected 30mg, half the maximum dose, *into Michael's gluteus*. But one hour later the star claimed he was still in a lot of pain, so Evan administered the remaining half and instructed him to lie down and try to relax.

"Keep an eye on him," Evan told Jordie. "It'll take a few minutes to kick in. I'll be right back."

"When I went back to check on him, maybe ten minutes later," Evan recalled, "*He was acting weird, babbling incoherently and slurring his speech*. Toradol is a pretty safe drug, and I thought that either he was

775 Raymond Chandler, *All That Glitters: The Crime and the Cover-Up* (Windsong Press, Ltd., 2004) 46.

having a rare reaction or had taken another drug and was having a combination reaction."

Other than *the drunk-like symptoms*, Michael's pulse and respirations were normal and he appeared to be in no real danger. So Evan took no further action.

But Jordie was scared. He had seen his friend "acting strange" before, but never like this.

"Don't worry," Evan assured his son, "Right now *Michael's the happiest person in the world*. All we need to do is keep him awake and talking until the drug wears off."

Four hours and a serious case of cottonmouth later, Michael began to sober up. While Jordie was downstairs fetching water, *Evan decided to take advantage of Michael's still uninhibited but somewhat coherent condition.* "Hey, Mike, I was just wondering...I mean, I don't care either way, but I know some of your closest people are gay, and *I was wondering if you're gay too?*"

"You'd be surprised about a lot of people in this town," Michael mumbled, as he rattled off the names of a few prominent Hollywood players who were still in the closet.

Evan tried to get back on track before Jordie returned. *He stroked Michael's hair* and reassured him, "I don't care if you're gay, Mike. I just want you to know you can tell me if you are."

"Uh-uh", Michael slurred. "Not me."

Given Michael's willingness to talk openly about everyone else's sexuality, *his consistent denial about being gay reinforced Evan's belief that the singer was asexual.* [776]

There is a lot here, even though the full account as presented by Raymond Chandler is disingenuous at parts. Because Michael, who has spent the night at Evan's house with Jordan, complains of a headache, Evan calls his and Barry Rothman's anesthesiologist friend Mark, who comes over and drugs Michael with an injection in his buttocks. Raymond claims the drug was Toradol, a non-

---

776 Chandler, *All That Glitters* 46-49.

steroid anti-inflammatory drug. But this can't be true. According to medical personnel Toradol does not produce the effects described: Michael babbled incoherently and had slurred speech, with drunk-like symptoms that lasted four hours. That was not Toradol. Evan all but admits this when he assures Jordan: "Don't worry, *right now Michael's the happiest person in the world.*" They doped Michael, clearly. The actress Carrie Fisher, Evan's celebrity patient, noted in her autobiography entitled *Shockaholic* that both Evan Chandler and Mark Torbiner were two shady Hollywood doctors who abused medications. At one time, according to journalist Mary Fischer, the U.S. Drug Enforcement Administration probed Torbiner's practice under the suspicion he inappropriately administered drugs during paid house calls.[777]

Once Evan and Torbiner has Michael nice and doped up, they "take advantage of Michael's still uninhibited but somewhat coherent condition" by probing him about being gay. We can discern here the preoccupation of Victor Gutierrez and the Pedophile Agenda, because Evan presented himself as having a different personal viewpoint:

> **Chandler:** [tape irregularity] I mean, I'm young, I'm really liberal. As far as I'm concerned, anybody could do anything they want. That's my philosophy. You guys can do whatever you want. Just be happy. Don't get hurt. So…

But Michael clears that up: "Uh uh. Not me."

That was May 29th. By July 8th, the day of the three secretly recorded phone calls, we know that the "certain plan" by a group of people including Evan Chandler to "get rid of Michael Jackson" by "destroying" him, "humiliating him beyond his worst nightmare" was already operationalized to some extant: "**Chandler**: Because the thing's already — the thing has already been set in motion…it's out of my hands. I do nothing else

---

777 Fischer, "Was Michael Jackson Framed? 18.

again…I'm not even in contact anymore." And then July 16th happens. The boy Jordan, with his father and Torbiner, is drugged.

> In the presence of Chandler and Mark Torbiner, a dental anesthesiologist, the boy [Jordan Chandler] was administered the controversial drug *sodium Amytal*—which some mistakenly believe is a truth serum. And it was after this session that the boy first made his charges against Jackson. A newsman at KCBS-TV, in L.A., reported on May 3 of this year [1994] that Chandler had used the drug on his son, but the dentist claimed he did so only to pull his son's tooth and that while under the drug's influence, the boy came out with allegations. Asked for this article about his use of the drug on the boy, Torbiner replied: "If I used it, it was for dental purposes."[778]

Claiming he was sedating his son in order to pull a baby tooth, Evan injected Jordan with sodium amytal. Why is this significant?

> "It's a psychiatric medication that cannot be relied on to produce fact," says Dr. Resnick, the Cleveland psychiatrist. "People are very suggestible under it. People will say things under sodium Amytal that are blatantly untrue." Sodium Amytal is a barbiturate, an invasive drug that puts people *in a hypnotic state when it's injected intravenously*…Scientific studies done in 1952 debunked the drug as a truth serum and instead demonstrated its risks: False memories can be easily implanted in those under its influence. "It is quite possible to implant an idea *through the mere asking of a question*," says Resnick. But its effects are apparently even more insidious: *"The idea can become their memory, and studies have shown that even when you tell them the truth, they will swear on a stack of Bibles that it happened,"* says Resnick.[779]

Thus, Evan confesses that after he drugged his son with sodium amytal: "When Jordie came out of the sedation *I asked him to tell me about Michael and him.*"[780] And Evan says to Jordan, oddly: "Look, Jordie, lots of famous   people are bisexual and nobody gives a shit. They're not embarrassed. It's sorta cool, in a way." Huh? Evan is still presenting the idea of a sexual encounter

---

778 Fisher, "Was Michael Jackson Framed."16.
779 Fisher, "Was Michael Jackson Framed."16.
780 Diane Dimond, *Be Careful Who You Love*, 60.

between Michael Jackson and his 13-year old son as a simply matter of "bisexuality," which, he says, is sorta cool. These were apparently enough seeds planted for the drugged Jordan, who now for the first time "confesses" that Michael touched him sexually. Before this drugging, "The boy repeatedly denied that anything had happened."[781] However, after being injected by his father with a drug that can induce false confessions by the mere asking of certain questions, Jordan for the first time allegedly confessed that Michael "touched" him, according to Raymond Chandler's account. Scott Lilienfeld writes in *Psychology Today*

> So what crucial fact has most of the press coverage omitted? It's that Jordan Chandler apparently never made any accusations against Jackson until his father, a registered dentist, gave him sodium amytal during a tooth extraction. Only then did Jackson's purported sexual abuse emerge; Jordan Chandler's reports became more elaborate and embellished during a later session with a psychiatrist.
>
> Sodium amytal is a barbiturate and one of the most commonly used variants of what is popularly known as "truth serum," a spectacular misnomer. There's no scientific evidence that sodium amytal or other supposed truth serums increase the accuracy of memories. To the contrary, as psychiatrist August Piper has observed, there's good reason to believe that truth serums merely lower the threshold for reporting virtually all information, both true and false. As a consequence, like other suggestive therapeutic procedures, such as guided imagery, repeated prompting, hypnosis, and journaling, truth serums can actually increase the risk of false memories—memories of events that never occurred, but are held with great conviction."[782]

We know that subsequently Victor Gutierrez was personally meeting with Jordan Chandler, according to his admission.[783] During the police investigation of the case, Gutierrez was one of

781 Fisher, "Was Michael Jackson Framed." 13.
782 Scott Lilienfeld, "Michael Jackson, Truth Serum, and False Memories," *Psychology Today* July 7, 2009.
783 Sandall, "Michael Jackson Was My Lover"*:* "Thanks to the intervention of someone he will only identify as 'a very good source within the house', Gutierrez was able to arrange meetings with Jordie while the terms of the legal settlement were being hammered out."

the first people the LAPD "interviewed," and they did so for several hours over two days.

> During the early stages of the Chandler investigation, Gutierrez "spoke to LAPD officers for two hours on Thursday and was interviewed again on Friday." "He would not disclose what transpired during those sessions, but he told The Times that he has interviewed for his book some of the same youngsters being sought for questioning by the LAPD."[784]

In other words, Victor Gutierrez and the Pedophile Agenda's fingerprints are *all over this case*.

IV.   *The Sham Investigation*

The investigation of the Chandler case was launched in August and by November neither the Santa Barbara nor the Los Angeles police departments found *any corroborating evidence* to support Jordan Chandler's *drug-induced* allegation. This frustrated the authorities.

> Police ended up confiscating a total of fifty boxes filled with photographs, notebooks, files, and documents and broke into a safe belonging to the star...*The police had reached a dead end in their investigation*. They had failed to turn up any evidence to corroborate Jordan Chandler's claims. [785]

The smoking gun which the Santa Barbara D.A. Tom Sneddon desperately desired had eluded him. Then on November 19, 1993 it was delivered to him – or so he thought. And it was Dr. Arnold Klein who willingly handed it to him. On that day Sergeant Deborah Linden of the Santa Barbara County Sheriff's Department

---

784 Charles P. Wallace and Jim Newton, "Jackson Back n Stage; Inquiry Continues: Investigation: Singer resumes Bangkok concerts after two-day absence. Officials here are now looking into extortion claims," *Los Angeles Times* August 28, 1993.
785 Ian Halperin, *Unmasked: The Final Years of Michael Jackson.*

Sergeant Deborah Linden

tried to serve a search warrant on Dr. Klein's Beverly Hills office looking for Michael Jackson's medical records, which had been *removed from the premises* by Klein. Nevertheless, Sergeant Linden "spoke with Dr. Klein" and apparently Debbi Rowe, his nurse assistant.[786] Dr. Klein offered Sergeant Linden some of Michael's medical information which Tom Sneddon and the Santa Barbara police used to make Michael Jackson endure "the most humiliating ordeal" of his life, a "horrifying nightmare": the shameful body search of December 20, 1993.

In the Spring (April or May) of 1993, Michael reportedly attempted to use the cream Benoquin on his scrotum and ended up causing some burning. Michael called Dr. Klein and told him, and Klein had Debbie Rowe tend to him.[787] Klein shared this information with Sergeant Linden while she "spoke with" him on November 19, 1993 during the service of the search warrant.[788] In addition, Debbie Rowe said that because she gave Michael massages to help him sleep "she could identify any markings on

786 "Jackson Doc Hid Medical Records, Deputy Says," *TMZ* July 13, 2009.

787 J. Randy Taraborrelli, *Michael Jackson: The Magic, The Madness, The Whole Story, 1958-2009*; Seal, "The Doctor Will Sue You Now."

788 Orth, *The Importance of Being Famous*: "according to the affidavit, in April or May 1993… 'Jackson told Dr. Klein that he had gotten Benoquin on his genitals and it burned. Dr. Klein told Jackson not to put Benoquin on his genitals." Emma Parry, "'He Did Not Deny It': Michael Jackson 'refused' to answer when asked: 'Are you f***ing my kid?' by first accuser Jordan Chandler's dad, police document reveals," *The Sun* February 15, 2019: "in an un-redacted section (of the affidavit), Jackson's doctors claim that the star suffered vitiligo, a disease which causes depigmentation of the skin, which gave him blotches and areas of discolouration on his body and legs. The same doctor - dermatologist Dr Arnold Klein also claimed that Jackson once put his vitiligo cream - which helps to even out the skin's colors - on his genitals, which "burned" them."

310

his buttocks".[789] The real reason Dr. Klein's nurse assistant could identify markings on Michael Jackson's buttocks is because, according to medical and police records, she gave Michael "repeated injections of Demerol" in his buttocks in 1993, creating the scars.[790] These medical revelations were then put in a sworn affidavit signed by Sergeant Linden and known as the "Linden Affidavit." Interestingly, in this "Linden Affidavit" these medical revelations of Klein and Rowe appear with *alleged descriptions by Jordan Chandler of distinctive marks on Michael's genitals and buttocks!* However, Jordan specifically admitted to Private Investigator Anthony Pellicano on July 9, 1993 that *he never saw Michael's genital area or buttocks*:

> According to Pellicano, [Jordan] told him a lot in 45 minutes. "He's a very bright, articulate, intelligent, manipulative boy." Pellicano, who has fathered nine children by two wives, says he asked [Jordan] many sexually specific questions. "And I'm looking dead into his eyes. And I'm watching in his eyes for any sign of fear or anticipation—anything. And I see none," Pellicano says. "And I keep asking him, 'Did Michael ever touch you?' 'No.' *'Did you ever see Michael nude?'* 'No.' He laughed about it. He giggled a lot, like it was a funny thing. *Michael would never be nude...* 'Did you and Michael ever masturbate?' 'No.' 'Did Michael ever masturbate in front of you?' 'No.' 'Did you guys ever talk about masturbation?' 'No.'
>
> "So you never saw Michael's body?" "One time, *he lifted up his shirt and he showed me those blotches.*"[791]

Nevertheless, Tom Sneddon now had his "smoking gun" and the "Linden Affidavit" with its Klein and Rowe-derived information and its clearly manufactured or *coached* Jordan descriptions was the basis upon which court permission to "photograph Jackson's

---

789 "Debbie Rowe Injected Jackson with Drugs," *TMZ* July 13, 2009.
790 Harvey Levin with Dr. Arnold Klein on TMZ Live, November 5, 2009.
791 Fisher, "Was Michael Jackson Framed," 13; Lisa D. Campbell, *Michael Jackson: The King of Pop's Darkest Hour* (Boston: Branden Publishing Company, Inc., 1194) 52; J. Randy Taraborrelli, *Michael Jackson: The Magic, The Madness, The Whole Story, 1958-2009.*

private parts" was secured.[792] The result was a search warrant ordering officials to "search Jackson's body 'including his penis' – saying that the star had no 'right to refuse.'"[793] That body search occurred on December 20, 1993.

Present during the profoundly intrusive procedure were police photographer Gary Spiegel, Michael's personal photographer Louis Swayne, the D.A.'s doctor Dr. Richard Strick, and Michael's dermatologist Dr. Arnold Klein. What is remarkable is that it *was Klein who gave Michael all of the instructions on behalf of the police department during this humiliating, nightmare procedure.* The D.A. photographer Gary Spiegel recalled in a declaration to the court:

> Dr. Klein made a statement [to Jackson] that we were interested in photographing Jackson's genital area *and directed Jackson* to stand and remove the robe he had on. Jackson protested, saying things like "What do I have to do that for?" and "Why are they doing this?" In my opinion, Jackson's demeanour was a combination of hostility and anger. Jackson complied with Dr. Klein's request...As Mr. Jackson was complying with Dr. Klein's request, Dr. Klein made the statement that others in the room should turn their heads so as not to view Jackson's genital area. At the time, I found this peculiar because the only persons in the room at the time were Mr. Jackson, the two doctors, me, and the other photographer. Dr. Klein also made a statement that he was not going to look. He said he had never seen Mr. Jackson's genital area and he was not going to do so at this time.[794]

Klein's "peculiar" volunteering of the information that *he* never saw Michael's genital area seems to be a common theme of his during this case. During the grand jury that was impaneled in Santa Barbara he again voluntarily insisted "he had never seen" Michael's genital area.[795] Such voluntary insistence is suspicious. We do know that it was Klein who gave the key information about

---

792 "The Telltale 'Splotch,'" *the smoking gun* January 6, 2005.
793 Emma Parry, "'He Did Not Deny It': Michael Jackson 'refused' to answer when asked: 'Are you f***ing my kid?' by first accuser Jordan Chandler's dad, police document reveals," *The Sun* February 15, 2019.
794 Dimond, Be Careful Who You Love, 14.
795 Taraborrelli, *Michael Jackson.*

genital discoloration in the Linden Affidavit which was the pretext for the humiliating body search. What's more, according to Santa Barbara Detective Russel Birchim's declaration to the court, at some point Michael Jackson struggled to leave the room where the body search was taking place *but Arnold Klein physically restrained him*. "Dr. Klein was successful in pulling Jackson back into the room and the door was once again closed,"[796] so Michael Jackson's "horrifying nightmare" continued.

With all of this violation of Michael Jackson and the hope and excitement which DA Tom Sneddon placed in it, Sneddon *failed to get his smoking gun*! Why? Because as the *Los Angeles Times* reported, Michael's appearance "does not match a description provided...by the alleged victim."[797] In other words, with all of the assistance that Jordan Chandler had in describing Michael's private areas thanks to the tip that Arnold Klein offered, Jordan Chandler *still got it wrong*. For this reason, Tom Sneddon had no choice but to lobby for banning the body search photos from the trial.

With Tom Sneddon's "smoking gun" going up in smoke, the case had no foundation other than the uncorroborated word of a boy who first denied and then affirmed the allegations only *after being drugged*. Trial was scheduled to begin March 1994 and Michael Jackson no doubt would have won the case just as he did later in 2005. However, Michael Jackson *was robbed* of his day in court. How? Because his team of lawyers, who were friends with his accusers' team of lawyers, settled the case with the Chandlers. It is reported that Michael never wanted to settle because he knew he could win in court, as he won in 2005.

By the time of the second child molestation case of 2005, during which Michael Jackson was *acquitted* and *exonerated*, Jordan Chandler had *confessed that he and his parents lied*. We learn this from Michael's 2005 attorney Thomas Mesereau, who spoke at Harvard on November 29, 2005, and revealed that, had

---

796 Halperin, *Unmasked*, 72-73.
797 Jim Newton, "Grand Jury Calls Michael Jackson's Mother to Testify," *Los Angeles Times* March 16, 1994.

the prosecution succeeded in forcing Jordan to testify in the new case, Mesereau had witnesses that were going to testify under oath that Jordan told them Michael Jackson *never* molested him. Mesereau said:

> Now the one you're talking about [Jordan Chandler] never showed up [to the 2005 case]. He's the one who got the settlement in the early 90s. And my understanding is prosecutors tried to get him to show up and he wouldn't. If he had, *I had witnesses who were going to come in and say he told them it never happened.* And that he would never talk to his parents again for what they made him say. And it turned out *he had gone into court and gotten legal emancipation from his parents.* His mother testified that she hadn't talked to him in 11 years.

One of Mesereau's listed potential witnesses was Josephine Zohny who attended New York University with Jordan Chandler. Zohny testifies that Jordan *openly* said Michael Jackson *was not capable of doing what his father (and later mother) accused him of,* and that his parents made him do things that he didn't want to do.[798]

V.   *The Attempt To Frame Michael With Child Pornography*

> [Michael Jackson] was very vulnerable to blackmail, having already paid out millions to settle one case. A gay pornographer had infiltrated his entourage with the possible goal of setting up the star and then blackmailing him.[799]

After the 9/11 attacks in 2001 Michael Jackson organized the *What More Can I Give* charity single for the 9/11 victims. The contributors to the song were big: Beyonce, Ricky Martin, Mariah Carey, Carlos Santana, and others come contributed vocals. McDonalds agreed to a $20 million deal to sell the charity record.

---

798 "Square One: New Witness in Michael Jackson Case," 2019 Documentary @ https://www.youtube.com/watch?v=ZxNDb2PVcoM.
799 Breitbart and Ebner, *Hollywood, Interrupted*, 174.

However, after the *New York Post* ran a story on the McDonalds deal on October 13 the white "American moms" complained and McDonalds pulled out of the deal. Behind the scenes, though, an even bigger scandal was brewing.

The executive producer of the song and its subsequent videos was Marc Schaffel. Michael, at that time, didn't really know who Schaffel was. But the celebrity sleuth Paul Barresi did. Because Barresi had been involved in Hollywood's gay pornography scene he knew Marc Fred Schaffel, who reportedly made gay porn with young boys imported from Eastern European countries like Hungary and the Czech Republic.[800] According to Barresi, former Schaffel associate/employer David Aldorf in a taped interview on November 19, 2001 gave him some information: Schaffel shared with Aldorf a plan to blackmail Michael Jackson for $25 million by framing him "by planting kiddy porn on him."[801] Aldorf also revealed that he possessed a video tape of Schaffel filming a gay porn video in Budapest with young Hungarian boys. Aldorf gave Barresi a copy of the video.[802]

Barresi admits to trying to sell this information to Michael's personal accountant and business manager Barry Siegel. Barresi gave a copy of the video of Schaffel to the LAPD (whom he worked with in the past) and the FBI. Barresi also admits that he said to Eric Mason, a private investigator for Michael Jackson: "How much is it worth to save a pop star's ass?"[803] Barresi claims Seigle and Mason refused to cooperate. However, John Branca received the video and set up a meeting with Michael to play the tape. Michael was angry and immediately fired Schaffel. "That same night, Jackson called Schaffel and told him he was off the

---

800 Breitbart and Ebner, *Hollywood, Interrupted*, 175.
801 Breitbart and Ebner, *Hollywood, Interrupted*, 178.
802 "Jackson Kids In Danger? Debbie Rowe's New Fiancé Was Named As Co-Conspirator In MJ Child Molestation Indictment — PLUS His Secret Gay Porn Past Revealed!" *Radar Online* April 28, 2014.
803 Breitbart and Ebner, *Hollywood, Interrupted*, 182.

charity project, acknowledged Schaffel..."[804] Yet, for some reason some of Jackson's people *kept Schaffel around.* [805]

Barresi then gave the info to the legal department of Sony and to Sony head Tommy Mottola (he would not be "terminated" until January, 2003). This potential scandal was to Sony's advantage because "The revelations could call into question [Michael's] credibility in the dispute with Sony."[806] Right in the middle of Michael's dispute with Sony and a month after Michael called Mottola a devil in London, Barresi leaked the story to the *USA Today* which ran it on July 14, 2002. Barresi gave the video to NBC's *Dateline* and to Andrew Breitbart and Mark Ebner. The theme of the headlines went something like this: "Peter Pan had picked a [child] porn producer to be his private videographer in Neverland."[807]

Michael reportedly accused Sony of blocking the release of the song as part of their ongoing dispute. "But," the *Los Angeles Times* says, "internal records and interviews indicate that it was Jackson's own advisers who quietly asked Sony to bury the charity project..."[808] It is said that it was John Branca who pressed Sony to kill the *What More Can I Give?* project by refusing permission to stars scheduled to be own it. Barresi also desired to get the *What More Can I Give* project killed, which he ultimately did.[809]

After being fired by Michael in 2001 Schaffel sued him for $3 million in November 2004. When the two legal teams met in London, Jackson made the statement about why he fired Schaffel: "I was shown a videotape by the lawyer [Branca] and I was shocked. He was *in that whole circle*, and I didn't know." [810] "That whole circle" which Marc Schaffel was reputedly in was the Gay

---

804 Tanya Caldwell, "Former Jackson Lawyer Testifies," *Los Angeles Times* July 11, 2006.
805 Caldwell, "Former Jackson Lawyer Testifies."
806 Chuck Philips, "Producers Porn Ties Said to Derail Jackson's Song," *Los Angeles Times* July 12, 2002.
807 Breitbart and Ebner, *Hollywood, Interrupted.*
808 Chuck Philips, "Producers Porn Ties Said to Derail Jackson's Song," *Los Angeles Times* July 12, 2002.
809 Breitbart and Ebner, *Hollywood, Interrupted*, 183.
810 Sullivan, *Untouchable*, 38.

Pedophile circle! How did he infiltrate Michael Jackson's team? Through Arnold Klein.

Marc Schaffel was Dr. Arnold Klein's "friend and patient."[811] It was coincidently (?) at an amfAR (American Foundation for AIDS Research) fundraiser – the foundation which Arnold Klein founded in his house with David Geffen and others[812] – when Schaffel "ran into" Michael Jackson. However, "He and Jackson didn't have their first real conversations…until the year 2000, when they met at the home of the famous dermatologist they shared, Arnold Klein, a friend of Schaffel's…"[813] In June 2001 Michael Jackson and Marc Schaffel met again at Klein's home. Evidently knowing Michael's film dreams Schaffel "Boast[ed] of his background in film production and flashing a bank account that approached eight figures, Schaffel pledged to organize Michael's various film and video projects through a company the two formed, called Neverland Entertainment. There was talk of building a movie studio at the ranch, of making short films, perhaps producing an animated television series."[814] Schaffel was thus able to make himself – or someone made him – "the official videographer at Jackson's Neverland Ranch" and "despite Schaffel's total lack of music production experience, Jackson handed him the reins to oversee the recording of his 9/11 single "What More Can I Give," and its subsequent music video, later that year."[815] Marc Schaffel

---

811 Sullivan, *Untouchable*.
812 " 'Don't forget, I founded AmFAR in my house," [Klein] told me, referring to the American Foundation for AIDS Research, which he helped establish with Dr. Mathilde Krim, Elizabeth Taylor, and David Geffen in 1985": Mark Seal, "The Doctor Will Sue You Now," *Vanity Fair* February 2, 2012; "Jackson's Dermatologist Says Murray Fallout Hurts," *The Telegraph* October 15, 2011: "Klein teamed with other physicians, Taylor and Geffen to form the respected American Foundation for AIDS Research, AmFAR…"
813 Randall Sullivan, Untouchable: The Strange Life and Tragic Death of Michael Jackson (New York: Grove Press, 2012) 16.
814 Sullivan, *Untouchable*, 17.
815 "Jackson Kids In Danger? Debbie Rowe's New Fiancé Was Named As Co-Conspirator In MJ Child Molestation Indictment — PLUS His Secret Gay Porn Past Revealed!" *Radar Online* April 28, 2014.

the reputed gay pedophile pornographer who reportedly planned to frame Michael Jackson with "kiddy porn" in order to extort $25 million out of him did successfully infiltrate Michael's camp and it was Dr. Arnold Klein who introduced Schaffel to Michael in the first place.

In addition, according to Schaffel, Tommy Mottola had already known about his background: "Tommy Mottola knew [about my past] too. He brought Usher to the studio to sing on 'What More Can I Give?' and Tommy was sitting and joking with me about some girl in the porn business he knew, to see if I knew her too."[816]

---

816 Sullivan, *Untouchable*, 21.

Part 8

A Conspiracy That Leads To Death

Chapter Thirteen

Motive For Murder

I.   *The Billion Dollar Asset*

The Music Mafia is the tightknit group of predominantly Jewish and Italian New Yorkers who have controlled this business for decades. Some really are members of the official Mafia...Some are not. But in terms of running the music industry, these boys are a brethren. Outsiders (as well as women) aren't welcome in this clan...without a fair understanding of Yiddish or Italian, there's no way to land a good job in music. The hit men who run the record labels, law firms, management companies and promotion agencies that steer the business may dislike -- even despise -- each other, but in the end they'd rather keep it all to themselves than allow access to newcomers.[817]

    In the 1980s Michael Jackson had an informal investment committee, a council of advisors, if you will, with which he met once every few months. The committee/council included music and movie mogul David Geffen, founder of *Ebony* John Johnson, and superlawyer John Branca, Michael's lawyer. "Had the organization been officially incorporated, it might have been called Michael Jackson, Inc."[818] In 1985, against the objection of advisers such as David Geffen, Jackson instructed Branca to purchase ATV, the company which housed the prized music catalog of the Beatles. For $47.5 million Michael purchased ATV from Australian billionaire Robert Holmes à Court. This purchase made Michael Jackson one of the *best business minds in the industry.* By the time Michael Jackson died in 2009, the ATV catalog would be worth over $1 billion and some estimates have

---

817 Deborah Wilker, "Out From Under The Rock of the Music Business," *South Florida Sun-Sentinel* September 30, 1990.
818 Zack O'Malley Greenburg, "Buying The Beatles: Inside Michael Jackson's Best Business Bet," *Forbes* June 2, 2014.

said $2 billion. Thus, this purchase *also* made Michael Jackson one of *the most marked men* in recent history.

The plot to separate Michael from this tremendously valuable asset started early. Mickey Schulhof, the CEO of Sony Corp. of America, had designs on the catalog. A brief visit once to Michael's Century City apartment — a fantasyland of overstuffed animals —convinced Schulhof that Sony's star singer someday would "spiral toward the poor house and be forced to sell everything," thereby allowing Sony to fully acquire Michael's catalog in the process.[819]

> That's always been Sony's dream scenario, full ownership. "But they don't want to do that [repossess Michael's half of the catalog] as *they're afraid of a backlash from his fans*. Their nightmare is an organised "boycott Sony" movement worldwide, which could prove hugely costly. It is the only thing standing between Michael and bankruptcy."[820]

If Michael's fan-base could be weakened – maybe by some widely publicized fabricated scandal, for example – Sony's fear of an organized "boycott Sony" movement could be allayed.

For years prior to the 1993 False Allegations Sony had been pressuring Michael to sell them his catalog but he refused. However, the False Allegations was the first step in helping Sony claw their way into full ownership. The consequences of the 1993 False Allegations put Michael in dire need of cash. He was making no money according to his lawyer John Branca.[821] The child molestation scandal cost Michael $20 million (through his insurance company) in the private settlement. Michael owed promoters a fortune after having to suspend his world tour *due to his drugging by Dr. Arnold Klein.*[822] So John Branca proposed his

---

819 Johnnie L. Roberts, "Fired, the Superlawyer Returns to Bail Jackson Out – for a Price," *The Wrap* December 8, 2010.
820 Ian Halperin, " 'I'm better off dead. I'm done': Michael Jackson's fateful prediction just a week before his death," *Daily Mail* June 29 2009.
821 Pete Mills, "Sony exec claims Michael Jackson's 'image and likeness' worth less than a second-hand car," *Orchard Times* February 18, 2017.
822 Johnnie L. Roberts, "Fired, the Superlawyer Returns to Bail Jackson Out – for a Price," *The Wrap* December 8, 2010.

"brilliant idea" to Michael: sell half of your catalog to Sony through a merger and live off of the $150-million check. [823] The circumstances forced Michael to sell half of his catalog *and take out loans.*

> In August 1994 — five months after *Time* magazine reported Jackson had paid a multimillion-dollar settlement after a 14-year-old boy claimed he had molested him — the King of Pop signed loan papers with Sony in which he used his catalog of songs to secure a loan. [824]

But Sony would not stop there. The dream was for "full ownership" of Michael Jackson's most valuable asset. In 2002 Michael Jackson and Sony were embroiled in a nasty public dispute. Michael believed that Sony deliberately sabotaged the success of his *Invincible* album that was released in 2001. Sony *did* have something to gain by Michael's career failing: they hoped he would have to sell his share of the catalog and at a low price. During the height of the 2002 Michael Jackson vs. Sony standoff the press reported that Sony chief Tommy Mottola would *threaten to ruin Michael by destroying his career*: "I'll ruin you," he said to Michael on conference calls.[825] As Roger Friedman of *Fox News* reported:

> The basis for all this (i.e., the threats)? "The Beatles catalog," says my source. "That's it in a nutshell. This has all been done by Tommy in an effort to squeeze Michael financially. Tommy wants the Beatles catalog."[826]

It should also be noted that during the 1993 False Allegations a Mottola aide at the time recalled hearing Mottola bagger Michael: "I knew it was your problem. But you better @#%$ stop. You hear

---

823 Roberts, "Fired, the Superlawyer Returns to Bail Jackson Out"; Pete Mills, "Sony exec claims Michael Jackson's 'image and likeness' worth less than a second-hand car," *Orchard Times* February 18, 2017.
824 Roger Friedman, "Jackson May Claim 'Threats' by Mottola," *Fox News* July 12, 2002
825 Friedman, "Jackson May Claim 'Threats' by Mottola."
826 Friedman, "Jackson May Claim 'Threats' by Mottola."

that Michael? You better @#%$ stop."[827] All the while, Mottola likely knew the charges were false.

With Tommy Mottola threatening to ruin Michael Jackson on group conference calls, Michael began publicly exposing Mottola. At Al Sharpton's National Action Network in New York on June 2, 2002, Michael revealed Mottola's racism and called him "devilish." At a fan club event in London on June 15, 2002 however, Michael told the crowd, "Tommy Mottola is a devil." His larger remarks there are very revealing.

> And… Sony…Sony… Being the artist that I am, at Sony I've generated several billion dollars for Sony, several billon. They really thought that my mind is always on music and dancing. It usually is, *but they never thought that this performer — myself — would out think them.* So, we can't let them get away with what they're trying to do, because now I'm a free agent… I just owe Sony one more album. It's just a box set, really, with two new songs which I've written ages ago. Because for every album that I record, I write — literally, I'm telling you the truth — I write at least 120 songs every album I do. So I can do the box set, just giving them any two songs. So I'm leaving Sony, a free agent,… owning half of Sony! I own half of Sony's Publishing. I'm leaving them, and they're very angry at me, because I just did good business, you know. So the way they get revenge is to try and destroy my album! But I've always said, you know, art — good art — never dies. …Thank you. *And Tommy Mottola is a devil!* I'm not supposed to say what I'm going to say right now, but I have let you know this. (Points to crowd). Please don't videotape what I am going to say, ok? Turn it off, please. Do it, do it, I don't mind! Tape it!

> Mariah Carey, after divorcing Tommy, came to me crying. Crying. She was crying so badly I had to hold her. She said to me, "This is an evil man, and Michael, this man follows me." He taps her phones, and he's very, very evil. She doesn't trust him. *We have to continue our drive until he is terminated.* We can't allow him to do this to great artists, we just can't.

On January 9, 2003 – six months after Michael Jackson led a *drive to terminate Tommy Mottola at Sony* - Mottola was "terminated,"

---

827 Robert Sam Anson, "Tommy Boy," *Vanity Fair* November 1996.

forced to resign as CEO of Sony. Michael Jackson won but he earned an enemy for life.

Who is Tommy Mottola?

> "When Tommy has it in for somebody he can be unbelievably petty. He'll call maître d's to make sure people aren't given tables," says an acquaintance. Mottola's tactics were often brass-knuckle, but those who've known him for many years describe him as a gangster groupie who purposefully adopted the shiny-suited look of a Mafia lieutenant.[828]

Tommy Mottola is an Italian who converted to Judaism in 1971 when he married the daughter of the Jewish "Music Mob" figure Sam Clark. Mottola had his own mob associations as well, including Jewish industry mobster Morris Levy, longtime associate of the Genovese crime family. Mottola also had a friendship with Father Louis Gigante, who was introduced to Mottola by his brother, Mob Boss Vinnie the Chin Gigante. Mottola showed up in a 1986 NBC report on the Mob infiltration of the music industry.[829]

Equally important are Mottola's association with the reputed head of the "Gay Mafia". Roger Friedman of *Fox News* informs us: "David Geffen…is an ally of Tommy Mottola in the often brutal, warlike atmosphere of the record industry."[830] In 2016 the *Observer* asked Mottola who he considered as the one person who *made* his career. His answer: David Geffen and Clive Davis.

> *If you could pick one person who you think gave you a leg up at a critical moment and made your career, who would you thank today?* Well, there are a couple of people. When I managed Hall & Oates in the late 70s and early 80s, I was very close to David Geffen, and he really taught me a lot. Clive Davis was an inspiration. But I used to look at him sort of on a pedestal cause the guy was sort of untouchable.[831]

---

828 Phoebe Eaton, "Tommy Mottola Faces The Music," *New York Magazine* February 21, 2003.
829 Anson, "Tommy Boy."
830 Roger Friedman, "Jacko Will Get His Albums Back After All," *Fox News* July 19, 2002.
831 David Wallis, "Tommy Mottola: Strong Execs Need Someone to Say 'Shut the Fuck Up'," *Observer* December 12, 2016.

Geffen and Mottola

This makes sense as it was David Geffen who helped orchestrate the *coup* that removed Walter Yetnikof as chief of CBS in 1990. Mottola was Yetnikoff's number two man.

> Geffen staged a commando raid on Yetnikoff's own turf…Agreeing that Walter had gone off the rails, a loose-knit alliance of Geffen, [Allen] Grubman, Mottola, [Bruce] Springsteen manager Jon Landau and [Irving] Azoff staged a palace coup. Yetnikoff resigned in September 1990, a month after Mottola was honored at the annual City of Hope dinner on the Sony lot…[832]

While Mottola was not immediately installed as Yetnikof's replacement, with Yetnikof out of the way eventually Mottola did assume the top spot. He owes much to David Geffen. Thus, two enemies of Michael Jackson – David Geffen ad Tommy Mottola – happened to be besties. This could not work out well for Michael.

---

832 "The Same Old Song, Part Three," *Daily Double* April 3, 2017; Dannen, *Hit Men*, 330ff.

II.   Betrayal: Sony and the Interfor Report

> Additionally, Interfor's investigation found a tight business relationship between Branca and Tommy Mottola, primarily in regard to the affairs of Jackson. Interfor has begun investigating the flow of funds from Jackson through Mottola and Branca into offshore accounts in the Carribean. Interfor believes that, at this stage of the investigation, if we had additional time and a proper budget we could develop intelligence which would uncover a scheme to defraud Jackson and his empire by Mottola and Branca by diverting funds offshore.

In 2003, Michael Jackson retained the services of Intefor Inc. to investigate the people in his inner circle. Intefor Inc. is a Manhattan-based corporate espionage and international investigative intelligence firm founded by Israeli-American security consultant Juval Aviv, a former major in Israel's Defense Force and former Mossad assassin. Aviv was retained by Pan Am in 1989 to investigate the bombed Pan Am flight 103, and his leaked report concluded that the Lockerbie Bombing was a CIA gun- and drug-smuggling operation gone wrong. The results of Aviv's investigation for Michael Jackson were shared in February and March and were compiled in a dossier known as the "Interfor Report," the final version of which is dated April 15, 2003 and was submitted to Michael as "Confidential." According to the Report the investigation found an insidious betrayal afoot within Michael's inner circle; specifically Aviv found a "tight business relationship between [Michael's lawyer] Branca and [Michael's enemy] Tommy Mottola, primarily in regard to the affairs of Jackson." The investigation uncovered evidence of "the flow of funds from Jackson through Mottola and Branca into offshore accounts in the Carribean (*sic*)," and "a scheme to defraud Jackson and his empire by Mottola and Branca diverting funds offshore." It is reported that the results of this investigation prompted Michael to fire his attorney John Branca.[833] According to Michael's manger

---

833 Johnnie L. Roberts, "The Secret Probe That Got Branca Fired," *The Wrap* December 5, 2010.

Leonard Rowe, "The Interfor Report caused Michael Jackson great anguish and Michael demanded that Branca *was never to have anything to do with him, his business, his family, or his personal life again.*"[834] Yet, a week before Michael Jackson was killed Branca pops back up and is later made executor of Michael's estate. It should be pointed out that Mottola abruptly resigned – was "terminated" - as CEO from Sony a month prior to the release of the Interfor Report.

III.   *The Nation of Islam Pushes The Jewish Mafia Back*

Michael Jackson sitting with Al Malnik

In the year 2000 Michael Jackson developed a relationship with Florida attorney and businessman Al Malnik, son of Russian Jewish immigrants. Al Malnik was Mafia. He was an employee of Jewish Mobster Meyer Lansky and when Lansky died in 1983 at the age of 81 *Reader's Digest* named Malnik his "heir apparent." Between 2000 and 2002 Michael and Malnik developed a close relationship. Malnik is said to have loaned Michael up to $70 million, and he led a consortium that put together financial rescue

---

834 Leonard Rowe, What Really Happened to Michael Jackson The King of Pop: The Evil Side of the Entertainment Industry (n.p: Linell-Diamond Enterprises, LLC, 2010) 238.

plans to get Michael out of debt. However, by 2003 Michael ended his relationship with the Jewish Mobster because he came to believe that Malnik, whom he found out had Mafia associations, was conspiring with Sony's Tommy Mottola and film director Brett Ratner to wrangle the catalog from him. John Branca and Al Malnik were longtime friends as well. In 2005 Michael hired an investigator to verify his suspicions, Gordon Novel. Novel worked in the Lyndon Johnson administration and spent years as an investigator for former U.S. Attorney General Ramsey Clark. Before that, he assisted former New Orleans District Attorney Jim Garrison investigate the J.F.K. assassination. Michael believed this Mottola-Ratner-Malnik-Branca conspiracy was behind the 2005 child molestation charges, which Michael was ultimately acquitted and exonerated of. As Maureen Orth detailed in 2009:

> According to Novel, the Jacksons believed that it was all a grand conspiracy, that the accuser's mother was being paid by Jackson's enemies, who wanted to take control of his major economic asset, the Sony/ATV Music catalogue, which holds publishing rights to 251 Beatles songs and works by scores of other pop artists. Jackson claimed that the main conspirators were Sony Records; its former president, Tommy Mottola; and Santa Barbara County district attorney Tom Sneddon, the prosecutor, who also investigated Jackson in 1993. The catalogue is held jointly by Jackson and Sony, and Jackson's share is mortgaged for more than $200 million. If Jackson defaults, Sony has first chance to buy his half as early as this coming December. (A Sony spokesperson said, "We are not going to comment on any aspect of this.")

> Jackson explained to Novel that the conspirators had introduced him to Al Malnik, a wealthy Miami attorney who had once represented Meyer Lansky...According to Novel, Jackson said he was lured to Malnik's house in Miami Beach by film director Brett Ratner to see a house so beautiful it would make him catatonic. He said that once he was there, however, Malnik, who Jackson claimed had Mafia ties, wanted to put his fingers in the singer's business. Jackson also said he received a call from Tommy Mottola while he was there, which aroused his suspicion, but he did not tell Novel that he later put Malnik on the board of the Sony/ATV Music partnership. (Reached by telephone, Malnik scoffed at the idea of a conspiracy or of his having any Mafia ties. He said, "It does not make any sense." Ratner confirmed that he took Jackson to Malnik's house and that he considers Malnik a father figure.)

Jackson and Mottola have been at odds for years. In New York in July 2002, Jackson staged a public protest against Mottola with the Reverend Al Sharpton, calling him a racist and "very, very devilish." He called for a boycott of Sony, which is believed to have contributed to Mottola's ouster from the company six months later. Jackson is reportedly so frightened of Mottola that one of the reasons he surrounded himself with Nation of Islam guards in 2003 was that he thought Mottola could put out a hit on him. (Mottola could not be reached for comment.)

Jackson wanted Novel to find the links among these characters. Novel told me in March that "he believes he'll get convicted."[835]

Bob Norman who interviewed Novel says further:

"The whole thing centered on Tommy Mottola setting him up," Novel told me. "Mottola and him were at odds, and Jackson's information was that Mottola and Malnik got together to fuck him. He said he believed Malnik was representing the Mob."

I asked Novel if he believed Jackson's theory about the conspiracy against him. He said that he thought Jackson was not guilty of the criminal charges and that he was probably set up, but he had no idea if Mottola was involved.

"He thought that Mottola was Mob-connected and that Malnik was representing the Mob, but I can't vouch for any of that shit," Novel said. "I don't have anything against Tommy Mottola and don't know if what he thought was true or not. *I don't want to get on Mottola's bad side.* My sources in New York say he's a dangerous guy."[836]

It was around this time that Michael Jackson surrounded himself with the Nation of Islam. The Nation not only provided

---

835 Maureen Orth, "C.S.I. Neverland," *Vanity Fair* July 2005.
836 Bob Norman, "The Malnik Family's Michael Jackson Photo Dump," *Broward Palm Beach New Times* June 29, 2009.

soldiers as a security detail for Michael but also reportedly lent him the Chief-of-Staff of the Nation, Leonard Farrakhan, to help with Michael's business and legal affairs. According to *The New York Times*, "Officials from the Nation of Islam...have moved in with Michael Jackson and are asserting control over the singer's business affairs, friends, employees and business associates of Mr. Jackson said."[837] This is I'm sure a significant overstatement. The

The Honorable Minister Farrakhan and Michael Jackson

word did go out, though: "Farrakhan and the Nation of Islam; those people are very protective of Michael."[838] At this point, the presence of the Nation of Islam in Michael Jackson's world was now so palpable that Michael's official spokesman, Stuart Backerman, resigned claiming, "I quit because the Nation of Islam had infiltrated Michael's world."[839] This is a skewed perspective. There was no "infiltration" of Michael's world. The fact of the matter is, Michael Jackson would become very close friends with the Honorable Minister Louis Farrakhan, current leader of the Nation of Islam. Others now left Michael's camp. "Michael LePerruque, Jackson's chief of security, and other top advisers, were soon gone. *Malnik was done*."[840] This strong presence of the

---

837 Sharon Waxman, "Dispute on Michael Jackson Camp Over Role of the Nation of Islam," *The New York Times* December 30, 2003.

838 Roger Friedman, "Claim: Jacko's Rep Threatened Harm From Nation of Islam," *Fox News* March 24, 2009.

839 "Michael Jackson's aide 'quit due to Nation of Islam," *Telegraph* July 7, 2009.

840 Gerald Posner, "Michael's Missing millions," *The Daily Beast* August 2, 2009.

Nation around Michael removed the immediate threat from Michael's world.

> More costly [in terms of Michael's affiliation with the Nation of Islam] in the short term, …was that Muhammad and his henchmen were destroying Jackson's relationships with almost everyone who had done anything to help him (*sic!*) in recent years. [**read: almost everyone who had done anything to hurt him in recent years. - WM**] The most expensive exclusions were those of *Marc Schaffel…and Al Malnik…*"I told Michael that it was the worst mistake of his life when he allowed the Nation of Islam to come in and convince him to stop speaking to Al Malnik," Schaffel said. With Leonard Farrakhan and associates whispering in Michael's ear, *the relationship with Malnik deteriorated far beyond the point of not talking to one another.* By the spring of 2004, Jackson…was convinced that Malnik was part of a conspiracy against him that included Sony, Bank of America, and Tom Sneddon and that all of them were after the Beatles songs.[841]

Not only did Al Malnik and Marc Schaffel disappear from Michael's circle around 2003, so too did Dr. Arnold Klein. He told TMZ's Harvey Levin in 2009:

> **Levin**   Well, you know, but you were in contact with him at that time (2005).
> **Klein**   Not at that time. Not during the whole second trial. I was not.
> **Levin**   You never talked to him?
> **Klein**   Not during that trial.
> **Levin**   You had a falling out?
> **Klein**   No, it wasn't a falling out but he was up there in that trial and I never talked to him during that trial whatsoever. There were periods of time, vast periods of time, from 2003 to now that I never spoke to him. You know that. I hadn't spoken to him since 2003…[842]

In other words, despite the negative spin by the press, the Nation of Islam's presence in Michael Jackson's life at this critical time was a positive influence.

---

841 Sullivan, *Untouchable.*
842 November 5, 2009 Harvey Levin Interview.

Chapter Fourteen

AEG Live: Setting The Stage For Murder

I.   *50 Dates By Hook or By Crook*

His aides weren't the only ones who recognized that a 50-concert run was foolhardy. In May, Jackson himself reportedly addressed fans as he left his Burbank rehearsal studio. "Thank you for your love and support," he told them. "I want you guys to know I love you very much. "I don't know how I'm going to do 50 shows. I'm not a big eater. I need to put some weight on. I'm really angry with them booking me up to do 50 shows. I only wanted to do ten."...Whatever the final autopsy results reveal, it was greed that killed Michael Jackson. Had he not been driven – by a cabal of bankers, agents, doctors and advisers – to commit to the grueling 50 concerts in London's O2 Arena, I believe he would still be alive today.[843]

After his exoneration during the 2005 False Allegations trial, Michael Jackson spent eleven months in Bahrain as a guest of the royal family. Upon his return to the U.S. Michael took up residence in Las Vegas. He had not performed for four years when, in January 2009 he was approached by representatives from AEG Live about a string of concerts to take place at the new O2 Arena in London. Reportedly, Michael or his team twice rebuffed Randy Phillips, CEO of AEG Live, and his concert proposal.[844] As is clear from internal emails that surfaced during the 2013 trial, AEG Live executives had a disdain for Michael Jackson the person: while trying to "hook" him they were yet referring to him as a "creepy" "freak,"[845] and among themselves they disrespectfully called him

843 Ian Halperin, "'I'm better off dead. I'm done': Michael Jackson's fateful prediction just a week before his death," *Daily Mail* June 29 2009.
844 Halperin, "'I'm better off dead."
845 On January 28, 2009 AEG Live Senior VP and General Counsel Shawn Trell to his boss Ted Fikre, AEG's chief legal officer. Alan Duke, "AEG exec

"Mikey."[846] They were also deceiving him from the very beginning by deliberately presenting an exaggerated earning potential and deceptively downplaying the labor on Jackson's part involved. "AEG tried to mislead Michael Jackson about how hard his concert tour would be, e-mails imply…Greedy concert promoters tricked…Michael Jackson into signing up for his grueling final concert."[847] Michael signed the contract. The deception didn't stop there. Michael Jackson agreed to a 10-concert deal. That is what in January 2009 Michael was confident he could pull off. However,

> Before long…ten concerts had turned into 50 and the potential revenues had skyrocketed. The vultures who were pulling his strings somehow managed to put this concert extravaganza together *behind his back*, then presented it to him as a fait accompli,' said one aide… "We knew it was a disaster waiting to happen," said one aide. "I don't think anybody predicted it would actually kill him but nobody believed he would end up performing."[848]

II. *A Healthy Michael Jackson Chemically Assaulted…Again*

It is extremely important to point out that, in January 2009, *"Michael Jackson was not abusing pain medication in years leading up to comeback tour deal with AEG Live*, says doctor"[849] As the *New York Daily News* reported in 2013

---

called Michael Jackson 'freak' before signing concert contract," *CNN* May 23, 2013.

846 Alan Duke, "AEG drops Michael Jackson insurance claim," *CNN* September 10, 2012.

847 Richard Johnson, "Concert promoters pulled fast one on Jackson, emails imply," *New York Post* May 29, 2013.

848 Ian Halperin, "'I'm better off dead. I'm done': Michael Jackson's fateful prediction just a week before his death," *Daily Mail* June 29 2009.

849 Nancy Dillion, "Michael Jackson was not abusing pain medication in years leading up to comeback tour deal with AEG Live, says doctor," *New York Daily News* July 3, 2013.

"Michael Jackson apparently *was clean and not abusing pain medication* in the years leading up to his comeback tour deal with concert promoter AEG Live, a Connecticut doctor testified Wednesday.

Dr. Sidney Schnoll based his opinion on medical records stating the King of Pop only needed 100 milligrams of the narcotic pain medication Demerol to knock him out for a dermatology procedure in late 2008.

Schnoll said Jackson would have built up too much tolerance for that dose to work if he frequently abused opioids during the era of his 2005 molestation trial and subsequent travels abroad.

"He would have to take a much higher dose of Demerol to get the (necessary) effect for the surgery," Schnoll told jurors." [850]

This is because Michael fought this addiction and apparently won. To help him battle the Demerol addiction which doctors such as – and reportedly *primarily* – Arnold Klein *created*, Michael Jackson was in 2003 fitted with a "secret medical implant" called the Narcan Implant which stopped its user from getting enjoyment from opiates, effectively making drug-taking pointless. The Narcan Implant releases into the patient doses of Narcan (Naloxone) which blocks pleasure receptors in the brain. According to court papers in the 2013 Katherine Jackson v. AEG Live case the implant was discovered in Michael's body after his death.[851] So Michael Jackson *could not have been* a Demerol addict; he got no pleasure from Demerol. Rather, Michael Jackson would be *deliberately drugged with Demerol (and other drugs)* by AEG Live employees.

Thus, at the start of Michael's relationship with AEG Live in 2009 he was *a healthy, non-drug addict*. This is confirmed by the physical exam conducted on February 4, 2009, by the London insurance company Lloyd's of London. AEG Live was seeking insurance for the (at first) ten shows in London which covered cancellation or postponement of the shows or illness of the singer

---

850 Dillion, "Michael Jackson was not abusing pain medication."
851 "Michael Jackson 'had secret implant to prevent him getting enjoyment form opiates', court papers reveal," *Daily Beast* April 11, 2013.

or death of the singer.[852] Remarkably, the insurance policy AEG Live was seeking included a *drug overdose* provision as well! Before Lloyd's of London would approve such policy, they required Dr. David Slavit from New York to conduct a physical examination of Michael Jackson in his Los Angeles home. Blood samples were drawn which, upon examination by Westcliff Medical Laboratories, resulted *in normal and consistent findings*! Dr. Slavit found Michael Jackson to be in excellent condition and notified AEG Live that he "passed with flying colors". The insurance policy for ten shows was thus completed in April 2009.[853]

Michael Jackson was a *healthy, non-drug abuser* at the start of this process with AEG Live in January and February, until in March *Dr. Arnold Klein was brought back into Michael's life after being absent for six years.*[854] The pretext or pretense was that Klein would "rebuild" Michael's face for the "This Is It" tour. As an employee of AEG Live Klein *immediately* began pumping Michael with "insane" amounts of Demerol, just as he did in 1993. For example, over a three-day period in May Klein pumped Michael with *900 milligrams of Demerol* and according to the medical testimony during the Dr. Conrad Murray trial these "stiff doses" of Demerol *were not* required for the Botox and Restylane treatments that were listed in the medical records.[855] "Dr. Robert Waldman, an addiction specialist, was of the opinion that Jackson had exhibited signs of developing tolerance to Demerol by late April and by early May he believed the singer was dependent on

---

852 "Michael Jackson's estate, Lloyd's of London settle insurance dispute," *Reuters* January 15, 2004; "AEG boss: Jackson insurance covers overdose," *Today* July 2, 2009.
853 Richards and Langthorne, *83 Minutes*, 111-112.
854 Klein claims that in October 2008 Michael Jackson first contacted him after three years requesting a doctor's note to get out of a court appearance. Seal, "The Ugly world of Dr. Arnie Klein"; "Lawsuit Accuses Doctor Arnie Klein of Fueling Michael's Jackson's Drug Addiction," *TMZ* August 4, 2011. This does not imply, however, that Michael became a patient of Klein's again. That would not happen until March 2009.
855 Matthew Perpetua, "Doctor: Michael Jackson Was Dependent on Demerol," *Rolling Stone* October 28, 2011.

Demerol and possibly addicted to opioids."[856] Klein's medical documents reveal he injected Michael with Demerol *51 times* in three months, mostly for minor procedures like acne treatments, lip treatments and Botox.[857]

> In a highly unusual and unorthodox protocol—in fact, a number of medical professionals consulted with for this piece had never heard of such a thing before—Klein administered 100mg to 200mg of the highly addictive painkiller Demerol to Jackson when he was getting injections of the cosmetic fillers Botox and Restylane, according to medical records. Setting aside that Botox and Restylane are supposed to last for at least two months and no one this writer or any dermatologist consulted knows has ever received anything but "numbing cream" (or in one instance a half a Vicodin) for the same treatment, according to medical documents Arnie Klein gave Restylane and Botox to Jackson almost every other day accompanied by a total of 2,475 mg of Demerol in April 2009 and in a two-week period in May, more than 1,400 mg of Demerol. This has led some medical professionals familiar with the records to wonder if some of the Botox and Restylane injections listed on the medical billings were simply "cover."[858]

Dr. Arnold Klein reportedly made Michael Jackson a Demerol addict in 1993, which Michael successfully overcame; and Klein made Michael a Demerol addict again in 2009! In the three months that Klein worked to "rebuild" Michael's face Klein injected 6,500 milligrams of Demerol into Michael. [859] And during these three months (March 23-June 22) of injecting Michael with medically non-warranted amounts of Demerol Klein submitted his invoice totaling $48,000 to AEG.[860] As he admitted: "AEG and not the Jackson Estate was to pay me."[861]

---

856 Richards and Langthorne, *83 Minutes*, 119.
857 "MJ and Klein – Affection for Injections," *TMZ* October 28, 2009.
858 Amy Ephron, "Conrad Murray Michael Jackson Trial: The Evidence the Public Won't Hear," *The Daily Beast* September 29, 2011.
859 Alan Duke, "'Perfect storm' of drugs killed Michael Jackson, sleep expert says," *CNN* October 14, 2011.
860 Roger Friedman, "DEA 'Inspected' Office of Michael Jackson's Dr. Klein Last Week: Exclusive," *Showbiz 411* June 30, 2010.
861 Initially on his web page @ http://www.arnoldwklein.com/?p=2128

III.　　*Enter Dr. Conrad Murray*

And *then* came Conrad Murray. On May 8, 2009, AEG Live co-CEO Paul Gongaware called Dr. Murray to officially retain his services. Dr. Murray was AEG Live's employee, not Michael Jackson's employee. So too was Dr. Arnold Klein AEG Live's employee. Dr. Murray was to be paid *not* from Michael Jackson's advanced budget but from AEG Live's own budget.[862] On May 12, Dr. Murray ordered the drug Propofol which was to be used on Michael Jackson. Propofol is an intravenously administered *hypnotic drug*. While AEG Live was paying (in theory) Dr. Arnold Klein, who was loading Michael Jackson with Demerol, AEG Live was also paying (in theory) Dr. Conrad Murray who was pumping Michael with Propofol as well as a "cocktail" of other drugs, which we will discuss below.

Michael Jackson was a healthy, non-drug abusing man in January. By May, under the "medical care" of AEG Live's two employees Dr. Conrad Murray and Dr. Arnold Klein, Michael Jackson was suffering the effects of drug abuse.

In May and June, Michael Jackson was confused, easily frightened, unable to remember, obsessive, and disoriented. He had impaired memory, loss of appetite, and absence of energy. He was cold and shivering during summer rehearsals for his show, and as shown in photographs and motion pictures of him, he uncharacteristically wore

---

But that's now removed. The post can be currently found here: https://www.michaeljacksonhoaxforum.com/forums/index.php?topic=23648.0
862 "AEG Live controller Julie Hollander … her testimony about the company's budgeting, which she acknowledged included $1.5 million approved to pay Dr. Murray. The doctor's costs were listed as production costs — expenses that AEG is responsible for paying — and not as an advance, which Jackson would ultimately be responsible for giving back to the company, she testified. The controller's testimony appears to contradict the argument AEG lead lawyer Marvin Putnam made in a CNN interview days before the trial began (that Murray was an employee of Michael Jackson rather than of AEG Live)." "AEG files claim for losses from Michael Jackson's death the day he died," *Fox* * May 20, 2013.

heavy clothing during the rehearsals, while other dancers wore scant clothing and were perspiring from the heat.[863]

While leaving his Burbank rehearsing studio in May Michael addressed some of his fans and one of his employees at the time recalled to Ian Halperin of *Daily Mail*:

> "The way he was talking, it's like he's not in control over his own life anymore," she told me earlier this month. "It sounds like somebody else is pulling his strings and telling him what to do. Someone wants him dead. They keep feeding him pills like candy. They are trying to push him over the edge. He needs serious help. The people around him will kill him."[864]

Why would AEG Live take a healthy Michael Jackson, sign a contract with him for a series of *50 concerts* at *their* newly renovated arena in London and then deliberately drug him to the point of incapacitation? The answer is a simple, two-part answer.

"The Plan" was clearly to drug Michael Jackson and then take advantage of his reduced mental capacity. The incapacitation made Michael incompetent to make rational decisions, and this served AEG Live's interests. Michael was indeed *chemically controlled*. As the 2013 complaint stated:

> AEG's control of Jackson's person was further extended by the drugs being administered by Murray, which weakened Jackson's physical and mental health, rendering him vulnerable, confused, *and subject to direction*.[865]

Family friend Terry Harvey describes the effects of this intentional *drugging* of Michael Jackson:

---

863 Superior Court of California, County of Los Angeles, *Joseph* Jackson v. Conrad Murray et al. Case No. BC450393, 30 November 2010, pg. 12.
864 Ian Halperin, " 'I'm better off dead. I'm done': Michael Jackson's fateful prediction just a week before his death," *Daily Mail* June 29, 2009.
865 Superior Court of California, County of Los Angeles Katherine Jackson v. AEG Live LLC et al., Case No. BC445597 September 15, 2010, 10-11.

[Michael] had a sharp mind, but he was deluded, hampered by the drugs. He didn't know what he was saying to people. To make his life easy *he would just say 'yes'*. He was walking around in a daze like a zombie." Another friend said: "He shouted out, 'They are punishing me and I can't take it anymore. They are gonna kill me.'"[866]

It appears that Michael was chemically maintained in a state of continuous confusion and compliance. Detectives Orlando Martinez, Dan Meyers and Scott Smith said in the 2019 documentary *Killing Michael Jackson* that Murray "purposefully kept [Michael Jackson] under the influence."[867] He allegedly did so on AEG's orders. By the time of his death on June 25th Michael had already been suffering from chronic pneumonia, chronic respiratory bronchitis, anemia, and brain swelling.[868] The respiratory problems could have been caused by his severely damaged lungs (the autopsy revealed there was widespread inflammation and extensive scarring), which damage could be due to Michael's noted discoid lupus or it could have been caused by his Demerol drugging.[869]

The days before Michael was killed his mental incapacitation was clear to everyone. He was described by the show director on June 19 as a "basket case," who was "trembling, rambling, obsessive," and the stage manager said "My layman's degree tells me [Michael] needs a shrink"[870] He was disoriented and Karen Faye testified that "He kept repeating, 'why can't I choose.'"[871] According to other testimony Michael told Kenny

---

866 "'Drugged, exhausted' MJ 'could barely walk' during This Is It rehearsals," *Thaindian News* October 31, 2009.

867 Adam Starkey, "Michael Jackson's doctor waited 25 minutes to call police after finding singer's body, claims new documentary," *Metro* June 21, 2019.

868 Superior Court of California, County of Los Angeles, *Joseph* Jackson v. Conrad Murray et al. Case No. BC450393, 30 November 2010, 12.

869 Colin Vickery, "Michael Jackson should have died earlier, autopsy report reveals," *News Corp Australia* June 25, 2014.

870 "AEG Live CEO Randy Phillips Testifies About Emails on Michael Jackson's Condition," *Billboard* June 7, 2013.

871 Alan Duke, "Witness: Michael Jackson was paranoid, talking to himself in last days," *CNN* May 9, 2013

Ortega the show director, "God keeps talking to me."[872] This latter "uttering," however, just may have been true.

IV.   *The Chemical Leash and the Return of John Branca*

A most illuminating illustration of AEG taking advantage of Michael Jackson's mental incapacitation occurred within days prior to Michael's death. Remember the Interfor Report of April 15, 2003, repoted that Michael's attorney John Branca had been colluding with Michael's enemy Tommy Mottola to rob Michael. Michael thus fired Branca and according to Michael's manger Leonard Rowe, "Michael demanded that Branca *was never to have anything to do with him, his business, his family, or his personal life again.*"[873] But on the eve of Michael's death, while he was drugged, mentally incapacitated, zombified and chemically controlled by the AEG Live executive team, a treacherous event occurred:

> At around 7 o'clock one evening during the third week of June 2009, John Branca arrived in Michael Jackson's dressing room at L.A.'s Fabulous Forum, where rehearsals were under way for the performer's "This Is It" concert.

> It was their first meeting in three years. They immediately hugged, before *Branca handed Jackson a letter to be signed, formally rehiring the superlawyer.*

> It was an abrupt reunion after a bitter split — and *just days before the show business legend died.*

> "They hadn't really spoken since 2006," says CEO Randy Phillips of AEG Live, the promoter of Jackson's "This Is It" concert series.

---

872 Duke, "Witness."
873 Leonard Rowe, What Really Happened to Michael Jackson The King of Pop: The Evil Side of the Entertainment Industry (n.p: Linell-Diamond Enterprises, LLC, 2010) 238.

341

So how did Branca's and Jackson's epic relation come full circle, as if according to a Hollywood script?

In fact, Branca had begun to seek a return to the fold no sooner than Jackson wrapped up the press conference unveiling "This Is It" in early March 2009. The lawyer phoned [Randy] Phillips. "'I'd do anything in the world to be involved,'" Phillips remembers Branca saying. The AEG executive was noncommittal then.

Later, however, Phillips and Frank DiLeo, Jackson's manager from the 1980s glory days, phoned Branca. *DiLeo himself had only recently been invited back onto the brain trust, exactly two decades after Jackson fired him in 1989*, a year before Branca was booted for the first time.

...

After the dressing-room meeting, Jackson headed off apparently to his intravenous Propafol drip and Branca to a Mexican vacation, where a few days later, on June 25, his phone rang with (fellow attorney Joel) Katz on the line. Jackson had just died after Dr. Conrad Murray, his private physician, administered the drug.

"Does anyone have a will," Katz wondered?

"I have one," he says Branca answered. "If it's valid."

It was, in fact, the will that installed Branca, along with longtime Jackson family friend John McClain, as co-executor of the Jackson estate.[874]

As Johnnie L. Roberts writes: "in June 2009, within a week of Jackson's death, Branca...returned to the fold after a three-year break-up. Six days after Jackson's drug-fueled death – having spoken to [Branca] only once in three years – he, along with longtime Jackson family friend John McClain, emerged as co-executor of the tragic icon's extraordinary holdings."[875]

---

874 Johnnie L. Roberts, "A Superlawyer Return, A Pop Icon Dies – a Will is Discovered," *The Wrap* December 9, 2010.
875 Johnnie L. Roberts, "How Michael Jackson Nearly Lost his Prized Music Catalog," *The Wrap* December 5, 2010.

V. *Chemically Incapacitating Michael*

"The Plan" was also *to make Michael Jackson physically incapable of performing.* The 2010 Complaint of Katherine Jackson v. AEG Live LLC et al. asserts.

> The AEG-JACKSON AGREEMENT provided that AEG would have the exclusive right to manufacture and sell Michael Jackson merchandise associated with the Tour. In exchange for these and other revenues associated with the Tour, as well as for the prestige associated with sponsoring the This Is It Tour, AEG advanced Michael Jackson substantial sums of money, which it was to recoup through revenue from the Tour. *If, however, Jackson failed to perform,* or failed to generate the revenue to cover the advances, then AEG would have the right to collect the advance against security provided by Michael Jackson and his company, Michael Jackson LLC. *The assets from which AEG could seize from Michael Jackson include the Sony/ATV song catalogue owned by Jackson...*his assets stood security if he failed to perform.[876]

AEG Live personell can be said to have deliberately made Michael Jackson physically unable to rehearse for the show, and then used his absence from rehearsal as the pre-text for "pulling the plug" or cancelling the tour, thereby seizing Michael's assets as collateral.

> AEG threatened that if Jackson missed any further rehearsals, they were going to "pull the plug" on the show, Jackson's house, the doctor, and all the expenses for which they paid. If AEG called off the Tour, Jackson would be required to repay AEG for its advances to him. If he could not repay AEG, AEG would be entitled to collect the collateral Jackson had put up to secure his obligation to perform.[877]

But co-CEO Paul Gongaware admitted in court that, per the contract between AEG Live and Michael Jackson, Michael *was NOT obligated to attend ANY rehearsals*.

---

876 Superior Court of California, County of Los Angeles Katherine Jackson v. AEG Live LLC et al., Case No. BC445597 September 15, 2010, 4-5.
877 Superior Court of California, County of Los Angeles Katherine Jackson v. AEG Live LLC et al., Case No. BC445597 September 15, 2010, 4-5.

Gongaware explained MJ didn't have to attend rehearsals, since it was not part of his deal. He said they never required an artist to rehearse. "I didn't have any expectation", Gongaware said regarding MJ rehearsing. He said that during the HIStory tour, MJ didn't rehearse, nailed it.[878]

So the "rehearsal mandate" was a false pretext. In fact, the insistence by Randy Phillips was tantamount to nothing short of *weaponizing the rehearsals* against Michael. The concurrent drugging of Michael Jackson with Demerol by Klein and Propofol by Murray as well as with the other drugs made Michael progressively unable to physically rehearse. On June 2, 2009 Randy Phillips and Frank DiLeo confronted Michael Jackson at his home about missing rehearsals and Michael

attended the meeting wearing a surgical mask and layers of clothing as he was complaining about feeling very hot, then extremely cold. These are classic withdrawal symptoms of an addict coming down from Demerol and it's possibly no coincidence that Jackson visited Dr Klein twice in the first week of June and received two injections, totaling 400mg of Demerol. [879]

Nevertheless, Michael's AEG Live handlers showed him no sympathy at all.

[Michael's chef] Kai Chase suggested that Jackson was an emotional wreck at the time; that he was scared, fearful and anxious about the meeting. She had to go in and out of the room refilling beverage glasses but didn't overhear anything while she was briefly in the room but did, however, hear raised voices when she had left. On one occasion when she returned to fill the glasses she noticed a vase was lying on the floor and it wasn't long after that Dr Murray stormed into the kitchen having escaped the meeting and exclaimed: "I can't handle this shit!" before leaving via the back door.[880]

---

878 Testimony during Katherine Jackson et al. v. AEG Live, Monday June 3, 2013. DAY 22.
879 Richards and Langthorne, *83 Minutes*, 135.
880 Richards and Langthorne, *83 Minutes,* 135

June 19, 2009, can be considered the day the die was set. That date marked the beginning of the end for Michael Jackson. Battling the devastating effects of the forced drug abuse, Michael showed up at the Staples Center for rehearsal at 9:30 p.m. and in bad condition: "trembling, rambling and obsessive." The show director Kenny Ortega sent Michael home without setting foot on stage. Stage manager John Houghdahl emailed Phillips and Gongaware informing them that Michael was sent home from rehearsal and also candidly stating: "I have watched [Michael] *deteriorate in front of my eyes over the last 8 weeks.* He was able to do multiple 360 spins back in April. He'd fall on his ass if he tried it now."[881] Michael could do 360 spins eight weeks prior because, before he fell into the clutches of AEG Live's drug pushers Klein and Murray, Michael was healthy. In eight weeks Michael did not deteriorate on his own; he was chemically assaulted.

Hougdahl also revealed that earlier that night after watching a pyrotechnics demonstration, Michael said, "You aren't going to kill the artist, are you?" Hougdahl wrote to Phillips that Michael, whose scalp was badly burned while shooting a Pepsi commercial in 1984, *didn't appear to be referring to the fireworks.*"[882] Associate producer Alif Sankey after the rehearsal called Kenny Ortega: "I kept saying that 'Michael is dying, he's dying, he's leaving us, he needs to be put in a hospital...Please do something. Please, please.' I kept saying that. I asked [Ortega] why no one had seen what I had seen. He said he didn't know."[883] What Ortega *did* know on that day is that they were "pulling the plug" on Michael Jackson: "The situation came to a head after the June 19, 2009, rehearsal, when Ortega sent an email to Phillips saying that they should consider 'pulling the plug' on the upcoming

881 Hannington Dia, "Katherine Jackson Leaves Court In Tears During M.J. Civil Trial," *News One* May 24, 2013.
882 "AEG Live CEO Randy Phillips Testifies About Emails on Michael Jackson's Condition," *Billboard* June 7, 2013.
883 Alan Duke, "Witness: 'Everybody was lying' after Michael Jackson died," *CNN* May 13, 2013.

concert dates."[884] In fact, according to Karen Faye's text messages that were read to the court on September 9, 2013 Ortega and Randy Philips that night "told [Michael] they will PULL THE PLUG IF HE DOESN'T GET HIS SHIT TOGETHER. IF HE DOESN'T DO THIS, HE LOSES EVERYTHING, **PROBABLY EVEN HIS KIDS**."

VI.   *Pulling The Plug on Michael Jackson*

The AEG Live executives showed *zero* sympathy for Michael Jackson's rapidly deteriorating physical and mental condition. They threatened even to take his children away. The next day on June 20th Phillips and Ortega confronted a physically and mentally suffering Michael Jackson at his home during a so-called "crisis meeting" and verbally and mentally assaulted him further. During the meeting AEG Live threatened to "pull the plug."[885] Murray, who was present, recounts details from the meeting during a November 2011 interview:

> The producer Kenny Ortega made several statements. He was going to quit; this could not go on if Michael was not going to do what he was expected to do, they cannot have a show. And they could not get Michael to conform to what they wanted. Michael on the other hand was saying they were working him too much. He was …He did not want to be worked as a machine. He felt like a machine…
>
> That's when I got the shock. Randy Phillips asked that they just step out of the living room when the meeting had ended. This is him, grinding his teeth. "He does not have a fucking cent, a fucking cent. What's this bullshit all about? Listen, this guy is next to the skid row, he's going to

---

884 Kimberly Potts and Tim Kenneally, "Michael Jackson Producer Wanted to Pull Plug on Concert Tour," *The Wrap* October 25, 2011. "Kenny Ortega feared Michael Jackson's tour would fail days before death," *Our Weekly* July 11, 2013: "Ortega said: 'On the 19th, I had more than a serious concern. I didn't think it was going to go on."
885 Richard Johnson, "Michael Jackson cut off financially by promoters in final days because he was missing rehearsal," *New York Post* June 7, 2013.

be homeless, the fucking pop sickles that his children are sucking on… Look, those kids…what's that all about? Nine security guards, why does he need that? I'm paying for that shit. I'm paying for the toilet paper he wipes his ass with. He has never a fucking cent. And if he don't get his show done, *he's over.* This is it. This is the last chance that he has to earn any kind of money. He is ruined. Financially he has *nothing. Zero.*[886]

And then the move was made: the plug was officially pulled.

Michael Jackson was cut off financially by promoters of his last concert tour days before he died (June 20th) and told he couldn't have another advance of $1 million because he was missing rehearsals, according to testimony today. Five days before Jackson died in 2009 of an anesthetic overdose, AEG was threatening to 'pull the plug' on his 50-concert tour, *and cut him off,* testimony and e-mails revealed in court.[887]

The reference is to the request sent to Randy Phillips by Michael's lawyer Michael Kane on June 19th for a $1 million advance so Michael could pay staff. For the first time, Phillips refused the request, announcing in his response email to Kane: "it is impossible to advance any $$$. He may, unfortunately, be in *anticipatory breach* at *this point.*"

AEG Live executives feared Michael Jackson would sabotage his comeback concerts five days before his death, the company's CEO testified Thursday. Randy Phillips refused to advance money to help Jackson pay his staff because he believed the singer was "in an anticipatory breach" of his contract because he had missed rehearsals, he testified.[888]

An anticipatory breach refers to an action that shows a party's *intention to fail* to perform or fulfill its contractual obligations to another party. An anticipatory breach negates the counterparty's

---

886 See also Caroline Graham, "NO, I didn't kill Michael. He did it himself…with a massive overdose using his own stash," *Daily Mail* November 24, 2013.
887 Richard Johnson, "Michael Jackson cut off financially by promoters in final days because he was missing rehearsal," *New York Post* June 7, 2013.
888 Alan Duke, "AEG exec feared Michael Jackson would sabotage his comeback tour," *CNN* June 7, 2013.

responsibility to perform its requirements under the contract. Phillips is here claiming that, because the physically incapacitated Michael Jackson was missing some rehearsals *which he was NOT contractually mandated to attend*, Michael showed *intent* to fail to honor the terms of his contract!!!!

> the chief executive of AEG LIVE thought Jackson might be preparing to breach his contract by not rehearsing...Phillips said he thought Jackson might be preparing to break his contract by not showing up for rehearsals. "You felt Mr. Jackson's not going to rehearsal...may have placed him in breach of the contact. That's why you wouldn't advance him any more money?" [Jackson attorney Brian] Panish asked. "Yes," replied Phillips.[889]

But this was all a big ruse. As Alan Duke of *CNN* pointed out:

> Phillips' testimony that he believed Jackson was contractually obligated to attend rehearsals contradicted AEG Live Co-CEO Paul Gongware's previous testimony that Jackson *was not required to rehearse.*[890]

On June 20, 2009, the plug was officially pulled on Michael Jackson. And as Karen Faye noted in a September 26, 2013, tweet: "When [Randy Phillips] threatened to 'pull the plug' it meant a lot more than stop the show." That morning Randy Phillips spoke to Dr. Murray on the phone. In Phillip's video deposition that was shown to the jury in 2013 he claimed that the conversation lasted only three minutes. However, he was shown phone records that showed it lasted 25 minutes. Phillips was caught in a lie. When he was then asked what he and Murray discussed on that 25- minute call the morning of June 20th, he claimed that "he did not recall."[891] Of course not. However, in an email he sent to Ortega that afternoon he hints: "I had a lengthy conversation with Dr. Murray, who I am *gaining* immense respect for as I get to deal

---

889 Jeff Gottlieb, "Michael Jackson was 'trembling, rambling,' director said," *Los Angeles Times* June 7, 2013.
890 Duke, "AEG exec feared Michael Jackso."
891 Jeff Gottlieb, "Michael Jackson case: AEG exec admits Murray characterizations wrong," *Los Angeles Times* June 10, 2013.

with him more".[892] Whatever conversation transpired on that call, it endeared Murray to Phillips.

On June 23rd – two days before Michael Jackson was killed by drugs delivered to him by AEG Live employees - AEG Live moved to finalize the new insurance policy on Michael Jackson's life.[893] While the first policy was approved in April, it only covered the original ten shows. When AEG Live expanded the run to 50 shows, Lloyd's of London the insurance company required Michael Jackson to undergo a second medical exam, four hours that involved three doctors, heart-monitoring and blood work.[894] AEG Live did everything they could to avoid that second physical, because they *knew* that the newly "drug-addled" Michael would *never* have passed that second physical exam. And a lot was at stake. While the original policy that covered 10 shows had the potential to net AEG Live $17 million, a successful claim on the expanded policy covering the 50 shows may have netted AEG Live 300 million euros, according to *The Guardian*.[895] Murray was called in to assist AEG Live lie to the insurance company about Michael Jackson's health.[896]

> AEG's insurance broker tried to persuade Lloyd's to drop the physical, according to the email discussions. AEG suggested that Jackson's physician, Dr. Conrad Murray, could give an oral recitation of Jackson's recent medical history instead, the Times reported. Lloyd's refused.

---

892 Jeff Gottlieb, "Michael Jackson case: AEG exec admits Murray characterizations wrong," *Los Angeles Times* June 10, 2013.

893 Corina Knoll, "AEG sought life insurance on 'basket case' Michael Jackson," *Los Angeles Times* May 21, 2013: "In days before Michael Jackson's death, AEG executives were still attempting to secure a life insurance policy on the performer who had been acting erratically at rehearsals for his comeback tour, according to testimony and emails…"

894 Steve Starr, "Promoter emails say Michael Jackson was out of shape, consumed with doubt," *Today* September 2, 2012.

895 Sean Michaels, "Michael Jackson concert insurer refuses $17.5m payout," *The Guardian* June 8, 2011.

896 Andrew Gumbel, "Conrad Murray – the man who supplied Michael Jackson's lethal dose of propofol," *The Guardian* November 7, 2011.

A Lloyd's underwriter wrote that repeated requests for written records and details about Jackson's daily fitness program were met "always with no response."

Murray responded to the last of the requests June 25 at Jackson's Southern California home, according to emails presented at the doctor's criminal trial. He wrote that he had talked to Jackson and "Authorization was denied."

Jackson died less than an hour later, according to a timeline Murray gave investigators.[897]

Indeed, less than an hour later Michael Jackson was dead by the hand of AEG Live's hired doctor Conrad Murray. And only hours after that *AEG LIVE filed their insurance claim to collect the payout!*

AEG Live filed an insurance claim to recover losses from Michael Jackson's death the same day he died, according to a lawyer for Jackson's family…AEG's insurance claim…was filed with Lloyds of London on June 25, 2009 — hours after Jackson was pronounced dead at UCLA Medical Center. [898]

The insurance policy was taken out to cover the cancellation or postponement of the London concerts in the case of the death, accident or illness of Jackson.[899]

---

897 Steve Starr, "Promoter emails say Michael Jackson was out of shape, consumed with doubt," *Today* September 2, 2012.
898 "AEG files claim for losses from Michael Jackson's death the day he died," *Fox* * May 20, 2013.
899 "Michael Jackson's estate, Lloyd's of London settle insurance dispute," *Reuters* January 15, 2004.

Concert promoter AEG Live's chief executive says insurance will help cover any losses on the now-cancelled Michael Jackson concert series if the pop star died accidentally, *including of a drug overdoes*, but not if he died of natural causes.[900]

A most revealing detail was reported on June 26, 2009, by Katherine Blackler on the U.K. insurance page *Insurance Post*: according to sources within Lloyd's of London the much resisted second physical exam on Michael – which he was sure to fail – *was scheduled for June 26th,* the very day after Michael Jackson was killed by AEG Live's hired doctors![901] In other words, Michael Jackson was killed the day before his scheduled physical exam that most certainly would have blown AEG Live's chance of *any* insurance payout! Who is naïve enough to believe this is a mere coincidence? Just as thinking Elvis Presley being killed by a mysterious drug overdose the day before he was schedule to testify against the Mafia is a mere coincidence is naïve. Incidentally, two weeks after Michael was killed, on July 5, 2009 Paul Gongaware who was a part of Elvis Presley's tours when he was likely killed by a Mafia "syringe job" wrote in emails: "I was on the Elvis tour when he died so I kind of knew what to expect [with Michael Jackson]."[902] Indeed, he did know what to expect. In some ways the murder of Elvis Presley was the prototype of the murder of Michael Jackson.

Former X Factor judge Sharon Osbourne revealed on The Talk what she was told by AEG Live people:

There were people at the company who knew he was not well but didn't care. *Whether he performed or not, they'd still make money.* I

900 "AEG boss: Jackson insurance covers overdose," *Today* July 2, 2009,
901 Katherine Blackler, "Claims for cancelled UK Michael Jackson concerts could cost industry up to £300million," *Insurance Post* June 26, 2009 @ https://www.postonline.co.uk/reinsurance/1406311/claims-for-cancelled-uk-michael-jackson-concerts-could-cost-industry-up-to-ps300million.
902 Richards and Langthorne, *83 Minutes*, 120.

had conversations with people who said exactly that. I will tell people who said it (if subpoenaed).[903]

By August 2009 Randy Phillips would be bragging in an email: "Michael's death is a terrible tragedy, but life must go on. *AEG will make a fortune from merch sales, ticket retention, the touring exhibition and the film/dvd.*"[904] In addition, "The promoter (AEG)…said at the time that it was reimbursed by Jackson's estate for its concert-related losses."[905] Randy Phillips did not lie about the fortune that Michael Jackson's death meant for them. On June 21 2010, a year after Michael was killed, it was reported that

> since the singer's death a year ago, the King of Pop's assets have grossed more than $1 billion, *Billboard* reports, thanks largely to a new record contract *with Sony*, renewed interest in his catalog and *the concert rehearsal documentary This Is It*, already the most successful film of its kind in history.[906]

Michael's estate and legacy – and thus his fortune – was hijacked. Why did Randy Phillips bring Michael's enemy John Branca back into Michael's camp while Michael was drugged? To present a fraudulent will.

> On the day the will was brought and shown to Katherine Jackson, the signature page was not presented. It was missing. When the will was supposedly signed in Los Angeles by Michael Jackson, *the singer was provably thousands of miles away* – protesting in New York against his perceived mistreatment at the hands of Sony Music. Following his ex-

---

903 "'They knew he was not well and didn't care': Sharon Osbourne reveals she will testify in Michael Jackson wrongful death trial," *Daily Mail* April 6, 2013.
904 "Tour Executive's E-Mail After Michael Jackson Died: We're Going To Make A Fortune From Merchandise Sales," *Radaronline* June 11, 2013: "Michael Jackson's death was seen as an opportunity to make a fortune off the singer, according to an email from the CEO of the company promoting his tour."
905 "Michael Jackson's estate, Lloyd's of London settle insurance dispute," *Reuters* January 15, 2004.
906 Daniel Kreps, "Michael Jackson Estate Earned $1 Billion Since Death," *Rolling Stone* June 21, 2010.

client's death, John Branca is on record as stating, "I am Michael Jackson now".[907]

In 2012 Michael's siblings (Jermaine, Janet, Randy, Tito, Rebbie) sent a letter to Branca and John McClain demanding their resignation as executors of the Michael Jackson estate for, among other things, *using a fraudulent will with a forged signature* to secure their position over the estate. In the letter they state:

We know there is most certainly a conspiracy surrounding our brother's death and now coarse manipulation and fear are being used to cover it up...THIS HAS TO STOP NOW: NO MORE!! You will not succeed. John Branca, after our brother passed, you said to our mother: "I AM MICHAEL JACKSON NOW". How dare you. Make no mistake, Mr. Branca, before we hit the stage, we were a family and still to this day we are a family. We're not going to let anyone abuse our mother, nor will we tolerate any further attempts to divide us.[908]

907 Pete Mills, "Sony exec claims Michael Jackson's 'image and likeness' worth less than a second-hand car," *Orchard Times* February 18, 2017.
908 "Michael Jackson's Family Demands Executors of Estate Resign: Report," *ABC News Radio* July 18, 2012; "THIS HAS TO STOP NOW": Michael Jackson's family claim singer's will was forged," *FACT Magazine* July 19, 2012

Chapter Fifteen

The King Is Dead

I.   *Cause of Death?*

As Michael Jackson's life slipped away, his personal physician delayed calling 911, hid evidence of his medical treatment, misled paramedics and doctors, and then abruptly left the hospital before police could question him, prosecutors and the pop star's employees said in court Tuesday...[Dr. Conrad] Murray initially did not return police calls, but two days after Jackson's death he met with police...[Before calling 911] Murray ordered another security guard, Alberto Alvarez, to help collect pill bottles and medical paraphernalia in a bag.[909]

Detectives Orlando Martinez, Dan Meyers and Scott Smith in the 2019 documentary *Killing Michael Jackson* claim that

Murray spent 25 minutes clearing away medical supplies, making phone calls, and sending emails before assisting Jackson with CPR and calling the police. 'Mr Murray started cleaning up the mess that he had left, covering up the medical treatment that he was giving,' Martinez said. 'He put that away, called for help from security, and directed them to call 911 while he gave ineffective, one-handed CPR.' Detective Martinez argues Murray attempted to cover up Jackson's death by hiding receipts worth up to the value of five gallons of propofol at his girlfriend's apartment, saying that 'at that point we knew this was not an honest mistake, but that this was on purpose, bad medicine'.[910]

The Coroner's Office conducted an autopsy on Michael on June 26, 2009, but did not release its official conclusions until

---

909 Harriet Ryan and Victoria Kim, "Michael Jackson's doctor frantically tried to cover up singer's treatment," *Los Angeles Times* January 5, 2011.
910 Adam Starkey, "Michael Jackson's doctor waited 25 minutes to call police after finding singer's body, claims new documentary," *Metro* June 21, 2019.

September 18, 2009. There is good reason to believe that the results that were ultimately published in September are not completely consistent with what was discovered during the autopsy on June 26. "Acute propofol intoxication with a contributory benzodiazepine effect" is the established cause of death. This means that Michael died from an overdose of the drug propofol combined with other drugs of the benzodiazepine class. This is the September 18th conclusion. Propofol was the primary killer and Dr. Conrad Murray was the sole administrator. However, almost every bit of the early press focused on a different drug and a different doctor – Demerol and Arnold Klein.

"Jackson Family: Demerol Shot Caused Death," *TMZ* June 26, 2009:

> A close member of Michael Jackson's family has told us Jackson received a daily injection of a synthetic narcotic similar to morphine — Demerol — and yesterday he received a shot at 11:30 AM. Family members are saying the dosage was "too much" and that's what caused his death.

"Michael Jackson Death Caused By A Demerol Shot?," *The Examiner* June 26, 2009:

> New reports are in that say Michael Jackson may have died from a Demerol overdose. Many news agencies and websites are reporting that Michael Jackson died from receiving an overdose of Demerol. Toxicology results will take 4 to 6 weeks to confirm cause of death. *The Sun* reports an Emergency Room source at UCLA hospital said Jackson aides told medics he had collapsed after an injection of potent Demerol. A Michael Jackson source said: "Shortly after taking the Demerol he started to experience slow shallow breathing. His breathing gradually got slower and slower until it stopped…Shortly after the Demerol shot was given 911 was called.

Susan Donaldson James, "Friend Says Michael Jackson Battled Demerol Addiction," *ABC News* June 26, 2009:

> The Los Angeles police were told that Jackson received a Demerol injection one hour before his death, according to a senior law enforcement official. Paramedics at the Los Angeles hospital where Jackson died Thursday, according to the British tabloid the Sun, said the star's breathing got 'slower and slower until it stopped.'

Anita Singh, "Video: Michael Jackson's weird and wonderful life," *Telegraph* June 26, 2009.

> He last performed on Wednesday night, 12 hours before the emergency services were called to his Los Angeles home. Following that performance he reportedly took a painkilling injection of Demerol, a commercial name for the morphine-based drug pethidine. Pethidine is known to have dangerous side effects including cardiac arrest if used wrongly.

Fox News,[911] *ABC News*,[912] and *The Sun*,[913] all reported that by July 15 police have confirmed that Demerol was one of the many drugs found in Michael's home, thus giving credence to the "Death by Demerol" reports. Propofol was found as well and an early theory developed of the relation between the two drugs in the death of Michael Jackson.

> Both of pop superstar Michael Jackson's arms were scarred with track marks, investigators probing his death say, and the marks are consistent with the finding of the potent sedative propofol (trade name Diprivan) in his home -- a drug that is increasingly at the center of their probe into what caused Jackson's death, ABC News has learned...

> Medical experts point out that the abuse of Demerol could have set the stage for cardiac arrest, by increasing Jackson 's risk.

> One pharmacologist blogged about Propofol this week and explained in his science blog how Demerol abuse could have caused cardiac problems and could have increased his risk for heart rhythm disturbances from the Propofol: "As I wrote last week in my blog post on Demerol ® (meperidine), Jackson's reported long-term use of this analgesic for back pain may have already primed him for cardiac problems due to the accumulation of a toxic metabolite, normeperidine," Dr. David Kroll said. "However, most relevant to the Jackson case is that propofol can cause cardiac tachyarrhythmias (rhythmic disturbances at high heart rate), especially in people predisposed to cardiac problems." ...

---

911 Jana Winter, "At Least Nine Doctors Who Treated Michael Jackson Under investigation," *Fox News* July 15, 2009: "Law enforcement sources confirmed to FOXNews.com that Demerol, propofol (Diprivan) alprazolam (Xanax), Percocet and antibiotics were found in Jackson's rented Holmby Hills mansion after he died."

912 Russell Goldman, "The Accident that Sparked Jackson's Addiction," *ABC News* July 15, 2009: "Police investigating Jackson's June 25 death have confirmed that his home was filled with powerful prescription drugs including the painkillers Oxycontin and Demerol and the hospital-grade anesthetic Diprivan..."

913 As reported in Vic Walter and Richard Esposito, "Michael Jackson's Arm's Marred by Track Marks Consistent with Potent Sedative Use," *ABC News* July 1, 2009: "The Sun has reported there were at least 20 drugs found in Jackson's home, and many of these can be injected, including Methadone, Fentanyl, Demerol, Versed, and Lidocaine."

The Sun has reported there were at least 20 drugs found in Jackson's home, and many of these can be injected, including Methadone, Fentanyl, Demerol, Versed, and Lidocaine.[914]

It was reported that Michael's mother Katherine Jackson and other members of Michael Jackson's family gave the LAPD a list of doctors whom they believed misprescribed drugs to Michael: Dr. Conrad Murray and Dr. Arnold Klein topped the list.[915] Dr. Steven Hoefflin announced on July 22nd:

"Over the last few days I have been with the family when the police were present and obtaining their information from the family about Michael. The evidence, as it is mounting, is horrifying." Dr Hoefflin said Mrs Jackson believes two doctors are responsible for her son's death and up to eight more could have their medical licenses reviewed.

"In my understanding of this case, from being present when police talk to the family, there are two, who if found guilty of the acts suspected of them, could go to jail...It is my professional opinion that - although there are successful and much safer ways of treating these problems - some of his doctors chose to use large doses of Demerol for his pain and administer Propofol to induce sleep."[916]

Dr. Hoefflin was a Government Witness working with the State Attorney General's Office in the Investigation of Michael Jackson's death.[917] On July 23 he spoke to *Access Hollywood*:

Dr. Steven Hoefflin, a longtime friend and doctor of Michael Jackson, has claimed that the King of Pop "had lethal amounts of Demerol and Propofol in his body" at the time of his death...Hoefflin claimed to *Access* that according to a reliable source of his, Jackson's toxicology report indicated Michael "had lethal amounts of Demerol and Propofol in his body" when he died on June 25. Results from the LA Coroner's official autopsy of Jackson have yet to be publicly

914 Vic Walter and Richard Esposito, "Michael Jackson's Arm's Marred by Track Marks Consistent with Potent Sedative Use," *ABC News* July 1, 2009.
915 "Jackson Family Gave LAPD Doctor List," *TMZ* July 8, 2009.
916 "Michael Jackson 'left to die on drugs drip after a doctor fell asleep', his plastic surgeon claims," *Daily Mail* July 23, 2009.
917 See below.

released…Hoefflin claimed that the Demerol came from Dr. Arnold Klein – Michael's dermatologist – and the Propofol came from Dr. Conrad Murray, Jackson's personal physician in the weeks before his death.[918]

On June 30 *TMZ* reported: "We've learned that the LAPD wants to talk to Michael Jackson's longtime dermatologist Arnold Klein about drugs he may have prescribed or given Michael Jackson. We're told Klein has already gotten a lawyer but as far as we know the LAPD has not spoken with him."[919] On July 2 the Coroner's Office requested medical records from Klein's office and on July 10 the Coroner's office subpoenaed Klein's records.[920] On July 15, 2009 *The Sun* reported:

> Michael Jackson's skin doctor is under investigation over the singer's death, it was announced yesterday. Assistant Chief Coroner Ed Winter barged into Dr Arnold Klein's office to seize medical records - as the doc told of "rebuilding" the star's face. Cops will probe the dermatologist's prescription practices with regard to the vast amount of drugs [Michael Jackson] was taking. They will investigate whether medication was given to aliases. Dr Klein admitted "occasionally" giving him the sedative Demerol, but said: "That was the strongest medication I ever used."

Of course, it is demonstrable that Klein is not being forthright here, as we will show.

But Dr. Arnold Klein was an "eminence in Los Angeles" and well-connected as a member of Hollywood's Gay Mafia. So he was protected – at first. When the Coroner's Report was released on September 18, 2009, *there was no mention of Demerol as a contributing factor to Michael's death*, only propofol and the contributory benzodiazepines. This is no doubt because if *Klein* is connected to Michael Jackson's death through his Demerol injections, this might possibly have brought David Geffen and

---

918 "Former Jackson Doctor Claims Michael 'Had Lethal Amounts of Demerol & Propofol'," *Access Hollywood* July 23, 2009.
919 "Cops Interested in Another Michael Jackson Doc," *TMZ* June 30, 2009
920 "Jackson Doc Did Not Fully Cooperate," *TMZ* July 14, 2009.

other members of the Gay Mafia into view as well. So, Klein's Demerol legally disappears.

Dr. Conrad Murray was charged with involuntary manslaughter for the death of Michael Jackson in February 2010. As part of his defense Murray contended that while he was giving Michael propofol for his insomnia Klein was (allegedly unbeknownst to Murray) at the same time giving Michael Demerol; that Klein made Michael dependent on Demerol and *caused* Michael's insomnia with the Demerol; and that Klein should be a co-defendant with him as he is at least partly to blame for Michael's death as well.[921]

But Dr. Conrad Murray was never able to make that case in court. Why?

> The judge in the forthcoming trial of Michael Jackson's doctor Conrad Murray has barred the singer's dermatologist from giving evidence. Dr Murray's lawyers had wanted to argue that Arnold Klein injected Jackson with the painkiller demerol "for no valid medical purpose" and that the star became addicted to the drug. The judge said it was "not relevant".[922]

Indeed, Judge Michael Pastor "dealt a crushing blow" to Murray's defense by disallowing Klein to be called to testify. The justification that Klein's testimony "isn't relevant to the case, and that it could confuse the jury,"[923] is of course ridiculous.

> lead defense attorney Ed Chernoff invoked Klein's name seven times during his opening statement and has referred to the dermatologist

---

921 Matthew Perpetua, "Doctor: Michael Jackson Was Dependent on Demerol," *Rolling Stone* October 28, 2011; Alice Gomstyn and Chris Connelly, "Michael Jackson's Secret World: Willing Doctors, Hospital-Grade Sedatives," *ABC News* November 4, 2011; Alan Duke, "'Perfect storm' of drugs killed Michael Jackson, sleep expert says," *CNN* October 14, 2011; Caroline Graham, "NO, I didn't kill Michael. He did it himself…with a massive overdose using his own stash," *Daily Mail* November 24, 2013; "Dr. Murray Targets Arnie Klein in MJ Death," *TMZ* September 5, 2010.
922 "Michael Jackson judge bars skin doctor from testifying," *BBC News* August 30, 2011.
923 Jen Heger, "Dr. Conrad Murray Dealt Crushing Blow In Upcoming Michael Jackson Trial," *Radar Online* August 29, 2011.

repeatedly throughout the trial. The defense, which is expected to begin presenting its side next week, sought to call Klein as a witness but was blocked by Los Angeles Superior Court Judge Michael Pastor, who ruled Klein's testimony was not relevant to the case. [924]

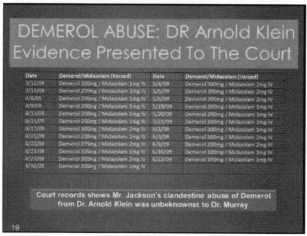

At this time Klein was still protected. His emotions, his hubris, and his mouth will cost him this protection, however, and likely his life.

---

924 "Jackson's Dermatologist Says Murray Fallout Hurts," *The Telegraph* October 15, 2011.

II.   Death By Polypharmacy

"It was a pharmaceutical experiment on Michael Jackson. It was an obscene experiment in 2009..." - Prosecutor David Walgren (2013)

The toxicology report that was finally released revealed that "there was a bewildering number of drugs coursing through his veins at the time of his death."[925] And while Demerol mysteriously "disappeared" from the conversation as totally as did the second shooter who was apprehended during the Malcom X assassination, propofol became known as *the killer* of Michael Jackson. But the toxicology report reveals *a much darker* picture of what was being done to Michael Jackson. It might even be said in fact that propofol, like Conrad Murray who wielded it, was but the *fall guy (drug)* for a much more complex conspiracy.

billboard

Doctor: Drug 'Cocktail' Killed Michael Jackson

Dr. Conrad Murray's use of a cocktail of drugs on Michael Jackson as he struggled to fall asleep on the day he died was a "recipe for disaster" and ultimately caused his death, a UCLA sleep therapy expert testified Thursday.

Like Elvis Presley, "Michael Jackson had a 'polypharmacy' of drugs in his system."[926] In addition to propofol the examiner also found traces of **lorazepam** (a benzodiazepine drug, also called Atvian); **midazolam** (another benzodiazepine, also called Versed); **lidocaine** (a local anesthetic often included with propofol to relieve injection pain); **diazepam** (a benzodiazepine to treat anxiety, insomnia and alcohol withdrawal, also called Valium); and **nordiazepam** (a benzodiazepine-derived

925 Colin Vickery, "Michael Jackson should have died earlier, autopsy report reveals," *News Corp Australia* June 25, 2014.
926 Superior Court of California, County of Los Angeles, *Joseph* Jackson v. Conrad Murray et al. Case No. BC450393, 30 November 2010, pg. 12; Jeff Gottlieb, "Michael Jackson had several drugs in his system when he died," *Los Angeles Times* May 7, 2013; "The drugs found in Michael Jackson's body after he died," *BBC Newsbeat* November 8, 2011.

sedative, often used to treat anxiety) in Michael's bloodstream. It was AEG Live's hiree Dr. Conrad Murray who administered this fatal polypharmacy to Michael Jackson.

> On June 22, 2009, three days before Michael died, Dr. Murray gave him a 25mg dosage of propofol, along with ativan (=lorazepam) and versed (=midazolam). The next night, on June 23, 2009, Murray gave him ativan and versed. And on that fateful mourning of mornings, Dr. Murray gave Michael a 10mg tab of valium [1] at the wee time of 1:30 in the morning. Then, a half hour later (2:00 am), he gave him a 2mg IV of Ativan [2]. Then, just an hour later (3:00 am), he gave him a 2mg IV of versed [3]. Another two hours later (5:00 am), he gave him yet another 2mg IV of ativan. Then, two and a half hours later (7:30 am), he gave him still another 2mg IV of versed. Now, you don't have to be a medical professional to know, as one medical expert said, that *this much dosage "is enough to put an elephant down"*!"[927]

And the frail, emaciated Michael Jackson was the furthest thing from a bull elephant. This combination of drugs administered to Michael Jackson was so strong it "could bring down several people"; it "'was the perfect storm' that killed him."[928] Dr. Nader Kamanger, a UCLA sleep therapy expert and prosecution witness, said it was the "cocktail of drugs" - diazepam (Valium), lorazepam (Ativan) and midazolam (Versed) and propofol – that was the "recipe for disaster" and "ultimately caused [Michael Jackson's] death."[929] Longtime friend Frank Cascio said Michael once confided in him that he feared he would die from a gunshot. But, Cascio said, "no one would have ever thought that a shot of a prescription drug would claim Jackson's life so prematurely." [930] But death by gunshot is only *one* method of a Mafia hit. Another is the so-called *syringe job* – death by a shot of prescription drugs. Just like Elvis Presley's death, Michael's has all of the earmarks

---

927 Dr. Firpo W. Carr, "The Drug-Induced Death of Michael Jackson," *Los Angeles Sentinel* August 27, 2009.
928 Duke, "'Perfect storm' of drugs."
929 Anthony McCartney, "Doctor: Drug 'cocktail' killed Michael Jackson," *Associated Press* October 13, 2011.
930 Alice Gomstyn and Chris Connelly, "Michael Jackson's Secret World: Willing Doctors, Hospital-Grade Sedatives," *ABC News* November 4, 2011.

of a syringe job. Family friend Terry Harvey gave an interview to the *News of the World* on July 19, 2009 and said "Michael was poisoned," a position Michael's brother Jermaine Jackson expressed as well:

Terry Harvey: "Michael was poisoned"

Monday, 20/07/2009 11:14 AM (GMT +7)

According to the News of the World, the autopsy report shows that Michael was murdered.

Police told Michael's family that their investigation will focus on one or several people who took care of Michael's treatment in his final days. In the near future a criminal trial will be open to hear who is responsible for Michael's death.

This means the doctor who was treating and caring for Michael will be included in the list for the investigation. Police are conducting an investigation in order to quickly find the guys who injected high doses of pain medication into Michael's body.

Last week, La Toya Jackson – Michael's sister said to the News of the World that she knows who killed her brother. And the amazing thing is yesterday, 19/7, Terry Harvey – a longtime friend of the Jackson family also gave an exclusive interview to the News of the World.

Terry said: "According to the survey results Michael died from an overdose of painkiller Diprivan and many other poisonous drugs. The investigators found very much of the drug in his stomach. The body of Michael had a lot of scars from injections ".

It should be pointed out that Conrad Murray's claim that he was injecting Michael with Propofol every night for two months in order to "treat insomnia" is medically dubious. "Propofol is an intravenously administered *hypnotic drug.*"[931] Beverly Phillip, professor of anesthesia at Harvard Medical School, says Propofol is "not a sleeping aid at all. What it is is a general anesthetic (i.e. it numbs pain)...So the use as a sleep aid is way off the mark...Everyone has been saying, 'Michael Jackson wanted to sleep.' No one talked about relaxing drugs. With this drug in unskilled hands, this sleep is permanent. It induces general anesthesia, which is not like a night's sleep."[932]

III.   *The CIA's Hypnosis Drug*

But there is one drug within this deadly cocktail that was administered to Michael Jackson which hints at a poisoning operation originating from a source much higher than Dr. Conrad Murray and even higher than AEG: the drug Midazolam (Versed). Recall that, according to his own accounting (which, giving how many times Murray has lied and changed his story,[933] must be assumed to *not* give the full story) on the night that Murray killed Michael Jackson, the polypharmacy Murray administered included 10mg of Valium, 4mg of Atvian and 4mg of Versed, along with 25mg of propofol. We learn also that Murray administered this "polypharmacy of drugs" to Michael over *several weeks*, not just on that fateful night.[934] The presence of Versed/Midazolam in this cocktail is quite alarming.

931 Superior Court of California, County of Los Angeles Katherine Jackson v. AEG Live LLC et al., Case No. BC445597 September 15, 2010, pg. 6.

932 Katherine Harmon, "What is Propofol—and How Could It Have Killed Michel Jackson?" *Scientific American* October 3, 2011.

933 Superior Court of California, County of Los Angeles, *Joseph* Jackson v. Conrad Murray et al. Case No. BC450393, 30 November 2010.

934 Superior Court of California, County of Los Angeles Katherine Jackson v. AEG Live LLC et al., Case No. BC445597 September 15, 2010, pg. 6, 8: "The 'cocktail' Murray provided was similar to the medicaitons he had given Jackson for the prior five (5) weeks".

Versed is the most commonly used drug in a group of drugs called benzodiazepines...This class of drugs is designed to provide for sedation, *hypnosis-like compliance*, relieve anxiety, muscle relaxation, and anticonvulsant activity. The "side effect" that medical professionals most like about these drugs is that they generally induce *anterograde amnesia* (prevent memory by blocking the acquisition and encoding of new information). In other words, medical professionals like these drugs because most people *will not remember what happens to them while under their effect even though they are "awake."*

In medical terms, this is called conscious sedation. While under the influence of these drugs, patients ... will therefore *be very compliant* with medical professionals (they will not advocate for themselves), and they will most likely not remember anything about what happened. It is these last two consequences that most appeal to the healthcare industry. If you're given Versed prior to being brought into the Operating Room, you will likely not remember who is in the room, being placed on the OR table or being prepared for anesthesia. Further, once surgery is over, you will likely be given a few more doses of Versed, again that means you will likely not remember being in the PACU... Keep this in mind: Versed or similar sedative drugs legally invalidates any patient testimony regarding their treatment...Also note that Versed is also known as a date-rape drug. Versed is perfect for predators because *it makes the recipient completely compliant* and generally induces memory loss of traumatic events.[935]

Versed/Midazolam has the ability to bend the mind of the patient and make him obedient and compliant. It is thus used as a "patient control drug." Patients have testified that Versed/Midazolam turned them into "compliant zombies" with no will of their own.[936] Dr. Conrad Murray, as a hired hand of AEG Live, injected Michael Jackson with this drug on a regular basis. Recall that Terry Harvey described Michael in his final days under the influence of the drugs as "walking around in a daze like a zombie," and simply telling people "yes" to their demands – being compliant.[937] By June

---

935 "Sedation, *Versed*, and Your Procedure," *Medical Patient Modesty* @ http://patientmodesty.org/versed.aspx.
936 http://versedbusters.blogspot.com/2005/12/introduction.html
937 "'Drugged, exhausted' MJ 'could barley walk' during This Is It rehearsals," *Thaindian News* October 31, 2009.

during rehearsals Michael appeared "very stoic."[938] Recall also that, according to Karen Faye, Michael stoically kept repeating, "why can't I choose,"[939] but he offered no resistance.

Versed/Midazolam as a "patient control drug" due to its ability to bend the mind into compliance or as a "date-rape" drug due to its amnesia effect are only two of the drug's scary characteristics.[940] The drug is also used "as part of a cocktail of chemicals for executions,"[941] in certain jurisdictions in the U.S. Usually, it is part of a three-drug protocol during execution by lethal injection, also including an opioid. Experts say "the drug in effect paralyzes the brain."[942] Versed/Midazolam acts as a sedative to render the condemned prisoner unconscious, at which time the vecuronium bromide and potassium chloride are administered, stopping the prisoner's breathing and heart, respectively.[943]

Dr. Conrad Murray delivered a three-drug cocktail to Michael Jackson the night of June 24th: Valium, Atvian and Versed/Midazolam. At some point the opioid Demerol was added to this cocktail. There occurred a "reaction" that succeeded in killing Michael. We will consider that below.

---

938 Colin Bertram, "The Final Days of Michael Jackson," *Biography* June 24, 2019 @ HTTPS://WWW.BIOGRAPHY.COM/NEWS/MICHAEL-JACKSON-FINAL-DAYS.
939 Alan Duke, "Witness: Michael Jackson was paranoid, talking to himself in last days," *CNN* May 9, 2013
940 "New date rape drug hits Sydney nightclubs," *The Sydney Morning Herald* February 2, 2003.
941 Tom Porter, "What Is Midazolam and Why Do Protesters Claim Its Use in Executions Is Cruel," *Newsweek* July 26, 2017.
942 Porter, "What Is Midazolam."
943 Ben Bryant, "Life and Death row: How the lethal injection kills," *BBC* March 5, 2018.

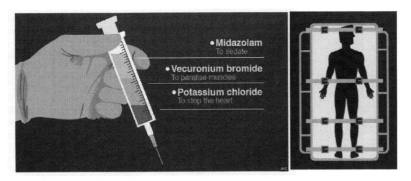

The drug midazolam – a sedative used by several states to cause unconsciousness – has proved so controversial that, in 2017, Alabama inmate Thomas D Arthur asked to be executed by firing squad. Arthur lodged an appeal with the Supreme Court to postpone his execution on the basis that midazolam, one of the drugs in Alabama's three-drug lethal injection combination, could contribute to 'prolonged torture'. The Supreme Court denied the appeal, and Arthur was executed (by lethal injection) in May 2017.[944]

During Conrad Murray's manslaughter trial in 2011 the prosecutor David Walgren in his closing argument described Murray's polypharmacy administration to Michael Jackson as an "obscene" "pharmaceutical experiment on Michael Jackson."[945] There are strong grounds for believing that this choice of language is appropriate…and revealing.

After the 9/11 attacks in 2001 in New York, so-called terrorism suspects that were detained in U.S.-controlled facilities were subject to a U.S. "torture program." Part of that program was spearheaded by the C.I.A.'s Office of Medical Services (OMS). OMS conducted a drug-research program called "Project Medication," in which the detainees were chemically experimented on. Project Medication lasted "officially" from 2001 to 2003 (though we have reason to believe it had a longer

944 Bryant, "Life and Death row."
945 Alice Gomstyn and Chris Connelly, "Michael Jackson's Secret World: Willing Doctors, Hospital-Grade Sedatives," *ABC News* November 4, 2011.

"unofficial" existence). Project Medication was heir to the CIA's MK-Ultra program of the 1960s and the Soviet experimental program of the 1950s, both of which were studied by the Project Medication researchers. OMS chose a specific drug to experiment with on prisoners during Project Medication: Versed/Midazolam.[946]

One of the purposes of Project Medication was to test the CIA's theory of "learned helplessness."[947] *Learned helplessness* is a condition in which a person suffers from a sense of *powerlessness* arising from a traumatic event or *persistent failure* to succeed. It is thought to be one of the underlying causes of depression, resulting from a real or perceived *absence of control* over the outcome of a situation. The C.IA. spent $81 million investigating learned helplessness as "a technique of stripping someone of their will" by exposing people to aversive events which they cannot control.[948] The scientific aim is to *induce the apathetic attitude that one's actions do not have the power to affect one's situation.* "But it's also more than that. Learned helplessness occurs when a subject is so broken he will not even attempt escape if the opportunity presents itself," *The Washington Post* reports.[949] The C.I.A.'s experimentally induced "learned helplessness" on terrorist detainees such as Abu Zubaydah successfully produced "compliance":

> When the interrogator "raised his eyebrow," without instructions, Abu Zabaydah "slowly walked on his own to the water table and sat down,"

---

946 Eli Rosenberg, "The CIA explored using a 'truth-serum' on terrorism detainees after 9/11, newly released report shows," *The Washington Post* November 13, 2018; Dror Ladin, "Secret CIA Document Shows Plan to Test Drugs on Prisoners," *ACLU* November 13, 2018 @ https://www.aclu.org/blog/national-security/torture/secret-cia-document-shows-plan-test-drugs-prisoners.
947 "CIA considered potential truth serum to force suspects to talk," *CBS News* November 13, 2018.
948 Terrence McCoy, "'Learned helplessness': The chilling psychological concept behind the CIA's interrogation methods," *The Washington Post* December 11, 2014.
949 McCoy, "'Learned helplessness'."

one account said. "… When the interrogator snapped his fingers twice, Abu Zabaydah would lie flat on the waterboard"… He had been trained. Like one of [the laboratory] dogs."[950]

Through their "learned helplessness" techniques the C.I.A. successfully trained Abu Zubaydah "Like one of [the laboratory] dogs."

One of the apparent aims of Project Medication was to experiment with Versed/Midazolam, "the preferred drug," in the production of the C.I.A.'s "learned helplessness." Project Medication's "preferred drug" was also one of the drugs that Dr. Conrad Murray, as a part of his work for AEG Live, regularly injected into Michael Jackson. The result: Michael Jackson's learned helplessness.

AEG's control of Jackson's person was further extended by the drugs being administered by Murray, which weakened Jackson's physical and mental health, rendering him vulnerable, confused, *and subject to direction.*[951]

In May and June, Michael Jackson was confused, easily frightened, *unable to remember*, obsessive, and disoriented. He had *impaired memory*, loss of appetite, and absence of energy.[952]

"The way he was talking, it's like *he's not in control over his own life any*more," she told me earlier this month. "It *sounds like somebody else is pulling his strings and telling him what to do.* Someone wants him dead. They keep feeding him pills like candy…The people around him will kill him."[953]

[Michael] had a sharp mind, but he was deluded, hampered by the drugs. He didn't know what he was saying to people. To make his life easy *he would just say 'yes'.* He was walking around in a daze *like a zombie.*"

---

950 McCoy, " 'Learned helplessness'."
951 Superior Court of California, County of Los Angeles Katherine Jackson v. AEG Live LLC et al., Case No. BC445597 September 15, 2010, 10-11.
952 Superior Court of California, County of Los Angeles, *Joseph* Jackson v. Conrad Murray et al. Case No. BC450393, 30 November 2010, pg. 12.
953 Ian Halperin, " 'I'm better off dead. I'm done': Michael Jackson's fateful prediction just a week before his death," *Daily Mail* June 29 2009.

Another friend said: "He shouted out, 'They are punishing me and I can't take it anymore. They are gonna kill me.'"[954]

Emotionally frail and physically thin, Jackson was described by *This Is It* makeup and hair artist Karen Faye as paranoid, shivering from chills and repeating himself during his last days...He was "very upbeat, but he was on the thin side," Faye said of an earlier, April 2009 meeting with Jackson. Come June, everything had changed. "He was not the man I knew," Faye testified. "He was acting like a person I didn't recognize"...Jackson appeared "*very stoic*" but "frightened"..."He kept repeating, '*why can't I choose*,' it was one of the things he repeated over and over again," Faye said...[955]

By June 2009 Michael Jackson was *clearly* put in a state of *learned helplessness* which was chemically induced, and one of the main chemicals used is the very "preferred drug" of the C.I.A.'s Project Medication: Versed/Midazolam. Michael was chemically controlled by being chemically maintained in a state of continuous confusion and compliance. And then, he was killed – the day before he was scheduled for a physical examine that would have killed AEG Live's insurance application hopes, costing them a potential 300 million euros.

Murray had been administering this drug cocktail to Michael Jackson for several weeks before the night of June 24, 2009. This is no doubt how Michael was chemically controlled and manipulated during the months of May and June. But something specific happened on the morning of June 25, 2009, that caused Michael's *death*. Murray injected Michael with something that morning. After Michael was found dead, according to the testimony of Michael Jackson's personal assistant Michael Amir Williams, Murray called him and said Michael Jackson "had a bad reaction."[956] If Murray only injected Michael Jackson with 25mg

954 "'Drugged, exhausted' MJ 'could barley walk' during This Is It rehearsals," *Thaindian News* October 31, 2009.
955 Colin Bertram, "The Final Days of Michael Jackson," *Biography* June 24, 2019 @ HTTPS://WWW.BIOGRAPHY.COM/NEWS/MICHAEL-JACKSON-FINAL-DAYS.
956 Harriet Ryan and Victoria Kim, "Michael Jackson's doctor frantically tried to cover up singer's treatment," *Los Angeles Times* January 5, 2011;

of propofol, it is hard to see how such a fatal "bad reaction" could have all of a sudden occurred. It should be pointed out that the combination of propofol and Versed/Midazolam helped with sedation and even has a synergistic effect: "Clinical and animal studies indicate that the combinations of propofol and midazolam...have a synergistic interaction with respect to their ability to *produce hypnosis.*"[957] The combination of Midazolam and propofol thus increases the *hypnotic effect*!

On the other hand, the combination of Versed/Midazolam and Demerol *can be deadly*.

> Using meperidine (Demerol) together with midazolam may increase side effects such as drowsiness, dizziness, lightheadedness, *confusion, depression*, low blood pressure, *slow or shallow breathing*, and *impairment in thinking, judgment*, and motor coordination. Occasionally, *severe reactions may result in coma and even death.*[958]

This perfectly describes Michael Jackson's state and condition in his final days as well as the moments of his death as we are told.

> *The Sun* reports an Emergency Room source at UCLA hospital said Jackson aides told medics he had collapsed after an injection of potent Demerol. A Michael Jackson source said: "Shortly after taking the Demerol he started to *experience slow shallow breathing. His*

---

957 David C. Oxorn et. Al, "The Effects of Midazolam on Propofol-Induced Anesthesia: Propofol Dose Requirements, Mood Profiles, and Perioperative Dreams," *Anesth Analg* 85 (1997): 553-559 (554); S. McClune et al., "Synergistic interaction between midazolam and propofol," *Br J Anaesth* 69 (1992): 240-5; T.G. Short and P.T. Chui, "Propofol and midazolam act synergistically in combination," *Br J Anaesth* 67 (1991): 530-545; T.G. Short, J.L. Plummer and P.T. Chui, "Hypnotic and anaesthetic interactions between midazolam, propofol and alfentanil," *Br J Anaesth* 69 (1992):162-7; E. Taylor, A.F. Ghouri and P.F. White, "Midazolam in combination with propofol for sedation during local anesthesia," *J Clin Anesth* 4 (1992): 213-6.
958 "Drug Interactions between Demerol and Versed," *Drugs.com* @ https://www.drugs.com/drug-interactions/demerol-with-versed-1557-939-1628-3562.html.

*breathing gradually got slower and slower until it stopped...*Shortly after the Demerol shot was given 911 was called.[959]

It is very conceivable that the "bad reaction" that Conrad Murray informed Michael Amir Williams about was caused by an injection of Demerol at 11:30 A.M., as has been claimed, which then interacted with the Versed/Midazolam which Murray had already injected Michael with at 3:00 A.M and again at 7:30 A.M.

---

959 "Michael Jackson Death Caused By A Demerol Shot?," *The Examiner* June 26, 2009.

Chapter Sixteen

Whodunit

We know that Dr. Conrad Murray was convicted of involuntary manslaughter on November 7, 2011. Mother Katherine Jackson demanded that the charge of manslaughter be upgraded to second degree murder.[960] "Second degree murder requires malice aforethought, which can be implied by the conduct of the defendant" in interrupting CPR on Michael Jackson in order to conceal drug evidence, said attorney Adam Streisand. This is most appropriate. Conrad Murray's actions throughout the months of May and June 2009 and culminating with his deeds on June 25th surely meet the requirements of the State of California's Depraved Heart Murder crime. Joe Jackson, LaToya Jackson and Jermaine Jackson have gone on record with their belief that Dr. Murray's role in the death of Michael Jackson was a part of a larger conspiracy in which Murray was but the fall guy, the patsy.[961] Much evidence strongly supports – even vindicates – their belief. Who else was involved in the conspiracy to *murder* Michael Jackson?

---

960 Nancy Dillon, "Katherine Jackson demands upgraded charge of second-degree murder against son's doctor Conrad Murray," *Daily News* March 23, 2010.
961 Daniel Kreps, "Joe Jackson Hints at Michael Jackson Murder Conspiracy, Calls Murray 'Fall Guy,'" *Rolling Stone* February 9, 2010; Sean Michaels, "Michael Jackson was murdered, says his sister La Toya," *The Guardian* June 23, 2011; Katie Hodge, "Michael Jackson murdered for hit catalogue, claims LaToya," *Independent* June 24, 2010; Chris McGreal, "After the tributes, the twist: was Michael Jackson's death murder?" *The Guardian* July 15, 2009; Jermaine Jackson with Larry King, *CNN* June 25, 2010.

HOLLYWOOD STAR WHACKERS

Randy Quaid is an Oscar-nominated and Golden Glove winning Hollywood veteran and his wife Evi Quaid is a former model and one-time Hollywood "It Girl." Today, however, they are both fugitives from the law in Canada, having once sought asylum in Vancouver, to which they fled in October 2010.

> [Quaid's] fleeing prosecution in California and seeking refugee status north of the border because he and Evi, 47, believe they are being hunted by Hollywood "star whackers," the same mysterious "they" who *offed Michael Jackson* and Heath Ledger and David Carradine.[962]

TODAY   f 🐦 ✉ •••

NEWS

Randy Quaid, wife flee 'Hollywood 'star whackers' '

Oct. 27, 2010, 3:48 PM CDT / Source: msnbc.com news services

Actor Randy Quaid and his wife told Canada's immigration board Friday they are seeking refuge in Canada because they are afraid of a shadowy group responsible for killing their Hollywood friends.

Quaid, 60, and his wife, Evi, were released on cash bonds of $10,000 each after they appeared before an Immigration and Refugee Board hearing in Vancouver, British Columbia.

They were arrested Thursday afternoon in a shopping area of an affluent Vancouver neighborhood on U.S. warrants related to vandalism charges.

The pair told an adjudicator that the actor has had eight close friends murdered in recent years and fear they could be next.

"We feel our lives are in danger," Evi Quaid told the board hearing.

Get the latest from TODAY

Sign up for our newsletter

SUBSCRIBE

---

962 Nancy Hass, "The Deeply Strange Saga of the Quazy Quaids," *GQ* December 1, 2010.

According to the Quaids, Hollywood is home to a "celebrity-killing cult,"[963] a shadowy cabal of what they called "Star Whackers" who "whack[ed] celebrities for their money."[964] The Quaids believed that the group had killed several of their personal friends including Heath Ledger and David Carradine and were now targeting Randy. Before Canada's Immigration and Refugee Board in Vancouver, British Columbia they said they were seeking refuge in Canada "because they are afraid of a shadowy group responsible for killing their Hollywood friends."[965] Evi Quaid told the board hearing, "We feel our lives are in danger." In a Vancouver interview Randy Quaid said:

We believe there to be a malignant tumour of star whackers in Hollywood. It's possible for people to gain control of every facet of your life. We're not faking it. I am being embezzled by a monstrous ring of accountants, estate planners and lawyers who are mercilessly slandering me and trying to kill my career and, I believe, murder me in order to gain control of my royalties.

His wife added: "We are refugees. Hollywood refugees. I genuinely feel these people are trying to kill us. They are businessmen. It's the mafia, it's organised crime."[966] "Hollywood is murdering its movie stars."[967] The Quaids believe they are running from a Mob hit; that a former business manager took out a million-dollar life-insurance policy on Randy and hired the Mafia to kill both Quaids, making it look like a murder-suicide.[968] According to them, this group has done that before:

963 "What Happened to Randy Quaid?" *The Week* November 3, 2010.
964 Philip Sherwell, "Why actor Randy Quaid and wife Evi Fled the Hollywood 'star whackers' to Canada," *Telegraph* November 6, 2010.
965 "Randy Quaid, Wife flee 'Hollywood 'star whackers'"," *Today* October 22, 2010.
966 Philip Sherwell, "Why actor Randy Quaid and wife Evi Fled the Hollywood 'star whackers' to Canada," *Telegraph* November 6, 2010.
967 Mike Von Fremd and Sarah Netter, "Randy Quaid, Wife Seek Asylum in Canada, Saying They Fear for Their Lives," *ABC News* October 20, 2010.
968 Diane Dimond, "Hollywood's Nightmare Couple," *The Daily Beast* September 28, 2009.

"They"—the aforementioned Hollywood Star Whackers—"decide, O.K., if we knock off David [Carradine], then what we can do is simply collect the insurance covering his participation in the television show he was working on overseas," Evi said. "It's almost moronic, it's so simple." She said she also suspected Jeremy Piven's falling ill from mercury poisoning was another sign of a dastardly plot by the Broadway producers of *Speed-the-Plow* to collect insurance money. "It was an orchestrated hit," she said. "They could have put mescaline in his water bottle." Jeffrey Richards, one of the producers of the play, declined to comment.[969]

The Quaids are convinced that their friends Heath Ledger and David Carradine were victims,[970] but also that "the web of intrigue…somehow involved the death of Michael Jackson and the 'framing' of Mel Gibson."[971] Michael Jackson was "set up" and murdered by the Star Whackers, they allege. "'It's a conspiracy with the police in Santa Barbara,' Evi insisted… '[Santa Barbara Detective Ron] Forney was heavily involved in the Michael Jackson setup,' Evi alleged."[972] It was in fact shortly after the death of Michael Jackson in June 2009 that the Quiads trouble with the law first occured. The Quaids have a very interesting connection to Michael Jackson. According to Becky Altringer, a private investigator hired by the Quaids, Evi, who reportedly heavily used Demerol, shared doctors with Michael Jackson – *Dr. Conrad Murray! She got her Demerol from Dr. Murray.* "[Evi Quaid] told me she and Michael Jackson had the same doctors."[973] This "bizarre connection between the couple and Michael Jackson"[974] means that there is only "one degree of separation between…Evi

969 Nancy Jo Sales, "The Quaid Conspiracy," *Vanity Fair* December 1, 2010.
970 Moriah Gill, "Randy Quaid Claims Hollywood Star Whackers Killed Heath Ledger," *Rare* September 11, 2019.
971 Nancy Jo Sales, "The Quaid Conspiracy," *Vanity Fair* December 1, 2010.
972 Sales, "The Quaid Conspiracy."
973 "P.I. Says Evi Quid & Michael Jackson Had Drug Connection: Conrad Murray," *Radar Online* September 27, 2009.
974 "P.I. Says Evi Quid & Michael Jackson."

Quaid and Michael Jackson: Dr. Conrad Murray and His Magical Prescription Pad."[975]

Another interesting connection with Michael Jackson may be through the Gay Mafia. It seems that at least some of the Quaids' troubles in Hollywood may have begun with a neighborly dispute – with the Gay Mafia. Sandy Gallin was their Beverly Hills neighbor in the mid-2000s. The Quaids believe Gallin was part of a plot to financially scam Randy, and some time in 2006 when Gallin threw one of his famous star-studded parties, the Quaids deliberately tried to sabotage it with music from *Home on the Range* blasted from speakers lodged in trees.[976] They laughed about what they did that night, but a year later Randy Quaid was permanently expelled from the Actor's Equity Association, Hollywood's union.

Susan Donaldson James for *ABC News* makes the ominous observation that, like Michael Jackson "Both rock icon Elvis Presley and movie star Heath Ledger died of combination overdoses."[977] Elvis Presley's was no doubt a Mob Hit via "Death by Polypharmacy" (a syringe job). A New York medical examiner ruled that a cocktail of six different painkillers, sleeping pills and anti-anxiety drugs killed Heath Ledger as well in 2008, just as a similar cocktail killed Michael Jackson in 2009. According to the information the Quaids are attempting to spread, both Ledger and Michael Jackson were killed by the Hollywood Mafia of "Star Whackers." There is strong, additional support to the claim of the Quaids.

FRANK DiLEO AND THE MAFIA HIT

All of the suspicious activities that had transpired months and weeks prior to his death played out in my mind over and over again. People

---

975 "Evi Quaid used Michael Jackson's doctor, Conrad Murray, to get Demerol and other drugs," *Starcasm* September 27, 2009.
976 Sales, "The Quaid Conspiracy."
977 Susan Donaldson James, "Friend Says Michael Jackson Battled Demerol Addiction," *ABC News* June 26, 2009.

that Michael vowed to never do business with again such as John Branca and Frank DiLeo had suddenly been brought back into his life by Randy Phillips of AEG. Michael and I could never figure out why...Michael Jackson, The King of Pop, in my opinion was murdered, and his words still haunt me to this day: "They want my catalogue (music publishing rights) Rowe and they will kill me for it." – Leonard Rowe, Michael Jackson manager

Leonard Rowe, who was close to Joe Jackson, was retained by Michael Jackson in March 2009 to oversee Michael's financial and business affairs and to keep an eye on AEG, who had just backdoored Michael with a 50-show tour.[978] Rowe says that Randy Phillips refused to work with him and instead brought back Frank DiLeo, whom Michael fired years earlier, and

Leonard Rowe

then Phillips practically blackmailed Michael Jackson into accepting DiLeo over Rowe by threatening to "pull the plug" on the London shows and demand all of the advances back if Michael didn't give in.

Frank DiLeo

Randy Phillips knew he had to do something about me, when Michael asked me to come and work with him and to watch over his financials and other business affairs. This also included the shows that were scheduled for London. Michael told me that Randy Phillips had said to him that he refused to work with Leonard Rowe, and that he was calling in Frank DiLeo to manage him. If he didn't accept this, then he was going to pull the plug on everything. He knew he had Michael trapped. From that point on, Michael and I began speaking a lot less

---

978 Leonard Rowe, What Really Happened to Michael Jackson The King of Pop: The Evil Side of the Entertainment Industry (n.p.: Linell-Diamond Enterprises, LLC, 2010) 125.

often. I received a phone call from Michael a day or so later and he said to me, "I want you to meet and work with Frank DiLeo...Randy Phillips and Frank DiLeo claim that Michael had hired Frank DiLeo to be his manager and he was to replace me. I never heard any of this from Michael. When it came to Michael Jackson it appeared that Randy Phillips had a tendency to make things like he wanted them to be without having a signed agreement or a contract in place. I have asked numerous times where is Frank DiLeo's management contract signed by Michael. They surely would have one if that was Michael's wish, but it wasn't. In my opinion, this was an act forced on Michael by Randy Phillips. Michael told me himself that he would never hire Frank DiLeo again. He could have hired Frank DiLeo before he signed an agreement with me but he didn't. In my opinion, and the words of Michael, this was a move being forced on him by Randy Phillips in an effort to get rid of me.[979]

So, right before the murder of Michael Jackson, Randy Phillips brought back both John Branca and Frank DiLeo, both of whom were fired years ago by Michael Jackson and whom Michael declared to be enemies who were never to be hired again. No, it is not a coincidence.

Frank DiLeo shared his bosses' Randy Phillips' and Paul Gongaware's disdain toward Michael and total indifference to his heath degeneration. Karen Faye testified in 2013 that during Michael's final days she tried to warn DiLeo about the singer's health *on that fateful night of June 19th*, but his response was cold.

"Frank was saying pretty much, 'I got it under control, don't worry about it,'" Faye testified Friday.

"I said, 'But he's losing weight rapidly.' ... I said, 'Why don't you ask [costume designer] Michael Bush to verify taking in his pants and how much weight he's actually losing?'"

Faye said DiLeo went to speak to Bush and she overheard the manager say, "Get him a bucket of chicken." "It was such a cold response," she said. "I mean, it broke my heart."[980]

---

979 Rowe, *What Really Happened to Michael Jackson*, 144-147
980 Corina Knoll, "Jackson witness: Answer to health was 'Get him a bucket of chicken'," *Los Angeles Times* May 10, 2013.

Terry Harvey says that he also tried to get through to Frank DiLeo: "I told Frank, '[Michael] needs to get clean first', but [DiLeo] didn't want to know." Terry says he specifically told DiLeo: "You are going to kill Michael." [981]

Yet, *DiLeo gave Dr. Murray instructions regarding Michael's "medical care"!* This was made evident by a voice mail message DiLeo left Dr. Murray on June 20th, instructing Dr. Murray to get a blood test on Michael.

> I'm sure you're aware he had an episode last night. He's sick. Today's Saturday. Tomorrow, I'm on my way back. I'm not going to continue my trip. I think you need to get a blood test on him. I – I – we gotta see what he's doing. All right. Thank you.

Katherine Jackson's lawyer during the 2013 AEG Live lawsuit, Brian Panish, believed that DiLeo spoke with an AEG executive just prior to making the phone call.[982] This call was made the day after DiLeo mocked Michael's physical condition with "Give him a bucket of chicken"; the call was made the day after that fateful June 19th when Randy Phillips and AEG Live decided to "pull the plug" on Michael Jackson. This call was made five days before Michael Jackson was murdered via a chemical cocktail.

On August 24, 2011, Frank DiLeo died, two years after Michael Jackson's murder. DiLeo's cause of death was reported as complications following heart surgery – a surgery he had six months prior. At the time of his death, DiLeo was reportedly *feuding with the executors of the hijacked Michael Jackson estate* – John Branca and John McClain, whom DiLeo *helped with the hijacking.* But a falling out had apparently occurred, such that reportedly DiLeo's last days were "darkened" by his disenchantment with and feuds with Branca and McClain. One reason given for the feud is that DiLeo felt his power and his

---

981 James Desborough and Christopher Bucktin, "Michael Jackson could not sing and dance live at the same time, claim emails to be presented in court," *Mirror* May 13 2013.

982 Alan Duke, "Michael Jackson manger's e-mails found, could be key in AEG trial," *CNN* May 19, 2013; "Frank's Phonecall," *The Michael Jackson World Network* May 5th, 2013.

money were being cut, and he protested it.[983] And then he was dead.

There is another reason to be suspicious of DiLeo's reported cause of death. Before he died DiLeo let it slip out that he prepared a manuscript, a "tell-all" book. DiLeo reportedly declared before he died: "The truth has to be told. *I'm going to set the record straight once and for all.*"[984] "Frank knew where all the bodies were buried," said an insider.[985] What sort of bodies might be revealed by this "tell-all"? Mark Lamica, DiLeo's long time

Mafia planned to murder Michael Jackson, Goodfellas star Frank DiLeo reportedly claimed

DiLeo played the cigar-chugging Tuddy Cicero in Scorsese's mob movie

Jenn Selby | @JennSelby | Monday 9 February 2015 16:27 |

DiLeo and Jackson on the set of "Bad" in 1987

business partner, manager and producer, who is in possession of the manuscript, says that DiLeo told him to publish it "if anything happened to him."[986] Something did happen to him and Lamica is trying to put that book out: *DiLeo: I Am Going To Set the Record Straight*. Lamica says

> This book...promises to name and shame all of *those who ripped off and used Michael,* including some big names in the music business. It will include details of his dealings with his record label, his Neverland Ranch deal with Colony Capital, *plus a shocking mob hit on Michael* that was stopped by DiLeo. It will also *lift the lid on* the deal for his "This Is It"

---

983 Gatecrasher, "Frank Dileo, Michael Jackson's former manager, fed up with pop star's estate before death: source," *New York Daily News* August 25, 2011.
984 "Jackson trial breakthrough," *Page Six* July 8, 2013.
985 "Jackson trial breakthrough."
986 Emily Smith, "MJ had plastic surgery to not look like 'abusive' dad," *New York Post* February 7, 2015.

tour and *the final difficult months of Michael's life* (emphasis added – WM).[987]

This of course implies that there is something hidden under the lid over the AEG deal. According to Lamica, DiLeo shared with him that there was a *"planned Mafia contract to kill Michael Jackson"*.[988] Allegedly, DiLeo "managed to stop it from happening." "The Mafia planned to carry out a contract killing on Michael."[989] The claim is that "DiLeo used his influence to call off the hit."

Whoa. This is an extremely important confession: *there was a Mafia contract out on Michael Jackson!* This of course agrees with Randy and Evi Quaid's claim that Michael Jackson was in fact killed by the Mafia "Star Whackers" of Hollywood. The only difference is that, according to Lamica, DiLeo allegedly got the Mafia hit "called off" while the Quaids say the Mafia Star Whackers actually succeeded in "whacking" Michael Jackson for his money (=catalog). Lamica probably has good reason to add that embellishing (and likely fabricated) detail to the story, that DiLeo called off the Mob contract kill on Michael Jackson: Lamica is probably aware that DiLeo himself was likely killed after threatening to tell "where all the bodies are buried." DiLeo will be the first potential whistleblower who is killed, but he is not the last. Lamica no doubt read the handwriting on the wall and provided some "cover" for himself.

---

987 Smith, "MJ had plastic surgery."
988 Jenn Selby, "Mafia planned to murder Michael Jackson, Goodfellas star Frank DiLeo reportedly claimed," *Independent* February 9, 2015.
989 Paul Thomson, "Mafia planned to kill Michael Jackson in mob hit reveals Goodfellas star," *Mirror* February 8, 2015.

II. *A Government Witness Sounds The Alarm On The Conspiracy*

Dr. Steven Hoefflin at one time was known as "the favorite plastic surgeon of Hollywood celebrities."[990] This past President of the Los Angeles Society of Plastic Surgeons was Michael Jackson's surgeon for 25 years since 1979 when he performed Michael's first rhinoplasty after the singer broke his nose while rehearsing a dance routine. It was Hoefflin who performed the skin graft to Michael's scalp after the 1984 burning during the shooting of the Pepsi commercial.

But Hoefflin has another side as well. This UCLA-educated doctor with a genius IQ worked as a witness for the FBI,  DEA, CIA, and the Secret Service. Beginning at least in June of 2008 Hoefflin began exposing corruption within the LAPD. On June 13, 2008 he sent an email to the LAPD leadership warning about *organized crime's infiltration* of the LAPD, LAX Police, and the Sheriff's Department.[991] According to Hoefflin, while working on "undercover cases" he discovered the problem of "dirty cops" in Los Angeles. He went to California Governor Arnold Schwarzenegger and Daniel McMullen, the Special Agent in Charge of the L.A. office of the FBI. Hoefflin had in the past "work[ed] with the FBI on several investigations…" However, the California "establishment" had now iced Hoefflin: he clearly crossed a line attempting to expose the corruption of Los Angeles law enforcement and its relationship with the Mafia. Less than a week after Hoefflin communicated

990 Michael Sheldon, "The man who made Michael Jackson," *The Telegraph* April 2, 2001.
991 Diane Dimond, "Its Getting Even Weirder," *Daily Beast* August 5, 2009.

what he knew to the LAPD leadership in an email, the department's special Threat Assessment Unit was in Hoefflin's neighborhood, officers allegedly confronting Hoefflin up in a tree yelling at them about a conspiracy to assassinate him.

But Hoefflin ultimately proved to be too well-connected to be taken down. As an "established Government Witness" Dr. Hoefflin assisted the State Attorney General's Office of Jerry Brown as a "primary witness" in their Michael Jackson Death Investigation. Hoefflin interviewed 100 persons and examined medical records. He threatened to make public "all of the credible evidence in my possession on *the*

corruption in Los Angeles Law Enforcement pertaining to the Michael Jackson Investigation," and to expose members of law enforcement, claiming to possess "abundant incriminating evidence that is going to put a lot of people in prison."[992] Claiming to have evidence that various agencies and interests in Los Angeles were colluding to obstruct the Michael Jackson Death Investigation, Hoefflin demanded a cessation of the threats to him and his family. Hoefflin was so sure of his findings that he reached out to his "friend" former Secretary of State Colin Powell asking him to engage a congressional investigation into the LAPD and the Los Angeles Sheriff's Department and the corruption that is taking place in the Michael Jackson and other investigations.[993]

992 Klein v. Hoefflin, Decided April 3, 2012" @https://casetext.com/case/klein-v-hoefflin.
993 "Michael Jackson's Doctor Says He Has Evidence to Put People in Prison," *Radar-Online* September 17, 2009.

```
┌────────────────────────────────────────────────┐
│              Dr. Hoefflin's Findings              │
│                                                  │
│   •  Michael Jackson's death was the result of a │
│      "large conspiracy"                          │
│   •  Dr. Arnold Klein was part of this "large    │
│      conspiracy"                                 │
│   •  Corrupt elements within Los Angeles Law     │
│      Enforcement obstructed the investigation    │
│      into Jackson's death                        │
│                                                  │
└────────────────────────────────────────────────┘
```

According to Hoefflin's revelations, he not only possessed the evidence of the role of the corrupt/organized crime elements within Los Angeles law enforcement in obstructing the investigation into Michael Jackson's death, he also possessed the incriminating evidence against Dr. Arnold Klein and his role in the "larger conspiracy" that resulted in Michael Jackson's death itself. [994] On July 22, 2009 Dr. Hoefflin sent an email to Dr. Klein charging:

> Dr. Klein: Prior to his death, Michael Jackson asked you to send me a copy of his medical records. Those records were reviewed and *are now in the hands of the Los Angeles Police Department.*
>
> In your own writing and in your own public statements, is found evidence that you:
>
> (a) Ruined Michael's health.
> (b) Ruined his appearance.
> (c) Ruined him emotionally.
> (d) You caused his Demerol and other prescription pain medicine addiction.
> (e) You instructed Debbie Rowe to inject large quantities of Demerol while she was alone in his home.

---

994 "Plastic surgeon airs conspiracy theory for Jackson's death," *Mirror* September 18, 2009.

(f) You prevented him from entering a drug rehabilitation program.
(g) You prevented him from continuing his Dangerous Tour.
(h) You administered IV Diprivan [a brand name for propofol] to him in your own office.
(i) You instructed others to unsafely administer IV Diprivan
(m) You are definitely not the father of his two older children and are making fraudulent claims that you are.
(n) You contributed to the death of Michael Jackson.[995]

On that day Hoefflin aired his explosive charges in an interview with *Access Hollywood*:

Dr. Steve Hoefflin, a longtime friend and doctor of Michael Jackson, has claimed that the King of Pop "had lethal amounts of Demerol and Propofol in his body" at the time of his death…Hoefflin claimed to *Access* that according to a reliable source of his, Jackson's toxicology report indicated Michael "had lethal amounts of Demerol and Propofol in his body" when he died on June 25. Results from the LA Coroner's official autopsy of Jackson have yet to be publicly released…

Hoefflin claimed that the Demerol came from Dr. Arnold Klein – Michael's dermatologist – and the Propofol came from Dr. Conrad Murray, Jackson's personal physician in the weeks before his death. Further, Hoefflin claimed it was Jackson himself who told him about his heavy drug intake — at the time of his intervention. "Michael told me Dr. Klein was injecting him with massive amounts of Demerol" in 2002, Hoefflin claimed…

"Dr. Klein is the one who made his face white by using Benoquin, a permanent bleaching agent," Hoefflin claimed. "[Michael] had Lupus and it was made worse by Dr. Klein's massive injections of collagen. Patients who have lupus should not have collagen… For many years, Dr. Klein was using the very powerful cortisone Celestine to inject into the deep pimples on Michael's face and nose – cortisone injections can thin out tissue in the face. I told him that he should not have any further injections… as it was thinning out his face and nose… [And Klein] was prescribing him narcotics under an alias name, Omar Arnold." …

Denying the gay allegation, Hoefflin, who Michael lived with the doctor during the time surrounding his 1987 album "Bad," also said he previously took the singer to the Playboy mansion.

---

995 Seal, "The Ugly world of Dr. Arnie Klein."

"All the time, Michael was commenting on the beautiful women," he said. [996]

On July 24 Dr. Klein's attorney Bradley P. Boyer sent Dr. Hoefflin an email demanding that he "immediately agree to retract all false information which you have disseminated about Dr. Klein and not to publish any further such false statements.'" Hoefflin responded by suggesting to Klein's attorney that he and Klein sit down and Klein be "interviewed openly covering his medical records and other materials in my possession"[997]: "On July 24th, 2009…I invited Dr. Klein and Mr. Boyer to sit down with me and go over all of the evidence that I had on Dr. Klein's criminal activities and that I would delete anything that they proved to be false. I never heard back from them."

Note also that Debbie Rowe, Dr. Klein's long-time nurse assistant, also accused Klein and contributing to Michael's death.

Michael Jackson's ex-wife Debbie Rowe blamed his former doctor, Arnold Klein, for his death when she first heard about it…She then called him, saying: "What the f**k did you give him? He's dead and *it's your fault.*"[998]

On August 26, 2009, Dr. Hoefflin was interviewed by reporter David Willets of *The Sun* and was told that, on the day of Michael's death Dr. Murray called Dr. Klein.[999] According to phone records, between the time that Dr. Murray initially said he found Michael Jackson not breathing (10:52 a.m.) and the time the Los Angeles Fire Department recorded the 911 telephone call

---

996 "Former Jackson Doctor Claims Michael 'Had Lethal Amounts of Demerol & Propofol'," *Access Hollywood* July 23, 2009; "Former Jackson Doctor Claims Michael 'Had Lethal Amounts of Demerol & Propofol'," *KNBC-TV* July 23, 2009.
997 "Klein v. Hoefflin, Decided April 3, 2012" @https://casetext.com/case/klein-v-hoefflin.
998 "Arnold Klein blamed for Jackson death," *Contactmusic* July 26, 2013
999 David Willetts, "Jacko 'dead 47 mins' as doc made 3 calls," *The Sun* Aug 26 2009; "Lawyers For 'Dermatologist' to the Stars' Argue Against Defamation Case," *Waven Newspapers* June 16, 2011.

(12:22 p.m.), Murray spent 47 mins on three phone calls – two in-state calls and one out-of-state call. Three journalists and the editor of *The Sun* told Dr. Hoefflin:

> that there were phone records in their possession indicating that Dr. Murray had called Dr. Klein on June 25, 2009 ***prior*** [to] Michael's Death. I was also told that Dr. Klein was one of the doctors who showed Dr. Murray how to administer Propofol. I had no reason to doubt the veracity of what they said especially in light of the ongoing investigation of Dr. Klein by the Los Angel[e]s Police Dept. I was further advised that they had turned over this information to the police.[1000]

Of course, Dr. Klein and his office personnel (who had now gone into "protection mode" for Klein[1001]) denied talking to Dr. Murray on the day of Michael Jackson's death.

> According to Klein, on the day Jackson died, Klein was working with patients. He received no telephone calls from Murray or anyone claiming to act on his behalf. His office manager, Jason Pfeiffer (Pfeiffer) was fielding all his telephone calls, and Pfeiffer was the one who told him about Jackson after a patient called the office with the news.

> Pfeiffer explained in his declaration that Klein's office switchboard did not refer incoming calls to Klein but the calls went first to Pfeiffer. When Klein was working, Pfeiffer answered calls on Klein's cell phone. Pfeiffer never received a call from Murray or anyone claiming to be from Murray's office. "More specifically, any statement that Conrad Murray or anyone claiming to be calling on behalf of Conrad Murray spoke to, or called, Dr. KLEIN on the morning that Michael Jackson died is false. I received no such calls and I have personal knowledge that Dr. KLEIN, who spent the entire morning with patients, took no such calls.[1002]

1000 Klein   v.   Hoefflin,   Decided   April   3,   2012"
@https://casetext.com/case/klein-v-hoefflin.
1001 Mark Seal, "The Ugly world of Dr. Arnie Klein, Beverly Hills' King of Botox," *Vanity Fair* February 2, 2012: ""According to Khilji, Klein's office staff went into protection mode to keep the doctor away from the press. "He really wanted to take the opportunity to go to the media and exploit it," said Khilji. "Our plan was to try to tell him this was not a good idea."
1002 Klein   v.   Hoefflin,   Decided   April   3,   2012"
@https://casetext.com/case/klein-v-hoefflin.

But Hoefflin doubled down. In a sworn declaration Hoefflin claimed that *The Sun* reporters told him that Dr. Klein showed Murray how to administer propofol.[1003] According to Hoefflin, "They [*The Sun*] check their facts with an electronic microscope. There is factual evidence that the statements that I made are true. They have in their

possession phone records, recordings, documents and other evidence that confirms facts in their stories before they're published."[1004] Hoefflin thus declared: "I know that one of those individuals that Dr. Murray called during those 47 minutes was indeed Dr. Klein."[1005] Hoefflin said he expected Klein to be "arrested and indicted for contributing to Michael's death"[1006]

Dr. Hoefflin presented the allegedly incriminating evidence against Dr. Klein to the executors of the Jackson estate, Howard Weitzman and John Branca, and both stated that they "did not condone me providing evidence to the public about Dr. Klein's criminal activities, that may have actually contributed to Michael's death, the very person who's estate they now represent." Hoefflin will later reveal that Weitzman and Branca colluded with Klein's attorneys to protect Klein. At this point – September 2009 – Klein is still a protected "eminence" in Los Angeles and member of the

---

1003 "Lawyers For 'Dermatologist' to the Stars' Argue Against Defamation Case," *Waven Newspapers* June 16, 2011.
1004 "Michael Jackson Doc Sues," *TMZ* September 15, 2009.
1005 Klein v. Hoefflin, Decided April 3, 2012" @https://casetext.com/case/klein-v-hoefflin.
1006 Klein v. Hoefflin, Decided April 3, 2012" @https://casetext.com/case/klein-v-hoefflin.

Gay Mafia of Hollywood. Dr. Hoefflin thus got no assistance from the hijackers of Michael Jackson's estate in exposing the conspiracy behind Michael Jackson's death and Dr. Arnold Klein's alleged role in it.

On September 14, 2009, Dr. Klein filed a complaint against Hoefflin alleging causes of action for slander, defamation, etc.[1007] In his defense, Dr. Klein through his attorneys told a demonstrable lie:

> "Dr. Klein and Conrad Murray have never met, spoken, nor communicated with each other," read a statement from Klein's attorneys, Richard L. Charnley and Bradley P. Boyer. "Indeed, Dr. Klein did not know that Conrad Murray even existed until his name came out in the press. Further, Dr. Klein did not provide Propofol to Conrad Murray and obviously did not teach him how to administer it."[1008]

Dr. Klein stated in his declaration that "he had never met or spoken to Murray."[1009] As we shall show below, this claim that Klein never met or spoke to Dr. Murray and didn't even know of his existence until his name appeared in the press is wrong, which makes one wonder what the *point* of the lie was.

Responding to the lawsuit filed against him, Hoefflin published a long and very revealing Statement on September 16, 2009. *Mirror* reported that Dr. Hoefflin has made a "series of damning conspiracy-like allegations" that "the King of Pop's death was part of a larger conspiracy."[1010] Below is his full statement.

1007 "Michael Jackson Doc Sues," *TMZ* September 15, 2009.
1008 Josh Grossberg and Claudia Rosenbaum, "Jackson's King of Collagen: I Didn't Help Kill Michael," *E News* September 15, 2009.
1009 Klein v. Hoefflin,Decided April 3, 2012" @https://casetext.com/case/klein-v-hoefflin.
1010 "Plastic surgeon airs conspiracy theory for Jackson's death," *Mirror* September 18, 2009.

Statement from Steven M. Hoefflin, M.D., F.I.C.S., F.A.C.S.[1011]

I am personally going to put a stop to all of the threats on my life and the threats against my family.

I am now bringing out to the public *all of the credible evidence in my possession on the corruption in Los Angeles Law Enforcement pertaining to the Michael Jackson Investigation.*

I am going to personally stop all of the threats from the LAPD on my life and the threats against my family. These are occurring because *those members of law enforcement know that I possess abundant incriminating evidence that is going to put a lot of people in prison.*

I am not going to allow and will expose those people who are colluding together, such as Diane Dimond of Entertainment Tonight, with the police to use false documents to threaten me, obstruct my independent investigation into Michael's death and to stop me from providing evidence to the proper authorities.

All of the people that have been threatening my family and I that I have incriminating evidence on are going to be exposed with this evidence in the public eye so they will stop their attempts on my life that I have been experiencing for too long. For me to wait for the slow wheels of government investigations to catch on and bring these people to justice is no longer feasible.

Colin Powell is a friend of mine. I have already called his house and left a message for him. *I am asking him to engage a congressional investigation into all of the LAPD and Los Angeles Sherriff Department Law Enforcement Corruption in Los Angeles that is taking place in the Michael Jackson and other important investigations* that is ruining our city. I want a Congressional Committee to subpoena these people, put them under oath, gather credible evidence for a good District Attorney, and bring them to proper justice. I have already asked Bob Woodward to report on this matter in the Washington Post.

I am going to put an end to these threats now. I owe it to my family. I owe it to myself. But, most of all, I owe it to the public who always wants to know the truth and especially the truth about what happened to Michael Jackson. In reference to yesterday's lawsuit filed against me by Dr. Arnold Klein, *I am established Government Witness in the Michael Jackson Death Investigation.* It is my clear opinion that Dr. Arnold Klein

---

1011 See "Michael Jackson's Doctor Says He Has Evidence to Put People in Prison," *Radar-Online* September 17, 2009.

and his attorneys are attempting to prevent me from discussing incriminating evidence that I possess on Dr. Klein.

They know that I have provided this evidence to the authorities. They also know that credible, incriminating evidence is going to be *shortly released in my book*. In my opinion and that of others, they desperately want me to stop any further investigation and to stop providing the public and the authorities the evidence that I acquire. It is my opinion that Dr. Klein is using a letter with falsified information sent to him by Howard Weitzman, Esq. In July 2009, I was asked to have a privileged meeting with Mr. Weitzman and another attorney.

I shared incriminating evidence that I possessed on Dr. Klein and that he was under investigation by multiple agencies of the Department of Justice. Mr. Weitzman told me that he would neither talk with Dr. Klein, would not provide him any defense, nor would he assist his defense attorneys. On August 1st, 2009, after that privileged legal meeting, Mr. Weitzman prepared a letter with false information to Dr. Klein's defense attorney, Mr. Charnley, in an attempt to discredit me. The false information in his letter was known to be false by both he and Mr. John Branca.

Mr. Weitzman had told me he had discussed it with Mr. Branca. Mr. Weitzman falsely stated that I had no permission nor right to talk about Michael or his mother. He also stated that *he and Mr. Branca did not condone me providing evidence to the public about Dr. Klein's criminal activities, that may have actually contributed to Michael's death, the very person who's estate they now represent*. Shortly after the publication of his letter containing false information, I had left Katherine Jackson's home, and Mr. Weitzman, my wife and I had a telephone conversation.

We requested that he provide a corrected letter to Mr. Charnley, to the media who requested a correction, and to send a copy to me. He already had the hand-written and signed consents from both Michael Jackson in March 1999 giving me permission to publically discuss his medical records and from Katherine and Rebbie Jackson from July 18, 2009 giving me permission to talk with the media about Michael. He told me that he had discussed the issue with Mr. Branca and that both of them agreed to provide me, Mr. Charnley and the media with a corrected letter. Both of them failed to do this despite having documents proving the information in Mr. Weitzman's letter was false.

On July 24th, 2009, [I] had corresponded about the issue of slander and defamation with one of Dr. Klein's lawyers, Mr. Boyer. I invited Dr. Klein and Mr. Boyer to sit down with me and go over all of the evidence that I had on Dr. Klein's criminal activities and that I would delete anything that they proved to be false. I never heard back from them. His client, Dr. Klein, also had knowledge of my being given consents by Michael Jackson and by Katherine and Rebbie Jackson to discuss Michael and his medical records. Dr. Klein, all of his attorneys Richard Charnley, Bradley Boyer, Susan Wootton and the firm "Ropers, Majestic, Kohn, and Bentley" together with Howard Weitzman and now apparently John Branca knew of the falsity of Weitzman's letter, yet are attempting to use it in their attempts to bring a frivolous lawsuit against me, obstruct my testimony, and to discredit me.

With this evidence, I have contacted the Attorney General of California, Jerry Brown. I expect that he will put a stay on this lawsuit because he would never allow a court to proceed in an action that would obstruct one of *their primary witnesses (myself) in a federal investigation.* In addition, I expect that he will now open an additional investigation into probable felonies that all of these individuals have committed in attempting to obstruct justice, intimidating a government witness with a document that is known to be false, and possibly other crimes. I believe that with this evidence, I now have a legal standing to bring a lawsuit against all of them, which I certainly will, for possible felonies committed against me.

I am going to start providing the media and Michael Jackson's fans all of the evidence that I have involving *the Michael Jackson Death Investigation, the Corrupt Los Angeles Law Enforcement, and others colluding together to obstruct Justice.* If anyone wants to file another slander and defamation suit, I suggest that they send a copy directly to the Attorney General of California Jerry Brown. Those trying to hurt my family and I should stop because all of the evidence that we possess will not be with us but with the public.

Steven M. Hoefflin, M.D., F.I.C.S., F.A.C.S.
Sincerely,
Steven M. Hoefflin, MD, FACS
Immediate Past President
Los Angeles Society of Plastic Surgeons

Chapter Seventeen

The Whistleblower And His Fall

Frank DiLeo threatened to "blow the lid" off of the conspiracy against Michael Jackson but he was dead before he could do any blowing (2011), 2 years after Michael's death. Dr. Arnold Klein lasted longer, but his death in 2015 was much more ignominious than DiLeo's. This is no doubt because, before his death, Klein *did a lot of whistleblowing.*

Klein fell hard and fell far from his position of eminence in Hollywood. Once a protected member of Hollywood's Gay Mafia, he fell so hard that even David Geffen could not halt it, even though he offered a lame and transparently disingenuous show of public support during Klein's darkest hour. I think it can be confidently said that Klein's tremendous fall was precipitated by three factors: his emotionalism, his hubris, and his big mouth that came with no filter.

In November of 2009 Klein was still a member of the Gay Mafia in good standing. Certainly, at that time he was still helping to carry out the agenda of the Gay Mafia against Michael Jackson. Part of that agenda was to make Michael "gay" in the public view. This of course was part of the Pedophile's Agenda against Michael. On August 14, 2009, less than two months after his "friend's" death Klein and his office manager Jason Pfeiffer sold a salacious story to the Australian tabloid *Women's Day* claiming that Michael Jackson was gay and he and Jason were lovers.[1012]

1012 "Clinic worker claims to have had homosexual love affair with Michael Jackson," *The Telegraph* August 21, 2009. Mark Seal, "The Ugly world of Dr. Arnie Klein, Beverly Hills' King of Botox," *Vanity Fair* February 2, 2012: "On April 30, 2010, Klein told the Web site TMZ that Michael Jackson was a homosexual and that Klein's office manager, Jason Pfeiffer, had had an affair

Klein publicly supported this lie until April of 2011 when he confessed that "Allegations about...Jason being Michael Jackson's lover are ridiculous. *That story was made up...*"[1013] However, up until November 2009 Klein was still peddling that "ridiculous...made up" story about Michael Jackson.

November 5, 2009, I think must be considered the day Arnold Klein crossed the Rubicon River. He spoke for 90 minutes to TMZ's Harvey Levin and there was no way his life could have been the same afterwards. No doubt wounded in some ways by his feud with Dr. Hoefflin and the latter's exposure of him, Klein's emotionalism got the best of him and during that hour and a half that he sat with Levin Klein dug his grave with his mouth. He does lie throughout the interview, mainly to protect himself by obfuscating his crimes; but he drops bombs on others, such that at one point in the interview he knows he has crossed the line and he thinks out loud, "I'll probably get shot on the way out." Here are examples of Klein's lying during the interview:

Levin   Did you know Murray?
Klein   No, I never met him. *I didn't know he existed.*
Levin   Ever talk to him on the phone?
Klein   No. I only knew he existed from Michael telling me he'd met him in Las Vegas...
Levin   And he was treating his kids?
Klein   Yeah, he primarily told me...he wanted to know, very strangely...he called me up and he said what I thought of Afro-American black doctors and I said I don't really judge doctors by color, and he said, "What do you think? Are they good doctors"? I said anyone could be a good doctor. The great doctors are black doctors. I mean, orange doctors, yellow doctors, white doctors. I mean, it doesn't matter the colour, it matters the

---

with him. Pfeiffer was "the love of [Jackson's] life," Klein said. The television show *Extra* had just aired an interview with Pfeiffer, who declared, "I was Michael Jackson's boyfriend He was very passionate, he was very sexual." On May 1, 2010 Klein called in to Harvey Levin on TMZ Live to support the Pffeifer lie.
1013 Arnold Klein, "TMZ Torture" Facebook post dated April 18, 2011; "Arnie Klein -- My Buddy Was Not Michael's Lover," *TMZ* April 22, 2011; Seal, "The Ugly world of Dr. Arnie Klein."

quality of the doctor. Is he a good doctor? And he said, "He's a cardiologist" he tells me. He was a heart doctor. I said, "Are you sure that he's a good doctor?" He said, "Well, I think he's a great doctor." I said, "Fine, then he's a good doctor" and that's the last we ever discussed Dr Murray until I read his name in the newspaper when everyone knew about him…

Of course, this is just a repeat of what Klein through his lawyers proclaimed in 2009 in response to Hoefflin's charges: "[Dr. Klein] had never met or spoken to Murray." However, in 2015 when the charade was long over Klein admits to having met Dr. Murray in 2007 and throwing him out of Michael's room! Speaking of himself in the third person he says:

> Klein went to see Michael In Vegas in 2007 and met Dr. Conrad Murray who Michael said was incompetent. Klein asked Murray to leave and had a long talk with Michael about Propofol.[1014]

> Michael had first met [Dr. Conrad Murray] in 2006 and *I threw him out of Michael's room at the Mirage.*[1015]

Klein was thus lying when he and his lawyers publicly proclaimed that he never met or knew Conrad Murray even existed until he heard of him from the press. Also, Levin asks Klein about propofol, which has by this time replaced Demerol in the press as the cause of Michael's death.

Levin   Okay. Did you ever administer propofol to Michael Jackson?
Klein   *Never.*
Levin   Did he ever ask you for propofol?
Klein   Yes. He called me one weekend and he asked me if I would administer propofol and I told him he was absolutely out of his mind.

We know from his nurse assistant since 1977 Debbie Rowe that this is not true. In her testimony during the 2013 AEG Live trial she testified under oath that Klein gave Jackson propofol: "Rowe

---

1014 Arnold Klein, "Michael Jackson and Arnold Klein," June 21, 2015 @ https://awkleinmd.wordpress.com/2015/06/21/470/

1015 Arnold Klein, "What Happened to Michael? Live From Los Angeles," October 23, 2015 @ http://mjhoaxlive.blogspot.com/2013/09/it-wasnt-michael-jackson-they-wanted-it.html.

was a nurse assistant to dermatologist Arnold Klein, who she said provided the painkiller Demerol and Propofol for many of the hundreds of treatments Jackson received over 20 years...[1016]

A final, quite hilarious example of Klein getting tangled up in his lie is this: that he nor his nurse ever injected Michael Jackson with Demerol for minor procedures such as acne in his office:

Klein   Debbie Rowe treated Michael at Neverland.

Levin   Well, she treated... Debbie Rowe treated Michael Jackson in your office in 1993 and gave him repeated injections of Demerol.

Klein   I don't know if I was even there. You have to understand this is according to records of Steve Hoefflin's trying to say...

Levin   No, no, no, no, no, I can tell you that that's not true. *This is according to records from the Santa Barbara County Sheriff's Department investigation* where Debbie Rowe is quoted by one of the officers, because I've seen the report, and the report talks about Debbie Rowe repeatedly injecting Michael Jackson in the buttocks, *in your office...*

Klein   Okay, I have to tell you one thing...

Levin   *...for acne treatments.*

Klein   No, we don't give...*I don't give Demerol for acne, ever.* She could have done it. You want to know why? Because she treated Michael at different times. Don't forget she posed for...

Levin   She said acne by the way.

So, Klein first tries to deny that he, through his nurse assistant, ever injected Michael with Demerol for acne. Then Levin reveals that Santa Barbara County Sheriff's Department records prove that it *was done* and in *his office*, not at Neverland. Then Klein tries to distance himself personally from the act by declaring: "I don't give Demerol for acne, *ever.*" But then, *this happens.*

1016 "Michael Jackson trial: Debbie Rowe cries during testimony," *ABC7* August 14, 2013; Jeff Gottlieb, "Debbie Rowe: Michael Jackson's doctors competed to give pain eds," *Los Angeles Times* August 14, 2013.

Levin   The LAPD has some of the records...

Klein   Yes.

Levin   ...that the Coroner took from the office. At least one of the records involves...it talks about *you filling acne scars and putting him under with Demerol.*

Klein   **Yeah.** *You know how many acne scars he had?* You know how terrible his acne was, that he wouldn't go to school?

So now, the truth comes out! Klein is forced to *admit that he DID* inject Michael Jackson with Demerol for acne – *you know how many acne scars he had?!*

So much for "ever."

But of course, it was not Klein's lies to Harvey Levin that got him into so much trouble: it was his truthful disclosures, surely made in a period of frustration. The two biggest disclosures – at this point more Freudian slips than whistleblowing – have to do with AEG's complicity in the death of Michael and with the three phone calls made by Dr. Murray during the 47 minutes that Michael Jackson lay dead or dying.

Klein   I think if we just sit here and we talk about the drugs, it's a terrible thing. I think the horror of this whole thing is that AEG hired Murray, and we will agree with that, will we not?

Levin   Well, what do you know about that? I mean...

Klein   It was...I read the article in People magazine that AEG hired Murray and I think that if I would hire a doctor for a very famous person I would make sure that the doctor was qualified to be the physician to this patient...

Klein ...I think what we have here though is a situation where this Dr Murray existed and I feel this man is responsible for his death...AEG hired Murray.

Levin   Do you think Dr Murray should be prosecuted?

Klein   Of course he should be prosecuted I feel, but I think also...*I think the people responsible for hiring him are culpable also because I think they didn't do a background check to know enough...*

Klein   ...And then when AEG has every satellite truck around the place, rented, every satellite space rented and then wants to charge us, the City of Los Angeles, it's totally ridiculous. Then AEG films the funeral and they feed it to CNN, don't you begin to think about how much AEG was involved in this? *I'll probably get shot on the way out but*, I mean, how much is their money involved in this whole thing. And then they own the movie, which they released through John Branca.

Levin   You're not suggesting there was foul play here?

Klein   *No, I don't think there's foul play* but I think they're making a lot of money there and I don't think they should have the City of Los Angeles pay for the funeral. That's what I'm saying. Why should we pay nickels and dollars for the funeral when AEG's making money off of this whole thing and rented out the satellite spaces all around the Staples Centre when they filmed this. So I don't think there's anything here but I think they're culpable in this because they should have known the background of Dr Murray when they hired him.

This is pretty stunning. Klein must have developed some frustration with AEG executives, as Frank DiLeo would as well, and this frustration hindered Klein's filter. We do know that Klein was still trying to get not only the $48,000 invoice to AEG Live paid, but he claimed that AEG Live owed him over $100, 000 for the work he did on Michael Jackson for them.[1017] So here we have Klein totally impeaching AEG Live's legal covering in the case of the death of Michael Jackson. AEG was claiming that it has no culpability in the death because Dr. Conrad Murray, who killed Michael, was *an employee of Michael Jackson and NOT an employee of AEG Live*. Klein is here saying on national television that it was *AEG* who hired Murray and *shares culpability in Michael's death*, and then made money off of the death! Klein seems to instantly realize that he has messed up: ***I'll probably get***

1017 Arnold Klein, "What Happened to Michael? Live From Los Angeles," October 23, 2015 @ http://mjhoaxlive.blogspot.com/2013/09/it-wasnt-michael-jackson-they-wanted-it.html.

shot on the way out but… He then tries to pull back by saying that there was no foul play. However, once Klein goes *full* whistleblower he will explicitly reveal the foul play.

And then, the whopper:

> **Levin** …about a phone call that came to your office during the emergency when Michael Jackson was taken to the hospital, by one of Michael Jackson's people.
>
> **Klein** Yes. *Frank DiLeo called the office.* Now here's the question that always remains. *Who was called by Dr Murray?* We know I wasn't called, contrary to what a certain doctor said. Again, this lovely doctor said I was called. But who was called? And, I mean, is it public who was called? Do people publicly know who was called?
>
> **Levin** No.
>
> **Klein** Okay. But there's been conjecture about many people who's been called.
>
> **Levin** Right.
>
> **Klein** And one was a conjecture was that *the head of AEG was called.* That's a conjecture. *One was Frank DiLeo*, who used to be his manager, was called and whoever the third call was, was supposedly a patient who was suing Dr Murray. Okay? That was supposedly what the third call was about and *that's my knowledge.* I can't say for a fact and it maybe a big lie but *that's what I was told.*
>
> *I was told* one call went to a patient who was suing Dr Murray – that's the first person he talks to after his patient has died, *next thing went to the head of AEG, then **they talked** to Frank DiLeo* and those were the three calls. And I know fairly well, *I was assured yesterday* that the first call was to this patient who was very angry. So I don't know where these calls…
>
> **Levin** What happened when Frank DiLeo called to your office?
>
> **Klein** Well, he was telling us that it didn't look very good. Now I didn't take the call. I mean, Jason, who's my office manager, took the call.

403

Levin   And what did he say.

Klein   He said that it didn't look very well, it didn't look very good.

Levin   *Did it…my understanding is there was something said about what caused Michael Jackson to have an emergency.*
Klein   Yeah, and I mean you have to repeat it…I mean, I wish Jason was around to repeat it but he's not here right now to repeat it…

Levin   Okay, fair enough.

Two extremely important revelations here. The first is that Arnold Klein doesn't conjecture but *was told* and was *assured* of the identity of those whom Dr. Murray called after he killed Michael Jackson with his cocktail of drugs, **before he called 911**: the first call was to an as yet unidentified "patient" of Dr. Murray who was suing Murray at the time. Who was he and *why was he the first call* after Murray killed Michael? The second call after Michael was killed was to Randy Phillips of AEG Live! The third call was from both Murray *and Phillips* to Frank DiLeo, who later revealed his closeness to a Mafia contract hit on Michael Jackson! There is here the *strong* impression that, after killing Michael Jackson Murray called his bosses to tell them: mission accomplished! Only then, after cleaning up the crime scene, did Murray have 911 called. And then we learn that Frank DiLeo *called Arnold Klein!* Thus,

1. Murray kills Michael Jackson
2. Murray makes mystery call
3. Murray calls Randy Phillips of AEG Live
4. Murray and Randy Phillips call Frank DiLeo
5. Frank DiLeo calls Arnold Klein

When Klein insists that he wasn't one of the three calls made after the death of Michael, he no doubt is correct and this does not contradict the records in the possession of *The Sun* because their records actually showed, reportedly, "that Dr. Murray had called

404

Dr. Klein on June 25, 2009, *prior* [to] Michael's Death."[1018] This would mean that sometime in the morning of June 25, 2009 Dr. Murray called Dr. Klein. At around 11:30 a.m. Murray possibly administered to Michael a fatal injection of Demerol or propofol or maybe both, which may have reacted negatively to midazolam already in Michael's system. It is possible that such a reaction caused Michael's death. At this point, Dr. Murray does *not* call 911 but instead calls the "patient" that is suing him, then Randy Phillips, then he and Phillips call Frank DiLeo. Later, Frank DiLeo calls Arnold Klein. It is interesting how Klein shuts down the question above about Frank DiLeo's call, and Harvey Levin seems happy to oblige him.

It was not long before the "powers that be" started responding to Klein's "loose lips." That next month on December 18, 2009 Dr. Klein's former office employee Bruce Ayers, "Dr. Klein's research assistant and confidant," was found dead on a sidewalk. Klein claims he fired Ayers in February 2009,[1019] but he also suspected that Ayers was murdered by his (Klein's) own enemies.[1020] On June 30, 2010, the DEA conducted an Administrative Inspection Warrant on Klein's Beverly Hills office, "a rather stringent regulatory examination" in which they "went through all his logs, and did extensive checking to make sure what drugs are being administered to which patients."[1021]

It was 2011 when Dr. Arnold Klein became a full-fledged whistleblower, and the circumstances are pretty transparent. Like Randy Quaid before him, after that 2009 interview Klein claimed to be the victim of a financial conspiracy that forced him to file bankruptcy in January of that year.[1022] While Klein is having a

---

1018   Klein   v.   Hoefflin,   Decided   April   3,   2012"
@https://casetext.com/case/klein-v-hoefflin.
1019 "Michael Jackson's Doc—Ex-Employee Dies," *TMZ* December 30, 2009.
1020 Diane Dimond, "Doctor Demerol: Michael Jackson Dermatologist Arnold Klein Under Investigation," *Daily Beast* December 5, 2011.
1021 Roger Friedman, "DEA 'Inspected' Office of Michael Jackson's Dr. Klein Last Week: Exclusive," *Showbiz 411* June 30, 2010.
1022 "EXCLUSIVE DOCUMENTS: Michael Jackson Doctor Arnold Klein Files For Bankruptcy; Owes Creditors $3.5M -- Read His Petition," *Radar Online* January 25, 2011; Klein v. Khilji, United States Bankruptcy Court

public meltdown, he is spilling all of the beans in the process. In a September 22, 2011, interview with the *Associated Press* Dr. Klein announced he is writing a book about Michael.[1023] This book "will expose the people whose greed killed Michael" and "even if no one reads this book in this generation I have to leave behind the truth," Klein said. On October 14, 2011, David Geffen breaks his silence regarding his friend's troubles, but says really *nothing*:

> Dear Arnie, in light of all that is being said about you in the press I feel compelled to add my truths. I have never known a doctor who tries to know and learn everything as completely as you do, a doctor who has always been there for me.[1024]

And those were apparently the only "truths" Geffen was prepared to share publicly about Klein, and they do not speak to or even help Klein's current situation. On December 5, 2011 the Medical Board of California subpoenaed Klein, "reportedly for pumping the singer full of prescription painkillers," and Klein's lawyer Herbert L. Weinberg resigned.[1025] Klein's former ally in the press Diane Dimond is now calling him "Doctor Demerol."[1026]

And so, he lashes out with details. Mark Seal, who covered Klein's fall for *Vanity Fair*, reported:

> In his phone call with me, Klein insisted that he's not the villain but the victim of a vast conspiracy. *"If you don't think everything's interconnected—it is,"* he said. He implied that the powers behind

---

Central District of California Los Angeles Division, November 4, 2015 CV15-8713-JAK.
1023 "Jackson's Dermatologist Says Murray Fallout Hurts," *The Telegraph* October 15, 2011
1024 "Jackson's Dermatologist Says Murray Fallout Hurts."
1025 "MJ's Skin Doc: The Med Board Is On My Ass…And My Lawyer Just Quit," *TMZ* December 5, 2011.
1026 Diane Dimond, "Doctor Demerol: Michael Jackson Dermatologist Arnold Klein Under Investigation," *Daily Beast* December 5, 2011; Diane Dimond, "Dr. Arnold Klein, Michael Jackson's Longtime Physician, Courts Substance-Abuse Allegations," *Daily Beast* August 25, 2011.

Jackson's comeback were engaged in dark maneuvers. "A.E.G. was behind the whole thing," he said. [1027]

Klein now comes clean, announcing "I am very much aware of the events surrounding Mr Jackson's death"[1028] and "The Death of Michael Jackson was not accidental…Michael Jackson's death was caused by a group of people or an investment consortium who were more interested in Michael's Immense Music Catalogue than his survival"[1029]; "Michael Jackson's death was caused by a group of people who were more interested in Michael's Immense Music Catalogue than his survival"[1030]; "Michael Jackson's death was about money not him as a performer."[1031] According to Klein, Michael Jackson was "murdered…by an incompetent physician who was nothing short of *a hired hit man* employed by a Rich Entertainment Conglomerate. They only wanted his music Catalogue."[1032]

Klein names names. "Phillip Anscutz is an evil man who was deeply involved in the death of Michael Jackson."[1033] Who is Phillip Anscutz? He is the Jewish billionaire head of AEG, the parent company of AEG Live. According to Klein's revelations,

---

1027 Seal, "The Ugly world of Dr. Arnie Klein."
1028 Arnold W. Klein, M.D., "Corrupt Officials Exposed: $30 Million Embezzlement Cover-up Surrounding the Death of Michael Jackson" www.arnoldwklein.com February 28, 2013.
1029 Arnold Klein, "The truth about Jackson's death, the 2003 Will," June 22, 2015 @ https://awkleinmd.wordpress.com/2015/06/22/the-truth-about-jacksons-death-the-2003-will/
1030 Arnold Klein, "Michael Jackson and Arnold Klein," June 21, 2015 @ https://awkleinmd.wordpress.com/2015/06/21/470/
1031 Arnold Klein, "The Destruction and Death of Michael Jackson, the Theft of His Catalogue and Attempted Destruction and Resurrection of Dr. Klein," February 3, 2015 @ https://awkleinmd.wordpress.com/2015/02/03/the-destruction-and-death-of-michael-jackson-the-theft-of-his-catalogue-and-attempted-destruction-and-resurrection-of-dr-klein/
1032 Arnold Klein, "What Happened to Michael? Live From Los Angeles," October 23, 2015 @ http://mjhoaxlive.blogspot.com/2013/09/it-wasnt-michael-jackson-they-wanted-it.html.
1033 Arnold Klein, "What really happened to Michael (there is much more)." February 2013 post @ https://www.michaeljacksonhoaxforum.com/forums/index.php?topic=23648.0.

Anschutz was good friends with Tom Barrack (Lebanese Christian parents) who owned Colony Capital, Inc. In 2008 Barrack bought the $23 million loan on Michael Jackson's Neverland Ranch, thus saving it from foreclosure. The terms of Barrack's rescue of Michael were: Barrack's Colony Capital agreed to bail Michael out and in return Michael had to agree to allow Barrack's friend, Phillip Anscutz and his AEG, to stage Michael's comeback.[1034] AEG had just completed renovations on their O2 Arena in London and they wanted to open with a series of Michael Jackson concerts. While Michael was not eager to tour again, the terms of Barrack's/Colony Capital's bail out put a lot of pressure on him to agree to the concerts.

Tom Barrack was also co-owner with William Bone of Sunrise Colony, who owned the mortgage on Conrad Murray's $1.2 million mansion in the Red Rock Section of Las Vegas.[1035] Barrack and Sunrise Colony were foreclosing on the property, as Dr. Murray had fallen $100,000 behind in mortgage payments. Murray was indebted to Barrack, and thus beholden to Barrack. So according to Klein, "That is how they found the incompetent Murray to care for Michael"[1036]; "Murray was totally incompetent and hired by Tom Barrack because Barrack was foreclosing on his home in the Red Rock Section of Las Vegas and Murray was up to his neck in debt and had to take the Job. Barrack hired him for Phillip Anschutz of AEG."[1037]

1034 Arnold Klein, "What really happened to Michael (there is much more)." February 2013 post @ https://www.michaeljacksonhoaxforum.com/forums/index.php?topic=23648.0.
1035 Langthorne, *83 Minutes*, 100.
1036 Arnold Klein, "What really happened to Michael (there is much more)." February 2013 post @ https://www.michaeljacksonhoaxforum.com/forums/index.php?topic=23648.0.
1037 Arnold Klein, "who killed Michael Jackson?" November 8, 2014 @ https://awkleinmd.wordpress.com/2014/11/08/howard-weitzman-and-the-first-molestation-why-did-you-; Arnold Klein, "The truth about Jackson's death, the 2003 Will," June 22, 2015 @ https://awkleinmd.wordpress.com/2015/06/22/the-truth-about-jacksons-death-the-2003-will/.

The conspiracy gets deeper, according to Klein's revelations. While the terms of Barrack's bail out of Michael's Neverland Ranch stipulated that Michael agree to allow Anschutz's AEG to stage Michael's comeback with a series of planned concerts, according to Klein *"The plan was never for the concerts it was for the catalogue."*[1038] Klein exposes:

> Murray was not licensed in England because England was never in their plan.[1039]

> Murray was not Licensed in England? England was never a part of their plan...[They] killed Michael for his Catalogue...[1040]

> They want the Catalogue and [the] person Michael was not totally necessary. The Catalogue was their main interest...The death of Michael Jackson rests on whoever allowed Murray to care for him. He was not licensed in California. For this reason alone Anschutz, Barack, Phillips and Tome Tome should be on trial for Michael Jackson's death as accomplices because commonly criminal offences involve individuals who act at a distance, providing information, transportation, and supplying the Propofol. They all knew what Murray was doing up there for that is the reason the long-standing Nanny Grace quit.[1041]

Actually going to London was "never in the plans." Wow. We said above:

> Why would AEG Live take a healthy Michael Jackson, sign a contract with him for a series of *50 concerts* at *their* newly built arena in London and then deliberately drug him to the point of incapacitation? ... The Plan was clearly to drug Michael Jackson and then take advantage of his

---

1038 Arnold Klein, "What Happened to Michael? Live From Los Angeles," October 23, 2015 @ http://mjhoaxlive.blogspot.com/2013/09/it-wasnt-michael-jackson-they-wanted-it.html.
1039 Arnold Klein, "The truth about Jackson's death, the 2003 Will," June 22, 2015 @ https://awkleinmd.wordpress.com/2015/06/22/the-truth-about-jacksons-death-the-2003-will/
1040 Arnold Klein, "Michael Jackson and Arnold Klein," June 21, 2015 @ https://awkleinmd.wordpress.com/2015/06/21/470/
1041 Arnold Klein, "What Happened to Michael? Live From Los Angeles," October 23, 2015 @ http://mjhoaxlive.blogspot.com/2013/09/it-wasnt-michael-jackson-they-wanted-it.html.

reduced mental capacity. The incapacitation made Michael incompetent to make rational decisions, and this served AEG Live's interests. Michael was indeed *chemically controlled*...A most illuminating illustration of AEG taking advantage of Michael Jackson's mental incapacitation occurred within days prior to Michael's death [- the resigning of his enemy John Branca].

Klein's revelations confirm our suspicions and gives details. He says:

Additionally Michael's resigning with Branca makes no sense in that He hated Branca and Sony as I, Lisa Marie Presley and everyone close to him knew. However during the last week of his life Murray had taken to skin popping him with Propofol (which means giving him little or large shots under the skin.) This would make Michael incompetent to make any rational decision. Through these illegal acts, Anschutz, Branca and Weitzman now own Michael Jackson and his catalogue. John Branca was very close to Sony. Sony recently bought Epic so with the amount held by the Prince of Bahrain Michael's Legacy is the property of Anschutz, Branca and Weitzman.[1042]

(Michael) called Branca a Monster a month before he died.[1043]

Now remember Branca=Sony. You know how Michael hated Sony! He was drugged from shots of Propofol by Murray into his muscles. That's the reason he re-signed with Branca. Levin, Philips, Branca, Weitzman did not care if they got his rights dead or alive. Who bought the drugs [?] AEG. Tell everyone this will is a total fraud.[1044]

Michael's resigning with Branca makes no sense...However during the last week of his life Murray had taken to skin popping him with Benzodiazpines
(which

1042 Arnold Klein, "What really happened to Michael (there is much more)." February 2013 post @ https://www.michaeljacksonhoaxforum.com/forums/index.php?topic=23648.0.
1043 Arnold Klein, "What Happened to Michael? Live From Los Angeles," October 23, 2015 @ http://mjhoaxlive.blogspot.com/2013/09/it-wasnt-michael-jackson-they-wanted-it.html.
1044 Facebook comment date June 12, 2011.

explains the body marks.) This would make Michael incompetent to make any rational decision.[1045]

Thus, Klein declares that Michael Jackson was "**murdered…by an incompetent physician who was nothing short of *a hired hit man* employed by a Rich Entertainment Conglomerate. They only wanted his music Catalogue.**"[1046] Klein said the Conrad Murray manslaughter trial in 2011 "was an absolute hoax."[1047]

By 2012, the press was officially declaring of the "dermatologist of the stars" that his own "star has faded"[1048] and they began eulogizing his "dramatic" and even "astonishing fall from grace."[1049] "Everything unraveled for Klein when Michael died" and his "life went into a tailspin and he ended in financial ruin."[1050] Once a very wealthy, powerful "eminence in Los Angeles" with an endowed chair named after him in UCLA's medical school,

> The perfect face Klein long presented to the world is now sagging. The man once touted as the "dermatologist to the stars" is bankrupt. Palatial homes where he entertained celebrity clients are in foreclosure. Mementos bestowed by grateful Hollywood friends are to be auctioned off to pay bills… "The assets that Dr. Klein worked long and hard to build have been decimated…"[1051]

1045 Arnold Klein, "What Happened to Michael? Live From Los Angeles," October 23, 2015 @ http://mjhoaxlive.blogspot.com/2013/09/it-wasnt-michael-jackson-they-wanted-it.html.
1046 Arnold Klein, "What Happened to Michael? Live From Los Angeles," October 23, 2015 @ http://mjhoaxlive.blogspot.com/2013/09/it-wasnt-michael-jackson-they-wanted-it.html.
1047 Seal, "The Ugly world of Dr. Arnie Klein.".
1048 Harriet Ryan, "A-List doctor's star has faded." *Los Angeles Times* January 1, 2012.
1049 "From chauffeured Bentleys and mansions to foreclosure and insolvency: The dramatic fall of Jacko's dermatologist," *Daily Mail* January 3 2012; "Dr. Klein Michael Jackson's Physician & Friend Dies," *TMZ* October 23, 2015.
1050 "Dr. Klein Michael Jackson's Physician & Friend Dies," *TMZ* October 23, 2015.
1051 Harriet Ryan, "A-List doctor's star has faded." *Los Angeles Times* January 1, 2012.

But the financial ruination of Dr. Arnold Klein The Whistleblower was only the opening act.

During the four days between Monday October 19 and Thursday October 22, 2015, Klein reportedly suffered severe abdominal pains. Finally on Thursday he called 911 himself and was taken to a Palm Springs hospital. However, he had to waite for a bed to become available to him, and while waiting he had a heart attack and died at 7:50 p.m. October 22. The coroner issued a brief press release which failed to mention a cause of death and no investigation was listed.[1052] According to an autopsy report obtained by *Radar Online* Klein died after "suffering in excruciating pain" from a "mysterious" "cocktail of medications" found in his system.[1053] How ironic. According to *Radar Online*, "Eight meds over the three or four his doctor prescribed were found in his system". Further irony: one of the drugs found in Klein's system was midazolam. There was a hole in Klein's bowel, "a side-effect of multiple drug interactions which caused excrement to seep into his stomach." What is the source of these extraneous medications that were interacting in Klein's system? There is a remarkable detail cited in the Coroner's Report:

> On 10/23/15 coroner personnel received disturbing information from Arnold's husband, Shaun Anderson, that he had concerns regarding an incident that occurred in 2014 involving Arnold's caregiver was mixing Arnold's medications. The Palm Springs Police Department interviewed Shaun on 11/28/14. The investigative report was written and was documented as "Information Only."[1054]

Klein had himself claimed to have been poisoned through the unauthorized "mixing" of his medications in an attempted homicide. He claimed to have discovered that a potentially fatal

---

1052 "Michael Jackson's dermatologist Dr. Arnold Klein dies," *CBS News* October 23, 2015.
1053 " 'Slow Suicide'? Alleged Biological Father of Michael Jackson's Kids Died an Excruciating Death," *Radar Online* April 13, 2016.
1054 Riverside Counter Sheriff – Coroner Division. Coroner Investigation Case # 201510769 November 30, 2015.

dose of the antipsychotic drug Moban was daily hidden in his lunchtime medications by an office worker.[1055] *Radar Online* quotes some interesting reflections of "an insider":

> Now, the insider is demanding answers to what really was happening behind the scene's during Klein's final hours. "Was there no one there to say look you're in such excruciating pain we need to call an ambulance? No. He suffered for four days in excruciating pain so finally 911 was called — and who called? He was the one!" blasted the insider. "Where are these people [who were supposed to care about Dr. Klein] when this guy was suffering for four days?"

> Tragically, Klein died after he had a heart attack while waiting for help in a Palm Springs medical facility. "By the time he got to the hospital he didn't even make it to the bed," said the insider. "The responsibility falls on whoever was closest to him. The [coroner] ruled it a natural death but I think it was a slow suicide." [1056]

Or, a slow homicide.

Nobody claimed Klein's body – no family or friends. For two weeks it remained on ice in the morgue and when the body was finally released to a funeral service for burial no burial plans information was given.[1057]

The words of friend and patient of Dr. Klein, Sandy Gallin, regarding the Gay Mafia's "code of silence" comes to mind:

> Gallin admits that because of his place in this family he has been an eyewitness to some remarkable events in show-business and pop history. At one point he muses aloud about the bestseller he may write one day. "You're going to ask a question—why don't I write a book about all my

1055 Arnold Klein, "Elder Abuse And Money Laundering Penal Code Section 186.9-186.10," October 28, 2014 @ https://ebolausadotme.wordpress.com/2014/10/28/145/.
1056 "'Slow Suicide'? Alleged Biological Father of Michael Jackson's Kids Died an Excruciating Death," *Radar Online* April 13, 2016.
1057 Regina F. Graham, "The body of Michael Jackson's doctor Arnold Klein remains on ice at the coroner's office," *Daily Mail* October 28, 2015; "Arnold Klein's Body Released for Private Burial," *Extra* November 2, 2015.

friends and the things I've done? "My answer is: *Where would I live?*"[1058]

That was a code that, ultimately, Arnold Klein couldn't keep and he apparently paid a very steep price for it. However, partly because of Klein's leaky mouth, we know what happened to Michael Jackson.

1058 Matthew Trynauer, "Sandy's Castle," *Vanity Fair* April 1996.

Made in the USA
Middletown, DE
30 January 2024

48599847R00253